Eastern Perspectives on Women's Roles and Advancement in Business

Ela Burcu Uçel
İzmir University of Economics, Turkey

A volume in the Trending Topics Book Series (TTBS) Book Series

IGI Global
PUBLISHER of TIMELY KNOWLEDGE

Published in the United States of America by
IGI Global
Information Science Reference (an imprint of IGI Global)
701 E. Chocolate Avenue
Hershey PA, USA 17033
Tel: 717-533-8845
Fax: 717-533-8661
E-mail: cust@igi-global.com
Web site: http://www.igi-global.com

Library of Congress Cataloging-in-Publication Data

Names: Ucel, Ela, 1975- editor.
Title: Eastern perspectives on women's roles and advancement in business / Ela Ucel, editor.
Description: Hershey, PA : Information Science Reference, [2022] | Includes bibliographical references and index. | Summary: "This book offers real life stories of women in business in Eastern countries, specifically focusing on how they overcame challenges and broke the glass ceiling and handled situations of discrimination and inequality"-- Provided by publisher.
Identifiers: LCCN 2021035421 (print) | LCCN 2021035422 (ebook) | ISBN 9781799887423 (hardcover) | ISBN 9781799887430 (paperback) | ISBN 9781799887447 (ebook)
Subjects: LCSH: Women in the professions--Developing countries. | Businesswomen--Developing countries.
Classification: LCC HD6054.2.D44 E27 2022 (print) | LCC HD6054.2.D44 (ebook) | DDC 331.409172/4--dc22
LC record available at https://lccn.loc.gov/2021035421
LC ebook record available at https://lccn.loc.gov/2021035422

This book is published in the IGI Global book series Trending Topics (TTBS) (ISSN: pending; eISSN: pending)

British Cataloguing in Publication Data
A Cataloguing in Publication record for this book is available from the British Library.

All work contributed to this book is new, previously-unpublished material.
The views expressed in this book are those of the authors, but not necessarily of the publisher.

For electronic access to this publication, please contact: eresources@igi-global.com.

Trending Topics Book Series (TTBS) Book Series

ISSN:pending
EISSN:pending

MISSION

Every day all over the world, researchers are making groundbreaking discoveries that address current challenges and solve complex problems across a variety of fields. Due to advancements in technology, changes in demographics, adjustments to societal norms, the development of political and economic structures, and more, new theories, methods, strategies, techniques, and applications are constantly being established in response to both existing and evolving issues.

Based on the success of IGI Global's latest Trending Topics Campaign, which provides news snippets and trending research breakthroughs relevant to IGI Global content, IGI Global has launched this new book series, titled the **Trending Topics Book Series**, which offers small anthologies of reprinted IGI Global book chapters and journal articles hand-selected by IGI Global's Executive Editorial Board on topics currently trending and stirring up discussion and/or controversy.

Spanning across topics such as the multigenerational workforce, legislation for sustainability, emotional branding, privacy on mobile devices, robotics in healthcare, and bio-based product development, this book series aims to provide researchers, academicians, professionals, and students with the most up-to-date studies in order to advance knowledge across all industries.

COVERAGE

- Emotional Branding
- Environmental Legislation and Sustainability
- Multi-Generational Workforce
- Library Budget Challenges
- Business Sustainability
- Privacy on Mobile Devices
- Bio-Based Product Development
- Plan S and Open Access Movements
- Inclusive Learning
- Millennials

The Trending Topics Book Series (TTBS) Book Series (ISSN pending) is published by IGI Global, 701 E. Chocolate Avenue, Hershey, PA 17033-1240, USA, www.igi-global.com. This series is composed of titles available for purchase individually; each title is edited to be contextually exclusive from any other title within the series. For pricing and ordering information please visit http://www.igi-global.com/book-series/trending-topics-book-series/228608. Postmaster: Send all address changes to above address.

Titles in this Series

For a list of additional titles in this series, please visit:
www.igi-global.com/book-series/trending-topics-book-series/228608

Improving the Safety and Efficiency of Emergency Services Emerging Tools and Technologies for First Responders
Information Resources Management Association(USA)
Information Science Reference • © 2020 • 464pp • H/C (ISBN: 9781799825357) • US $195.00

Innovations in Global Maternal Health Improving Prenatal and Postnatal Care Practices
Information Resources Management Association (USA)
Medical Information Science Reference • © 2020 • 437pp • H/C (ISBN: 9781799823513) • US $285.00

Alternative Pain Management Solutions for Avoiding Prescription Drug Overuse
Information Resources Management Association (USA)
Medical Information Science Reference • © 2020 • 388pp • H/C (ISBN: 9781799816805) • US $245.00

Developing Safer Online Environments for Children Tools and Policies for Combatting Cyber Aggression
Information Resources Management Association (USA)
Information Science Reference • © 2020 • 416pp • H/C (ISBN: 9781799816843) • US $215.00

Five Generations and Only One Workforce How Successful Businesses Are Managing a Multigenerational Workforce
Information Resources Management Association (USA)
Business Science Reference • © 2020 • 364pp • H/C (ISBN: 9781799804376) • US $215.00

Developing Eco-Cities Through Policy, Planning, and Innovation Can It Really Work?
Information Resources Management Association (USA)
Engineering Science Reference • © 2020 • 374pp • H/C (ISBN: 9781799804413) • US $195.00

IGI Global
PUBLISHER of TIMELY KNOWLEDGE

701 East Chocolate Avenue, Hershey, PA 17033, USA
Tel: 717-533-8845 x100 • Fax: 717-533-8661
E-Mail: cust@igi-global.com • www.igi-global.com

Table of Contents

Detailed Table of Contents

everyday work narratives, which in turn shapes both the meaning we attribute to work and the meaning we get out of it.

The purpose of this chapter is to bring a more holistic, inclusive, and critical perspective to discussions on the politics of the female body and dress in workplace settings. It aims to explore the struggles and experiences of women in the business environment with regards to 'looking the part' and the role dress and bodily adornment play in construction and expression of their workplace identities. It will further discuss the role dress might have as signifier of status and power and the ambiguities related to age, body image, sexuality, and identity at work. Furthermore, most of the prior studies on dress acknowledge fashion as a Western phenomenon ignoring the role of dress in non-Western cultures. Therefore, this chapter also aims to discuss how might these conflicts differ in a non-Western context. Finally, considering that during the COVID-19 pandemic image management has shifted to a virtual world, creating further challenges for women, the chapter will conclude by shedding light on these struggles and presenting ideas for the future of work dress code.

As can be seen in most Eastern or Middle Eastern countries, the primary role of women has been defined as motherhood or to be a wife to a man. The fact that women have a role apart from these is seen as a radical change. In Turkey, where the base of this chapter is, there have been many struggles to change this situation from past to present and to maintain the male-female equality. Yet, this "equality" cannot be seen in some broad areas in life such as work-life. The aim of this chapter is to make visible what women have encountered in order to advance in academia through some real-life stories.

The aim of this study is to examine and understand the experiences of women who have token status in their profession based on the news reflected in national news agencies. In the study, 10 professions were determined, including military service, pilot, prison director, firefighter, driver, driving instructor, pumper, house painter/ electrician/car mechanic, postal officer, fisher, where women are numerically a minority. The method of the research was determined as the qualitative research method, and the research design was determined as descriptive content analysis. It reaches conclusions about the occupational gender typing for women in Turkey. The research also tries to understand the roles attributed to these individuals in the context of occupations attributed to the female gender. Finally, images of women in the mentioned professions are also examined in terms of the way the news about token women is presented.

This chapter questions whether the women who have been under the pressure of choosing pink-collar jobs imposed by patriarchal societies would choose white-collar, blue-collar, or some other type of jobs instead of pink-collar ones. This paper uses data from a survey conducted on respondents aged ≥15 years in Turkey. In total 114 people participated in this study. The survey was conducted online due to the COVID-19 pandemic. Participants were expected to answer various questions, such as their personal information to their knowledge about the pink-collar job concept. This chapter aims to figure out whether higher education levels and appropriate vocational education affect female labor decisions positively or not.

Section 2
Eastern Women and Entrepreneurship

In the second section, five chapters are presented which that are by researchers from Morocco, Bangladesh, and Turkey. Each chapter focuses on female entrepreneurship with a specific viewpoint: women entrepreneurs and the challenges they face in Morocco; , how the female mind is enslaved by the patriarchal system; , the profile of women entrepreneurs in Antalya region in Turkey; , Generation X women entrepreneurs' social intelligence, and women entrepreneurs and the entrepreneurship ecosystem in Turkey. These studies contribute to the female entrepreneurship literature through providing insights from Turkey and Morocco and challenging the patriarchal system and understanding which that attempts to force women to stay behind in the entrepreneurial ecosystem.

Despite the various reforms undertaken by the state, women entrepreneurship in Morocco barely constitutes 10% of all businesses in the country whereas the average in the rest of Africa is of 24%. Based on these figures, this chapter seeks to study the evolution and characteristics of female entrepreneurship in Morocco. It examines the motivation behind an entrepreneurial project as well as the environment around it and the struggle to adjust to a male-dominated ecosystem. By exploring a few examples from the eastern region of the country, the study shows that entrepreneurship in Morocco is mainly urban, non-innovative, and merely of a subsistent nature. Indeed, women entrepreneurs, mostly in socially conservative regions (as is the case of the region under study), show a great adaptability to their socio-economic context. While enhancing their leadership skills, autonomy, and self-confidence, the business models adopted by women entrepreneurs focus on their own well-being and that of their families and community. Therefore, the indicators of success are not the usual business and profit growth, but financial autonomy coupled with family responsibility and well-being.

The woman who fought for the liberation of women in the Indian subcontinent from the state of "other" is Rokeya Sakhawat Hossein (1880 – 1932). Another lady icon can be named in this occasion, Fatima al-Fihri, who, in the Moroccan city of Fez, founded a mosque that developed into the famous al-Qarawiyyin University, which has come to be recognized as the oldest existing university in the world. Many inspiring stories come along such as the one like Haya Faisal's from Pakistan who became a female cab driver for the sake of supporting her family. The issue of subversion or reversal of gaze is addressed by throwing light on Simone de Beauvoir's "Myth and Reality" and Michel Foucault's "Concept of Power" in The History of Sexuality. The chapter finally considers different endeavors of different Eastern women like Rokeya, Fatima, Haya, and the like to show women's participation or treatment of gender roles in organizational behavior, strategic management, and entrepreneurship.

This chapter focuses on motivations, problems, and future needs of Turkish women entrepreneurs. The study uses a quantitative research methodology. A self-administered questionnaire is applied to a randomly selected group of urban women entrepreneurs in Antalya region, Turkey. One hundred and nineteen responses are statistically analyzed. Findings indicate that women entrepreneurs are driven mostly by psychological and economic motivators such as working independently, achieving economic independence, and doing the job she wants which suited her abilities. Obtaining capital is the primary problem they faced. In addition, the majority of women entrepreneurs need support in marketing and branding.

Social intelligence has been recognized as a remarkable factor affecting individuals' success and performance on the job with intent engagement. This research explores the social intelligence's impact on job engagement of Generation X women entrepreneurs who operate in the TR62 region, covering Adana and Mersin provinces. Business scholars and industry leaders have widely recognized the importance of women's entrepreneurship. Thus, research aimed to shed light on women entrepreneurship in the Turkish business ecosystem. Social intelligence can have a catalyst role on job engagement to advance entrepreneurship skills. As a part of social intelligence, there was a moderate relationship between the social information process and social awareness. Social intelligence had a moderate correlation with emotional and cognitive job engagement. Also, there was a moderate relationship between social information processing and physical job engagement being collaborated with emotional job engagement on account of Generation X women entrepreneurs' active role in a social and business environments.

While women's entrepreneurship preserves its traditional entrepreneurial mission from a neo-liberal perspective, it has also been accepted as an essential tool in ensuring equality and empowering women with a gender perspective. It is seen that supranational institutions are trying to realize these two perspectives together, at least working in this direction. This study aims to conceptualize "women's entrepreneurship" and bring it to the agenda in Turkey form a gender perspective. Evaluating the literature on women's entrepreneurship from a historical perspective and examining the fundamental inequalities embedded in entrepreneurship, especially in a developing economy such as Turkey that still has structural gaps, is the study's main contribution.

Preface

Justice is about making sure that being polite is not the same thing as being quiet. In fact, often times, the most righteous thing you can do is to shake the table. – Alexandria Ocasio-Cortez

Women, half of the world's population, systematically ignored, suppressed, and left behind. Eastern women, limited with domestic roles and responsibilities largely by culture, tradition, and religion. These words should have belonged to the previous century, but the unfortunate fact is, they apply to this day and age.

The modern society is pretty two-faced, it seems to acknowledge gender equality but strives to maintain status-quo: the subordinate position of women. The patriarchal system ensures the sustainability of this status-quo by not only raising boys as the rulers but also conditioning girls to be the submissive servers. Thus, referring to Ocasio- Cortez, for women, it is no longer the time to be silent, it is just the time to shake the table. This book will attempt to do that by providing diverse perspectives from international researchers all of whom focused on women and their presence in the workplace.

WOMEN IN THE WORKPLACE

Either an employee, manager or entrepreneur, women increasingly take part in organizational settings. But the pace of this increase is not enough, Labor Organization (ILO) dataset shows that the male to female labor force participation rate is just three to two (ILO, 2019). The Global Gender Gap Report by World Economic Forum indicates the fact that only 34% of all managers are female globally (World Economic Forum, 2018). When it comes to entrepreneurship, women are surpassed again: only 1 in 3 businesses are owned by female entrepreneurs (World bank Gender Data Portal, 2020).

These numbers are the reflections of a globally unequal system, as women face greater challenges in getting access to financial resources compared to men (World bank Gender Data Portal, 2020); they are not given equal chances of promotion with men (ILO, 2019) and they are not paid equally with men (Global Wage Report, 2018/2019). When women decide to give birth to a baby, the discrimination they face gets even worse: short parental leaves, unpaid parental leaves, loosing career chances and the unequal distribution of childcare duty and responsibilities (ILO, 2019).

Despite the ever increasing interest and attention on gender equality, "through supposedly gender neutral but often very masculine norms and practices, organizations not only become gendered but are also places in which one gender is consistently seen as second best." (Kaushik, Sharma and Kumar Kaushik, 2014, pp.90.). The gendered workplace and gendered employment relations unsurprisingly, set invisible barriers in front of women of all professions and levels.

This unpleasant portrayal of the current state is essentially hindering global economic welfare and development. When women and girls are not provided with equal education and business opportunities, the world is devoid of the economic contributions of and the potential value created by half of the population. When women actively participate the business life and have their independent income, they not only improve their own well-being but also contribute to their children's well-being (Sen, 2000). When women take the entrepreneurial risks and have their own businesses, they create jobs and wealth, contribute to economic growth and development and reduce poverty (Byrne et al., 2019; Neumeyer et al., 2019; Akehurst et al., 2012). Women, different than men, tend to share their achievements with others. They provide gains to the others in the community, in areas like health and education (Orser et al., 2006). Thus they contribute the nation's sustainable development.

Eastern women's situation is no different than the other women of the world: a constant struggle to have a voice in domestic and business life. The difference lies in the fact that there is limited research on Eastern women's workplace experiences and entrepreneurship (Welsh et al, 2018; Kimosop, Korir, and White, 2016; Mas-Tur, Pinazo, Tur-Porcar, and Sánchez-Masferrer, 2015).

The Western dominated research cannot be generalized to Eastern contexts, as Metcalfe states that different nations have different "specificities of socio-cultural and political processes and their impact on gender systems" (Metcalfe, 2008, p. 86). There is a need to provide more insights on Eastern women and their workplace experiences.

Thus, this book aimed to contribute enriching the literature on the topic of concern. Through ten different chapters each of which focus on women's experiences in organizational contexts, it will provide a diverse collection of findings and a colorful set of understandings to the reader.

The book will come in useful for students studying gender equality, gender mainstreaming, gender relationships, social construction of gender and women in organizations. It will also serve instructors teaching gender related topics, researchers studying gender and workplace relationships, policy-makers devoted to gender mainstreaming, gender equality activists fighting the patriarchy and the curious reader who wants get a broader perspective on the issue.

To make the reading experience satisfying, the book is organized in two sections. The first section presents five chapters that focus on Eastern women's experiences in the workplace:

CHAPTER 1: NARRATIVE PRACTICING OF THE MEANING OF WORK – THE GENDER WE THINK AND TALK

Authors Ünlüoğlu, Çangarlı and Gaggiotti aimed to present how gender asymmetry is produced, by analyzing work-related narratives of 28 people from different occupations in Turkey. The findings show how these people positioned their jobs in their lives and how they positioned themselves in the work life. The chapter contributes our knowledge by providing an order of gender in how people experience and make sense of their work lives.

CHAPTER 2: HOLISTIC AND CRITICAL PERSPECTIVE TO POLITICS OF DRESS AND THE FEMALE BODY IN WORKPLACE SETTINGS

Author Ertekin provides a holistic, inclusive and critical perspective to politics of female body and dress in the workplace. The chapter enriches our knowledge by exploring the role dress and bodily adornment play in the construction and expression of women's workplace identities. The dress emerges as an indicator of status and power in organizational settings. The chapter also brings changes in women's work dress code during the Covid-19 pandemic to our attention.

CHAPTER 3: WHAT TURKISH WOMEN NEED TO ADVANCE IN ACADEMIA

Author Tatarlar presents real-life workplace experiences of a number of women academicians from Turkey. These stories show how demanding, challenging, irrational and irrelevant can the superior expectations from women academicians be. In addition to making research, teaching and completing administrative work, women academicians are also expected to satisfy their superior's personal needs and wants. The chapter contributes our knowledge by providing examples of workplace bullying that women face in everyday work life.

CHAPTER 4: TOKEN IMAGE IN MALE-DOMINATED PROFESSIONS AND OCCUPATIONAL SEGREGATION BASED ON GENDER – A STUDY ON THE CASES REFLECTED ON NATIONAL NEWS

Authors Yılmaz and Sürgevil, in their attempt to understand the experiences of token women, analyzed 86 news items about women's token image in male-dominated professions, which were published on national and local newspapers in Turkey. Their findings present that token men do not attract as much attention as token women do. The study also reveals that token women had the following experiences: gender identity as performative, insufficient instruction, perceived hostility and resistance, close and punitive supervision, lack of support and stereotyping and differential treatment. This chapter improves our understanding about tokenism and token women in Eastern parts of the world.

CHAPTER 5: FALLING FOUNDATION OF PATRIARCHAL SOCIETIES – PINK-COLLAR FEMALE LABOR FORCE

Authors Göksel and Çolak conducted a survey with a sample from Turkey and examined people's awareness about and knowledge on pink-collar jobs. The results showed that participants with a college degree are more likely to break free from the concept of pink collar jobs than others. Female participants, when informed about the concept, are estranged from it. One particular finding attracts attention for further research: 38% percent of female participants reported that they believe they will not be approved by the society even if they choose a pink-collar job. The chapter sheds light on the influence of patriarchal system on women and girls and how it makes them internalize the oppressive and inhibitive thoughts even when they are not aware.

Second section presents Eastern women's entrepreneurship by providing insights from different countries: Morocco, Bangladesh, and Turkey.

CHAPTER 6: WOMEN ENTREPRENEURS IN THE EASTERN REGION OF MOROCCO – CHALLENGES AND OPPORTUNITIES

Author Boutkhil presents a thorough profile of female entrepreneurship in Morocco to the reader: evolution and characteristics of women entrepreneurs and the motivation behind women's entrepreneurial projects. It shows how women entrepreneurs in socially conservative regions of the country successfully adopt the socio-economic context; and reports that profit and business growth are not the indicators of success, but well-being and financial autonomy coupled with family responsibility are, for women entrepreneurs in Morocco. This chapter adds to our knowledge of Eastern female entrepreneurship and the entrepreneurship ecosystems that they operate in.

CHAPTER 7: EASTERN WOMEN'S ENTREPRENEURSHIP – LIBERATING THE ENSLAVED MIND BEYOND THE PATRIARCHAL GAZE

Author Akmam offers an examination of the life and works of the famous Bengali writer of the Indian subcontinent, Rokeya Sakhawat Hossain, who struggled to bring social changes all through her life, from an entrepreneurial point of view and a distinctive literary perspective. She touches on the patriarchal gaze and the stereotyped female, the creation of the enslaved mind and studies *Stories of Aporajita.* This chapter enriches the book through providing the audience a good read on Bengali literature and women's entrepreneurship.

CHAPTER 8: THE PROFILE OF WOMEN ENTREPRENEURS – A CONTEXTUAL ANALYSIS FROM A DEVELOPING COUNTRY

Author Atsan focuses on the motivations, problems and expectations of women entrepreneurs in Antalya, Turkey. Based on the fact that female entrepreneurship has a significant impact on the growth and stability of the national economy, the study presents a profile of women entrepreneurs in the region, the reasons why they decided to have their own businesses and the multidimensional problems they face in running their businesses. It also provides a guidance on the areas that women need support in their quest of entrepreneurship.

CHAPTER 9: EXPLORING THE SOCIAL INTELLIGENCE IMPACT ON JOB ENGAGEMENT – A RESEARCH ON GENERATION X WOMEN ENTREPRENEURS AT TR62 REGION

Author İnan studied the impact of social intelligence on job engagement of generation X women entrepreneurs at TR62 region, namely the Adana and Mersin provinces in Turkey. Referring to the fact that female entrepreneurs contribute the exponential growth of the national economy, the study focuses on social intelligence and job engagement, as they empower entrepreneurial skills. Findings present a noticeable relationship between the sub-dimensions of social intelligence and job engagement of generation X women entrepreneurs based on women's intention to thrive in their business and social lives. This provides a sound managerial implication to female entrepreneurship practice as a sign of the importance of using and improving social intelligence on success.

CHAPTER 10: CRITICAL CONCEPTUALIZATION OF WOMEN ENTREPRENEURSHIP – REFLECTIONS ON TURKISH ENTREPRENEURSHIP ECOSYSTEM

Authors Seckin-Halac and Samur-Teraman conceptualize women's entrepreneurship in the Turkish entrepreneurship ecosystem with a gender perspective. They provide a critical discussion of female entrepreneurship globally, and a review of female entrepreneurship in Turkey. They also discuss the embedded inequalities in the entrepreneurship ecosystem and present a portrayal of women entrepreneurs and the context that they operate in Turkey, now. The chapter is closed with a discussion of how women's entrepreneurship in Turkey needs to be expanded into four particular themes: (1) not being able to use the female workforce potential, (2) cultural variables, (3) as a political intervention tool, (4) disinformation/data access difficulties in detecting the current situation, and (5) gender inequality both in a general sense and in entrepreneurship activities.

As a collection of the above summarized studies, this book aims to create an opportunity to present Eastern women's unique experiences as organizational members and entrepreneurs in business life. Through the ten chapters written by authors from Turkey, Morocco, England, Bangladesh and Netherlands, it provides different views, perspectives and ideas on how Eastern women experience their work lives. The fundamental contribution of the book to the literature is, it stands as an humble attempt to make Eastern women's voices heard in a world where West is always noisy and loud.

The editor wishes to end with a nice couple of words from the acclaimed Indian author and political activist Arundhati Roy, to inspire all the readers and women fighting their own battles out there.

Another world is not only possible, she is on her way. On a quiet day, I can hear her breathing. – Arundhati Roy

Ela Burcu Uçel

REFERENCES

Akehurst, G., Simarro, E., & Mas-Tur, A. (2012). Women entrepreneurship in small service firms: Motivations, barriers and performance. *Service Industries Journal, 32*(15), 2489–2505. doi:10.1080/02642069.2012.677834

Byrne, J., Fattoum, S., & Diaz Garcia, M. C. (2019). Role models and women entrepreneurs: Entrepreneurial superwoman has her say. *Journal of Small Business Management, 57*(1), 154–184. doi:10.1111/jsbm.12426

ILO. (2018). *Global Wage Report 2018/19*. International Labor Organization.

ILO. (2019). *Maternity Protection and Work-Family Policies (The Care Economy)*. Retrieved from https://www.ilo.org/global/topics/care-economy/parental-leave/lang-- en/index.htm

Kaushik, N., Sharma, A., & Kumar Kaushik, V. (2014). Equality in the workplace: A study of gender issues in Indian organisations. *Journal of Management Development, 33*(2), 90–106. doi:10.1108/JMD-11-2013-0140

Kimosop, J., Korir, M., & White, M. (2016). The moderating effect of demographic characteristics on the relationship between strategic capabilities and firm performance in women-owned entrepreneurial ventures in Nairobi, Kenya. *Canadian Journal of Administrative Sciences, 33*(3), 242–256. doi:10.1002/cjas.1399

Lewis, P., Simpson, R., & Sealy, R. (2010). Meritocracy, difference and choice: Women's experiences of advantage and disadvantage at work. *Gender in Management, 25*(3), 165–169. doi:10.1108/17542411011036374

Mas-Tur, A., Pinazo, P., Tur-Porcar, A. M., & Sánchez-Masferrer, M. (2015). What to avoid to succeed as an entrepreneur. *Journal of Business Research, 68*(11), 2279–2284. doi:10.1016/j.jbusres.2015.06.011

Metcalfe, B. (2008). Women, management and globalization. *Journal of Business Ethics, 83*(1), 85–100. doi:10.100710551-007-9654-3

Neumeyer, X., Santos, S. C., Caetano, A., & Kalbfleisch, P. (2019). Entrepreneurship ecosystems and women entrepreneurs: A social capital and network approach. *Small Business Economics, 53*(2), 475–489. doi:10.100711187-018-9996-5

Orser, B. J., Riding, A. L., & Manley, K. (2006). Women entrepreneurs and financial capital. *Entrepreneurship Theory and Practice, 30*(5), 643–665. doi:10.1111/j.1540-6520.2006.00140.x

Sen, A. (2000). *Development as freedom / Amartya Sen.* Anchor Book.

Welsh, D. H. B., Kaciak, E., & Shamah, R. (2018). Determinants of women entrepreneurs' firm performance in a hostile environment. *Journal of Business Research, 88*, 481–491. doi:10.1016/j.jbusres.2017.12.015

World bank gender data portal. (2020). *World Bank.* https://blogs.worldbank.org/opendata/women-entrepreneurs-needed-stat

World Bank. The global gender gap report 2018. (2018). World Bank.

Acknowledgment

The editor wishes to sincerely thank fellow researchers and academicians who contributed this book as authors and reviewers:

Selen Kars-Ünlüoğlu, University of the West of England, UK

Burcu Güneri Çangarlı, İzmir University of Economics, Turkey

Hugo Gaggiotti, University of the West of England, UK

Zeynep Özdamar Ertekin, İzmir University of Economics, Turkey

Ceren Deniz Tatarlar, Tilburg University, The Netherlands

Benan Kurt Yılmaz, Sinop University, Turkey

Olca Sürgevil Dalkılıç, Dokuz Eylül University, Turkey

İdil Göksel, Izmir University of Economics, Turkey

Yiğitcan Çolak, Izmir University of Economics, Turkey

Soumia Boutkhil, Mohammed Premier University, Morocco

Jannatul Akmam, Jamia Ahmadia Sunnia Mohila Fazil Madrasah, Bangladesh

Nuray Atsan, Akdeniz University, Turkey

İbrahim İnan, Çukurova University, Turkey

Duygu Seckin-Halac, Yaşar University, Turkey

Seray Begum Samur-Teraman, Istanbul Kültür University, Turkey

Cansu Yıldırım, Dokuz Eylül University, Turkey

Feride Deniz Zaptçıoğlu Çelikdemir, Yaşar University, Turkey

Acknowledgment

Dicle Yurdakul, Altınbaş University, Turkey

Mert Günerergin, İzmir University of Economics, Turkey

This book is dedicated to my late mother Aygen Yücel and to my biggest motivation to fight the patriarchy, my daughter Leyla Bade Uçel.

Ela Burcu Uçel
İzmir University of Economics, Turkey

Introduction:
Women in the Workplace – A Glimpse Into the History

Until the end of early 20th century, women existed primarily in the domestic sphere. They mostly didn't have wage work. They were handling housework and child rearing responsibilities and were contributing to family businesses run at home. Domestic work, which is a full time job, was not accepted as work and was seen as not having an economic value. Women were not seen as workers and housework not seen as working.

With the Industrial Revolution, family's role as the center of production was taken over by factories. This change distinguished jobs as, work done for wages and work done at home. The first was assigned to men and the latter to women. Thus, roles related with work for both genders were established. In that period of time, women were accepted to have a natural inferiority: they were sensitive and delicate, caring and compassionate, they had smaller brains and weaker bodies. They were anticipated to have certain personality characteristics, behaviors and to meet society's expectations. They were defined as being subordinate and existing in the domestic sphere (Kessler-Harris, 1981).

Women were destined to be at home, handling family responsibilities. They had to perform several vital functions at home to maintain men's working ability: preparing and serving meals, providing clean cloths and a comfortable home to rest, ensuring emotional and sexual relief, absorbing the stress and tension, raising children and buying stuff for all family members (Milkman, 2016).

This definition of woman was coupled with a definition of man: strong and independent, working at competitive and demanding wage jobs, supporting the family and requiring a serving wife at home (Kessler-Harris, 1981).

At first, the new understanding may have sounded nice to some women, as they were both working at home and at the family business or farm, before the Industrial Revolution. Now they were responsible of housework, only. Herewith, they became dependents of men. They were defined through men. Trivializing housework, as it was not accepted as a job and it was unpaid, contributed to women's so called "inferiority" and dependency.

When the system needed more employees, women started to work at the mills and the factories in large numbers. But they were seen as subordinate and paid less than men. As women's pay were low, they were unable to sustain their families alone and men remained to be the primary breadwinners.

In the meanwhile, men were not happy with women working: they were holding the wages down. If there were no women workers, there would be more and better paying jobs and men could have made more money. Working with low wages and under menial conditions, women needed to fight for their rights, but they were not successful in organizing around unions. Because they were expected to be kind and submissive and society made them believe that their primary roles were wife and mother, and working was only temporary. Sometimes women had to work, but it must be guaranteed that their domestic roles are not neglected, as jobs were transitory and the primary responsibility was the family (Kessler-Harris, 1981).

When women were working at the factories, as the working conditions were poor and workplaces were hazardous, they were treated badly and injured very often. This led to a tendency to keep women away from certain jobs, with the aim of protection (www.britannica.com), but it ended up engaging women only to domestic roles.

The system wanted the women at home and men at work. This not only made women dependent, but also turned men into captives of heavy responsibilities: working very hard to support their families. A man having a working wife was almost a failure, a sign of not being able to take care of his family. A working wife was a threat: a woman who is no longer dependent. The men faced an endless struggle to work harder and harder in order to provide better conditions to their families and, women faced a dependent life at home, busy with mothering and housework. Men were stabilized and controlled with the responsibility of supporting their families, women were trapped in their houses and submissive roles.

In time, with the changes in the society, women were demanded as workers in education as teachers and healthcare as nurses. With the expansion of the service industry, more and more women were employed in restaurants, cafes and shops. After 1970s, women were able to find positions in traditional "men's jobs". They were educated, they had plenty of different occupations and started pursuing competitive careers (www.britannica.com).

In certain spheres, like education, gender equality was almost maintained, but in others the differences between men and women remained as barriers (Leeuwena & Zijdemanb, 2014). Gender regimes, which are the structures of inequalities (Tomlinson, 2007), continued existing in these domains. In many societies, cultural norms continued leading women out of the labor force, or towards jobs with lowest income, prestige and nonfinancial rewards, no matter how qualified they were. (Brinton et al., 1995).

Despite Western women's relatively improved position, Eastern women still have a lot to strive for. In that part of the world, cultural factors and structures, patriarchal norms, stereotypes, societal expectations, established gender norms and limited representation continue hindering women's advancement in business life (Cooke, 2010).

In the following chapters, a rich variety of research will be provided to the audience, all of which study Eastern women's presence in the workplace and attempt to inspire policy makers, managers, human resources specialists and women in general in removing barriers and facilitating women's success in business circles.

REFERENCES

Brinton, M. C., Lee, Y. J., & Parish, W. L. (1995). Married women's employment in rapidly industrializing societies: Examples from East Asia. *American Journal of Sociology*, *100*(5), 1099–1130. doi:10.1086/230633

Cooke, F. L. (2010). Women's participation in employment in Asia: A comparative analysis of China, India, Japan and South Korea. *International Journal of Human Resource Management*, *21*(12), 2249–2270. doi:10.1080/09585192.2010.509627

Kessler-Harris, A. (1981). *A woman has always worked: a concise story*. University of Illinois Press.

Leeuwena, M. H. D., & Zijdemanb, R. L. (2014). Digital humanities and the history of working women: A cascade. *The History of the Family*, *19*(4), 411–425. doi:10.1080/1081602X.2014.955517

Milkman, R. (2016). On gender, labor and equality. University of Illinois Press.

Tomlinson, J. (2007). Employment regulation, welfare and gender regimes: A comparative analysis of women's working-time patterns and work–life balance in the UK and the US. *International Journal of Human Resource Management*, *18*(3), 401–415. doi:10.1080/09585190601167466

Section 1

Eastern Women in the Workplace

In this section, five chapters by researchers from Turkey, England, and the Netherlands are presented. The studies focus on Eastern women's workplace experiences from different perspectives: how gender is structured in the workplace;, the role dress plays in women's workplace experiences;, the challenges women face in the academia;, women's token image in male- dominated professions, and women's perceptions on of pink-collar jobs and their career choices. Each study uniquely contributes to the literature and our knowledge on gender- related issues in organizational settings.

Chapter 1
Narrative Practicing of the Meaning of Work:
The Gender We Think and Talk

Selen Kars-Unluoglu
University of the West of England, UK

Burcu Güneri Çangarlı
https://orcid.org/0000-0003-3396-2217
Izmir University of Economics, Turkey

Hugo Gaggiotti
University of the West of England, UK

ABSTRACT

This chapter shows how gender asymmetry is produced through narrative practices. By analyzing the work-life narratives of 14 men and 14 women working in a variety of occupations ranging from personal care to finance, from crafts to health, from creative and performing arts to sales and marketing, this chapter demonstrates the ways in which the narrators positioned themselves within the world of work, and the work within their personal lifeworld. The analysis brings about an order of gender in how work is approached, made sense of, experienced, and narrated. Recognizing these dynamics helps organizations and their members to be more aware that gender is not a natural attribute of people but something we create and recreate in our everyday work narratives, which in turn shapes both the meaning we attribute to work and the meaning we get out of it.

DOI: 10.4018/978-1-7998-8742-3.ch001

INTRODUCTION AND BACKGROUND

In recent decades labor market participation by women has increased, with the alleviation of many material, social and psychological barriers that confined women to domestic responsibilities. However, women's continued disadvantage in the experiences of work persists (Lewis, Simpson & Sealy, 2010).

One of the reasons could be attributed to the lack of analysis of how narratively the meaning of work is gender-constructed. The way of experiencing work was addressed by the academic tradition enrooted in sociology and anthropology – from different perspectives, but always with the tendency of keeping women invisible. Under these initial conceptions, the so-called *labor market* was socially influenced by how work is conceived, but keeping women obscured as social actors. As Victor Strazzeri (2015) suggested, seminal sociologists like Max Weber were interested more on worker's attitude towards labor (service, obedience, dependence) and workers' wages and their living conditions (Engels, 1892 [1844]). When examining these attitudes, this literature was inspired on the analysis of men's manual work, originally agrarian and later industrial. Similarly, the initial anthropological research on work in industrial settlements, was focused on how the construction of the meaning of work was central when defining cultural identities and establishing a sense of community independent of gender roles or adscriptions (Warner & Lunt, 1941). For example, Elton Mayo's work in the Western Electric Company, a subsidiary of the American Telephone and Telegraph Company (AT&T), considered foundational of the disciplines of organization studies and anthropology of work, was based on 21,000 structured interviews mostly with women workers. However, a gender perspective of the construction of the meaning of work was invisible in Mayo's analysis. John Hassard (2012) has emphasized the central and crucial role of women in transforming the Hawthorne factory from a working place to a *social center* thanks to their understandings of work differently. However, a gender-based explanation of how work is understood still seems a sterile field for most of the academic tradition.

Indeed, many of contemporary explanations of the problem of segregating and discriminating women when analyzing working practices are not able to address the experience of gender asymmetry in the workplace sufficiently (Durbin, 2015). For example, the economic explanation would consider this phenomenon as the '*natural* product of differing investments' by men and women to the development of their human capital (i.e., education) (Becker, 1964). However, as Vinnicombe (2000) observes, young women who today seek to enter the world of work are just as well educated, or even more so, than men – an observation that questions the validity of the economic explanation. The structural explanation emphasizes the numerical composition of men and women in organization, arguing that the differing career opportunities of men and women can be explained by the fact that women are in the numerical minority (Kanter, 1977). The growing labor market presence of women which is unaccompanied by an equivalent redistribution of career opportunities nullifies this structural explanation.

The shortcomings of these explanations have promoted a search for new routes to understanding the complexities of gender issues in the labor market. Work-life literature focuses on the systemic elements inherent to women's continued disadvantage. For example, scholars like Brewis and Warren (2001), Greenberg, Ladge and Clair (2009) and Miller (2017) observe that contemporary narratives about intensive mothering pressure mothers to prioritize children above else with implications for experiences at work (Gatrell, 2013). Gatrell (2010) highlights that work-life *choices*' regarding job opportunities are not neutral and are heavily influenced by social position, that requires the individual to fit with the dominant norm of the labor market, a norm which tends to march with the experiences of men.

The dominant norm of what *choices* are realistically available to gender roles and how gender asymmetries are experienced in the workplace were also studied by analyzing supra-organizational cultures, like the nation state. It has been suggested that the national culture, a concept defined during the 1980's as 'the collective programming of the mind' (Hofstede, 1984), affects – among many things – the meaning attributed to work and how people talk about and do gender at work (Beham et al., 2000). Most recent literature has suggested that national cultures are strongly permeated with the role religion plays in the organization of the state (Dingley & Catterall, 2020). In the context of what some literature defines as Eastern national state organizing, for example, Dale (2005) shows that Pakistani and Bangladeshi women, even those who 'work hard and get educated', often feel closely bound to religion, in particular Islam, and related family customs, obliging them to seek parental and spousal blessings, including their in-laws' to pursue and continue in employment (p. 235). Similarly, Arifeen and Gatrell (2020), in their study of British Pakistani women professionals showed that women's perceptions of their professional selves are bound, metaphorically, to faith and family customs, which precludes them from accessing certain workplace opportunities and acts a 'glass chain' when engaging in formal and informal networking events.

The aim of this chapter is to show how gender asymmetry is also produced through narrative practices, in addition to structural, motivational or cultural/ normative reasons. We demonstrate how men and women, through narratives, produce their sense of self at work and position themselves within the world of work. We use this exploration to gain further insights into the complexities of gender issues in the labor market to argue how gender asymmetry in organizations is evidenced when narratively representing practices of working. As Silvia Gherardi (1994) refers, 'the meaning of gender is constantly deferred and negotiated in discourse...The thought and language that separates the female from the male underpins a symbolic order of gender which expresses experiences unique to each gender' (p. 591).

METHODS

In keeping with Cochran's (1990) advice that narrative approaches are most appropriate for career research, we demonstrate the ways in which gender is *talked* at work by men and women. As social researchers, we are aware that we 'do not have direct access to another's experience' (Riessman, 1993, p. 8), however, we have access to the telling of these experiences. That has formed the focus of our methodological approach.

We take a symbolic-interpretive approach (Gherardi, 1995) inspired by Anthony Giddens' (1979) perspective of the articulation between practices and the discursive conscience of workers. This approach enables us to see how gender asymmetry at work is constructed and narratively justified through symbolic means, such as vocabularies expressing values, metaphors and images of the world of work. In this view, gender is not a simple property of people, but a social practice, something that we reproduce through talk in everyday reality as we give meaning to work through narratives. The importance of talk and language is crucial in this, through which stories are relayed about meanings individuals attach to their experiences. The role of narrative language, therefore, is crucial to the creation of meaning in the lived experiences of people in 'communal interchange' (Gergen 1985, p. 266) in the 'space between people' (Hoffman, 1992) throughout their lived social and personal experiences.

We engage in an inductive study grounded in narrative inquiry of personal stories of work and work lives, and within that, consider the influence of gendered narratives on organizational life experiences. We frame our study with narrative identity theory, which posits that a person's identity is internalized and is an evolving story they craft. We align ourselves with the 'linguistic turn' in social sciences (Alvesson & Karreman, 2000), to argue for the centrality of narratives in the lives of all of us, regardless of whether we are particularly self-conscious about it. According to Gergen (1999, p. 70) 'we identify ourselves through narration', through countless narratives we tell about our work, our career, our aspirations, our relations with and at work. By engaging with the multiplicity of possible meanings that might be attached to what our world is, what part we play in it, and what situations we found ourselves in, we actively (not necessarily consciously) construct and enact the story we want to tell the world about ourselves. Over time, these stories color our notion of self and the social identity that we present to the world, to the extent to which our sense of 'self is a perpetually rewritten story . . . in the end we become the autobiographical narratives that we tell about our lives' (Bruner, 1987, p. 15). Some of these will be internalized ("this is who I want to be"), but regardless how internalized they are, they will also play a part in the 'presentation of self' (Goffman, 1956), including how we actually behave in our work life and how we narrate, to others, the story of our lives and work.

Narratives, as such, 'connect the inner world to the outer world' – 'they bridge cultural history with personal biography' (Plummer, 2001, p. 395), and have the potential to bring into being everything from identities to organizations themselves (Grant et al., 2004). The use of narrative research involves focusing towards the more relational and emergent aspects of work lives and of lives of workers outside of work to understand their orientation to work and consequent work behavior (Goldthorpe, Lockwood, Bechhofer & Platt, 1968). It draws emphasis to the manner in which meaning and concepts of what it means to be a worker, a professional, a male worker or a female professional are constructed and harmonized within the social relationships which exist between people and their specific context within and beyond work. This dynamic emphasizes the role of human agency and allows us to better appreciate the complexities of work and employee processes, as well as human lives and identities more generally. Therefore, we seek to understand how someone narrates their work and their worker selves to identify key elements of gendered differences in one's orientation to work, their interactions, relations and feeling at work.

Sample

Narrative data can be collected through a variety of means, and can take many forms, including written, oral, and visual (Larty & Hamilton, 2011; Riessman, 2008). The source material to be examined here are narratives of work experiences of men and women published as an ethnographic appendix to Katrinli (ed., 2008)'s book titled *Real-Life Stories of How People Feel and Behave in Organizations*. The whole corpus of this rich ethnographic material was a compilation of 58 stories featuring the working narrations of men and women from a variety of occupations ranging from personal care to finance, from crafts to health, from creative and performing arts to sales and marketing. The 58 stories were collected through semi-structured qualitative interviews, from working people in Izmir (the third largest metropolitan city in Turkey located on the Western coast) identified by convenience sampling methodology. Despite all interviewees were working in the same city, as further elaborated below and in Table 1, they represent a diverse demographics with respect to gender, age, education, employment, household income, marital and family status, and socio-economic properties of the city they regard as their hometown.

As indicated in the preface of Katrinli (ed., 2008), Katrinli and her colleagues' main aim was to explicate organizational behavior issues with real-life stories. In line with this aim, the 58 real-life stories are used as examples to demonstrate how scholarly theories reflect themselves in practice, in chapters on work ethic, job involvement, organizational justice, stress, work and family balance, emotional labor, workplace bullying and success. Given Katrinli and colleagues' use of the stories as illustrative material, these stories were not analyzed qualitatively, nor they were approached from the perspective of gender, unlike we do in this chapter.

As Katrinli and her colleagues did not aim to develop or test theories, they used convenience sampling in identifying the interviews, which is suitable to generate the richest and the most sensitive data from willing participants who feel comfortable 'opening up' (Brewis, 2014). However, we are aware that with convenience sampling, people with specific characteristics may have been more likely to take part in the interviews, which can lead to under coverage and, consequently, estimate bias in the reporting of the results (Robinson, 2014). As a result, we have downsampled the 58 interviews using purposive criteria. Among the 58 interviews, we selected a sub-corpus of 28 stories: 14 men and 14 women. Consideration was given to have a representation of different occupational groups as outlined in the International Standard Classification of Occupations published by ILO (2012). Where possible, we aimed for a matched pair design by having men and women representing the same occupational group (e.g., occupations in craft, health services occupations, personal and protective services workers, clerical occupations, elementary occupations business and administrative professionals and so on). The selected stories and the participants who narrate them can also be considered as reflecting 'strategic' or 'survivalist' drawing upon a categorization employed by McCrone (1994). The individuals categorized as 'strategic' had undergone a process of investing in labor market futures by utilizing their resources, ambitions, and experiences. By contrast, 'survivalists' focused upon getting by with their existing qualification and skills in a restricted and restrictive labor market with limited occupational flexibility. The resulting sample and the profile of narrators are presented in Table 1 below.

As mentioned above, the participants were all working in Turkey, in the city of Izmir. The Turkish context is an interesting background to explore gender asymmetry. In the traditional analyses of practices of working in relation to national cultures, Turkey has been characterized as a society with strong in-group collectivism, uncertainty avoidance and power distance, but a lack of gender egalitarianism and long-term orientation (Hofstede, 1984). Gannon and Pillai (2013) described Turkish national culture through the metaphor of the coffee-house, which is highly distinctive in Turkey than their counterparts in other countries. Despite being open-to-public places suitable for passing time, genuine Turkish coffee-houses are men-only establishments, a hub of men's social life, a place where men of the

Table 1. Participant profiles

Occupation	Gender	Age	Education	Marital status	Employment status
Actor	M	50-59	High school	Married with children	Freelance
Advertiser	F	NA	University	NA	Employed
Aesthetician	F	20-29	NA	Single	Employed
Artist	M	30-39	University	Single	Freelance
Baby-sitter	F	30-39	NA	Single	Freelance
Banker	F	20-29	University	Single	Employed
Belly dancer	F	20-29	NA	Married with children	Employed
Caregiver	F	20-29	NA	Married with children	Freelance
Clinic secretary	M	40-49	NA	Married with children	Employed
Construction worker	M	NA	NA	Married with children	Freelance
Consultant	M	30-39	University	Married with children	Freelance
Dentist	M	30-39	University	Married	Employed
Fashion designer	F	30-39	Vocational School	Married with children	Shop owner
Film director	F	60-69	University	Married with children	Freelance
Firefighter	M	30-39	High school	Married	Employed
Fortune teller	F	20-29	NA	NA	Employed
Hairdresser	M	20-29	Secondary School	Married with children	Shopowner
Housekeeper	F	30-39	Elementary School	Widowed with children	Employed by a family
Jeweller	F	40-49	Vocational School	Married with children	Shop owner
Lobby attendant	M	20-29	High school	Single	Employed
Masseur	M	NA	NA	Married	Employed
Pharmacist	F	40-49	University	Married with children	Shop owner
Pharmacy technician	F	30-39	Secondary school	Married with children	Employed
Photographer	M	30-39	High school	Married with children	Shopowner
Radio presenter	M	40-49	NA	Married with children	Employed
Security guard	M	20-29	University	Single	Employed
Tailor	M	50-59	NA	Married	Shop owner
Teacher	F	30-39	University	Married with children	Employed

neighborhood, town or village gather day and night to talk about current events and produce and disseminate the oral culture of the community. Therefore, the coffee-house metaphor reflects, according to Gannon and Pillai (2013), a male-dominant, hierarchical and relationship-oriented culture that could permeate how work is represented. In isolation, the image could suggest gender exclusion, segregation, and discrimination. Despite Turkish women, in comparison with other Eastern Arabic neighbors, have more open access, improved conditions and equal rights with men in the legal sense (Kabasakal & Bodur, 2002), the traditions underlying gender role differences are prevalent at work and in family life. This again adheres to the complexities of the coffee-house metaphor – a public space yet not quite. For example, in Turkey, men are perceived as the breadwinners and decision-makers in families (Gannon & Pillai, 2013), in rural and urban areas alike. Even in marital relationships, in which women are as well educated as men and contribute family income considerably, housework and childcare responsibilities are seen to belong to women. Turkey, geographically located in between East and West, a crossroad model of state (Pearce, 2012), allowed us to capture complex and nuanced insights in the ways gender is *talked* in relation to work and self at work.

Approaches to Narrative Inquiry

Inherent in the narrative inquiry is an interpretive reflexive process called the double hermeneutic (Finlay, 2003). First, the participants try to make sense of their social and personal world when trying to decide what to include in their narration and what to exclude, and which words to use. Secondly, the researcher tries to make sense of the participants making sense of their worlds. This second reflexive process entails re-presenting the participant's narrative and then taking 'interpretive authority for going beyond, in carefully documented ways, its literal and conscious meanings' (Josselson, 2011, p. 227).

The re-presentation can be achieved using a diverse range of approaches (Larty & Hamilton, 2011), which mainly fall into two groups: those that focus on analyzing narrative structure, and those that focus on analyzing the content of narratives (Lieblich, Tuval-Mashiach, R., & Zilber, 1998). We took the latter approach which encompassed 'what a narrative communicates rather than precisely how a narrative is structured' (Riessman, 2008, p. 730). This choice is significant for the scope of this research which is to understand what these narratives tell us about how people produce their sense of self at work and position themselves within the world of work – 'a position is what is created in and through conversations as speakers and hearers construct themselves as persons' (Gherardi & Poggio, 2001, p. 247).

Moving from the whole to the specific (Josselson, 2011), we began by reading each transcript in its entirety and capturing overarching themes and impressions from the transcript. These were then captured in a 'global impression' document (Lieblich et al., 1998, p. 62) which is a combined commentary with extracts from the narrative by regularly referring back to the narrative itself.

The 28 unique global impressions for the 28 narratives were then reviewed to decide on themes to pursue further in the analysis. From this stage, data analysis consisted of two opposing strands of activities – fragmenting and connecting. The process of fragmenting involved capturing and ordering the themes in a 'partially ordered meta-matrix' (Miles & Huberman, 1994). We assembled all relevant data in a condensed format to a master spreadsheet, by placing themes in columns and individual narrators in rows. This forced us to think about individuals from different angles. Filling as many cells in the matrix as possible for all narratives allowed us to see new themes, new connections, overlaps and differences.

Once each narrative was considered thoroughly, we moved to the connecting stage. The main method employed for this stage was the constant comparative method (Strauss & Corbin, 1998). By comparing individual narratives for each theme, and paying particular attention to gender, status and occupational differences, we induced tentative propositions. Each narrative was then revisited to see the degree of support. Data analysis oscillated between the processes of fragmenting and connecting, between inductively building concepts from the data, and deductively searching for the data that would support and further refine the nascent patterns.

Additionally, we paid particular attention to our own phenomenological world, as researchers and as the 'interpretive authorities' (Josselson, 2011). This is of clear relevance to this study because in the authorship team we have a working mother, a working father and a childless working woman. We were cognizant of our role in reflective processes, during and throughout the research process, shaping our reactions to and interpretations of the data. This required us to ask ourselves not only "what do these narratives mean" but also "how do I interpret what these narratives mean". As Guillemin & Gillam (2004, p. 275) state:

Reflexivity involves critical reflection of how the researcher constructs knowledge from the research process—what sorts of factors influence the researcher's construction of knowledge and how these influences are revealed in the planning, conduct, and writing up of the research. A reflexive researcher is one who is aware of all these potential influences and is able to step back and take a critical look at his or her own role in the research process. The goal of being reflexive in this sense has to do with improving the quality and validity of the research and recognizing the limitations of the knowledge that is produced, thus leading to more rigorous research.

To achieve reflexivity, traditionally aimed at bracketing biases, we utilized a reflective diary during the analysis process. This helped us to raise our own self-awareness of the specific issues that would require bracketing, as well as to capture our reactions to them. We also used peer debriefing during data analysis where we met at regular fortnightly intervals to compare progress in coding and analysis, challenge assumptions, probe deeper understanding, consider alternative interpretations, and manage subjectivities and to explore 'aspects of the inquiry that might otherwise remain only implicit within the inquirer's mind' (Lincoln & Guba, 1985, p. 308).

In many ways this description of the analysis process is too straightforward and linear. In practice the analysis was complex, slow, and characterized by uncertainty. Whilst moving through the data and making sense of it, the common practices and key themes only tentatively became more tangible. The peer debriefing meetings played a key role in this. During these meetings, we exchanged anecdotes from coded interviews, shared data segments, codes and meanings attached to them. There were no conflicting interpretations and this deliberation resulted in a richer pool of codes that sensitized us into alternative ways of seeing and thinking about what the participants narrated about their works and work lives. For example, the third author (male) was the first one to note the use of qualifiers as "serious", "proper" by participants when narratively constructing their workplaces and their jobs, which then sensitized the other two authors to similarities and differences in other interviews. Similarly, the second author (female with children), in one of the meetings, shared the contrasting patterns she noticed of how "serving" was constructed by different participants. This made the author team to pay attention to the demographic construction of "serving" during coding and analysis. After some trial and error, further reflection and scrutinization in our peer debriefing meetings and writing drafts of analysis and findings, a point was reached where categorization and consideration of the themes and data appeared to have been adequately carried out. It is the results of this process to which we now turn.

FINDINGS

The data analysis established two contrasting patterns – sameness and difference, each discussed in turn below. As the data analysis progressed, more depth and complexity were uncovered. This complexity is captured in the following sub-sections.

Configurations of sameness

The analysis of the work and career narratives of men and women suggested a degree of sameness. Pursuing dreams and aspirations in career choices, the work orientations, the range of feelings felt towards the work, especially in the face of (perceived) challenges and the coping mechanisms used to work with these feelings, showed little variation across genders.

Orientations towards work

Women, as much as men, suggested they pursued their dreams and aspirations in their career choices, and they shape their life choices (past and present) to serve their career dreams. Both genders, when feeling strong identification towards their work, talked about how they arrange the rest of their lives based on the job demands, and somehow with pride. This is more prevalent in narratives of people who attach a sentimental or altruistic value to their jobs. The uses of metaphors to refer to work indicate how work is considered by men and women.

Both my work life and family life are channeled into my work. (Advertiser, F)

I never consider being separated from my work, because they each have a sentimental value to me. (Artist, M)

I consider my job sacred... Our job has a very intense tempo, is very stressful yet very exciting. I never know what I will face next. (Firefighter, M)

This is my first job, and I hope it's the last. This is what I wanted to do ever since I was a child. (Babysitter, F)

My work is a second spouse. I have worked non-stop for 33 years, and want to go on until I die. (Tailor, M)

The opposite is also correct; when people referred to their jobs as an obligation that they have to do because of financial need, women and men equally emphasized the negative implications of working. They declared their unhappiness clearly, and if positive sides of work were mentioned, they were followed by "but ..." to justify their unsatisfaction to themselves and to the interviewer.

Banking is still a very respectable profession. People perceive us as respectable people since the bank hires us after a couple of interviews and then trust us with their money. That's what I used to think before I was hired, too. Now I understand that this is not the kind of job for woman. I cannot get out of here before seven. (Banker, F)

Job satisfaction depended much on the extent the job was perceived to supply the things valued by the jobholder. The value attributed to the job, whether positive or negative, and the way its characteristics and demands were narrated, reflected those things that participants consciously or subconsciously want to seek or avoid.

I like religion, and I have a fear of God. I get really disturbed for doing what I do each day... I'm seriously planning to quit because of this. The job is all about feelings and interpreting people's future by looking at shapes... It is wrong to say that such and such will happen. We are not God. (Fortune Teller, F)

I can work here, in my office with the projects I choose, during the hours that I set for myself. Even though I have to work really late and travel occasionally, I can still come to work wearing shorts, and leave early on my motorcycle to go camping. Having such independence is sometimes more important than making more money. (Consultant, M)

Work as a Challenge

The most common challenge prevalent in narratives was unrealistic demands or capricious behaviors of customers. Both genders from a variety of occupations, whether high or low status, perceived that doing the job would be much easier if customers would not be that much capricious.

There are many patients who are ignorant and that made my job stressful. (Dentist, M)

I deal with the two most difficult things to handle in the world: people and money... I get really fed up with the ignorance of people. (Banker, F)

This was observed more prevalently amongst the participants who can be classified as 'survivalists' holding low-status jobs. These participants more commonly, vocally, and strongly expressed the feelings of anger and weariness as a result of customers' behaviors.

When I think to myself that I am a nobody here, I no longer feel enthusiastic. Sometimes, I reach a point when I want to say to hell with it all, whatever is going to happen, just let it happen. I am sick and tired of being a second-class citizen. (Security Guard, M)

As time went on, I grew colder towards people... I began to see the true nature of people and felt that I was getting tired of receiving their negative energy... This is really exhausting... No one would love doing this job. (Fortune Teller, F)

Although both genders complained about the unrealistic demands or capricious behaviors of customers, only men in our sample specified the gender of the difficult customer, noting that they found women customers more difficult to handle. Below we hear from two male skilled workers singling out female for not being stable, not knowing what they want or sticking on tiny details:

What is difficult about it is not the styling of the hair, but dealing with women... women have more ups and downs in their life, and whenever they feel down, they want to forget about it all by changing their hairstyle... when I tell people about what I do for a living, they pity me, saying that it's not easy to deal with women. (Hairdresser, M)

It is especially difficult to please women as they are suspicious about every detail. They find tiny faults through minute observation. Men, on the other hand, are more superficial about such things. They don't even notice that most of the time. (Photographer, M)

After the customers, another commonly mentioned challenge by both genders was the behavior of their managers. Managers' interventions to the routine, day-to-day operations were perceived as unnecessarily rude. These again resulted in feelings of anger, exhaustion, and weariness. The way to cope with these negative feelings was to hold onto the feeling of (financial) security, perceived prestige and status of the work/ workplace or the feeling of being useful. Aspects of security and safety, such as having a steady income and social security premiums paid, perhaps unsurprisingly, was voiced more frequently by workers classified as 'survivalists':

The boss is no good, not the kind of the man to work for, but here, even if we get no business, we still get a wage. (Belly Dancer, F)

However, this is not as linearly mapped to economic and social status. Highly skilled workers too emphasized job security and financial safety as aspects of the work that keeps them going in the face of challenges and difficulties. For example, the Artist (male) in our sample considered himself lucky to have a job by referring to his teaching position at a university, as if being an artist is not a "proper job" in itself. The Actor (male) also felt the need to justify his professional standing saying, "I work for a serious company, doing a serious job". Attaching high level of significance to income security is perhaps unsurprising given the business and economic context our participants inhabit, since the Turkish economy is recurrently being hit by deep financial crises once a decade.

I am lucky I have a job; this provides me with some kind of security. (Artist, M)

Prestige appears as the second most mentioned factor that keeps people at work despite negative feelings and difficulties. When it was referred as a high-status job, job holders were proud of the title or the impact they created. Deprived of occupational prestige, holders of lower ranking jobs, focused on the prestige of the workplace in their accounts. If work was performed in a well-known, reputable workplace in their sector, they would mention it by naming there "serious". They seemed to get a higher status than their counterparts, which is essential in a high-power distance culture, like Turkey (Hofstede, 1984).

We maintain a serious appearance. (Aesthetician, F)

… the parlor, which is of good quality, has been in business for 20 years, and we are never subject to such abuse. I am proud to tell people where I work. (Masseur, M)

Holding onto altruistic feelings emerged as a coping strategy towards the challenges of the job. It was mentioned by job holders who believe they can create positive impact on the lives of people by caregiving, helping out or just being responsive to their concerns and questions. As the quotes below suggest, holding onto care for and connection to people was shared by a variety of participants regardless of the true nature of their job and the scope the job holds for caring.

Assisting people and helping them become better informed are very nice things… I find night shifts more enjoyable than the daytime ones. (Pharmacy Employee, F)

I sometimes think about doing something else, like becoming a vendor in a marketplace. But when an old client calls and makes an offer, I forget about everything. I want to do the same thing since I like my job. (Construction Worker, M)

Configurations of Differences

The analysis of the narratives revealed nuances. The more we paid attention to the way the work was talked about, the more depth and complexity we unearthed around the gendered differences of people's relations to their jobs and at their workplaces. We now turn our attention to how differences were configured.

"Serving"

In the previous section, we argued that there are no gendered differences across people's orientation towards their jobs. Men and women equally phrased their jobs in terms of financial obligation (belly dancer, housekeeper, security guard) or something for the social good (actor, firefighter, radio presenter, pharmacist, pharmacy employee) or something entirely altruistic and selfless (caregiver, masseur). However, it is interesting to note that, for the latter, as soon as the job became something more than the money, men narrated the nature of their jobs, and their role in it, as a kind of a heroic tale. They talked about how they serve "the public", what impact they have on "the people" – an anonymized, generalized, faceless crowd.

We work for the public.... I have to be selfless. If a person is selfish and not courageous, he should quit this job. (Firefighter, M)

We provide public service. (Radio Presenter, M)

In contrast, women enriched their accounts with stories of real people they have helped. The other party, in women's narratives, was as human and as fragile as the narrator. Women told stories about the mutual relationship they have formed with the other party, mentioned their names, and reflected on how they touched each other's lives. The mutualism in these stories is striking, they helped out the other party, but they are enriched in return too.

Being able to go deep into elderly's inner world is a very good feeling. (Caregiver, F)

I used to be an introvert before I started working here and since then I have overcome myself. Just by telling patients "Welcome, come on in", I have become a different person. I have learned to treat everyone equitably in this place. Since I have listened about peoples struggles all day long, I have learned to talk about my own problems. (Pharmacy Employee, F)

I witness the happiest occasions in people's lives.... which is the part of my job that I like the most... I have the perfect job. (Fashion Designer, F)

The contrast between the Fashion Designer and the Photographer is perhaps the best illustration of this difference. Despite both are operating in the same industry, wedding, the Fashion Designer focused on sharing happy moments with her clients in her narrative while the Photographer narrated how difficult it is to work with brides and how perfect the shots should be. There was no human in his accounts, and this is something we will elaborate more later, when discussing the constructions of professionalism and the ideal worker.

Paradoxically, men first and foremost, were serving the self, whilst serving the social good:

When I give a massage, my soul is relaxed which is really incredible... I discover myself in this job. (Masseur, M)

For the self is absolutely silenced and made invisible in women's stories. The "I" in their accounts was only used in relation to care, help, relation, connection, feelings. For example:

The elderly and I share quite a lot... I listen to them all with genuine curiosity.... It is very important that they are pleased with you and say thank you.... Would get happy if I felt that I made them happy. I would care everything about them... I find even some of the things they do out of spite beautiful. When they get into a stubborn contest with me, I hug and kiss them. (Caregiver, F)

The "social" is such a strong theme in women's stories that they admitted they lie to protect their customers or correct the systemic crookedness, and align their actions and its impact with their inner value system. For example, the pharmacist admitted lying to customers for their own (or the social) good:

Poor old man has people read his prescription in the coffee house, and they tell him it's for cancer. Who is going to cover it up for him? Of course, I will. I have to tell him it is for something else, I offered him tea and we talked for hours... I don't sell over the counter medicine, which might cause addiction, to young people. If an old man asks for the same medicine for, say insomnia, I give it to him. However, if a young person asks for it, I don't even consider whether I should sell it or not... Some people wearing golden bracelets up to their elbows, come here with green cards in hands. They drive their cars here, holding their green cards which are meant for the really poor and needy... I tell them those drugs are unavailable in the market... This is not a supermarket. (Pharmacist, F)

Similarly, the caregiver admitted breaching the boundaries of her job role and contract by helping the other elderly patients in the same hospital ward as her patient.

Men lie, too. However, this had a more self-serving nature, as seen below in the narratives of the clinical secretary and the masseur.

Yes, I do a little bit of favoritism here and there. If the patient is going to be finished that day anyhow, I give the appointment for the same day. However, if it will be a while for them anyway, I give appointments for later... If I treat people according to as they wish, things could not be done. (Clinical Secretary, M)

[Customers] come in wearing tennis shoes, then they take them off: all of a sudden, a terrible odor permeates the room. What's really amazing is that they are not even bothered by it. I sometimes make different excuses, telling them to take a shower first in order to accelerate their blood circulation. (Masseur, M)

Relations With and at Work

As seen in the quotes above, the relational aspect is highly visible in women's stories that they seemed to perceive their responsibility as making the people they serve happy. They expressed empathy more, with phrases such as "what if he was my husband/child", "what if I was in the same situation" used frequently. Such reflection and evaluation allowed them to go the extra mile for the customers or employees by helping them or listening to their problems.

Before my husband had back problems himself, I would just give the patients with back pain their pain medicine, corsets, etc. And I would be done. After my husband's illness, however, I began to give them a little more attention, being even more careful. It is as if I can feel their pain now. (Pharmacy Employee, F)

Women put an emphasis on the personal bond that exists between them and their customers or managers. While men used a more professional language in talking about relations at work emphasizing how they are learning from each other, mentoring each other, managing or being managed; the language that women used when talking about relations revolved around trust, friendship, confidence and sharing. It is interesting to note that such language was more prevalent with low status job holders, arguably using good relations with superiors as a status marker in the absence of occupational prestige. Alternatively, this can be explained through the internalization of masculine values by men and women as they climb up the career ladder, through the tactics of normalization, micro-disciplining and self-disciplining through social structures and institutions. Especially, when their opinions about job-related issues were acknowledged and took on board by others at work, women recounted these incidents with genuine feelings of pride.

Now I feel like a member of the family... (being one from the family is mentioned several times)...These days [the employer] has some problems at work... She pours her heart to me... when the owner of the house is opening up to me as such, it feels hypocritical of me not to do the same. (Babysitter, F)

They ask for my opinion even in the smallest decision concerning the elderly. (Caregiver, F)

In contrast with the relation-focused language in women, men, on the other hand, used process- and control-driven language more.

Everything that is processed in this place is under my responsibility... I process about 300 patients each day...My job is to get appointments in order here...I abide by the rules strictly. If I say "no" that means no, and a "yes" is a yes. (Clinical Secretary, M)

If my employees have taken some shots which are less than satisfactory, I hold another shooting session. I have to check everything constantly. When we are doing artistic shots, if the tables' measurements are taken wrong, I go crazy.... Next year, I want to open up two more studios: one in Manisa, another in Aydın. I'm already working on the cost analysis. We have a total of 9 studios in Izmir and Istanbul, my goal is to establish a large company organizing events, rather than to open up new studios. This is a must for me to advance in my profession. (Photographer, M)

These observations point towards gendered differences in how success is semantically constructed in relation to work. Men's meaning of success when working is narratively justified by appealing to control ("Everything... is under my responsibility...") and ambition ("300 patients", "9 studios"), while women are inclined to refer to the wider aspect of stakeholder satisfaction (the owner, the employer, customers).

The Professional, the Personal and the Ideal Worker

Both scholarly literature and popular accounts suggest that modern organizations have blurred the boundary between personal and professional domains of life due to work intensification. As such, the pressures shaping the boundary between life domains is likely to be experienced similarly by men and women alike. However, when work intensification is talked about, women were more attuned to the impact the work demands have on their personal life. While men equally complained about the busyness of their jobs, no men in our sample recognized or at least verbally acknowledged how work impacted their personal life.

Both my work life and family life are channeled into my work. (Advertiser, F)

I will not be able to get married because of my job. (Babysitter, F)

I would have liked to do this many years ago, but I wanted to wait until my children grew up. (Caregiver, F)

Women reflected on how work demands interfered with their social lives, hindered their marriage prospects or eaten into the time they can spend with their children. "Inadequate performance" in the private life domain was recognized only in the stories of women with young kids, and only toward their kids. This is perhaps unsurprising as motherhood in the Turkish culture, but in other cultures too, has been embraced both by traditional and contemporary educational, social and religious discourses. The traditional *sacred* role of being a mother, which suggested motherhood as the sole and worthwhile career for women, has been morphed into a different yet similar discourse. The contemporary discourses of 'intensive mothering' (Gatrell, 2013) permeate through popular and social media selling the idea(l) of the *supermom* who dedicates their whole self to her children's physical, behavioral and cognitive development.

My own children are also very small, and I constantly worry about whether they are doing OK on their own or whether they made it home safely... Of course, I love the children of the family I work for, too; still when I think that I can't do for my own children what I do for them, I get sad... My children are still very young, and it is very difficult for them to come to terms with the loss of their father. I need to be both their mother and their father, but under these circumstances, I can't even be a proper mother. (Housekeeper, F)

As mentioned before, although women complained about not taking care of themselves properly, they did not feel guilty. This is probably because self-care is a novel concept for the Turkish people as this requires seeing the self as an individual rather than a part of a collective entity. Interestingly, women who are self-employed did not express any guilt for not taking care of their kids properly. When evaluated in conjunction with the earlier findings around personal development and self-betterment discussed in the previous section, we can postulate that this maybe because prioritizing the professional domain over the personal is seen as a mean for serving their own welfare and wellbeing, and through that their families'.

When I am here, I don't think much about home, but when I'm at home, my mind is always at store. I don't feel relaxed if I'm not at the store. (Pharmacist, F)

I can't get any sleep until I'm done, and I guide [the team] to be the same way. I sometimes wear them out. They suggest going to the neighboring village for lunch, but I turn them down and tell them to get a quick bite to eat and be ready to shoot again in half an hour. (Film Director, F)

Women expressed that work demands influence marital relationship too. When women perceived they can work without the interference of their husband or when they are "let" to manage their own money by the husband, they talked about feelings of appreciation and gratefulness. The husband was then labelled as a "good husband":

I like best about my husband is that he has never interfered with my business or the money I make... I guess this is lucky of me if he were the kind to meddle in my business, what would I do? Get a divorce after a child? (Pharmacist, F)

This also came with assumed helplessness when the husbands demanded the opposite as the divorce was not seen as an option after having had children. Such reflection on the marital relationship when talking about the personal and the professional domains was only visible in women's stories; no men in our sample mention feeling grateful to their wives for being able to manage their professional life domain as they wish. The professional life domain was assumed to have dominance in men's stories, as men societally were expected to make a living when they come to the age. No women in our sample mentioned such societal, normative pressures. For instance, the masseur explained his motivation begin as he was expected to make money by his family when he came to the age. Would he have felt the same way if he was a woman? Especially, among the 'survivalists', both women and men in their narratives imply that the responsibility of making money for the family belonged first to men; if they cannot make enough, women had to work to support.

I am thankful that my husband is not like those of my friends, even though he needs me to work. At least, he doesn't go through my purse; he doesn't ask me how much I earn; rather, he gives me money from his earnings. (Belly Dancer, F)

Although my husband is always here in the store as a male figure, I am actually the one running the business. (Jeweller, F)

Analysis of the narratives demonstrates how narratively the participants positioned themselves within the world of work, and the work within their personal lifeworld. The analysis brings about an order of gender in how work is approached, made sense of, experienced, and narrated. Recognizing these dynamics helps organizations and their members to be more aware that gender is not a natural attribute of people, but something we create and recreate in our everyday work narratives, which in turn shapes both the meaning we attribute to work and the meaning we get out of it. We now turn our attention to discussing implications of this analysis for theory and practice.

DISCUSSION AND CONCLUSION

Our analysis shows a similar but ambivalent construction of the meaning of work. Both women and men considered work as a way of pursuing their personal and professional aspirations, and how there is always a dependable relation between working life (paid job) and personal or family life. However, the way work is integrated to life is narratively constructed differently depending on gender practices. Specifically, the uses of organizational metaphors to refer to work like "family" and "second spouse" epitomize how working is considered a more collective experience *involving* others for women, in contrast to an individual experience *impacting* others for men. The intention of helping themselves but also others and at the same time being useful, contributes to women representation of a different working ethos than men. Doing gender differently in the context of working by creating community, resonates with Hassard's (2012) explanation of how transcendental could be to work for women in comparison to men in certain conditions. Carey (1967) has suggested that this is the case of ethnic contexts where the meaning of work is constructed in relation to family and community values, not only in relation to status or class. In contrast, men cannot escape to a *"do ut des"* (I give, so that you may give) rhetoric, even when doing something for others. This is expressed in the need to be retributed in any way, like to be considered "heroes" because of serving. As Dennis, Henriques and Slaughter (1969[1956]) have suggested, in their ethnography of working communities, pre- and post-industrial capitalism constructed the relation between men and work always around the figure of a wage-worker that has to be always retributed for everything he does.

Retribution and compensation have always been central to the discussion of how work is constructed, as they are embedded in the conception of freedom. As the anthropologist Olivia Harris (2007) has referred, 'the opposition between freedom and coercion plays a foundational role in Western ideas about work' (p. 158). Reactions to work demands is equally addressed by both women and men. Unrealistic demands or capricious behaviors of customers and managers have however been narratively negotiated differently, invariably resulting in feelings of alienation (Blauner, 1964). Both genders from a variety of occupations whether high or low status referred that doing the job would be much easier if customers would not be that much capricious and the behavior of their managers been different. Managers' interventions to the routine, day-to-day operations, were perceived as unnecessarily rude. Such management malpractice, in the form of patronization, was a source of burnout. Literature on management malpractice signposted that favoritism and patronization were a source of burnout and turnover of working women from the moment official statistics started to consider women as workers as men (Benson, 1929).

Why women stay at work? As Andrew Clark (1997) referred 30 years ago, by any standards, women's jobs are always worse than men, but women, particularly young, have more positive job expectations. The argumentation by our participants was constructed around topics like expected financial security, perceived prestige and status of the work/ workplace or the feeling of being useful. Aspects of security and safety, such as having steady income and social security premiums paid, perhaps unsurprisingly, was voiced more frequently by workers we classified as "survivalists", even when addressing the conflicting agendas of work and life.

This conflict between life and work domains is accompanied by a feeling of guilt, when the women interviewed had young children. This has been the case with industrial and post-industrial working women across all sectors. Care responsibilities of children have been constructed solely around a women-mother actor that could be socialized and culturally penalized if they do not put these responsibilities at the center of their life (Toffoletti & Starr, 2016). Women professional success could in fact suggests that a woman is not taking seriously her duties as mother (Blau, Ferber & Winkler, 2002; Brindley, 2005).

We noticed in our analysis that success is indeed constructed quite differently. When women talk about growth, it is more about bettering themselves and developing personally and socially. This stands in contrast to men's narratives which is more about climbing the metaphorical ladder, such as opening more stores (the Photographer), expanding networks and customer base (the Consultant), drawing up contracts with prestigious galleries who would support the production of the work (the Artist). As we referred above, women produce the meaning of success differently, as a more social and holistic space in need of construction.

Doing gender while working is intrinsically related with the presentation of the self in dynamic and ambivalent scenarios in permanent negotiation that do not follow the binary gender roles of working women - working men anymore (Rumens, 2017). Perhaps our analysis could serve to illuminate new ways of understanding this negotiation, that not only could conduce to construct working women at work as empowered and autonomous subjects whose lives are shaped by individual choice, but also help working men to reimage different kinds of masculinities than what is traditionally ascribed to them.

REFERENCES

Alvesson, M., & Karreman, D. (2000). Taking the linguistic turn in organizational research: Challenges, responses, consequences. *The Journal of Applied Behavioral Science, 36*(2), 136–158. doi:10.1177/0021886300362002

Arifeen, S. R., & Gatrell, C. (2020). Those glass chains that bind you: How British Muslim women professionals experience career, faith and family. *British Journal of Management, 31*(1), 221–236. doi:10.1111/1467-8551.12387

Becker, G. S. (1964). *Human capital.* National Bureau of Economic Research.

Beham, B., Drobnic, S., Präg, P., Baierl, A., & Lewis, S. (2020). Work-to-family enrichment and gender inequalities in eight European countries. *International Journal of Human Resource Management, 31*(5), 589–610. doi:10.1080/09585192.2017.1355837

Benson, M. B. (1929). Labor turnover of working women. *The Annals of the American Academy of Political and Social Science, 143*(1), 109–119. doi:10.1177/000271622914300113

Blau, F., Ferber, M., & Winkler, A. (2002). *The economics of women, men and work.* Prentice-Hall.

Blauner, R. (1964). *Alienation and freedom: The factory worker and his industry.* The University of Chicago Press.

Brewis, J. (2014). The ethics of researching friends: On convenience sampling in qualitative management and organization studies. *British Journal of Management, 25*(4), 849–862. doi:10.1111/1467-8551.12064

Brewis, J., & Warren, S. (2001). Pregnancy as project: Organizing reproduction. *Administrative Theory & Praxis, 23*(3), 383–406. doi:10.1080/10841806.2001.11643533

Brindley, C. (2005). Barriers to women achieving their entrepreneurial potential. *International Journal of Entrepreneurial Behaviour & Research, 11*(2), 144–161. doi:10.1108/13552550510590554

Bruner, J. (1987). Life as narrative. *Social Research, 54*(1), 11–32.

Carey, A. (1967). The Hawthorne Studies: A radical criticism. *American Sociological Review, 32*(3), 403–416. doi:10.2307/2091087

Clark, A. E. (1997). Job satisfaction and gender: Why are women so happy at work? *Labour Economics, 4*(4), 341–372. doi:10.1016/S0927-5371(97)00010-9

Cochran, L. (1990). Narrative as a paradigm for career research. In R. A. Young & W. A. Borgen (Eds.), *Methodological approaches to the study of career* (pp. 71–86). Greenwood Publishing.

Dale, A. (2005). Combining family and employment: evidence from Pakistani and Bangladeshi women. In D. M. Houston (Ed.), *Work–life balance in the 21st century* (pp. 230–245). Palgrave Macmillan. doi:10.1057/9780230373594_12

Dennis, N., Henriques, F., & Slaughter, C. (1969). *Coal Is Our Life*. Tavistock Publications. (Original work published 1956)

Dingley, J., & Catterall, P. (2020). Language, religion and ethno-national identity: The role of knowledge, culture and communication. *Ethnic and Racial Studies*, *43*(2), 410–429. doi:10.1080/01419870.2019.1587309

Durbin, S. (2015). *Women who succeed: Strangers in paradise*. Palgrave Macmillan.

Engels, F. (1892). *The condition of the working-Class in England in 1844*. Swan Sonnenschein & Co. (Original work published 1844)

Finlay, L. (2003). Through the looking glass: Intersubjectivity and hermeneutic reflection. In L. Finlay & B. Gough (Eds.), *Reflexivity: A practical guide for Researchers in health and social sciences*. Blackwell Publishing. doi:10.1002/9780470776094.ch8

Gannon, M. J., & Pillai, R. (2013). Understanding global cultures: Metaphorical journeys through 31 nations, continents, and diversity. *Sage (Atlanta, Ga.)*.

Gatrell, C. (2010). Who rules the game? An investigation of sex-work, gender, agency and the body. *Gender in Management*, *25*(3), 208–226. doi:10.1108/17542411011036419

Gatrell, C. (2013). Maternal bodywork: How women managers and professionals negotiate pregnancy and new motherhood at work. *Human Relations*, *66*(5), 621–644. doi:10.1177/0018726712467380

Gergen, K. J. (1985). Social constructionist inquiry: Context and implications. In K. J. Gergen & K. E. Davis (Eds.), *The social construction of the person* (pp. 3–18). Springer. doi:10.1007/978-1-4612-5076-0_1

Gergen, K. J. (1999). An invitation to social construction. *Sage (Atlanta, Ga.)*.

Gherardi, S. (1994). The gender we think, the gender we do in our everyday organizational lives. *Human Relations*, *47*(6), 591–610. doi:10.1177/001872679404700602

Gherardi, S. (1995). Gender, symbolism and organizational cultures. *Sage (Atlanta, Ga.)*.

Gherardi, S., & Poggio, B. (2001). Creating and recreating gender order in organizations. *Journal of World Business, 36*(3), 245–259. doi:10.1016/S1090-9516(01)00054-2

Giddens, A. (1979). *Central problems in social theory: Action, structure, and contradiction in social analysis.* University of California Press. doi:10.1007/978-1-349-16161-4

Goffman, E. (1956). *The presentation of self in everyday life.* Doubleday.

Goldthorpe, J. H., Lockwood, D., Bechhofer, F., & Platt, J. (1968). *The affluent worker: Industrial attitudes and behaviour.* Cambridge University Press.

Grant, D., Hardy, C., Oswick, C., & Putnam, L. (2004). *Handbook of Organizational Discourse.* Sage.

Greenberg, D., Ladge, J., & Clair, J. (2009). Negotiating pregnancy at work: Public and private conflicts. *Negotiation and Conflict Management Research, 2*(1), 42–56. doi:10.1111/j.1750-4716.2008.00027.x

Guillemin, M., & Gillam, L. (2004). Ethics, reflexivity, and "ethically important moments" in research. *Qualitative Inquiry, 10*(2), 261–280. doi:10.1177/1077800403262360

Harris, O. (2007). What makes people work? In R. Astuti, J. Parry, & C. Stafford (Eds.), Questions of anthropology. Berg.

Hassard, J. (2012). Rethinking the Hawthorne Studies: The Western Electric research in its social, political and historical context. *Human Relations, 65*(11), 1431–1461. doi:10.1177/0018726712452168

Hoffman, L. (1992). A reflexive stance for family therapists. In S. McNamee & K. Gergen (Eds.), *Therapy as a social construction* (pp. 7–24). Sage.

Hofstede, G. (1984). Culture's consequences: International differences in work-related values. *Sage (Atlanta, Ga.).*

ILO. (2012). *International Standard Classification of Occupations: Structure, group definitions and correspondence tables.* International Labour Organization. https://www.ilo.org/wcmsp5/groups/public/---dgreports/---dcomm/---publ/documents/publication/wcms_172572.pdf

Josselson, R. (2011). "Bet you think this song is about you": Whose narrative is it in narrative research? *Narrative Works, 1*(1), 33–51.

Kabasakal, H., & Bodur, M. (2002). Arabic cluster: A bridge between East and West. *Journal of World Business*, *37*(1), 40–54. doi:10.1016/S1090-9516(01)00073-6

Kanter, R. (1977). *Men and women of the corporation*. Basic Books.

Katrinli, A. (Ed.). (2008). *Real life stories of how people feel and behave in organizations*. BookSurge Publishing.

Larty, J., & Hamilton, E. (2011). Structural approaches to narrative analysis in entrepreneurship research: Exemplars from two researchers. *International Small Business Journal*, *29*(3), 220–237. doi:10.1177/0266242611401796

Lewis, P., Simpson, R., & Sealy, R. (2010). Meritocracy, difference and choice: Women's experiences of advantage and disadvantage at work. *Gender in Management*, *25*(3), 165–169. doi:10.1108/17542411011036374

Lieblich, A., Tuval-Mashiach, R., & Zilber, T. (1998). Narrative research: Reading, analysis, and interpretation. *Sage (Atlanta, Ga.)*.

Lincoln, Y. S., & Guba, E. G. (1985). *Naturalistic inquiry*. Sage. doi:10.1016/0147-1767(85)90062-8

McCrone, D. (1994). Getting by and making out in Kirkcaldy. In M. Anderson, F. Bechofer, & J. Gershuny (Eds.), The Social and Political Economy of the Household (pp. 68–99). Oxford University Press.

Miles, M. B., & Huberman, A. M. (1984). Qualitative data analysis: An expanded sourcebook. *Sage (Atlanta, Ga.)*.

Miller, T. (2017). *Making sense of parenthood: Caring, gender and family lives*. Cambridge University Press. doi:10.1017/9781316219270

Pearce, S. C. (2012). The "Turkish model" of sociology: East-west science, state formation, and the post-secular. *The American Sociologist*, *43*(4), 406–427. doi:10.100712108-012-9163-4

Plummer, K. (2001). The call of life stories in ethnographic research. In P. Atkinson, A. Coffey, S. Delamont, J. Lofland, & L. Lofland (Eds.), *Handbook of Ethnography* (pp. 395–406). Sage. doi:10.4135/9781848608337.n27

Riessman, C. K. (1993). Narrative analysis. *Sage (Atlanta, Ga.)*.

Riessman, C. K. (2008). Narrative methods for the human sciences. *Sage (Atlanta, Ga.)*.

Robinson, O. C. (2014). Sampling in interview-based qualitative research: A theoretical and practical guide. *Qualitative Research in Psychology*, *11*(1), 25–41. doi:10.1080/14780887.2013.801543

Rumens, N. (2017). Postfeminism, men, masculinities and work: A research agenda for gender and organization studies scholars. *Gender, Work and Organization*, *24*(3), 245–259. doi:10.1111/gwao.12138

Strauss, A., & Corbin, J. (1998). Basics of qualitative research techniques. *Sage (Atlanta, Ga.)*.

Strazzeri, V. (2015). Max Weber and the 'labour question': An initial appraisal. *Max Weber Studies*, *15*(1), 69–100. doi:10.15543/MWS/2015/1/5

Toffoletti, K., & Starr, K. (2016). Women academics and work-life balance: Gendered discourses of work and care. *Gender, Work and Organization*, *23*(5), 489–504. doi:10.1111/gwao.12133

Vinnicombe, S. (2000). The position of women in management in Europe. In M. J. Davidson & R. J. Burke (Eds.), *Women in management: Current research issues* (Vol. 2). Sage.

Warner, W. L., & Lunt, P. S. (1941). *The social life of a modern community* (Vol. 1). Yale University Press.

Chapter 2
Holistic and Critical Perspective to Politics of Dress and the Female Body in Workplace Settings

Zeynep Ozdamar Ertekin
Izmir University of Economics, Turkey

ABSTRACT

The purpose of this chapter is to bring a more holistic, inclusive, and critical perspective to discussions on the politics of the female body and dress in workplace settings. It aims to explore the struggles and experiences of women in the business environment with regards to 'looking the part' and the role dress and bodily adornment play in construction and expression of their workplace identities. It will further discuss the role dress might have as signifier of status and power and the ambiguities related to age, body image, sexuality, and identity at work. Furthermore, most of the prior studies on dress acknowledge fashion as a Western phenomenon ignoring the role of dress in non-Western cultures. Therefore, this chapter also aims to discuss how might these conflicts differ in a non-Western context. Finally, considering that during the COVID-19 pandemic image management has shifted to a virtual world, creating further challenges for women, the chapter will conclude by shedding light on these struggles and presenting ideas for the future of work dress code.

DOI: 10.4018/978-1-7998-8742-3.ch002

INTRODUCTION

Approaches to gender equality are largely ineffective and prejudices about women still dominate the workplace (Tastad and Bass, 2020). Hence, women all over the world are facing numerous challenges and obstacles in business life. One of these challenges is women's identity at work. The persistent masculine nature of organizations means that professional women often have to conform to a male norm (Acker, 1990; due Billing, 2011). Therefore, impression management and "dressing for success" at work can become a struggle especially for women. Products and consumption experiences are often used to construct identity in contemporary consumer culture and society (Firat and Dholakia, 2003). Similarly, clothes have an important role in construction, development and expression of identity and self-image, especially for women (Benn, 2004; Boden, 2006). Women often dress their bodies in line with their changing identities and senses of self (Rawlins, 2006; Stone, 1962). In this regard, fashion and dress help to reflect the ambivalence of identity management (Davis, 1992).

Relation of dress and identity have been discussed by earlier scholars, since dress is an effective tool for constructing one's desired appearance (Davis, 1992) and communicating identity (Crane, 2000; Entwistle, 2000; Goodman, Knotts and Jackson, 2007; Roach-Higgins and Eicher, 1992; Stone, 1962). Dress is a nonverbal means of communicating identity and it helps to make a statement about age, gender, social class, school affiliation, or religion (Roach-Higgins and Eicher, 1992). Occupational and organizational identity can be expressed via dress as well (Pratt and Rafaeli, 1997; Rafaeli and Pratt, 1993). Dress is not only related to clothing. It incorporates all aspects of appearance. Despite the importance of body and embodiment in understanding organizations (Wolkowitz, 2006) and the fact that dress and bodily adornment are important parts of the corporate landscape, it is relatively an under-researched topic (Parker and Warren, 2017; Warren and Parker, 2009). Therefore, the aim of this chapter is to bring a critical perspective to discussions on the essence of dress and female body at workplace, both in a Western and a non-Western context.

In *Adorned in Dreams: Fashion and Modernity*, Elizabeth Wilson (1985) addressed that fashion is a cultural phenomenon and an aesthetic medium to express ideas, desires and beliefs. Therefore, dress and fashion are critical in communicating multiple meanings (Boydell, 2004). Fashion and clothes play a crucial part in defining gender, and in construction and expression of femininity and sexuality (Entwistle, 2000; Morris-Roberts, 2004; Twigg, 2007). Women can exercise agency in dressing their bodies. However, they also have to abide with cultural and societal expectations and often try to avoid the 'disciplinary gaze', which Foucault (1979) describes as the social control that result from being under constant surveillance.

This disciplinary gaze and surveillance can become even more intense at work environment. Furthermore, we live in a society obsessed with youth and beauty. Today women, in many countries, need to place greater emphasis upon appearance and control how they should look to conform to the normalized ideal of beauty and youth (Carolan, 2005). The aspiration and pressure to present themselves as beautiful, young and feminine may contradict with their professional identity at work.

Consequently, the purpose of this conceptual study is to shed further light and critically discuss these concerns and arguments about politics of the female body and dress in workplace settings. The chapter aims to explore the struggles and experiences of women at business environment with regards to 'looking the part' and the role dress and bodily adornment play in construction and expression of their workplace identities. It will further discuss the role dress might have as signifier of status and power and the ambiguities related to age, body image, sexuality and identity at work. The topic is discussed in the context of fashion, as dress provides an arena in which debates related to age, body, identity and agency can be pursued and fashion and dress are culturally constituted as feminized (Twigg, 2007). Furthermore, most of the prior studies on dress or fashion acknowledge fashion as a Western phenomenon ignoring the role of dress in non-Western cultures (Welters and Lillethun, 2018). Therefore, this chapter also aims to discuss how might these conflicts, concerns and struggles differ in a non-Western context.

Especially at a time when both fashion and management studies started to raise concerns about diversity and exclusivity, and with the rise of cultural and critical studies showing the need for a global and inclusive view, the chapter aims to provide a more holistic, inclusive and critical approach to discussions on fashion, workplace identity and gender. Finally, considering that during the Covid-19 pandemic, image management has shifted to a virtual world and home as working space have become part of the professional identity, creating further challenges and struggles especially for women, the topic will benefit scholars by presenting ideas for future research. In this regard, the chapter is structured to include main issues, controversies and problems related to politics of the female body and dress in workplace settings and provide insight for emerging trends and suggest future research opportunities related to future of work dress code.

ISSUES AND CONTROVERSIES RELATED TO DRESS AND PROFESSIONAL IDENTITY

Role of Dress in Construction and Expression of Women's Identities

Gender identity is an important component of a consumer's self-concept and identity. Even though gender roles vary by culture, many societies still have traditional sex roles and people often conform to their culture's expectations of how their gender should act and dress. Accordingly, society's expectations of masculinity and femininity also help to determine the products consumers buy to meet these expectations (Solomon, 2018). Gender identity is often represented via visual symbols such as dress (Akdemir, 2018; Davis, 1992; Goffman, 1959). In this regard, clothes are a means to express identity and can help to exercise agency (Twigg, 2007). Similarly, Boydell (2004) highlighted the important role clothing has played in defining feminine and masculine identities. Young girls, from an early age, may pursue an ideal of femininity in order to become effective consumers (Russell and Tyler, 2002). However, this sexuality is not only promoted by consumer culture and marketing institutions. Practices such as dressing-up or bodily adornment and social institutions such as schools and families, also contribute to gendering and sexualizing of bodies (Martin, 1998). Furthermore, even though clothes have an important role in the presentation of acceptable appearance and in determining appropriate femininity, it is difficult to define what appropriate femininity is, as there are different versions of femininity (Boydell, 2004). Moreover, styles or items that become fashionable can challenge existing perceptions and expectations of gender identity, such as trousers that became popular and preferred by women who struggle against class and gender discrimination in the 1960s (Akdemir, 2018).

Even though women can exercise agency in dressing their bodies, they also have to abide with cultural and societal expectations and actually have little control over what is presented and offered to them by marketing institutions. Therefore, they consume many products to alter their appearance to be in line with these expectations (Solomon, 2018). Furthermore, identities communicated by dress are also influenced by moral and aesthetic standards of the society as they impose what is considered proper and improper to wear and display (Roach-Higgins and Eicher, 1992). Therefore, women are often concerned with social disapproval and try to avoid the 'disciplinary gaze' and surveillance. Even though the emphasis is often on being subject to and pleasing the male gaze (Oliver, 2017), women often tell other women what they must wear in order to be liberated (Scott, 2005). Consequently, women are often under surveillance of both male and female gaze. This surveillance and disciplinary gaze can become more intense at work environments and these cultural and societal expectations can become even more restrictive in non-Western cultures.

Moreover, the society today is obsessed with youth and beauty. Mass media plays a major role in cultural idealization of youthfulness by signifying the importance of looking beautiful, younger, and thinner (Ozdamar Ertekin and Atik, 2015). Beautiful body images shown in advertisements, press, television, and films emphasize the importance of appearance and body maintenance in consumer culture (Featherstone, 1991). Consequently, in many countries, women may feel the pressure to control how they should look to conform to the normative standards and normalized cultural ideals of beauty and youth presented to them (Bordo, 1993; Carolan, 2005). As a result, there is an increasing desire to stay forever young, so they push the limits of their body by using products and services to combat the aging process and to reconstruct a youthful and beautiful appearance (Featherstone, 1991, 2010; Gavish et al., 2008; Thompson and Hirschman, 1995). As less powerful cultures often adopt standards of beauty in dominant cultures (Solomon, 2018), The Western ideal of beauty and similar concerns related to ageism are also valid in non-Western contexts.

Consequently, adorning the body with attractive clothes is not enough anymore. Many women today are having cosmetic surgery for aesthetic reasons to achieve a desired image (Firat and Dholakia, 2003). As women, are constantly exposed to celebrities, models, and actresses with ideal body images and physical beauty, they eventually become unhappy with their own bodies and develop body consciousness, even at a young age (Thomas, 2007; Thompson and Hirschman, 1995). This early sexualization has psychological implications such as eating disorders, low self-esteem, and depression. Furthermore, it has negative effects on society, including an increase in sexism, increased rates of sexual violence and sexual harassment (Hardy, 2010), which can also become problems women face in work environments.

On the other hand, women can also use clothing as a means to exercise agency and to resist or redefine the dominant meanings of age (Twigg, 2007), since fashion and clothes can be significant elements in the constitution and experience of age (Cook and Kaiser, 2004; Klepp and Storm-Mathisen, 2005; Twigg, 2007). However, even though marketing institutions in their campaigns aimed at women often frame consumption of clothes, make-up, accessories, and cosmetic procedures as expressions of freedom, they are actually means to adapt to a lifetime of compulsory, expensive, and sometimes even harmful practices (Wade, 2012). Therefore, women may not be exercising agency by dressing and acting in a certain fashion. Instead, they may be manipulated by marketing institutions to believe that it is natural for them to aspire femininity, youth, and sexuality. This aspiration and pressure to present themselves as beautiful, young and feminine may contradict with their professional identity at work, as they also have the pressure to 'look the part' in business environments.

Struggles of Women Related to 'Looking the Part' in Business Environments

As addressed in the previous section, women in many societies both struggled and took advantage of the power of fashion. Apart from the controversies and problems related to age, body image, and sexuality, women also face ambiguities related to their identity at work and have struggles with regards to 'looking the part' in business environments. For instance, Wolkowitz (2006) acknowledges that in industries such as retail and airlines, there are often strict rules about dress code and how employees should look. Therefore, impression management and the formation of self-identity is highly significant in workplace life. In this regard, dress and adornment have an important role in women's construction of their workplace identities and in expression of occupational identity (Pratt and Rafaeli, 1997; Roach-Higgins and Eicher, 1992). Scholars also argue that both in general and in an organizational setting, women are more sensitive about dress and appearance compared to men (Kanter, 1977). This may be partly due to the greater need women have for legitimacy, credibility, acceptance, and self-confidence in male-dominated organizations (Gummer, 1998). However, despite the importance of dress and bodily adornment in corporate landscape, it is an under-researched topic (Parker and Warren, 2017; Warren and Parker, 2009). Therefore, this chapter aims to focus on presentational aspects of the female body and dress in workplace settings, both in Western and non-Western contexts.

Fashion is an important mode of expression and dress has a significant role as signifier of status and power in the workplace. Therefore, it is important to discuss the power of style and use of clothing, especially by women. Dress can be used both to empower and disempower the wearer. For instance, wearing a uniform at work can be empowering and signify superiority but it can also lead to suppression of individual expression of creativity and individuality, taking away the freedom to choose one's own clothes to wear (Scott, 2005). Imposition or forbidding of certain items of clothing can have a disempowering effect as well, such as forcing women to wear or to remove turban or hijab in certain countries. Consequently, dress often has a contradictory role, requiring a more complex interpretation and analysis. For instance, clothes can be used both to communicate belonging and resistance (Boydell, 2004). Similarly, body provides a tool to manifest power as well, such as body modifications or the control of body weight. This relationship with body is also complex and operates in both directions. These contradictory roles and complexities related to dress and female body are also observed in organizational settings.

Rafaeli and colleagues are among the researchers who examined the meaning of dress in organizational life. For instance, Pratt and Rafaeli (1997) studied the meaning of nurses' dress in the rehabilitation unit of a hospital and argued that organizational dress both affirms control and communicates identity. In another study, Rafaeli and colleagues explored the thoughts, feelings, and behaviors of female administrative employees in an academic organization regarding the clothes that they wear to work and how they relate to dress. The authors state that individuals use dress as a symbol to engage and execute their role in organizations (Rafaeli et al., 1997). The study also sheds light on women's experiences in a male-dominated institution by reflecting on the tension between the participants' gender role and their organizational role and how they use appropriate dress to manage this tension (Gummer, 1998). The authors argue that dressing in a too feminine or sexually attractive way was interpreted to be inappropriate and uncomfortable, and also challenge one's status in the organization (Rafaeli et al., 1997).

Women have been a part of the corporate world but the style and appearance of many work environments still remain quite masculine (Orchard and Burke, 2020). Professional women often have to conform to a male norm. Therefore, "Dressing for success" and impression management can become a struggle for women (Acker, 1990; due Billing, 2011). Many societies still divide labor by sex although what tasks are considered women's work varies from society to society (Scott, 2005). Appearance is a marker of the gender system at work signified by dress, which is often monitored and regulated. In order to show the differences between sexes women are expected to wear and show feminine attributes, while men are expected show masculine characteristics. Many of the earlier discussions on the career women focused on appearance underlining the importance of "dress for success" or "power dressing". Therefore, the look of the Modern Woman was presented as an ideal (Scott, 2005, p. 321). According to Joanne Entwistle (2007), power dressing marked a new development in the history of women and work. It addressed a new kind of female worker, not including all women, for instance the cleaning lady or the manual worker. This new code of dressing was associated with educated, professional middle-class career women who emerged in the 1970s (Scott, 2005).

In his book *Dress for Success*, John Molloy (1976) described the look of the successful professional woman. According to him, the clothing that would make woman successful in business environments are skirt suits, plain shirts, sensible shoes, ties or scarves and expensive accessories (Scott, 2005, p. 287). Similarly, according to social psychologist Gurung, women are perceived to be more competent when they wear formal attire (Mull, 2020). Consequently, the professional women have become the favorite target of popular culture. Elizabeth Cagan (1978), on the other hand, stated that the motivation that led women to adopt power dressing was contrary to true feminist objectives. In *Fresh Lipstick,* Linda Scott (2005) criticizes the feminist critique of fashion, as she finds it too simplistic and not inclusive, excluding different viewpoints on the politics of dress. She argues that the phenomenon is more complex and problematic and dress is never politically neutral. Scott (2005) disapproves the higher moral value given to simple, colorless and asexual dress.

She argues that wearing high heels and make-up, and doing your hair does not deny you the right to seek advancement. Women do not have to wear ugly or shapeless clothes to achieve empowerment and equality. A woman should be able to work and still be considered feminine (Scott, 2005, p. 247). According to Scott (2005), wearing everything from high heels to lipstick is not oppressive and associating fashion with sexual objectification only serves to control other women, not to free them. Therefore, she challenges feminists to move beyond appearances and focus on equality for all women everywhere.

Image Management and Meaning of Dress for Women During Covid-19

Choices and properties of dress in relation to communicating identity change due to economic, demographic, technological and other societal changes (Roach-Higgins and Eicher, 1992). Similarly, impression management and presentation of self, shifted to a virtual world and the spatial distinctions between office and home eroded due to increase in working from home with the Covid-19 pandemic (Orchard and Burke, 2020). As more work is carried out from home, it has become harder to associate work with a particular mode of dress (Mull, 2020). Coming home and changing the work outfit allowed people to be free from work, both mentally and physically. However, as many people now wear the same clothes to work and to do housework and other chores at home, the mind and body never disconnect from labor (Mull, 2020). According to a survey with 1,000 remote workers, nearly half of people working from home don't adhere to a defined dress code for remote working. Business-professional, business-casual and smart-casual dressers all reported higher levels of productivity than those who dressed in gym clothes and pajamas (Smith, 2020). Furthermore, social psychologist Gurung states that there is an association between being dressed well and credibility and knowledge. It shows that you're taking the job seriously (Mull, 2020). Similarly, according to Linda Scott (2005), maintaining grooming allows a person to be seen credible in the eyes of the community and to stop grooming is giving up on life. Maintaining one's own appearance expresses the will to survive and raises chances of survival (Scott, 2005).

On the other hand, end of the work dress code is not necessarily the abandonment of professionalism. Dressing in a formal manner can convey respect to others. However, some studies also found that employees were more productive when casual dress was permitted (Elan, 2020). It is also important to consider the meaning of appropriate dress and distinguish between organizational comfort and personal comfort. Organizationally comfortable dress is dress that is organizationally appropriate, but not necessarily physically comfortable (Gummer, 1998). Moreover, employees might even become happier with the simplified dress code or no dress code, as people do not have to spend additional resources to buy work wear and for some more-casual dress codes can be a morale booster as well (Mull, 2020). Therefore, attitudes to the workplace and workwear started to become more casual and an increase in more-casual workplaces and more relaxed dress codes were observed even before the pandemic. This trend is expected to continue, since many people may continue working from home or in a hybrid system and the nature of workplaces and dress codes will continue to be fluid in the post-pandemic period as well (Elan, 2020).

Consequently, the pandemic and this new era of working from home or in a hybrid system changed the way we perceive and construct professionalism. The Covid-19 has produced unexpected effects on both fashion and work environments. Since March 2020, the pandemic has been influencing fashion and its politics in many ways, leading to decrease in purchase of clothing and accessories among many others. It also initiated the emergence of new aesthetic ideals and preferences, such as the quest for functional and comfortable but elegant clothes for working from home. For instance, the export of formal workwear such as suits, trousers and jackets decreased, whereas the demand for houseware, loungewear, sweatpants and sweatshirts increased (TRT Haber, 2020). New items and terms are introduced both to our wardrobes and to fashion terminology, such as the 'house dress' (*Onedio*, 2020), 'nap dress' (Feldman, 2020) and the 'zoom shirt' (Elan, 2020).

Secondary data from the media already includes discussions on how the pandemic has changed work dress codes. For instance, according to an article in The Guardian, work dress codes have changed radically during the pandemic, focusing more on simplicity and comfort and some of these trends related with the new relaxed work attire, will stay even after returning to the office (Elan, 2020). Another article in the Huffpost examines «What People Wore to Work Before the Pandemic vs. Now» and includes examples of work outfits from pre- and post-lockdown periods. According to their findings, there are people who started to dress nicely from the waist up only; ones who experiment with their style, and others who only changed their outfit slightly, for instance, by adding personal protective equipment, such as masks (Feldman, 2020).

The way we feel and speak about our clothes changed as well (Elan, 2021). For instance, two new words were coined to describe the new attitude to fashion and changing relationship with clothes, due to the stresses and mundanity of lockdown. The New York Times's "hate-wear" refers to clothes that are "neither stylish nor particularly comfortable, yet constantly in rotation." These are items worn for their utility rather than their style. Esquire's term "sadwear" on the other hand, refers to "clothes that make us feel better when we're sad, specifically born out of the existential ennui of lockdown" (Elan, 2021).

Women's workplace experiences of the pandemic have been different compared to their male counterparts, mostly due to multiplicity of the roles they have at home and the pressure to look nicer on video calls. Their virtual and home-working spaces and the clothes and accessories they wear, become part of the 'new' professional female identity they construct and communicate. Even though some women have become less attentive to their grooming habits such as wearing less-styled hair, sweats and lounge wear, and /or less or no make-up, others still felt the pressure to look more "professional," either from fear of not being taken seriously or from cultural pressure (Davis, 2021). Secondary data from the media includes reports of women being told to attend to their appearance online in order to 'look nicer' on video calls. According to a new survey published by the law firm Slater and Gordon, women are being told to dress sexier or more provocatively and wear make up for video calls. This reveals that workplace sexism is still widespread and continuing despite remote working and that "sexism has instead found new and insidious ways to thrive online" (Sky news, 2020). Although both men and women are told to pay greater attention to their appearance, women are still more likely to face comments and requests about their appearance during video calls (Warhurst and Nickson, 2020). This increasing obsession with appearance and aestheticization of individuals is also driven by the growing importance of the beauty industry and the rise in cosmetic or aesthetic surgery. The growth of aesthetic economy raises concerns about unfair discrimination at work on the basis of looks. This concern may even worsen with the rise of unemployment due to the pandemic leading to better looking candidates to have a better chance in filling available positions, or to get better pay or promotion (Warhurst and Nickson, 2020).

Moreover, platforms such as Zoom is transforming how we observe one another and construct or reconstruct our identities during the COVID-19 pandemic. Being observed by people on the other side of the screen can increase our focus on the appearance and generate discomfort about how we look (Orchard and Burke, 2020). This discomfort is more apparent for women. For many women, the pre-pandemic pressure to look good at work hasn't gone away even while working from home (Davis, 2021). Therefore, either due to these appearance-related concerns or due to a desire to multi-task, women are less likely to turn their cameras on during video calls (Orchard and Burke, 2020). According to a survey conducted for Fast Company with 2,026 U.S. adults, in June 2020, 55% of women working from home due to COVID-19 "always" or "sometimes" enable video during videoconference meetings, compared to 65% of men. 39% of women disable the video feature during virtual work meetings because they don't like the way they look compared to 25% of men. When women use video, they get prepared: 85% do their hair, versus 74% of men, and 80% change their outfit versus 71% of men. Besides physical appearance, 83% clean the workspace that will show up on camera as opposed to 77% of men. Apart from appearance related issues, 41% of women said they disable the video feature, because they want to be able to multitask without people knowing as opposed to only

30% of men who said the same thing (Meyer, 2020). Consequently, women still feel the pressure to look the part and do not have the same freedom as men, even when working from home. This may be one of the reasons behind the increase in demand for cosmetic surgery and facial procedures since the "Zoom boom" (Orchard and Burke, 2020). The extended time working remotely could even change the beauty standards in the future (Davis, 2021). In a post-COVID world, some of these 'Zoom boom' trends related to dress and beauty are expected to stay (Took, 2020).

Conflicts, Concerns and Struggles in a Non-Western Context

Dress and adornment processes can differ across cultures. Therefore, it is also important to consider the role dress and adornment play in women's construction of their workplace identities and whether these processes might differ across cultures. Even though some of the recent scholars have a more pluralistic view of fashion, most of the prior studies on dress or fashion acknowledge fashion as a Western phenomenon, paying less attention to fashion in non-Western cultures (Ozdamar Ertekin, 2019). Niessen (2016) also argues that the Western bias is still dominant in fashion studies, even though more fashion studies started to embrace the global. Similarly, Welters and Lillethun (2018) raise concern for a definition of fashion beyond the modern West and in their book *Fashion History: A Global View,* they address this problem of exclusion and suggest to resolve it by reconceptualizing fashion history as a global phenomenon. They argue that if fashion is defined as changing styles of dress adopted by people at any given time and place, then the West cannot be the focus of fashion history (Welters and Lillethun, 2018). Therefore, it is critical to consider both Western and non-Western perspectives. Furthermore, the desire to embellish the human body is one of the main reasons for dress and as people often seek novelty or change, fashion is common to human nature (Ozdamar Ertekin, 2019; Welters and Lillethun, 2018). Moreover, the Western-centered fashion system and its innovations, suggestions and trends influence and shape people's experience with dress all around the world. Therefore, similar conflicts, concerns and struggles, which are raised in above sections can be valid in non-Western contexts as well. However, despite the importance of the topic, there are very few studies that address these issues in a non-Western context.

Humphreys and Brown (2002) are among the few researchers, who examined how dress is linked to group and organization identity and the dynamics of identity conflicts within organizations in a non-Western culture. By focusing on a specific item of clothing, which is the headscarf, they examine its role in collective identity maintenance and the challenges involved in an all-female Turkish university department. They provide an analysis of the key role that attire can play in collective identity construction. In this regard, their study makes several contributions to the literature on study of dress in organizations in a non-Western context. They discuss how dress is used as symbolic challenge and political instrument and how it is involved in debates regarding individual and organizational identity and politics. They demonstrate that even a single item of dress can signify a variety of different meanings, which are sometimes related and sometimes in conflict. These meanings in return foster individual and collective identities. The authors suggest that organization identity should be considered as a dynamic and reflexive process. Their case differs than Pratt and Rafaeli (1997), where two different dress styles helped to resolve conflict in the organization. Whereas in the Turkish case, dress does not aid organizational coherence. Instead, it is used as an expression of political agenda (Humphreys and Brown, 2002). On the other hand, the researchers found similarities between female 'power dressing' in Western organizations and headscarf wearing in Turkey. Both Western women who power dress and headscarf wearers may be interpreted as a threat by others and face negative reactions due to their chosen attire. However, they also suggest that this may be changing due to rising importance of identity diversity in organizations (Humphreys and Brown, 2002).

According to another recent study on dress and professional identity of women, which was conducted in Turkey, how you dress at work is associated with how much you respect and care about your job. Therefore, dressing well in a formal or at least in a business casual way signifies credibility and that you take your job seriously and this in return influences your performance and success. This pressure to be taken seriously especially at higher level corporate jobs, is more apparent for women as their dress style is assessed more; they are under surveillance of both male and female gaze; and they feel the need to show that they are as powerful as men with the clothes that they wear. Furthermore, if women wear too appealing or revealing clothes, they are afraid that their sexual identity takes precedence over their expertise and knowledge. Whereas for men this is hardly a problem as they are not perceived as object of desire because of what they wear and their masculinity does not get ahead of what they do (Ozdamar Ertekin et al., 2021).

Furthermore, the same study also shows that there are changes related to dress and work experience due to the pandemic. Some professional women complain about fluidity of time and place and multiplicity of roles when working from home and they are burn-out and exhausted as a result. Whereas others got used to this new normal and happier with this simpler life at home. The relation with dress and meaning of dress have changed as well. Some use dressing up as a coping mechanism to be motivated and even have a collection of clothes that look good on screen. Whereas others adapted to the new comfort look and enjoy and want to maintain the comfort dressing. On the other hand, there are also women who use shopping to get ready for the post pandemic period and they are ready to wear their high heels and blazer jackets to go back to the office (Ozdamar Ertekin et al., 2021). These findings are similar to some of the feedback shared from Western contexts. For instance, according to a recent article in Fashionista about the psychology of post-pandemic dressing, two types of post-pandemic scenarios are depicted. A group of consumers are expected to dress up, whereas others will dress down. The dresser-uppers are looking forward to leave behind the casual wardrobe they associate with the pandemic and use dress to enhance their mood. The dresser-downers on the other hand, will maintain the wardrobe they've developed in quarantine and continue wearing the loungewear and use dress to illustrate or maintain their current mood (Brannigan, 2021). Consequently, it is observed that similar struggles, conflicts and consequences exist during the pandemic in a non-Western context as well.

DISCUSSION, CONCLUSION, AND FUTURE RESEARCH DIRECTIONS

Explaining the appearance of women is a complex issue incorporating many factors and details. Self-presentation cannot be reduced only to sexual appeal (Scott, 2005). It requires taking into account the expectations of the culture and the society, the natural environment, the historical moment, the social hierarchy, and the personality, skills, resources, and psychological state and mood of the person. When we consider presentation of self at work, it is also related to the work environment, the type of industry and job, and the position and role within the company. As explained in the chapter, fashion has an important role in constitution of professional identity for women, both in Western and non-Western contexts. Fashioning the body can have critical consequences, as clothes can impress certain behaviors. Furthermore, dress can be interpreted as a form of silent communication (Barthes, [1967] 1983). Therefore, women's dress choices at work reflect and impact the professional identity that they want to construct and communicate.

As individual bodies started to be monitored and regulated with the rise of modernity women feel the pressure to control how they should look and try to conform to the normalized ideal of beauty (Carolan, 2005). On the other hand, in recent years, there has been change with regards to politics of personal appearance, with the increase in importance of diversity and inclusivity. In order to become independent, women are willing to exercise agency in their fashion choices and clothing preferences. However, they still seek social acceptance and therefore conform to the norms and rules both in their private and professional lives. Therefore, as Scott (2005) also signifies dress is never politically neutral and all human dress speaks of social order. Consequently, the politics of dress should recognize multiple strategies, different origins and aspirations and a more critical way of analyzing the power relations expressed through dress (Scott, 2005). In this regard, analysis of literature and secondary data, current happenings, and observations presented in this chapter have implications and importance for gender, identity, management and fashion studies, by providing a holistic and critical perspective to politics of dress and the female body in workplace settings and by presenting emerging insights related with the changing meaning of dress for working women during the pandemic, both in Western and non-Western contexts.

The meaning of dress and adorning habits varies for every woman, depending on their place in society and at work. Dress is a mode of self-expression. It enables to make a difference and fulfills desire for newness. It can be used to show creativity, resilience and/or submission. Therefore, our relationship with dress will always be complicated. Dress code at work was a standard to which all should abide with, whether it is wearing a uniform, a suit or following the rules of the office dress code. The association between competence, power and professional dress was strong as well (Mull, 2020). However, the pandemic and the new era of working from home started to reshape the meaning of work clothes and the concept of a dress code. The meaning and role of dress in constitution of professional identity has become fluid, especially for women. It is apparent that some of these changes that started with the pandemic regarding working from home and in a hybrid system, will continue in the post-pandemic period as well. In a post-COVID world, remote work can become the standard, which will change the way people dress for work. Even when people go back to the offices it may be difficult to get them back into the uncomfortable, formal clothes. It is also possible that after the pandemic, consumers will demand stylish clothes to reinvent themselves again (Sarwari, 2020). As a result, taking into account the different concerns and reactions stated in sections above, it is still not clear how these changes and transformations in our professional and personal lives will influence the new business dress code. Consequently, the meaning of dress and its relation to gender, identity and performativity will remain to be a critical and interesting topic to research in the future.

REFERENCES

Acker, J. (1990). Hierarchies, Jobs, Bodies: A Theory of Gendered Organizations. *Gender & Society*, *4*(2), 139–158. doi:10.1177/089124390004002002

Akdemir, N. (2018). Visible Expression of Social Identity: The Clothing and Fashion. *Gaziantep University Journal of Social Sciences*, *17*(4), 1389–1397. doi:10.21547/jss.411181

Barthes, R. (1983). *The Fashion System*. Hill and Wang. (Original work published 1967)

Benn, J. (2004). Consumer Education between 'Consumership' and Citizenship: Experiences from Studies of Young People. *International Journal of Consumer Studies*, *28*(2), 108–116. doi:10.1111/j.1470-6431.2003.00364.x

Boden, S. (2006). Dedicated Followers of Fashion? The Influence of Popular Culture on Children's Social Identities. *Media Culture & Society*, *28*(2), 289–298. doi:10.1177/0163443706061690

Bordo, S. R. (1993). *Unbearable Weight: Feminism, Western Culture, and the Body*. University of California Press.

Boydell, C. (2004). Review: Fashioning Identities: Gender, Class and the Self. *Journal of Contemporary History*, *39*(1), 137–146. doi:10.1177/0022009404039889

Brannigan, M. (2021). *The Psychology of Post-Pandemic Dressing*. https://fashionista.com/2021/05/covid-19-pandemic-fashion-psychology

Cagan, E. (1978). The selling of the Women's Movement. *Social Policy*, (May/June), 4–12.

Carolan, S. M. (2005). The Conspicuous Body: Capitalism, Consumerism, Class and Consumption. *Worldviews: Global Religions, Culture, and Ecology*, *9*(1), 82–111. doi:10.1163/1568535053628436

Cook, D. T., & Kaiser, S. B. (2004). Betwixt and be Tween: Age Ambiguity and the Sexualization of the Female Consuming Subject. *Journal of Consumer Culture*, *4*(2), 203–227. doi:10.1177/1469540504043682

Crane, D. (2000). *Fashion and Its Social Agendas: Class, Gender and Identity in Clothing*. The University of Chicago Press. doi:10.7208/chicago/9780226924830.001.0001

Davis, F. (1992). *Fashion, Culture, and Identity*. The University of Chicago Press. doi:10.7208/chicago/9780226167954.001.0001

Davis, K. (2021). *How the pandemic changed what it means to look 'professional' at work*. https://www.fastcompany.com/90618736/how-the-pandemic-changed-what-it-means-to-look-professional-at-work

due Billing, Y. (2011). Are Women in Management Victims of the Phantom of the Male Norm? *Gender, Work and Organization, 18*(3), 298-317.

Elan, P. (2020). *'The Zoom shirt': How the pandemic changed work dress codes*. https://www.theguardian.com/business/2020/jul/20/the-zoom-shirt-how-the-pandemic-changed-work-dress-codes

Elan, P. (2021). *'Hate-wear' and 'sadwear': fashion's new names for lockdown dressing*. https://www.theguardian.com/fashion/2021/jan/17/hate-wear-and-sadwear-fashion-new-names-for-covid-lockdown-dressing

Entwistle, J. (2000). *The Fashioned Body: Fashion, Dress and Modern Social Theory*. Polity Press.

Entwistle, J. (2007). *'Power Dressing' and the Construction of the Career Woman*. Routledge.

Featherstone, M. (1991). The Body in Consumer Culture. In M. Featherstone, M. Hepworth, & B. S. Turner (Eds.), *The Body: Social Process and Cultural Theory*. Sage.

Featherstone, M. (2010). Body, Image and Affect in Consumer Culture. *Body & Society*, *16*(1), 193–221.

Feldman, J. (2020). *What People Wore to Work Before the Pandemic vs. Now*. https://www.huffpost.com/entry/work-from-home-outfits_l_5f96feeac5b646c70e9b3475

Firat, A. F., & Dholakia, N. (2003). *Consuming People from Political Economy to Theaters of Consumption*. Routledge.

Foucault, M. (1979). *Discipline and Punish: The Birth of the Prison*. Vintage.

Gavis, Y., Shoham, A., & Ruvio, A. (2008). A Qualitative Study of Mother-Adolescent Daughter: Vicarious Role Model Consumption Interactions. *Advances in Consumer Research. Association for Consumer Research (U. S.)*, *35*, 732–734.

Goffman, E. (1959). *The Presentation of Self in Everyday Life*. Doubleday.

Goodman, J., Knotts, G., & Jackson, J. (2007). Doing Dress and the Construction of Women's Gender Identity. *Journal of Occupational Science*, *14*(2), 100–107.

Gummer, B. (1998). In the Eye of the Beholder. *Administration in Social Work*, *22*(4), 75–90.

Haber, T. R. T. (2020). *İhracat takım elbisede azaldı, eşofmanda arttı* [Export of suits decreased and sweats increased]. https://www.trthaber.com/foto-galeri/ihracat-takim-elbisede-azaldi-esofmanda-artti/31582/sayfa-1.html

Hardy, L. (2010). *From One Worried Mother, a Passionate Call to Arms... It's Time to Stop the Fashion Industry Dressing Girls of Ten Like This*. http://www.dailymail.co.uk/femail/article-1249538/from-worried-mother-passionate-arms--its-time-stop-fashion-industry-dressing-girls-like-this.html.

Humphreys, M., & Brown, A. D. (2002). Dress And Identity: A Turkish Case Study. *Journal of Management Studies*, *39*(7), 927–952.

Kanter, R. M. (1977). *Men and Women of the Corporation*. Basic Books.

Klepp, I. G., & Storm-Mathisen, A. (2005). Reading Fashion as Age: Teenage Girls' and Grown Women's Accounts of Clothing as Body and Social Status. *Fashion Theory*, *9*(3), 323–342.

Martin, K. A. (1998). Becoming a Gendered Body: Practices of Preschools. *American Sociological Review*, *63*(4), 494–511.

Meyer, Z. (2020). *Do you show your face in Zoom meetings? Your gender may play a role*. https://www.fastcompany.com/90514033/do-you-show-your-face-in-zoom-meetings-your-gender-may-play-a-role

Molloy, J. T. (1976). *Dress for Success*. Grand Central Pub.

Morris-Roberts, K. (2004). Girls' Friendships, 'Distinctive Individuality' and Socio-spatial Practices of (Dis)identification. *Children's Geographies*, *2*(2), 237–255.

Mull, A. (2020). *After the Pandemic, the Office Dress Code Should Never Come Back*. https://www.theatlantic.com/magazine/archive/2020/05/kill-the-office-dress-code/609070/

Niessen, S. (2016). Afterword: Fashion's Fallacy. In M. A. Jansen & J. Craik (Eds.), *Modern Fashion Traditions: Negotiating Tradition and Modernity through Fashion* (pp. 209–217). Bloomsbury Academic.

Oliver, K. (2017). The male gaze is more relevant, and more dangerous, than ever. *New Review of Film and Television Studies*, *15*(4), 451–455.

Onedio (2020). *Gelecek Yılın Yepyeni Moda Trendleri Belli Oldu: Pandemi Dönemi Bittiğinde En Çok Neler Giyeceğiz*? [Fashion Trends for next year seems obvious: What will we wear the most after the post-pandemic period?]. https://onedio.com/haber/gelecek-yilin-yepyeni-moda-trendleri-belli-oldu-pandemi-donemi-bittiginde-en-cok-neler-giyecegiz-926956

Orchard, T., & Burke, S. (2020). *On Zoom, men don't like feeling watched and judged—but women are used to it*. https://theconversation.com/on-zoom-men-dont-like-feeling-watched-and-judged-but-women-are-used-to-it-150594

Ozdamar Ertekin, Z. (2019). Linda Welters and Abby Lillethun, Fashion History: A Global View (2018). *Markets, Globalization &. Developmental Review*, *4*(1), 6.

Ozdamar Ertekin, Z., & Atik, D. (2015). Aging of Youth through Fashion: Influential Dynamics and Societal Implications. In *Proceedings of the 40th Annual Macromarketing Conference* (pp. 38-53). The Macromarketing Society, Inc.

Ozdamar Ertekin, Z., Ucel, E. B., Oflac, B. S., and Dalkilic, O. S. (2021, June). *Dress and Professional Identity: Changing Wardrobes of Women in the Pandemic-era)* [Paper presentation]. Fashion Tales 2020+1 Conference, Università Cattolica del Sacro Cuore.

Parker, L. D., & Warren, S. (2017). The presentation of the self and professional identity: Countering the accountant's stereotype. *Accounting, Auditing & Accountability Journal, 30*(8), 1895–1924.

Pratt, M. G., & an, d Rafaeli, A. (1997). Organizational Dress as a Symbol of Multilayered Social Identities. *Academy of Management Journal, 40*(4), 862–898.

Rafaeli, A., Button, J., Harquail, C. V., & Mackie-Lewis, S. (1997). Navigating by attire: The use of dress by female administrative employees. *Academy of Management Journal, 40*(1), 9–45.

Rafaeli, A., & Pratt, M. G. (1993). Tailored Meanings: On the Meaning and Impact of Organizational Dress. *Academy of Management Review, 18*(1), 32–55.

Rawlins, E. (2006). Mother Knows Best? Intergenerational Notions of Fashion and Identity. *Children's Geographies, 4*(3), 359–377.

Roach-Higgins, M. E., & Eicher, J. B. (1992). Dress and Identity. *Clothing & Textiles Research Journal, 10*(4), 1–8.

Russell, R., & Tyler, M. (2002). Thank Heaven for Little Girls: 'Girl Heaven' and the Commercial Context of Feminine Childhood. *Sociology, 36*(3), 619–637.

Sarwari, K. (2020). *Will the Covid-19 Pandemic Change How People Dress for Work in the Future?* https://news.northeastern.edu/2020/12/14/will-the-covid-19-pandemic-change-how-people-dress-for-work-in-the-future/

Scott, L. M. (2005). *Fresh Lipstick: Redressing Fashion and Feminism.* Palgrave Macmillan.

Sky news. (2020). *Coronavirus: Women Told to Dress 'Sexier' When Working from Home, Survey Finds.* https://news.sky.com/story/coronavirus-women-told-to-dress-sexier-when-working-from-home-survey-finds-12034520

Smith, A. (2020). *Dress-Code Policies Reconsidered in the Pandemic*. https://www.shrm.org/resourcesandtools/legal-and-compliance/employment-law/pages/coronavirus-dress-code-policies.aspx

Solomon, M. R. (2018). *Consumer Behavior: Buying, Having, and Being*. Pearson Education Limited.

Stone, G. P. (1962). Appearance and the Self. In A. M. Rose (Ed.), *Human Behavior and Social Processes: An Interactionist Approach* (pp. 86–118). Houghton-Mifflin.

Tastad, C., & Deanna, B. (2020). *The route to true gender equality? Fix the system, not the women*. https://www.weforum.org/agenda/2020/01/gender-gap-equality-income-wages-solution/

Thomas, L. (2007). *Why Do We Dress Children Like Tarts*? http://www.telegraph.co.uk/comment/personal-view/3640879 /why-do-we-dress-children-like-tarts.html

Thompson, J. C., & Hirschman, C. E. (1995). Understanding the Socialized Body: A Poststructuralist Analysis of Consumers' Self-conceptions, Body Images, and Self-care Practices. *The Journal of Consumer Research*, *22*(2), 139–153.

Took, J. (2020). *10 big changes to business casual you will see in the post-pandemic workplace*. https://www.theladders.com/career-advice/10-big-changes-to-business-casual-you-will-see-in-the-post-pandemic-workplace

Twigg, J. (2007). Clothing, Age and the Body: A Critical Review. *Ageing and Society*, *27*, 285–305.

Wade, L. (2012). *Waxing for Girls 15 and Younger*. https://thesocietypages.org/socimages/2012/07/25/waxing-for-girls-15-and-younger

Warhurst, C., & Nickson, D. (2020). *Lookism: beauty still trumps brains in too many workplaces*. https://theconversation.com/lookism-beauty-still-trumps-brains-in-too-many-workplaces-148278

Warren, S., & Parker, L. D. (2009). Bean counters or bright young things? Towards the visual study of identity construction among professional accountants. *Qualitative Research in Accounting & Management*, *6*(4), 205–223.

Welters, L., & Lillethun, A. (2018). *Fashion History: A Global View (Dress, Body, Culture)*. Bloomsbury Academic.

Wilson, E. (1985). *Adorned in Dreams: Fashion and Modernity*. I.B. Tauris.

Wolkowitz, C. (2006). *Bodies at Work*. SAGE Publications Ltd.

Chapter 3 What Turkish Women Need to Advance in Academia

Ceren Deniz Tatarlar
Tilburg University, The Netherlands

ABSTRACT

As can be seen in most Eastern or Middle Eastern countries, the primary role of women has been defined as motherhood or to be a wife to a man. The fact that women have a role apart from these is seen as a radical change. In Turkey, where the base of this chapter is, there have been many struggles to change this situation from past to present and to maintain the male-female equality. Yet, this "equality" cannot be seen in some broad areas in life such as work-life. The aim of this chapter is to make visible what women have encountered in order to advance in academia through some real-life stories.

INTRODUCTION

As can be seen in most Eastern or Middle Eastern countries, the primary role of women has been defined as motherhood or to be a wife to a man. The fact that women have a role apart from these is seen as a radical change. In Turkey, where the base of this chapter is, there has been many struggles to change this situation from past to present and to maintain the male-female equality. In fact, it is possible to say that the struggle is still given today, and this equality has not been reached fully. It is true that the revolutions regarding women at the time and the so-called modernity required by the age supported the participation of women in the labor force at least as much as men. However, when looking at the country in general, it is seen that this participation takes place only in some privileged situations. Among

DOI: 10.4018/978-1-7998-8742-3.ch003

these privileged situations, there are various examples such as being in the urban area, coming from relatively wealthy families, being a member of open-minded families, or choosing professions deemed appropriate for women. While the struggle of women to find a place in business life constitutes a separate problem, the fact that women who can enter the business life are deployed in certain professions evokes a different problem. Occupations that can be categorized as gendered professions, such as nursing, teaching, secretarial, flight attendance, administrative assistant, or any job in service industry are seen as more suitable for women and are preferred more by women. Looking at the job descriptions and nature of these professions, it is seen that there are actions generally attributed to women, such as caring, paying close attention, empathy, and emotional labor. Being an academician, which is seen as a different variation of teaching, is also mostly preferred by women. Although these are considered as gendered occupations, all these occupations again do not provide enough freedom for women to advance their careers.

ACADEMIA IN TURKEY

According to 2021 data released by Council of Higher Education (CoHE - YÖK), female academics rate in Turkey is 45%. This rate remains high compared to the rate in many European countries despite having the lower number of women graduates (Healy et al., 2005). One of the reasons why women turn to academia is due to the professional characteristics and the roles expected of women. However, when it comes to gender equality academia is not innocent either. It is possible to see that women who try to rise in the academia instead of trying to rise by competing with men in the private sector face many different and similar problems from the private industry. It is even possible to say that academia can be much crueler in terms of expectations in order to achieve higher status. In order to talk about expectations, it is necessary to talk about the functioning of the academia inside and the parts that cannot be known from the outside. There are certain universal and fundamental steps to starting a career within universities such as completing undergraduate education, then master's and doctorate education, being able to do research as well as teaching. However, each country also has its own legal stages. In Turkey academics has a long career path extending to a professorship by fulfilling later requirements starting with the position "research assistant". It is possible to say that Turkish academic system follows the infamous American model with three main steps – assistant professor, associate professor, and professor after completing the research assistant part (Neale & Ozkanli, 2010:547). After getting the title assistant professor (which was replaced with "*doktor ogretim uyesi/doctoral lecturer*" after March 2018) you need to achieve some requirements to get further titles. Although there are requirements that can be seen as usual, such as completing the necessary dissertations, publishing in well-ranked journals, providing language proficiency, receiving a certain number of citations, and having foreign experience among the official promotion criteria, it is seen that this is not the case.

The relationship among academics in Turkey, inspired by the culture of course, is arranged in the form of master-apprentice relationship. It is seen that this type of relationship is also dominant in other professions. It is possible to say that the business relationships in Turkey are strongly influenced by the interpersonal relationships. Turkey's social structure and culture also affect the business environment (Sargut, 2001). This situation is also the same in universities. The collectivist and paternalist structure of Turkish society, defined by many different studies (Hofstede, 1984; Sargut, 2001; House et al., 2004; Gannon & Pillai, 2010), also appears in the academic working environment (Tatarlar, 2019). Interpersonal relationships can create different effects on individuals in an organizational environment. The reasons underlying the purpose of establishing these relationships, the situations that arise because of these relationships, the way the relationships are organized, affect the individuals at many points, such as organizational commitment, job satisfaction, motivation or even their psychological state.

There are many valuable studies (Ozbilgin & Healey, 2004; Healey et al., 2005; Senturk, 2015; Altinoluk, 2018; Tuncer, 2019) on the place of Turkish women in academia, and these studies mostly focus on gendered institutions (Acker, 1992), women's work-life balance, cultural complexities, gender segregation and glass ceiling examples. In general, when we consider the integrity of the subject, it cannot be said that an independent study can be made that is separated from all these sub-titles. In this study, different from the others, it comes to the forefront to examine the experiences and problems in practice by listening to the experiences of individuals at first hand. Each participant has their own story, and each of them can be addressed as a real case study. The aim of this chapter is to make visible what women have encountered in order to advance in academia from the entrance through some real-life stories. The general content of this chapter will include career stories participants told in their own words and how they overcame the challenges. These stories can be held as different case studies and discussed in several courses.

METHODOLOGY

Given the topic's exploratory nature, qualitative methods were used in this study. Since the aim is to obtain as many insights as possible, in-depth interviewing was chosen as a data collection method. 4 women who work in various fields of academia have participated in in-depth interviews. Their positions and titles range from research assistant to associate professor. They are all from social sciences discipline and work in Izmir, Turkey. Since this study is based on storytelling and personal narratives of participants, no strict interview protocol was used. Semi-structured questions were asked with the aim of collecting demographical data and creating a warm atmosphere and to establishing trust. Each interview was conducted according to the ethical rules, participants all contributed with consent. Participants were asked about how they got into academia, how their relationships are with their professors and other senior academicians which are related to them, if they are already in an advanced position what kind of problems they encountered whilst waiting for being assigned to that position, what are others' expectations from them, and many other probing questions related to their answers through interviews. All the interviews took place in wherever participants felt comfortable. Each of them was about between 30 to 58 minutes. All the interviews were recorded with the consent of participant. After each interview, recordings were transformed into transcriptions and topic-relevant parts were taken into consideration. As seen in every story section, several interpretations were made aligned with the concepts that participants mentioned.

Stories and Outcomes

In general, participants were asked to tell their stories on obstacles that they encountered during trying to excel through their career paths. Here you will witness the difficulties women faced from their perspective, with the stories they tell in their own words. Each of them told stories about their own career paths and how they interpreted everything that they have encountered. It is seen that there are similarities between these stories, as well as many unique situations. Some stories are longer, some are shorter, but on the whole, there are many striking examples. At the beginning of each story, participant will be introduced to you briefly.

Story 1

Participant 1 is an associate professor in a public university. She works in department of advertising. She has been in that university since the beginning of her bachelor's education – which is almost for 22 years.

I am a journalism graduate. While studying in undergraduate, we had a class in the 2nd year, "public relations project applications". We had a competition within the scope of that lesson. It was such an intense competition. Groups were being formed and we were writing projects to it. The subject of this project was the university's 1-year public relations project for that year. The competition was held and as a result of that competition, our project came first. Then we joined the "young *communicators" and there we won a first place and a second place in 2 branches. An internship offer came from the Rectorate. They said, "Come and work here, your project is very much in line with our strategy" and as a team, we started working in the rectorate from the second year. There were only 3 people left and I continued to work in the rectorate after I graduated from the university. In 2007, they offered me to work as a lecturer at a vocational school. I said OK and went there. I worked there for 1 year, waiting for a tenure. Then I got my tenure. I already wanted to return to my faculty in 2008, I did. I have been working in my own faculty for 10 years. I have my master's and doctorate degrees in advertising, and I still work as an associate professor in advertising today.*

While describing the environment there, she refers to events likely to happen in public universities in large cities in general. Izmir, being the third largest city in Turkey, has the same problem as other cities – tenure and staffing related problems. As such, it is inevitable to see a highly competitive environment in the universities where these problems are experienced. She also stated that she works in such an environment.

During the previous rector's term, the dean changed, and the dean had behaviors such as mobbing. We had problems with it. He had our department head taken out of his room reluctantly, said similar threatening things to us and made us leave. I have no idea why this was done.

For example, if there is an election about a board of directors, if the person on the other side does not support the candidate you want, then serious disconnections occur. Immediately resentments, polarizations. These kinds of things can happen. There can be 2-3 separate poles. A great teacher tries to attract others, for example, there are situations like that. You have to watch out for yourself because you would not want to be on the "wrong" side. Otherwise, your things go definitely wrong. You have to support whoever they want.

For example, there are too many people in the faculty who do not exceed the fingers of one hand. If they were not in the faculty, I can say that this faculty would be a rosy place. These are some of the personalities that can be said to be defective in rough terms. Because these people only do business by teasing others. These are the people who falsely apply for CIMER (communications center of presidency) in cases related to the tenure. For example, there are people among us who sit and throw mud until the morning saying that this is a "FETO" supporter, this is a "PKK" supporter. If those types were cleaned up, this faculty could be rosy. The only reason for this is that when the head of our department was appointed as the dean, he did not make this person vice dean and did not assign him a duty.

If you want to come to a place and rise, you must be someone's "man". And you have to choose that person correctly. It doesn't matter what you publish or your achievements.

The participant mentioned before that the environment in which she works is an organizational setting with high competition. The competition here is mostly manifest at the point of getting the administrative title. In this story, it is possible to see an example of how someone who has waited for a long time to become powerful has treated others after reaching the power. Also there is another point for being other's "man". Rivals not only behave each other, but also behave similarly to others whom they refer as "the man of the rival" and associated with them. Besides the masculine language being used, it is possible to see an academic career that is damaged by uncontrollable egos.

Story 2

Participant 2 is an associate professor in a public university. She works in International Relations department. She has been in this profession since 2000's as she mentioned – which is almost 21 years.

I started this profession as a research assistant in the early 2000s. My field is international relations, I became an associate professor about a year ago.

The professor we worked with was both a meticulous one and a professor with high demands. It would take a lot of time. He was very difficult as a person. Apart from business labor, it also required personal labor. Meeting all kinds of expectations in both a business and personal sense could be psychologically tiring.

At that time, my friends who were assistants with me also had various symptoms. Not taking care of yourself, not even wanting to dress, carelessness, intimidation, tiredness... Even if the working hours were over during my assistantship period, my professor would not welcome us to leave work before him. At such times, he might have discourses such as "what are you going to do at home" or "do you have an important thing to do?" that would concern private life. It was very disturbing. We always had to wait for him to leave work first. We would be very uncomfortable. But if we wanted to excel or if we wanted to be able to defend our thesis, we had to obey these things. He would call a lot after work, even when the working hour was over. In the evenings, at night... We had to answer that phone. If we didn't answer, he wouldn't like it and then act accordingly. There was a total interference in my private life, and I could not oppose this so as not to throw my career away. So, I ended up changing my institution.

The story shows us another problem which needs to be addressed: intervening private life and damaging work-life balance. As the participant mentioned, her supervisor, who already showed herself the contaminative behavior with different tactics and who wanted Participant 2 to exist only for herself, also interferes with her private life. This intervention is manifested by behaviors such as filling the personal life with work, preventing her from spare time, and despising herself about her spare time. Which makes working hard, and which leads to another problem: doing more than what needs to be done officially in order to get what you exactly deserve. To obtain a degree, you should do more than just writing and defending an outstanding dissertation – but also to fit your supervisor's unexpected needs. Other than that, these situations make people quit or voluntarily leave their job – which is a final form of physical withdrawal from work. When people are out of hope about their organizational expectations, they tend to quit.

Story 3

Participant 3 is an associate professor in a public university. She works in the department of Business Administration. She changed three universities. Her stories consist of all three of them.

I graduated in 2003 in Business. I completed my master's degree in 2006. Then I started working in City X as a research assistant. Then I came to City Y with an assignment since there was no doctorate program there. Then, when my doctorate was finished in 2011, I came back to City X to do my compulsory service. I worked there for a certain period of time, and one year before the end of my compulsory service, an assistant professor job was posted here (at university where she's working now). That one year of obligatory service was also missing. There was a certain compensation obligation. I paid it and resigned. No consent was given at that time. So, here I am now. I had a lot of problems with the consent form. After all, the top management did not want to lose staff there. After all, they cannot find many faculty members there easily. Therefore, they did not want to, there was an earthquake 1-2 years ago, there were many teachers who wanted to leave because of the earthquake.

When I finished my doctorate and returned to City X, I had a few problems. I had no expectation of getting an assistant professor position. I was already 4 months pregnant at that time. Also, we were 2 friends that got back. When I returned, the dean greeted us spontaneously and said that they had two tenures and that he would allocate this to the first two people. Then he went around, one of those tenures – we were both in department of Business by the way - was transferred to one of the economics department. Because the dean was also from the department of economics. That's when I observed that there were such relations in City X. It's a bit organic, so how can I say... Some tribal families are more dominant... I think that the first tenure was registered for such a reason as far as I know. Then the management decided to give me the second tenure. Good and nice... However, I had other plans in my mind regarding my private life. I was planning to stay in City X until I'm 7-8 months old pregnant - until the last time I can get on that plane, then I come to City Y, I give birth, because my doctor is here to give me birth... My family came to City X to help me. Because my husband was also working in City Z at that time. We were going back and forth between the two cities. But all my other circles are in City Y. I have such a plan. Later dean said that this tenure will be announced in late July. My birth is expected at the end of July, beginning of August. Well, in this case, it's not a time for me to travel. I can give birth on the road at any time. How is it going to be? He said go get some air, see your hometown, but come back, because the tenure will be here, plan the birth here now. Now this has been a very stressful factor for me, frankly. Because I am unprepared. Anyway, somehow... If that's the case, okay, I came to City Y, Here the doctor checked, made recommendations, I found a doctor in City X by chance. An obstetrician doing his military service in a military hospital. He is examining, but there is no guarantee that I will give birth there. Because, it is very interesting, the hospital works between 9 am and 5 pm. If there is a c-section, they can do it, but otherwise the normal birth should only happen during working hours on weekdays... All of this is a serious pressure... There are a lot of rumors about private hospitals in City X, they do c-section whether it is necessary or not... OK, do it, if necessary, but why not if it's not? I wanted to stay strong because I think that I want to give a normal birth... Then my husband and I said OK, there is a maternity hospital, so we go there. Of course, time passes, we spend time in City X, right on the last day of July, my birth process started. We went to the maternity hospital, thank God my daughter is healthy, we got through the process but... I came back straight away. I went through a difficult birth...

Anyway, we got over it, we are trying to raise the child, a week passes, two weeks pass, August is over, and I still don't get the tenure. Of course, that tenure was never appointed to me. Because at that time, the dean's assistant finished his doctorate. As a matter of fact, that tenure was appointed to him. I decided to leave City X at that time, as a matter of fact. I made my clear decision on the injustice I experienced. And I had a very harsh speech with the dean that he was actually playing with our lives. Afterwards, I paid whatever my compensation was and left the institution at the first opportunity.

Of course, did I have an easy life while working in City Y? No. I have worked with professors who are very tough, have to be managed very hard, and can react to anything at any time. For example, when my daughter was younger, there was a period when I stayed in City Y after giving birth. Since I did my doctorate in City Y and also worked as an assistant, I was on good terms with my professors there. But we no longer had a business connection. Anyway, after all, there is a baby, and I don't work there anymore... But I still know that my professor didn't talk to me for a year just because I celebrated her birthday on the phone instead of face to face. Think about what she was doing while I was working with her who did this to me after I quit my job.

It is possible to say that this example is the one which provides richest psychological output. In this case, we can see multiple behavioral practices that can be examined under the concept of mobbing, such as the person who is in power, having various sanctions to keep the individual in his hand, giving and giving up various promises, turning work-life balance upside-down, making decisions on behalf of someone else and preventing the individual getting its right. It is a serious problem that a given promise of position influenced the life of the participant and the family of the participant. The behavior is not only resulted in psychological distress but also physical health problems. The fact that the position was transferred to the professor's assistant also led to a mobbing behavior in order to defer and decelerate what is right for the participant as well as the kind of unfair behavior.

I encountered many more. I passed a lot of trust tests in my first years as an assistant. I got scolded for trying to run my business professionally. My professor had the following conversation with me... "You hang out very professionally here, but there will be organic ties. Whether you like it or not...". That's when I realized: "Oh, there will be something else here, in other words, closer relations are expected". Since this is not very suitable for me, I will say that I did as much as I could. However, they met their wishes and demands better with a person suitable for their nature, and they talked more in their private lives. I was just trying to balance it, but she didn't like it, so she actually wanted me to be closer. She would say it too.

Well, another memory... She actually did me a huge favor when I first started. She gave me the key to her room so that I could work more comfortably. Because I did not have a room until the appointment was made. Of course, I use it nervously. Now the professor's room, her desk... I'll turn on her computer, I'll look, but I'm scared if something happens. I enter and exit without touching anything. Because I'm afraid that if I don't go, she will ask why I don't use it, I'm afraid if I work somewhere else... Like this... Then, after a while, a week or two later, during the lecture, she got angry with my doctoral classmates, namely, that one of our homework we did, the general group assignment, was inadequate. It started with a general, group-oriented anger that came out, then directed a personal anger at me. She said angrily: "You are using my room, but you have not washed my dirty glasses/cups". I... I saw those cups when I was entering the room, but... You know, if I drink it myself, I clean mine anyway... But now I refrain from touching it... Touching seems to me to be more wrong with the order there. It was very painful for me to be scolded for such a reason in front of the whole class. A very serious disappointment... I mean, when we were thinking that we were going to think about very scientific works or something... Of course, we were in that naivety... No, I remember being disappointed to see that it wasn't like that at all. We dealt with many private tasks, from going to get the glasses that our professor forgot at her house, to getting her medicines to be prescribed to the pharmacy.

Women academics have to spend much more effort than their male colleagues, who are at the same steps of the academic hierarchy, in order to rise in the academy. Because, on the one hand, women have to carry out the housework and care activities that they see as their own responsibility, and on the other hand, they have to try to fulfill the criteria for academic advancement, so they have to work double time (Senturk, 2015). Sometimes this total work needs to be tripled, or let's say "housework" should be doubled, as seen in the discourse of this participant. Even though their status is "assistant" this should not mean to work as a private assistant of someone who is in a higher status.

I would like to talk about another topic. My professor was a very flamboyant woman. She loved to dress up... She took great care of herself. You could say I was the complete opposite. Someone who dresses more comfortably, not too fancy. She would even warn me about this. She messed with my clothes. But it's not like saying "go put on some makeup". When I first worked with her, my husband and I were not married yet. She used to talk to me about it. "Look, if you're walking around like this, this boy will leave you, what a state. Go spruce it up" she would say.

Here there is another example of private life interruptions. It has been observed that the person's special relations with others, clothing, and choices about own life have been a target for her superiors. To sum things up, all the examples that were given by Participant 3 are related to emotional abuse in organizations (Keashly, 2001), which is again a serious problem to mention.

Story 4

Participant 4 is unemployed with a PhD degree. She was a research assistant before, but she had to quit due to staffing regulations.

I came here from the east. Actually, I don't want to describe it like that, but it's true that I come from a part of the country that is seen as a village. When I first came, I felt the loss of it. I was already feeling it, and they also made me feel it.

For example, when I first arrived, I was seated in the same room as those who came with the assignment. It was like an isolation room. Those who are not from here... Those who are marginalized... Then my professor got annoyed with this and changed my room and took me to the same room with other women. This place was like a nightmare for me, too.

There was M at that time. She later left the institution. We were 5 women in the room. I was getting extremely stressed about my outfit because of M. Actually, I didn't know much about dressing. I don't know if I understand now, but I used to be worse. I really don't know how to dress. I try to be beautiful, I try to dress well, you know, I don't care, but I can't do it and there is always something wrong with me. When we entered the room, everyone was first looking at each other's clothes. Her (M) presence made me very nervous. As soon as I entered the room, there was someone who was looking at me from head to toe and was looking at me in a judgmental way, so it always bothered me. I was so stressed, I can't tell. I wish she would criticize me openly. It would be more comforting. But she wouldn't. Think about it, someone who secretly makes fun of your outfit all the time. I've also become someone who thinks more about what to wear that morning than my job.

Here Participant 4 speaks about her struggles with her new roommates, especially one exact person M. She stated that her roommate was quite into fashion, and she judged others by what they wore. She did it behind others, so it was inevitable that Participant 4 also thought that she is showing the same behavior to her. She feels like her roommate is judging her by gazing, staring, gestures and facial expressions. She felt like she needed to get dressed in a style that others would approve, so she might blend into this group of women. This is another striking example. Given the situation, people would expect women to be in solidarity towards all the other obstacles they encounter, but here we see another point. Women intimidating other women.

My other female friends would also involuntarily put pressure on me. They were also very sarcastic. When I was with them, I always felt compelled to use my intelligence. I used to think that I shouldn't be ordinary. This time, I would tire myself out with it. Because of their pressure, I turned into a person I was not, I lost a bit of myself. Because I came from the East, there was a lot of assumption about my identity. They said I'm Kurdish, they said I support PKK (a terrorist organization). I was heartbroken until I convince that I wasn't. When I came here, I felt worthless than a dog. Professors humiliating and judging me... All of this caused me to undergo therapy for a long time. I'm still in therapy and trying to find myself

CONCLUSION

It is possible to say that interpersonal relationships lead individuals to problematic situations without discriminating between men and women at some point, also the interviews reflect that woman may have experienced these effects more than men in certain situations. In these organizations, where it is not sufficient to meet the legally required criteria, it has been observed that advancement and promotion mostly depend on how personally close you are with the person in power. It is possible to say that the discriminatory discourses and actions encountered in the private sector also take place in the academy. Participants stated that during the recruitment interviews, questions were asked about their marital status, and that they even went further and expressed their opinion on when to have a child. In addition, it has been revealed that there are expectations other than legal requirements from female academicians in order to be assigned to the position after completing a doctoral program. Working as a special assistant to the thesis advisor, paying special attention to his / her birthdays, babysitting his/her children, making own hair and clothing look like him/her, establishing relationships only with people they approve are just a few examples to these unrealistic expectations. It is possible to see that these expectations mostly coincide with the role of women in Turkish / Eastern culture. When these and similar expectations are encountered, in addition to being assigned to the position, there are some irreversible damages on female academicians such as psychological problems, withdrawal, loss of self-sense and even more suicidal thoughts.

Although there are many problems expressed in the literature, not many real-life experiences from the Turkish context are available. Thus, it is aimed to provide the stories of women academicians in this short chapter. The study is intended to present how theoretical knowledge is manifested in real-life experiences. The stories show that the dominating culture is inseparably embedded in business life. What is important for employees, managers or academics is to identify and implement the necessary elements to make these voices heard and to prevent these stories from multiplying.

REFERENCES

Acker, J. (1992). From sex roles to gendered institutions. *Contemporary Sociology, 21*(5), 565–569. doi:10.2307/2075528

Altınoluk, D. (2018). Kadın olmak mı, akademisyen olmak mı?: İşte bütün mesele bu. *Fe Dergi, 10*(1), 57–66.

Gannon, M. J., & Pillai, R. (2010). Understanding global cultures: Metaphorical journeys through 29 nations, clusters of nations, continents, and diversity. *Sage (Atlanta, Ga.)*. Advance online publication. doi:10.4135/9781452224886

Healy, G., Özbilgin, M., & Aliefendioğlu, H. (2005). Academic employment and gender: A Turkish challenge to vertical sex segregation. *European Journal of Industrial Relations, 11*(2), 247–264. doi:10.1177/0959680105053966

Hofstede, G. (1984). *Culture's consequences: International differences in work-related values* (Vol. 5). Sage.

House, R. J., Hanges, P. J., Javidan, M., Dorfman, P. W., & Gupta, V. (Eds.). (2004). *Culture, leadership, and organizations: The GLOBE study of 62 societies*. Sage publications.

Keashly, L. (2001). Interpersonal and systemic aspects of emotional abuse at work: The target's perspective. *Violence and Victims, 16*(3), 233–268. doi:10.1891/0886-6708.16.3.233 PMID:11437116

Neale, J., & Özkanlı, O. (2010). Organisational barriers for women in senior management: A comparison of Turkish and New Zealand universities. *Gender and Education, 22*(5), 547–563. doi:10.1080/09540250903524113

Özbilgin, M., & Healy, G. (2004). The gendered nature of career development of university professors: The case of Turkey. *Journal of Vocational Behavior, 64*(2), 358–371. doi:10.1016/j.jvb.2002.09.001

Şentürk, B. (2015). Çokuz ama yokuz: türkiye'deki akademisyen kadinlar üzerine bir analiz. *ViraVerita E-Dergi*, (2), 1–22.

Tatarlar, C. D. (2019). *Contamination at workplace* [Unpublished doctoral dissertation]. Izmir University of Economics, Izmir, Turkey.

Toren, N., & Kraus, V. (1987). The effects of minority size on women's position in academia. *Social Forces*, *65*(4), 1090–1100. doi:10.2307/2579024

Tuncer, S. (2019). Cinsiyetlendirilmiş bir kurum olarak akademi: Türkiye'de akademinin cinsiyet kültürüne bakmak. *Kültür ve İletişim*, (44), 173–208. doi:10.18691/kulturveiletisim.629082

Chapter 4
Token Image in Male-Dominated Professions and Occupational Segregation Based on Gender:
A Study on the Cases Reflected on National News

Benan Kurt Yilmaz
Sinop University, Turkey

Olca Surgevil Dalkilic
Dokuz Eylül University, Turkey

ABSTRACT

The aim of this study is to examine and understand the experiences of women who have token status in their profession based on the news reflected in national news agencies. In the study, 10 professions were determined, including military service, pilot, prison director, firefighter, driver, driving instructor, pumper, house painter/electrician/car mechanic, postal officer, fisher, where women are numerically a minority. The method of the research was determined as the qualitative research method, and the research design was determined as descriptive content analysis. It reaches conclusions about the occupational gender typing for women in Turkey. The research also tries to understand the roles attributed to these individuals in the context of occupations attributed to the female gender. Finally, images of women in the mentioned professions are also examined in terms of the way the news about token women is presented.

DOI: 10.4018/978-1-7998-8742-3.ch004

INTRODUCTION

While sex refers to the biological characteristics of the individual and classifies them as male and female, gender roles refer to social norms built on these biological characteristics. Although certain jobs and occupations seem to be shared according to gender in work life, this distribution is related to gender roles rather than biological differences between men and women. The socialization process that develops depending on the gender roles of women and men results in the fact that women are not being candidates for certain professions and/or certain jobs in business life. Because women, who tend to jobs and professions dominated by male employees, face certain limitations in these areas and are exposed to negative experiences.

Kanter (1977) defines token status as individuals who are 15% or less numerically in their group due to their gender, ethnicity or race; individuals in the same group who are 85% or more numerically have a dominant status.

According to Kanter (1977), women who are exposed to negative experiences of tokenism are working in male-dominated occupations. Due to the social norms and gender role expectations, there are mismatches of gender roles and occupations. While occupational gender segregation creates norms about which profession is suitable for women, it causes women who make a choice outside of normative expectations to encounter negative experiences. On the other hand, there are studies showing that men who turn to professions dominated by women are not exposed to these negative experiences (Heilman, 1983; Terborg, 1977; Sacket et al.,1991; Cohen, Swim,1995; Reskin, 1988; Kurt Yılmaz, 2019). In summary, male tokens do not encounter the negative experiences of female tokens (Yoder, 1991: 180). While social and cultural barriers make it difficult for women to exist in certain professions, they also cause inequality practices that are not allowed by the law to emerge through various experiences (such as glass ceiling, glass cliff, glass escalator).

The aim of this study is to examine and understand the experiences of women who have token status in their profession, based on the news reflected in national news agencies.

The study showed that the number of women who make career choices which are not suitable for occupational gender typing has increased. However, the speed and numerical rate of this increase is not sufficient. For this reason, women continue to be mentioned with adjectives such as "the only" and "the first" female in the analyzed news. On the other hand, these token women are exposed to stereotyping, discriminatory treatment, close and punitive supervision, insufficient support, insufficient instruction resistance and hostile behavior in their professions.

Considering that women in the Eastern region experience different difficulties and problems in business life and in different professions, it is important to understand the ways in which they are represented in different professions. So it is hoped that the study will contribute to the evaluation of male-dominated occupational groups, gender-based inequalities and the evaluation of occupational gender segregation in Turkey. Thus, it will be possible to understand and discuss the different career paths, employment forms and conditions for women.

THEORETICAL FRAMEWORK: TOKENISM AND OCCUPATIONAL GENDER SEGREGATION

Tokenism

Rosabeth Moss Kanter published the book *Men and Women of the Corporation* in 1977, which expands and consolidates the work of social psychologists investigating the effects of group composition on group processes. This study of Kanter (1977a), which consists of case results of Fortune 500 companies, presents a new theory of gender unbalanced groups. Kanter (1977a) stated that less than 15% representation in workplaces or management levels means being a token and, she focused on the negative effects of being a person as a part of a small minority, up to a maximum of 15% (being a token). Kanter made this study on the basis of "people who are members of any minority or who are considered to have a disadvantageous characteristic are also considered as representatives of the categories they belong to, apart from being individuals in society or working life", and based on the determination that these people were put into stereotypes.

Kanter (1977a, 1977b) conducted a study with 20 sales executive women in a sales team of 300 people and drew attention to three negative experiences related to the representation of women in token positions: *performance pressure, boundary heightening,* and *role encapsulation.* In other words, while women who are proportionally below 15% in the organization and who have experienced these three negative processes are in token status, men who are proportionally above 85% are in the dominant status.

Performance Pressure. While the visibility of the individual in the organization produces positive results as promotion, bonus, etc., the visibility to be expressed in this dimension is the conspicuousness of the token. The expected performance from tokens is above what it should be and even falls into the "outstanding achievement" category. However, this performance expectation is normalized to tokens. It is impossible for these women to behave in a way that will escape the public's notice as they are exposed to constant scrutiny and observation in the workplace, trainings, meetings, and social events, As a matter of fact, token women are frequently faced with intense performance pressure, close control, harsh expressions and intonations.

Boundary Heightening. The second set created by the dominant group to restrict the behavior of tokens is expressed as boundary heightening. The token woman is constantly rejected by the dominant group member men, and her ties with other employees in the organization are cut off. As a matter of fact, men who are members of the dominant group perceive women with token status as a threat. There are two reasons why the dominant group perceives tokens as a threat and creates barriers. First, the dominant group tries to raise its own boundaries and exaggerate its ties against the desire of the "foreigner" coming from outside to change the culture and structure formed by the dominant group (Kanter, 1977b: 975). The second reason is that the existence of tokens in the organization and their efforts create awareness and lead to the loss of power of the dominant group.

Role Encapsulation. Tokens are often people with stereotypes about them. For this reason, they are evaluated within stereotypes and kept separate from the members of the dominant group. Token women are often constrained by expectations structured by gender roles. In this context, Kanter (1977a,b) states that token women are exposed to four different stereotypical role assignments as mother, pet, seductress, iron maiden.

Yoder, who conducted research on tokenism after Kanter, stated that tokenism can also manifest itself with different negative experiences other than the ones mentioned above (Yoder, 1991, 1996, 2002). In other words, Yoder drew attention to the fact that tokenism cannot be determined solely on a numerical ratio, and that there are different dimensions reinforce the negative experiences of tokenism. Yoder (1994) draws attention to the three-way interaction of the numerical ratio in the token group with gender status, occupational appropriateness, and instrusiveness.

Gender Status. Ethnicity, age, gender and occupation are the most common statuses but, since there is a hierarchical structure between social statuses, not all statuses are of equal value and do not provide the same prestige to the individual. Yoder (1994) states that the gender of the token affects the status of the token. In other words, male tokens do not encounter the negative experiences of female tokens (Yoder, 1991: 180). Researches (Heilman, 1993; Terborg, 1977; Sacket et al., 1991; Cohen and Swim,1995; Reskin, 1988) support that the gender of the token affects the experiences of the token.

Occupational Appropriateness. Gender segregation of a profession includes two dimensions, normative and numerical. Occupational gender segregation sets norms about which profession is suitable for women, and women who make choices outside of normative expectations face negative results (Schachter, 1951). However, this negative experience is not due to the 'fear of success' that the woman has about whether or not she is suitable for the profession she chooses, on the contrary, it is associated with underestimation of the woman (Cherry and Deaux, 1978). According to Reskin and Hartman (1986), occupational gender discrimination is so dominant that 53% of those who make career choices that are not suitable for occupational gender segregation, regardless of male or female, have to change their jobs. This research shows the power of stereotypes and represents the reflections of these socially formed judgments in business life.

Intrusiveness. Men are usually employed in high-paying and prestigious occupations with a limited number of employees. This situation causes these professions to be perceived as more suitable for men (Coser, 1981), and women's employment in these professions is made difficult by the social intervention of men. Because, while women's participation in these professions causes an increase in status and prestige for women, it also causes men to experience a loss of space (Zimmer: 1986). The majority who want to eliminate this threat develop intervention methods. Restricted opportunities, wage inequality, job harassment and boundary heighteining are some of these interventions. The way to reduce the interventions and pressure is to increase the numerical ratio. In other words, the experiences of minorities representing 10% and minorities representing 20% are different from each other. Proportionally increasing minorities increase their competitiveness and gain the power to cope with interventions (Blalock, 1976: 148).

Occupational Gender Segregation and Tokenism

Gender is beyond an individual's biological sex, it is a cultural construct imposed by society. In this context, gender creates constraints and frameworks on how each gender should act in society. It controls the roles of men and women in accordance with constraints and frameworks (Kelan, 2010), and individuals who go beyond gender roles are usually "marked" (Baxter, 2010; Ku, 2011). This duality directly affects the job roles that are considered appropriate for men and women. In other words, occupations are generally classified according to a gender (McDowell & Schaffner, 2011; Nilsson & Larsson, 2005).

Gender-based jobs are determined by the assumed skills and characteristics of men and women. Feminized jobs and occupations are determined by the stereotypical characteristics of femininity (as supportive, person-oriented). Masculine jobs and occupations are determined by the characteristics (as dominance, aggression, competitiveness) that are assumed to be related to masculinity (Baxter, 2010; Burke & Collins, 2001; Hendal et al., 2005; McDowell & Schaffner, 2011; Traut, 2002). Although women held more bachelor's degrees than men in the late 1990s, they are still underrepresented in many traditionally male-dominated professions such as engineering (18%), physical science (37%), mathematics/computer science (34%), chemistry (26%), and law (27%) (NCES, 1997, 2002).

Not only are women less likely to choose a career and occupation in these fields (Jacobs, Chhin, & Bleeker, 2006; Watt, 2010), they are also more likely than men to "leave" the job and/or profession (Mau, 2003). Also at each level of education, girls are more likely than boys to give up math and science. This situation, called the "leaky pipeline", refers to the pattern of women leaving male-dominated professions. The "leak" shows that token women who want to work in male-dominated fields are not fulfilling their potentials. These reasons have caused all tokenism research to date to focus on occupations that do not conform to normative gender segregation. For example, female doctors (Lorber 1984, 1991), female military personnel (Rustad 1982; Yoder, Adams, & Prince 1983), female academics (Young, Mackenzie, & Sherif, 1980), female auto workers (Gruber & Bjorn, 1982), female police officers (Gerber, 1996; Martin, 1994; Ott, 1989), female prison director (Jurik, 1985; Zimmer, 1986), and female transit operatives (Swerdlow, 1989) are some of these studies.

When the 1960s and 1980s are compared, occupational gender segregation has decreased in the USA and other developed countries, but the traces of classification continue (Yoder, 2002). In other words, efforts are increasing to remove the barriers to participation in jobs that are accepted as male and female occupations. However, since occupations are often categorized according to a one single gender by the society, occupational classification according to gender continues (Angouri, 2011; Holmes & Schnurr, 2006; Nilsson & Larsson, 2005).

Men often find it problematic to work in jobs that are considered low-paid and low-status (women jobs) if they work in more prestigious, challenging, and better-paying jobs (Lupton, 2000; Williams, 1995). However, due to the decline of relatively well-paid jobs in the industrial, business, and commerce sectors, men have started targeting jobs they typically view as "women jobs". For example, the number of men working in the nursing profession in England increased from 9.20% in 2002 to 10.73% in 2007 (NMC, 2008).

While the number of men increases in professions dominated by women, the number of women increases in professions dominated by men, as well. While these increases lead to a decrease in occupational gender segregation, they cause different experiences for men and women who go beyond the normative occupational segregation.

Researches indicate that women who go beyond the normative occupational segregation and are therefore considered tokens are exposed to discriminatory behaviors in their wage, promotion, performance evaluation, recruitment and assignment processes, and in their relations with their male colleagues (Day & Stogdill, 1972; Hagen & Kahn, 1975; Kanter, 1977; Patterson, 1975; Spangler, Gordon, & Pipkin, 1978; Terborg, 1977; Terborg & Ilgen, 1975). Similarly, these women are exposed to discriminatory experiences in family and social life, and therefore they have a dilemma about continuing their work.

METHOD

The aim of this study is to examine and understand the experiences of men and women who have token status in their profession, through the news reflected on national and local news sites. For this purpose, 10 professions, including military service, pilot, prison director, firefighter, driver, driving instructor, pumper, house painter/electrician/car mechanic, mail delivery man, fisherman, where women are numerically a minority were selected.

The method of the research was determined as the qualitative research method, and the research design was determined as descriptive content analysis. In content analysis, similar data are brought together within the framework of certain concepts and themes and interpreted in a form that the reader can understand (Creswell, 2013). Content analysis aims to measure the variables in a text and is a systematic, unbiased and numerical analysis performed for this purpose (Wimmer & Dominick, 2000: 135–136). In other words, the content analysis method aims to present the problem in a systematic and impartial way. In this study, scanning model was used in accordance with the stated purpose. The screening model aims to describe an existing situation as it exists without attempting to change it (Karasar, 1998: 77). This model screen the whole population or a sample taken from the population in order to make a general judgment about the population (Karasar, 2014: 79).

The population of the research is national and local news sites broadcasting daily in Turkey. The news in the occupation categories determined as female-dominated occupations reflected on the websites of national and local news agencies in Turkey between 1 January, 2020 – 30 July, 2021 constitute the sample of the study. In this study, the title and content of 86 news made on national and local news sites between the filtered dates regarding women who remained in token status due to the gender segregation of their job and profession were scanned.

Within the reference period determined for the research, content analysis was carried out on the given sample, and it is aimed to reveal how women in male-dominated professions are included in the news and framed. Within the scope of the research, for women in male-dominated professions, 86 news specific to 10 professions have been reached [military service (16), pilot (25), prison director (1), firefighter (7), driver (12), driving instructor (2), pumper (6) house painter/electrician/ car mechanic – pearl/copper/silver master (10), postal officer (6), fisher (1)].

It has been determined that there is no news reflected on national and local news sites between the dates in question regarding the professions of kindergarten teacher, cleaning, nursing and stewardess, which are included in the segregation of female-dominated occupation (Information about segregation of female-dominated occupation see Floge & Merill, 1985; Fottler, 1976; Greenberg ve Levine, 1971; Segal, 1962; Ott:1989; Croos & Bagihole; Jackson, 1974)

Table 1. Code System

Code System	Frequency
Thematic Coding	**85**
Stereotyping and Differential Treatment	**15**
Lack of Support	**6**
Close and Punitive Supervision	**2**
Perceived Hostility and Resistance	**8**
Insufficient Instruction	**7**
Gender Identity as Performative	**12**
Headlines	**35**

In the study, the frequency of yhe usage of some words together in the news published on national and local news sites was examined. The words in which the frequency of use was measured by making content analysis are as follows: Women (military service, pilot, prison director, firefighter, driver, driving instructor, pumper, house painter/electrician/car mechanic – pearl/copper/silver master, postal officer, fisher), first woman, only woman, rol model woman. After obtaining the title and contents of the news, expert opinion was taken and the data analysis was started.

Content analysis is the systematic analysis of printed or visual materials in terms of certain categories. The data obtained through content analysis were classified between each other and certain themes, thus revealing the relationships between the data (Yıldırım and Şimşek, 2011: 227). The news included in the scope of the study were analyzed within the framework of seven 'themes' (Information about themes see Yoder, 1994; Croos & Bagihole, 2002 ;McDowell,2015). These themes and their frequencies are presented in Table 1. MAXQDA Analytics Pro 2020, a qualitative data analysis program, was used to analyze the data obtained.

RESULTS

In this section, the findings obtained from the research are classified under themes. The findings obtained from these themes and content analysis are presented with visual figures, and then the findings are interpreted and discussed.

Within the scope of the study, 86 news items were subjected to content analysis[1-86]. Thus, it has been tried to determine how women who have token status in male-

Figure 1. The Most Used Combinations of Words in News

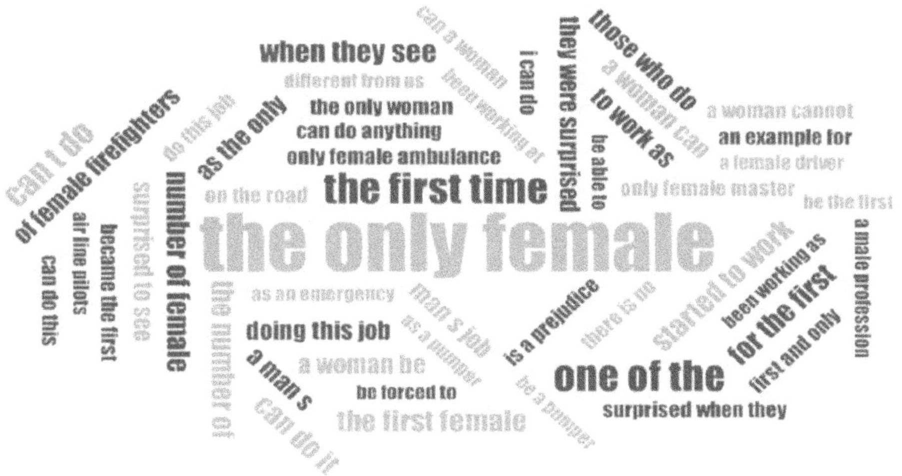

dominated professions are defined in the news in question and how they are presented to the reader who reads the news. It is striking that the expression "the only female" is frequently used in the news. The way the woman, who is the only/unique one in her profession or job, is reflected in the news is associated with her being "the only woman". However, another word combination that stands out in the news is the expression "the first time". Women who appeared in their profession for the first time in terms of their gender were brought to the news. Similarly, women who were the first in their region, province or institution were also highlighted in the news.

"For the first time, two female officers take part in the Sorgusky helicopter assigned by the Gendarmerie General Command".[8] The expression is an example of such usage. In addition, women who are the first/only in their profession and job also use this form of definition. This situation can be detected in the interview sections reflected in the news. *"As a few boyfriends and only a women from our era, we climbed and descended the tower".*[35] This statement is an example of the way women describe themselves. Another example is about the region in which the first or only women in the profession or work: *"The number of fisher women in Okçulu District, known as the first female fishing village, has reached 25. Women come back in the morning from the waters they opened in the evening".*[74]

In the study, 86 news items subjected to content analysis were classified with 7 thematic coding accompanied by expert opinion. One of these themes is news headlines, and these headlines are discussed in the following sections. In addition, the formation of the themes of *Gender Identity as Performative, Insufficient Instruction, Perceived Hostility and Resistance, Close and Punitive Supervision,*

Figure 2. Co-Created Codes

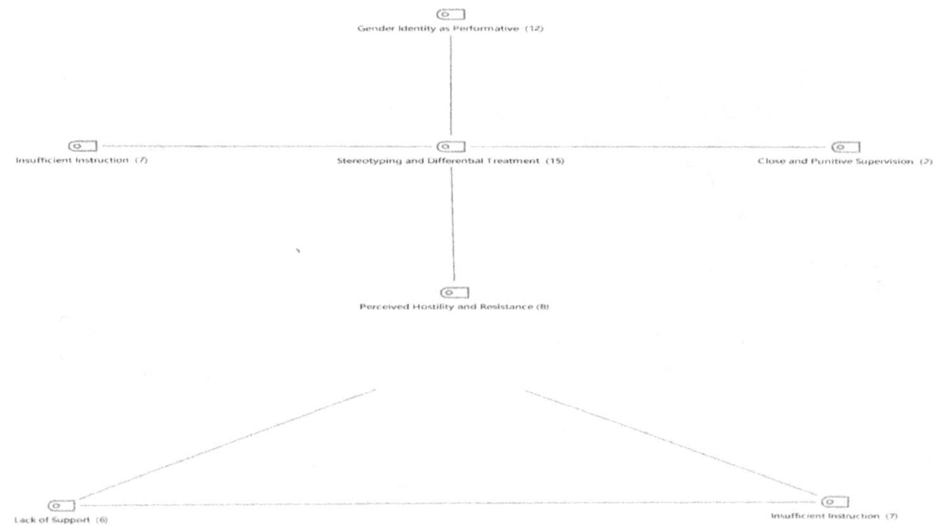

Lack of Support, Stereotyping and Differential Treatment were examined. In other words, while analyzing the news contents, it was tried to determine which themes occur together in the news contents. As a result of the analysis, it has been determined that some themes are in a structure that follows each other in terms of formation. It is determined that the themes of *Gender Identity as Performative Insufficient instruction, Close and punitive supervision, Perceived Hostility and Resistance* emerged in the same news text, along with the coding done by the researcher under the theme of *Stereotyping and Differential Treatment* in a news article. This situation shows an important information about news contents. In the news about women who have token status in their job and profession, some themes come together intensely. If there are discourses of *stereotyping and discriminatory treatment* regarding token women in the news, it can be said that the *gender identity of the woman comes to the fore before the professional identity* in the same text. Similarly, news of career choices that do not conform to the normative gender segregation of women give information about *perceived hostility and resistance* and also *insufficient support and guidance.* News about a women pumper can be given as an example: *"The drivers who came were making fun of me by saying, 'Would a woman be a pumper? but I had to work for my family. It is accepted in the society that pumping is a job done by men. But I believe that I will overcome this job even though I cannot get any support"*[51]

Similarly, as the first female prison director, A.B. says *"It gives pride. It's a nice title, but as I'm a female manager, I know all eyes are on me. I have to cope*

Figure 3. Headlines

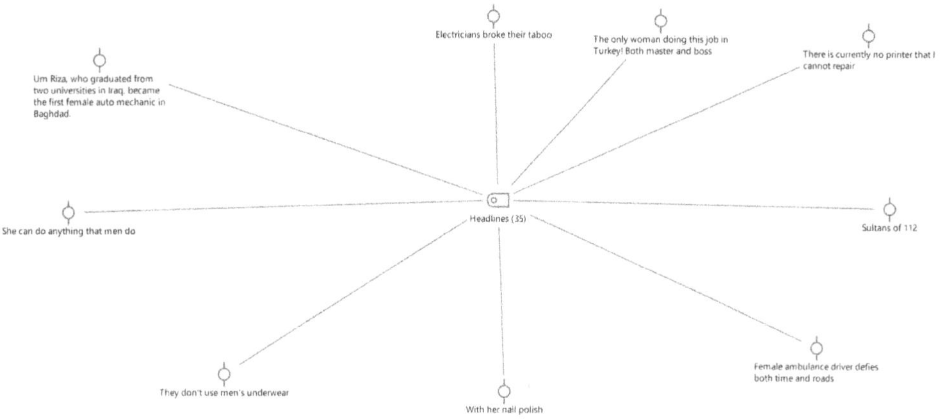

with this task successfully"[10] she states that she is subject to close control because of her gender identity.

It has been determined that 35 of the 86 news headlines examined in the study have a significant emphasis on women who are tokens in their profession. So much that even in situations where there are other women in the profession, the intensity of the expressions *"first", "only", "unique"* stands out. However, some of the titles visualized above differ because they emphasize gender identity beyond the fact that women are the first and only. Expressions such as *"sultans of 112", "repairing cars with nail polish", "women soldiers do not wear men's underwear", "can do anything that men do"*[19] stand out in particular.

In the analysis of the data obtained within the scope of the research, the Maxqda Analytic Pro 2020 Program, which provides the reader with ease of reading through visuals, was used. One of the conveniences offered by the program to the reader is the visualization of the content and expressions under the themes. In the next part of the study, the most striking expressions and contents are included under the 7 themes determined. The numbers in parentheses on the right of the themes indicate how many times the theme was coded in 86 news items. For example, 12 expressions were coded under the "Gender Identity as Performative" theme, and the most striking ones were presented to the reader under the theme modeling.

Figure 3, visualizes the contents under the *"Gender Identity as Performative"* theme. In this context, there are expressions that highlight women who are in token status in their profession, as women who perform female actionsnot related to job what they do. The expression of *"The woman who is an electrician with nail polish is funny to customers"* and the news as *"the law allowing female military personnel to grow their hair out"* can be given as examples of this theme.

Figure 4.

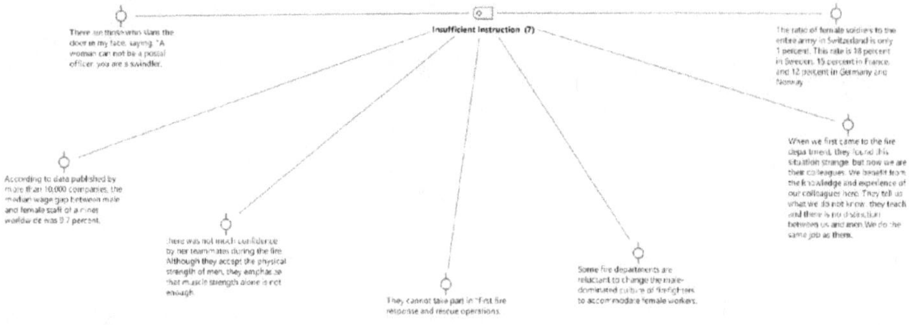

In Figure 4, the contents under the *"Insufficient Instruction"* theme are visualized. In this context, it is emphasized that women, who have token status in their profession, do not have any guides who have done this job/profession before them. For example, the woman working as a postal officer heard the words *"you are not a postal officer, you are a swindler"* from someone who has never seen a female postal officer before. Also the news of the reluctant attitude of firefighters, who did not have female firefighter colleagues before, to change the dominant culture can be given as an example of this theme.

Figure 5.

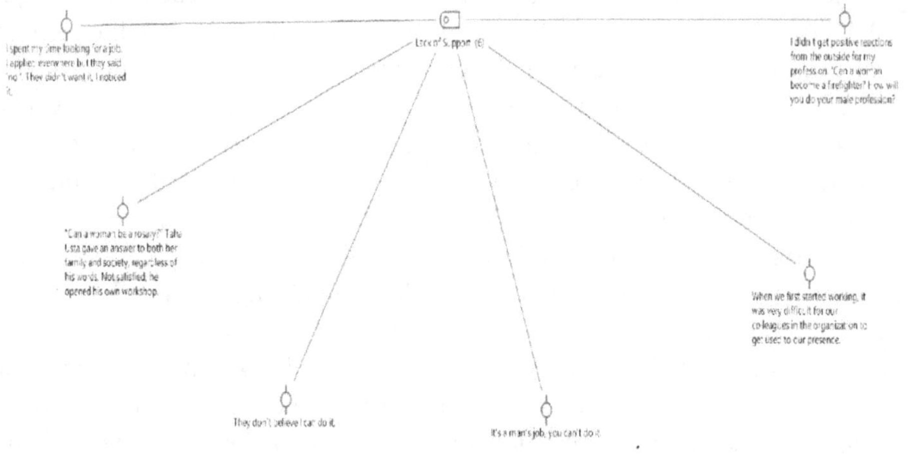

Figure 6.

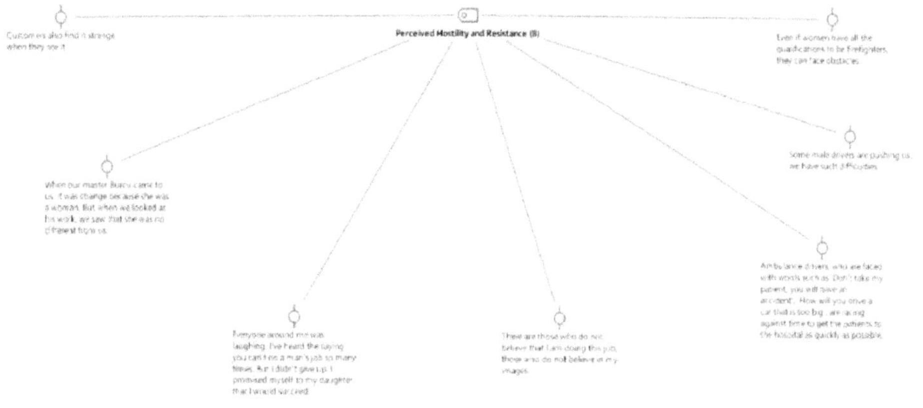

Figure 5 visualizes the contents under the *"Lack of Support"* theme. In this context, the experiences of women with token status in their profession due to lack of support while doing their jobs are emphasized. For example, the statements *"I applied everywhere but realized that they did not want me", "They did not believe that I could do it", "It was a very difficult process for my male colleagues to do this job and exist there"* can be given as examples of this theme.[43]

Figure 6 visualizes the contents under the *"Perceived Hostility and Resistance"* theme. In this context, the experiences of resistance and hostility experienced by women who have token status in their profession are emphasized. For example, the expressions *"those who did not believe in me would not believe in my dreams", "I do not want you to carry my patient because I do not believe you can drive this car", "I was forced to cause an accident by being squeezed by male drivers while driving an ambulance"* can be given as examples of this theme.[37-45]

Figure 7 visualizes the contents under the *"Stereotyping and Differential Treatment"* theme. In this context, the stereotyping and discriminatory behaviors experienced by women with token status in their profession are emphasized. For example, expressions such as *"People who saw me were shocked", "Driving a car is perceived as a male skill", "4 female health personnel work as an ambulance driver despite all the difficulties they face"* can be given as examples of this theme.[46,47]

In Figure 8, the contents under the *"Close and Punitive Supervision"* theme are visualized. In this context, the close control behaviors experienced by women who have token status in their profession are emphasized. Although there is no concrete example of close control in the news, the skills of women in this profession to do this

Figure 7.

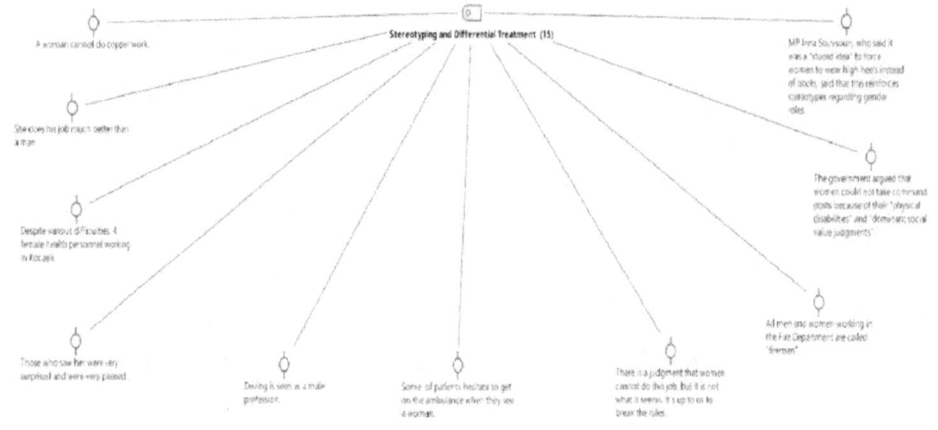

job are highly questioned. At the beginning of the phrases that women hear the most is *"Can you do it?"*. This is why all the behaviors of women are followed closely.[51,62]

Code clouds consist of the most used codes in content analysis. At the end of the thematic coding made in 86 news items that were subjected to content analysis, the code with the highest frequency is located in the middle of the code cloud. The other codes used are located around the most used code and thus a code cloud is formed. With the code clouds, the most used codes can be easily seen. Code clouds are important because they contain clues about the relationship between the research topic and the theme. In this study, the theme of *"Stereotyping and Differential Treatment"* is located in the middle of the code cloud as the most used code. In

Figure 8.

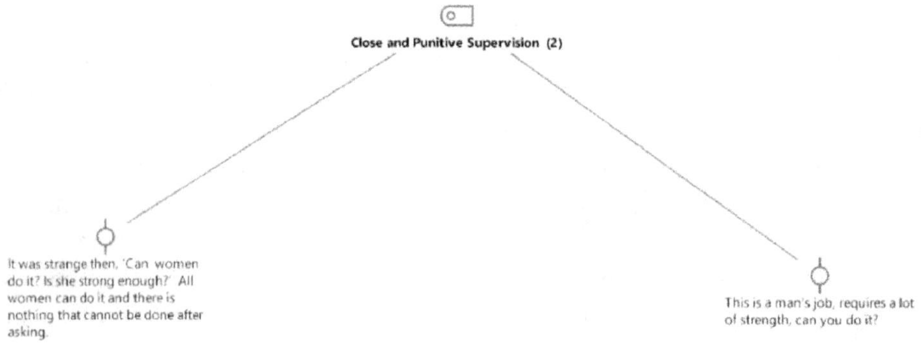

Figure 9.

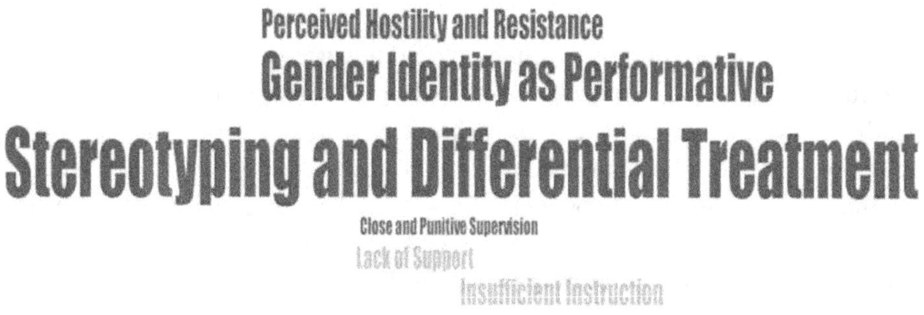

other words, it can be said that women with token status according to occupational gender typing are mostly exposed to stereotyping and discriminatory treatment, and this is mostly covered in the news.

CONCLUSION

The theory of tokenism was first put forward by Rosabeth Moss Kanter in her book "Men and Women of the Corporation" published in 1977.

The fact that the fact that there were no news available on token men during the research shows that the focus of attention is mostly token women. At this point, at this point, the current research overlaps with Yoder's research (1991, 1994, 1996, 2002), that stated the experiences of token groups differ. However, the fact that women's participation in the professions included in the study is new makes us think that the stories of these women are newsworthy. In other words, as military service, pilot, prison director, firefighter, driver, driving instructor, pumper, house painter/electrician/car mechanic, postal officer, fisher are the occupational groups in which women have just started to exist. For this reason, it can be considered that the value of these news is high.

Although the research supports that the number of women in male-dominated occupations has increased, it is possible to state that increase is slow. As a matter of fact, some of the token women in the news (such as the prison director) still maintain their feature of being the first and only in Turkey. Also the number of women in other professions (such as pilot) has not yet reached the desired level.

The research findings show that news about the token women include negative experiences in content and headlines like *Gender Identity As Performative*, Insufficient Instruction, Perceived Hostility And Resistance, Close And Punitive Supervision,

Lack Of Support, Stereotyping and Differential Treatment in news contents and headlines. The findings resemble with Kanter's negative experiences of tokenism (1977a,b).

The cultural pattern of jobs, occupations and organizations in which women are involved as tokens is also important. For example, in the firefighting profession, which has a history of almost 200 years, the process of women's acceptance progresses slowly. For example in the announcement of the institutions that will employ female firefighters, the sentence of "women firefighter will be recruited." can be seen. This situation causes women to experience both bewilderment and hesitation to be a part of the institution. In almost all of the news made in this context, women state that they have problems adapting to the organizational climate.

More support and guidance are needed to increase the number of women in the occupations included in the study. It is important to create flexibility for women in these professions, and to provide incentives (such as affordable childcare) for mothers who want to choose these professions. Since traditional housework culturally given to women continues, they tend to choose professions which would not give extra burden and create additional challenges to them.

As a final word, more studies are needed about the experiences of women and men in jobs and occupations that are contrary to occupational gender segregation. Actually, the fact that there was not a single news about token men in the specified date range arouses curiosity about the experiences of token men. Thus,it can be suggested for future studies to include more professions in their research by focusing on different date ranges.

REFERENCES

Angouri, J. (2011). 'We are in a masculine profession…': Constructing gender identities in a consortium of two multinational engineering companies. *Gender and Language*, *5*(2), 373–404. doi:10.1558/genl.v5i2.373

Angouri, J., & Bargiela-Chiappini, F. (2011). 'So what problems bother you and you are not speeding up your work?' Problem solving at work. *Discourse & Communication*, *5*(3), 209–229. doi:10.1177/1750481311405589

Baxter, J. (2010). *The Language of Female Leadership*. Palgrave Macmillan. doi:10.1057/9780230277915

Baxter, J. (2012). Survival or success? A critical exploration of the use of 'double-voiced discourse' by women business leaders in the UK. *Discourse & Communication*, *5*(3), 231–245. doi:10.1177/1750481311405590

Burke, S., & Collins, M. K. (2001). Gender differences in leadership styles and management skills. *Women in Management Review*, *16*(5), 244–256. doi:10.1108/09649420110395728

Cohen, L. L., & Swim, J. K. (1995). The differential ımpact of gender ratios on women and men: Tokenism, self-confidence, and expectations. *Personality and Social Psychology Bulletin*, *21*(9), 876–884. doi:10.1177/0146167295219001

Collins, P. H. (1986). Learning from the outsider within: The sociological significance of Black feminist thought. *Social Problems*, *33*(6), S14–S32. doi:10.2307/800672

Coser, R. L. (1981). *Women of a Certain Age: The Midlife Search for Self*. Academic Press.

Creswell, J. W. (2013). *Nitel Araştırma Yöntemleri*. Siyasal Kitabevi.

Day, D. R., & Stogdill, R. M. (1972). Leader behavior of male and female supervisors: A comparative study. *Personnel Psychology*, *25*(2), 353–360. doi:10.1111/j.1744-6570.1972.tb01110.x

Gerber, G. L. (1996). Status in same-gender and mixed-gender police dyads: Effects on personality attributions. *Social Psychology Quarterly*, 350–363.

Gruber, J. E., & Bjorn, L. (1982). Blue-collar blues: The sexual harassment of women autoworkers. *Work and Occupations*, *9*(3), 271–298.

Hagen, R. L., & Kahn, A. (1975). Discrimination Against Competent Women 1. *Journal of Applied Social Psychology*, *5*(4), 362–376. doi:10.1111/j.1559-1816.1975.tb00688.x

Heilman, M. E. (1983). Sex bias in work settings: The lack of fit model. Journal of Nursing Management, 13(2), 137–46.

Holmes, J. (2006). *Gendered Talk atWork: Constructing Social Identity through Work Place Interaction*. Blackwell Publishing. doi:10.1002/9780470754863

Jacobs, J. E., Chhin, C. S., & Bleeker, M. M. (2006). Enduring links: Parents' expectations and their young adult children's gender-typed occupational choices. *Educational Research and Evaluation*, *12*(4), 395–407.

Jurik, N. C. (1985). An officer and a lady: Organizational barriers to women working as correctional officers in men's prisons. *Social Problems*, *32*(4), 375–388.

Kanter, R. M. (1976). The ımpact of hierarchical structures on the work behavior of women and men. *Social Problems*, *23*(4), 415–430.

Kanter, R. M. (1977a). *Men and women of the corporation*. Basic Books.

Kanter, R. M. (1977b). *Some effects of proportions on group life, the gender gap ın psychotherapy*. Springer.

Kanter, R. M. (1987). Men and women of the corporation revisited: Interview with rosabeth moss kanter. *Human Resource Management, 26*(2), 257–263.

Kanter, R. M. (1994). Change ın the global economy: An ınterview with rosabeth moss kanter. *European Management Journal, 12*(1), 1–9.

Karasar, N. (1998). *Bilimsel Araştırma Yöntemi*. Nobel Yayın Dağıtım.

Karasar, N. (2014). *Bilimsel Araştırma Yöntemi*. Nobel Yayın Dağıtım.

Kelan, E. K. (2010). Gender logic and (un) doing gender at work. *Gender, Work and Organization, 17*(2), 174–194.

Ku, M. C. (2011). When does gender matter? Gender differences in speciality choice among physicians. *Work and Occupations, 38*, 221–262.

Lorber, J., & Farrell, S. A. (Eds.). (1991). *The social construction of gender*. Sage.

Lupton, B. (2000). Maintaining masculinity: Men who do women's work. *British Journal of Management, 11*(s1), 33–48.

Martin, S. E. (1994). "Outsider within" the station house: The impact of race and gender on Black women police. *Social Problems, 41*(3), 383–400.

Mau, W. C. (2003). Factors that influence persistence in science and engineering career aspirations. *The Career Development Quarterly, 51*(3), 234–243.

McDowell, J., & Schaffner, S. (2011). Football, it's a man's game: Insult and gendered discourse in The Gender Bowl. *Discourse & Society, 22*(5), 547–564.

Nilsson, K., & Larsson, S. U. (2005). Conceptions of gender: A study of female and male head nurses' statements. *Journal of Nursing Management, 13*(2), 179–186.

Ott, E. M. (1989). Effects of the male-female ratio at work: Policewomen and male nurses. *Psychology of Women Quarterly, 13*(1), 41–57.

Patterson, J. B. (1975). *Occupational Training for Mature Women: A Survey of the Enrollment of Women Over Age 35 in Proprietary Institutions in Cuyahoga County, Spring 1974*. Academic Press.

Reskin, B. F. (1988). Bringing the men back in: Sex differentiation and the devaluation of women's work. *Gender & Society, 2*(1), 58–81.

Rustad, M. L. (1982). *Women in Khaki: The American Enlisted Woman*. Praeger Publishers.

Sackett, P. R., Dubois, C. L., & Noe, A. W. (1991). Tokenism ın performance evaluation: The effects of work group representation on male-female and white-black differences ın performance ratings. *The Journal of Applied Psychology*, *76*(2), 263.

Spangler, E., Gordon, M. A., & Pipkin, R. M. (1978). Token women: An empirical test of Kanter's hypothesis. *American Journal of Sociology*, *84*(1), 160–170.

Swerdlow, M. (1989). Men's accommodations to women entering a nontraditional occupation: A case of rapid transit operatives. *Gender & Society*, *3*(3), 373–387.

Terborg, J. R. (1977). Women ın management: A research review. *The Journal of Applied Psychology*, *62*(6), 647.

Terborg, J. R., Peters, L. H., Ilgen, D. R., & Smith, F. (1977). Organizational and personal correlates of attitudes toward women as managers. *Academy of Management Journal*, *20*(1), 89–100.

Trauth, M. E. (2002). Odd girl out: An individual differences perspective on women in the IT profession. *Information Technology & People*, *15*(2), 96–118.

Watt, H. M. (2010). Gender and occupational choice. In *Handbook of gender research in psychology* (pp. 379–400). Springer.

Williams, L. C. (1995). *Still a Man's World: Men who Do 'Women's Work*. University of California Press.

Wimmer, D. D., & Dominick, J. R. (2000). *Mass Media Research: An Indroduction*. Wadsworth Publishing Company.

Yoder, J. D. (1983). Another look at women ın the army: A comment on woelfel's article. *Sex Roles*, *9*(3), 285–288.

Yoder, J. D. (1983). Another Look At Women In The Army: A Comment On Woelfel's Article. *Sex Roles*, *9*(3), 285–288.

Yoder, J. D. (1992). Rethinking Tokenism: Looking Beyond Numbers. *Gender & Society*, *5*(2), 178–192.

Yoder, J. D. (1994). Looking Beyond Numbers: The Effects Of Gender Status, Job Prestige, And Occupational Gendertyping On Tokenism Processes. *Social Psychology Quarterly*, *57*, 150–159.

Yoder, J. D. (2002). 2001 Division 35 Presidential Address: Context Matters: Understanding Tokenism Processes And Their Impact On Women's Work. *Psychology of Women Quarterly*, *26*(1), 1–8.

Yoder, J. D., Adams, J., & Prince, H. T. (1983). The price of a token. *Journal of Political and Military Sociology*, 325–337.

Yoder, J. D., Aniakudo, P., & Berendsen, L. (1996). Looking Beyond Gender: The Effects Of Racial Differences On Tokenism Perceptions Of Women. *Sex Roles*, *35*(7-8), 389-400.

Yoder, J. D., & Schleicher, T. L. (1996). Undergraduates Regard Deviation From Occupational Gender Stereotypes As Costly For Women. *Sex Roles*, *34*(3-4), 171–188.

Yoder, J. D., Schleicher, T. L., & Mcdonald, T. W. (1998). Empowering Token Women Leaders: The Importance Of Organizationally Legitimated Credibility. *Psychology of Women Quarterly*, *22*(2), 209–222.

Yoder, J. D., & Sinnett, L. M. (1985). Is It All In The Numbers? A Case Study Of Tokenism. *Psychology of Women Quarterly*, *9*(3), 413–418.

Young, C. J., MacKenzie, D. L., & Sherif, C. W. (1980). In search of token women in academia. *Psychology of Women Quarterly*, *4*(4), 508–525.

Zimmer, L. (1987). How women reshape the prison guard role. *Gender & Society*, *1*(4), 415–431.

Zimmer, L.(1988). Tokenism And Women In The Workplace: The Limits Of Gender-Theory. Social Problems, 35(1), 64–77.

ENDNOTES

"Doğuda Görev Yapan Kadın Komutanlar." 1 January, 2020. Retrieved from: https://www.ensonhaber.com/galeri/doguda-gorev-yapan-kadin-komutanlar
"Görenler Şaşırıyor, Yapamazsın Diyenlere İnat Hayalinin Peşinden Koştu." 9 January, 2020. Retrieved from: https://www.gzt.com/jurnalist/gorenler-sasiriyor-yapamazsin-diyenlere-inat-hayalinin-pesinden-kostu-3515787
"İlk Kadın Pompacılar." 27 January, 2020. Retrieved from: http://objektif17.com/haber/ilk-kadin-pompacilar-11358.html
"Elektrik Sektörünün Tabularını Yıktılar." 29 January, 2020. Retrieved from: https://www.cumhuriyet.com.tr/haber/elektrik-sektorunun-tabularini-yiktilar-1717042

"Gaziantep'te 6 Kadın Benzinci." 6 February, 2020. Retrieved from: https://enerjihaber.com/gaziantep-te-6-kadin-benzinci/951/

Göklerde Bir Kadın Pilot: İrem Poyraz. 14 February, 2020 Retrieved from: https://mezun.ku.edu.tr/news/irem-poyraz15/

"Türkiye'nin İlk Kadın Taarruz Helikopter Pilotu." 14 February, 2020 Retrieved from: https://www.egm.gov.tr/havacilik/turkiyenin-ilk-kadin-taarruz-helikopter-pilotu

"Hint Ordusunda Kadın Subaylar Artık Eşit Haklara Sahip Olacak, Komutanlık da Yapabilecek." 17 February, 2020. Retrieved from: https://www.bbc.com/turkce/haberler-dunya-51534006

"Türkiye'nin İlk Kadın Tır Şöförü." 18 February, 2020. Retrieved from: https://www.mersinkent.com/haber/1813/turkiyenin-ilk-kadin-tir-soforu-iveco-kiliclar-musterisi.html

"Karabük'ün Tek Kadın Posta Dağıtıcısı." 7 March, 2020. Retrieved from: https://www.sozcu.com.tr/2016/gundem/karabukun-tek-kadin-posta dagiticisi1125447/?utm_source=dahafazla_haber&utm_medium=free&utm_campaign=dahafazlahaber

"Sedefcilik Mesleğinin Tek Kadın Ustası." 7 March, 2021. Retrieved from: https://www.haberler.com/sedefcilik-mesleginin-tek-kadin-ustasi-13974731-haberi/

"Ordu'nun Tek Kadın Ustası." 8 March, 2020. Retrieved from: http://www.orduolay.com/yasam/ordunun-tek-kadin-ustasi/58381

"Burhaniye'de Kadın Pompacı İşbaşında." 9 March, 2020. Retrieved from: https://www.sondakika.com/haber/haber-burhaniye-de-kadin-pompacilar-isbasinda-12996045/

"Kadın Pompacılar İşbaşında." 9 March, 2020. Retrieved from: https://www.sondakika.com/haber/haber-burhaniye-de-kadin-pompacilar-isbasinda-12996045/

"Kadın Pompacı Benzin İstasyonuna Renk Kattı." 10 March, 2020 Retrieved from: https://www.bolgegundem.com/kadin-pompaci-benzin-istasyonuna-renk-katti-3350v.htm

"Ambulans Şöförü Nasıl Olunur?" 12 April, 2020. Retrieved from: https://www.milliyet.com.tr/kariyer/ambulans-soforu-nasil-olunur-ambulans-soforu-olma-sartlari-6186810

"Dünya Pilotlar Gününde Instagram Fenomeni Türk Kadın Pilotlar." 26 April, 2020. Retrieved from: https://www.ntv.com.tr/galeri/yasam/dunya-pilotlar-gununde-instagram-fenomeni-turk-kadin-pilotlar,Yv3tpsGVGk6NP3nrCfrByw

"İşte Sınırdaki Kadın Askerler." 26 July, 2020. Retrieved from: https://www.cnnturk.com/turkiye/iste-sinirdaki-kadin-askerler?page=11

"İspanya Büyükelçiliği'nden Kadın Pilota Sabiha Gökçen'li Övgü." 8 August, 2020. Retrieved from: https://t24.com.tr/haber/ispanya-buyukelciligi-nden-kadin-pilota-sabiha-gokcen-li ovgu,970805

"Çorum'un Kadın Posta Dağıtıcıları." 18 August, 2020. Retrieved from: https://www.memurlar.net/haber/769295/corum-un-kadin-posta-dagiticilari.html

"Cezaevine Kadın Elinin Değdiğini Göstermek İstiyorum." 10 August, 2020. Retrieved from:https://www.hurriyet.com.tr/kelebek/cezaevine-kadin-elinin-degdigini gostermekistiyorum7523128#:~:text=Yavuzy%C4%B1lmaz%2C%20 29%20ya%C5%9F%C4%B1nda%20T%C3%BCrkiye'deki,yani%202.%20 m%C3%BCd%C3%BCr%20olarak%20%C3%A7al%C4%B1%C5%9Facak

"Kadın Reisler." 3 September, 2020. Retrieved from: https://www.haberturk.com/ordu-haberleri/80553754-karadenizin-kadin-reisleriordunun-persembe-ilcesindeki-kadin-balikcilar-sezon-acilmasiyla

"Cezaevine Kadın Elinin Değdiğini Göstermek İstiyorum." 21 October, 2020. Retrieved from: https://www.hurriyet.com.tr/kelebek/cezaevine-kadin-elinin-degdigini-gostermek-istiyorum-7523128#:~:text=Yavuzy%C4%B1lmaz%2C%2029%20 ya%C5%9F%C4%B1nda%20T%C3%BCrkiye'deki,yani%202.%2-0m%C3%BCd%C3%BCr%20olarak%20%C3%A7al%C4%B1%C5%9Facak

"Tek Kadın Posta Dağıtıcısı." 25 October, 2020. Retrieved from: https://t24.com.tr/haber/nigdenin-tek-kadin-posta-dagiticisi,473453

"Kadın Pompacı Uyuşturucu ile Yakalandı." 7 November, 2020. Retrieved from: https://www.hurriyet.com.tr/gundem/kadin-pompaci-uyusturucu-ile-yakalandi-41656782

"Kadın Subaylar Turizm Başkentinin Trafiğini Havaden Denetliyor." 10 November, 2020. Retrieved from: https://www.aa.com.tr/tr/turkiye/kadin-subaylar-turizm-baskentinin-trafigini-havadan-denetliyor/2038199

"Türkiye'de Bu işi Yapan Tek Kadın: Hem Usta Hem Patron." 14 November, 2020. Retrieved from: https://www.milliyet.com.tr/galeri/turkiyede-bu-isi-yapan-tek-kadin-hem-usta-hem-patron-6354536

112'nin Kadın Ambulans Sürücüleri." 4 December, 2020. Retrieved from: https://www.iha.com.tr/haber-112nin-kadin-ambulans-suruculeri-880528/

"Otomobil Tamircisi Genç Kız Görenleri Şaşkına Çeviriyor." 9 December, 2020. Retrieved from: https://haberglobal.com.tr/yasam/otomobil-tamircisi-genc-kiz-gorenleri-saskina-ceviriyor-17737

"Usta Kadınları Hiçbir Şey Durduramaz." 20 December, 2020. Retrieved from: https://www.milliyet.com.tr/pazar/usta-kadinlari-hicbir-sey-durduramaz-6383458

"Edirne'nin Kadın Ambulans Söförü." 7 January, 2021. Retrieved from: https://gazetekolektif.com/edirnenin-ilk-kadin-ambulans-soforu-cicek-yalcin-yilmadim-israrci-oldum-ve-isi-kazandim/

"Hakkari'nin İlk ve Tek Kadın Ambulans Söförü Zeynep Sarı Zamana Karşı Yarışıyor." 7 January, 2021. Retrieved from: https://www.sabah.com.tr/video/yasam/hakkarinin-ilk-ve-tek-kadin-ambulans-soforu-zeynep-sari-zamana-karsi-yarisiyor-video

"Eskişehir İtfaiyesinin Tek Kadın Görevlisi." 11 January, 2021. Retrieved from: https://www.cnnturk.com/turkiye/eskisehir-itfaiyesinin-tek-kadin-gorevlisi?page=17

"THY Kadın Pilot Sayısında 211 ile Tarihi Rekor Kırdı."18 January, 2021. Retrieved from: https://www.hurriyet.com.tr/ekonomi/thy-kadin-pilot-sayisinda-211-ile-tarihi-rekor-kirdi-41422829

"İlk Kadın Usta Ordu'lu." 22 January, 2021. Retrieved from: http://www.orduolay.com/haber/ilk-kadin-usta-ordulu/58447

"Dünya'nın Çeşitli Ülkelerinde Orduda Görev Yapan Kadın Askerler." 27 January, 2021. Retrieved from: https://tr.sputniknews.com/foto/202101271043674597-dunyanin-cesitli-ulkelerinde-orduda-gorev-yapan-kadin-askerler/

"İzmir'in Kadın İtfaiyecileri." 28 January, 2021. Retrieved from: https://www.ensonhaber.com/galeri/izmirin-kadin-itfaiyecileri

"Kadın İtfaiyeciler Performanslarıyla Göz Dolduruyor." 28 January, 2021. https://www.trthaber.com/haber/turkiye/kadin-itfaiyeciler-performanslariyla-goz-dolduruyor-551685.html

"Denizli'de 25 Yaşındaki Genç Kadın 18 Yıldır Oto Tamircisi." 30 January, 2021. Retrieved from: https://www.denizli24haber.com/haber/denizlide-25-yasindaki-genc-kadin-18-yildir-oto-tamircisi-36218

"Tespih Tanelerinin Kadın Ustası." 31 January, 2021. Retrieved from: https://yeni1mecra.com/tespih-tanelerinin-kadin-ustasi/

112'nin Sultanı Yollarda." 7 February, 2021. Retrieved from: https://www.haberturk.com/gaziantep-haberleri/84547411-112nin-sultani-yollarda2-milyonluk-sehrin-tek-kadin-ambulans-soforuambulans-soforu-sibel

"Kadın İtfaiyeci İş Azmiyle Hemcinslerine Örnek Oluyor." 13 February, 2021. Retrieved from: https://www.aa.com.tr/tr/pg/foto-galeri/kadin-itfaiyeci-is-azmiyle-hemcinslerine-ornek-oluyor

"Kadın İtfaiyeci." 13 February, 2021. Retrieved from: https://www.aa.com.tr/tr/pg/foto-galeri/kadin-itfaiyeci-is-azmiyle-hemcinslerine-ornek-oluyor

"Şiddet Mağduru Kadın Hayata Dört Elle Sarıldı." 15 February, 2021. Retrieved from: https://www.aa.com.tr/tr/yasam/siddet-magduru-kadin-hayata-dort-elle-sarildi-/984726

"Irak'ta İki Üniversite Mezunu Um Rıza Bağdat'ın İlk Kadın Oto Tamircisi Oldu." 18 February, 2021. Retrieved from: https://www.aa.com.tr/tr/yasam/irakta-iki-universite-mezunu-um-riza-bagdatin-ilk-kadin-oto-tamircisi-oldu/2148976

"Yangını Kadınlar Söndürecek." 21 February, 2021. Retrieved from: https://www.sozcu.com.tr/hayatim/yasam-haberleri/yangini-kadinlar sondurecek/?utm_source=dahafazla_haber&utm_medium=free&utm_campaign=dahafazlahaber

"İzmir'in Şöför Nebahat Ablası Elif Hatlı Minibüste." 2 March, 2021. Retrieved from: https://www.haberler.com/izmir-in-sofor-nebahat-ablasi-elif-hatli-minibuste-13962239-haberi/

"Bu kadınlar Hayat Kurtarmak İçin Direksiyon Sallıyor." 6 March, 2021. Retrieved from: https://www.ozgurkocaeli.com.tr/video/6557942/bu-kadinlar-hayat-kurtarmak-icin-direksiyon-salliyor

"Kadın Ambulans Şöförü Erkek Meslektaşlarına Parmak Isırtıyor." 6 March, 2021. Retrieved from: https://www.sakaryadanhaber.com/haber/6557621/kadin-ambulans-soforu-erkek-meslektaslarina-parmak-isirtiyor

"Bu Kadınlar Hayat Kurtarmak İçin Direksiyon Sallıyor." 6 March, 2021. Retrieved from: https://www.ozgurkocaeli.com.tr/video/6557942/bu-kadinlar-hayat-kurtarmak-icin-direksiyon-salliyor

"Hava Yollarında Kaç Kadın Pilot Var?." 7 March, 2021. Retrieved from: https://boardinginfo.com/havayollarinda-kac-kadin-pilot-var/

"Hastamı Sen Götürme Kaza Yaparsın." 7 March, 2021. Retrieved from: https://www.dha.com.tr/istanbul/hastami-sen-goturme-kaza-yaparsin-diyen-de-oldu-yuhalayan-da-istanbulun-kadin-ambulans-soforleri/haber-1814730

"Kadın Sağlıkçılar Ambulans Direksiyonuna Geçecek." 7 March, 2021. Retrieved from: https://www.haberlisin.com/gundem/kadin-saglikcilar-ambulans-direksiyonuna-gececek-h60489.html

"İstanbul'un Kadın Ambulans Şöförü: Yuhalayan da Oldu, Hastasını Götürmemi İstemeyen de." 7 March, 2021. Retrieved from: https://www.mynet.com/istanbul-un-kadin-ambulans-soforu-yuhalayan-da-oldu-hastasini-goturmemi-istemeyen-de-110106748042

"Önyargıları Boşa Çıkaran Kadın Sürüş Eğitmeni." 8 March, 2021. Retrieved from: https://www.sehrivangazetesi.com/guncel/on-yargilari-bosa-cikaran-kadin-surus-egitmeni-erkeklere-de-h76508.html

"Kadın Direksiyon Eğitmeni Erkeklere Taş Çıkardı." 8 March, 2021. Retrieved from: https://www.sabah.com.tr/van/2021/03/08/kadin-direksiyon-egitmeni-erkeklere-tas-cikardi

"Kadın Ambulans Şöförü Yollara Meydan Okuyor." 8 March, 2021. Retrieved from: https://www.aa.com.tr/tr/yasam/kadin-ambulans-soforu-yollara-meydan-okuyor/1412419

""Kadın Usta 21 Yıldır Mobilya Döşemeciliği Yapıyor." 8 March, 2021 Retrieved from: https://www.haberler.com/kadin-usta-21-yildir-mobilya-dosemeciligi-yapiyor-13977186-haberi/

"Yoksa Siz İstasyonlardaki Kadın Enerjisini Hissetmediniz mi?." 8 March, 2021. Retrieved from: https://www.armanayse.com/yoksa-siz-istasyonlardaki-kadin-enerjisini-hissetmediniz-mi/

"18 Senedir Ellerinin Ojesiyle Araba Tamir Ediyor." 9 March, 2021. Retrieved from: https://www.haberturk.com/denizli-haberleri/84343240-18-senedir-ellerinin-ojesiyle-araba-tamir-ediyor18-yildir-oto-tamircisi-olan-25-yasindaki

"Malatya'nın Kahraman Kadın Ambulans Sürücüleri." 17 March, 2021. Retrieved from: https://www.haberturk.com/malatya-haberleri/85577821-malatyanin-kahraman-kadin-ambulans-suruculeri112-ambulans-servisinin-kadin-kahramanlari

"Kuaförlüğü Bırakıp Lokanta Açan Kadın Usta Adana Kebabına Lezzet Katıyor." 25 March, 2021. Retrieved from: https://www.trthaber.com/haber/guncel/kuaforlugu-birakip-lokanta-acan-kadin-usta-adana-kebabina-lezzet-katiyor-567498.html

"İsviçre Ordusunda Kadın Askerler Artık 'Erkek İç Çamaşırı' Giymeye Zorlanmayacak. 30 March, 2021. "Retrieved from: https://tr.euronews.com/2021/03/30/isvicre-ordusunda-kad-n-askerler-art-k-erkek-ic-camas-r-giymeye-zorlanmayacak

"Akaryakıt İstasyonunda Kadın Pompacı." 1 April, 2021. Retrieved from: https://www.ogunhaber.com/amp/genel/akaryakit-istasyonunda-kadin-pompaci-731241h.html

"Atak'a Kadın Pilot. 09 April, 2021. Retrieved from: https://www.yenisafak.com/gundem/ataka-kadin-pilot-polis-hava-ekibi-guc-kazandi-3617578

"Sivas'ta Zorlu Eğitimi Tamamlayan Kadın İtfaiyeciler Göreve Başladı." 9 April, 2021. Retrieved from: https://www.hurriyet.com.tr/gundem/sivasta-zorlu-egitimi-tamamlayan-kadin-itfaiyeciler-goreve-basladi-41783999

"Antalya'da Hızlı Postacılar Milli Takım İçin Yarıştı." 15 April, 2021. Retrieved from: https://www.ogunhaber.com/genel/antalya-da-hizli-postacilari-milli-takim-icin-yaristi-1064389h.html

"Kadın Ambulan Şöförü Hem Zamana Hem Yollara Meydan Okuyor." 17 April, 2021. Retrieved from: https://www.sesgazetesi.com.tr/haber/6954251/kadin-ambulans-soforu-hem-zamana-hem-yollara-meydan-okuyor

"Kadın İtfaiye Eri Aranıyor." 20 April, 2021. Retrieved from: https://www.kadinisci.org/2021/04/20/kadin-itfaiye-eri-araniyor/

"Sivas'ın İlk Kadın Ambulans Söförü." 1 May, 2021. Retrieved from: https://www.sivashaberler.com/sivasin-kadin/

"Akaryakıtta Pompanın Başına Kadınlar Geçti." 1 May, 2021. Retrieved from: https://www.cumhuriyet.com.tr/haber/akaryakitta-pompanin-basina-kadinlar-gecti-1832192

"Konya'nın Tek Postacı Ablası." 12 May, 2021 Retrieved from: http://arsiv.ntv.com.tr/news/4886.asp

"Özel Oğluna Destek İçin Başladı, 10 Yılı Geride Bıraktı." 28 May, 2021. Retrieved from: https://www.haberturk.com/eskisehir-haberleri/87589279-ozel-ogluna-destek-icin-basladi-yazici-tamirinde-10-yili-geride-biraktieskisehirdeki-tek

"Balıkesir'de Diplomalı Kadın Pompacı İlgi Odağı Oldu." 29 May, 2021. Retrieved from: https://www.acargazete.com/haber-balikesir-de-diplomali-kadin-pompaci-ilgi-odagi-oldu-8860.html

"Kentin Tek Kadın Ambulans Söförü Oldu." 1 June, 2021. Retrieved from: https://www.trthaber.com/haber/guncel/kentin-tek-kadin-ambulans-soforu-oldu-585162.html

"Manisa'nın Kadın Ambulans Söförleri Parmak Isırtıyor." 14 June, 2021. Retrieved from: http://www.manisadagundem.com/gundem/manisanin-kadin-ambulans-soforleri-parmak-isirtiyor-h32860.html

"İlk Türk Kadın Pilot Kimdir? İlk Türk Kadın Pilotun Hayatı."14 June, 2021. Retrieved from: https://www.hurriyet.com.tr/egitim/ilk-kadin-pilot-kimdir-ilk-turk-kadin-pilotun-hayati-41831674

"Bayan Askerler Makyaj Yapabilecek." 25 June, 2021. Retrieved from: http://arsiv.ntv.com.tr/news/160190.asp

"İşçi Bir Babanın Kızıyım Bu Koltuğa Oturmak İçin Tırnaklarımla Savaştım." 11 October, 2021. Retrieved from: https://www.sozcu.com.tr/hayatim/yasam-haberleri/isci-bir-babanin-kiziyim-bu-koltuga-oturmak-icin-tirnaklarimla-savastim/

"Ukrayna'da Kadın Asker Depremi." 3 July, 2021. Retrieved from: https://www.milliyet.com.tr/galeri/son-dakika-ukraynada-kadin-asker-depremi-6544759/1

"Ukrayna'da Kadın Askerler Topukluyla Yürütüldü." 3 July, 2021. Retrieved from: https://www.gazeteduvar.com.tr/ukraynada-kadin-askerler-topukluyla-yurutuldu-aptalca-bir-fikir-galeri-1527437?p=5

"Tekirdağ'ın ve Çerkezköy'ün Tek Kadın Minibüs Şöförü." 7 July, 2021. Retrieved from: https://www.cerkezkoyhaber.com.tr/haber/67978/tekirdagin-ve-cerkezkoyun-tek-kadin-minibus-soforu.html

"Suudi Kadın Askerler İlk Defa Hac Sırasında Görevde." 21 July, 2021. Retrieved from: https://www.diken.com.tr/suudi-kadin-askerler-ilk-defa-hac-sirasinda-gorevde/

"Kadın Boyacılar Her Yerde." 13 August, 2020. Retrieved from: https://www.sabah.com.tr/yazarlar/gunaydin/funda-karayel/2016/08/13/kadin-boyacilar-her-yerde

"Kırıkkale'nin Tek Kadın Posta Dağıtcısı." 15 October, 2021. Retrieved from: https://beyazgazete.com/haber/2012/10/15/kirikkale-nin-tek-kadin-posta-dagiticisi-ayvalik-aciklama-yapti-1454715.html

Chapter 5
Falling Foundation of Patriarchal Societies:
Pink-Collar Female Labor Force

Idil Goksel
Izmir University of Economics, Turkey

Yiğitcan Çolak
https://orcid.org/0000-0002-6604-647X
Izmir University of Economics, Turkey

ABSTRACT

This chapter questions whether the women who have been under the pressure of choosing pink-collar jobs imposed by patriarchal societies would choose white-collar, blue-collar, or some other type of jobs instead of pink-collar ones. This paper uses data from a survey conducted on respondents aged ≥15 years in Turkey. In total 114 people participated in this study. The survey was conducted online due to the COVID-19 pandemic. Participants were expected to answer various questions, such as their personal information to their knowledge about the pink-collar job concept. This chapter aims to figure out whether higher education levels and appropriate vocational education affect female labor decisions positively or not.

INTRODUCTION

Most of the women are not aware of the pressure they face during their career path. Due to social norms they believe what they live is what it ought to be. Sometimes these directions can be clearly seen; however in most of the cases it is done by social

DOI: 10.4018/978-1-7998-8742-3.ch005

pressure, and is considered to be normal as all females face more or less the same. This chapter aims to create awareness about one of the concepts about this issue, and analyze the Turkish case by conducting an online survey about pink-collar job concept. The concern of this chapter is to analyze the current situation in Turkey about the knowledge and perception of pink-collar jobs, and observe whether women change their attitudes when they are given the necessary information about the concept.

Although career planning education programs are prevalent worldwide, investigating the further utility outcome of occupations is scarce. It is crucial to examine the women who know about pink-collar jobs and their working conditions (wage, emotional display rules et cetera) among the women who have no idea about this concept and who have already accepted working without being aware of its conditions. The hypothesis was largely formed by delving into the bibliographic resources on why a person needs career planning training. Mastracci, S. H. (2016) states that “The non-college female population simply represents ordinary women. “Ordinary men and women seek alternatives to the four-year college degree path to advance themselves in the labour markets, but options are few relative to their demand…”. Labour market necessities enforce a person to stand out among other candidates. As mentioned before options are few. Either one must have a college degree -or above- or, preselected labour roles. Especially, women candidates have no choice other than being a pink-collar labour. Mastracci, S. H. (2016), also emphasizes “…Without an awareness of training alternatives, or without alternatives altogether, many women neither seek nor receive any formal post-secondary education at all and are therefore most likely to default into pink-collar occupations.”

In this chapter, we first briefly provide background on the concept of the pink-collar job in an effort to illuminate the ideas behind the terminology. The chapter continues with the explanation of the model and methodology which is used to carry out this study. Once the evaluation progress is understood, it will be easier to interpret and discuss the results. After gathering the results, the conclusion part of the chapter provides a detailed analysis of how our findings meet our initial claims.

BACKGROUND

The “pink-collar” concept has been popular since the end of the 1970’s. Social-critic Louise Kapp Howe used this term to indicate women working as nurses, secretaries, and teachers. The term was used to indicate clerical staff as well as non-professional office staff, which were largely held by women. Thus, the creation of the term “pink-collar,” which indicated the fact that it was not white-collar, was nonetheless an office job that was overwhelmingly filled by women.

The concept of a pink-collar job is a social contract that has existed since the beginning of civilized human life. While women started gathering food, men went hunting animals. From this point on, it began to shape its form up to today's perception of the gender of jobs. Societies have grown their sex-biased allegations about what women cannot do, while female workers have grown significant enough to fill our societies' workforce. Even though pink-collar workers are usually paid less and considered "light" workers by society and expected to act according to socio-ethical norms and values, they form the foundation of society.

LITERATURE REVIEW

A World Health Organization (WHO) study about the global burden of the disease reported that the risk of depression had the third-highest disease burden in 2004, and it is expected to have the highest burden by 2030 (Organization, 2008). Women who work as pink-collar labor, especially middle-aged women in their 50s and above, are more likely to develop depression compared to other age groups of women (Chun *et al*, 2020).

An analytical look at male-dominated occupations and female-dominated jobs, finds men and women have very similar occupational inputs like education, skill sets, motivation and commitment to the job. However, they have different, sex-biased outcomes such as low paying jobs with lower status, power, and prestige (Hunt, 1993).

Like adults, children are also aware of the status differences between jobs. Among the jobs which they know, children rate jobs known by the culture as masculine higher in status than jobs known by the culture as feminine (Liben, Bigler, & Krogh, 2001).

A wide-angled look-out to sociological differences between pink-collar jobs and white-collar job occupants might reveal additional information. Most pink-collar laborers complain that their jobs affect their social life. A structural equation modelling research proved that employees' financial well-being negatively affected job insecurity and had significant effects on employees' family's financial well-being positively (To, Gao, & Leung, 2020).

Most of the pink-collar laborers also complain about extra-financial conditions which affect their motivation, stress level and indirectly their social life. A study conducted on five female clerical workers revealed that when various elements are present, the female clerical workers' experience job stress. Green (2005), reported, "...several factors contribute to female clerical workers' experience of job stress, including difficult relations between workers and management (workplace bullying); too few staff and work overload (intensification of work); job insecurity; excessive monitoring; the increased pace of work; more complex and technical tasks; poor work organization; insufficient training; long work hours; and lack of decision-making and control over work."

In addition, pink-collar laborers usually have difficulties getting custom work conditions. Gupta (2019) reported "Since the job requirements of different types of collar job workers are different, so they need different quality of work-life at work. So, the employers have to change the QWL according to the nature of job of the workers only then they would be able to get maximum gain from their employees."

In patriarchal societies women are subject to economic and sociological constraints and discrimination. These are usually imposed on women more frequently than men, both within and outside of the family. Men superiorities appear nearly in any social subject, but some subjects are more closed to discussion inside the patriarchal societies. One cultural norm that maintains women's submissiveness and inferiority is reflected in the attitude that children cannot be raised in an appropriate and healthy way by one parent, and even more so if the mother raises them alone. (Haj-Yahia, M. M., 2005). Women are considered not capable of raising children alone, not to sustain a household economy, and moreover, they are considered to be dependent on men.

These attitudes begin while young females are being raised. Effects of these behaviours become clear when young women start to be active in social life. Andersen, S. *et al* (2013), reports "In most cultures, men are more likely to have a successful career outside the household than women. This has been attributed to men being more competitively inclined due to nature, or nurture, or both. An important open question in understanding the sources of the gender gap in competitiveness is at what stage the difference first arises and whether this interacts with the socialization process, or not. We show that girls become less competitive and boys are more competitive around puberty in a patriarchal society, whereas this difference never arises in the matrilineal society." This can be interpreted as women are clearly shaped and trimmed like sculptures to stay where men want them to stay. They are not allowed to compete or clearly state their differences in patriarchal societies.

Furthermore, despite being inactive social members, on scope of work-life they get complaints about "not being competitive", "not having any ambitions" etc. Socially constructed roles and constraints reveal themselves at the working environment as well. The entrepreneurial obstacles female entrepreneurs face is examined by Uluköy, M., & Bayraktaroğlu, S. (2014). They found that the ratio of female entrepreneurs being blocked by either their own families or male entrepreneurs is 24%. In the patriarchal Turkish society this ratio is considered to be low. They state that "But despite government policies protecting the women and supporting female entrepreneurship, female entrepreneurship is still being hindered. In the patriarchal Turkish society, obstacles imposed by families were expected to be higher, but it had the same rate with other obstacles.". (Uluköy, M., & Bayraktaroğlu, S., 2014). Regardless of their demographic conditions, all groups of women are imposed to

Table 1. Demographic groups of participants

Age	Males	%	Females	%	Prefer not to say	%
15-18	4	3%	8	7%	0	0%
19-25	25	22%	53	46%	0	0%
26-30	0	0%	2	2%	1	1%
31-49	4	4%	4	3%	0	0%
50-64	3	3%	10	9%	0	0%
65+	0	0%	0	0%	0	0%
Total	36	32%	77	67%	1	1%

these obstacles, behaviours, and attitudes. There is huge literature gap about this issue for Turkey, and this chapter aims to point out that 24% is a very optimistic value.

We can evaluate that most of the exerted pressure is built by patriarchal societies, however the question that must be asked is:

Would being aware of the pressure exerted by patriarchal societies overcome the concept of the pink-collar jobs in the future planning of women?

MODEL AND METHODOLOGY

This study uses data from a survey conducted on respondents aged ≥15 years in Turkey. The survey was conducted online due to the Covid-19 Pandemic. Participants were asked to answer questions about their knowledge of the pink-collar job concept and their expected behaviours on incidents that frequently happen to pink-collar workers. Also, male samples are included in the survey to understand their knowledge about and attitude towards pink-collar jobs. Table 1 shows the demographics of the participants who take the survey:

Although the identities of the participants were kept anonymous the questionnaire begins with personal questions such as name, marital status, salary et cetera. The participants were asked beforehand to consent to the use of the survey results in academic research.

Initially, the concept was directly asked to the participants to measure their knowledge. This was a "Yes" or "No" question with the extra option of "I do not remember". Then, a brief explanation was given about the concept, the idea behind this, and the suitable occupations. All participants responded to the question "Do you agree with that?" as a measure of awareness and the adequacy of a brief explanation. The available answers were "Yes", "No", "Partially".

Participants were also asked about how they decided about their major in college or how they decided what profession they would enter. The viable options were "I decided myself.", "I decided with my family/partner.", "My family told me what to choose.", "My partner told me what to choose.", and "My friends helped me to decide.". It was crucial to examine this situation in order to develop an idea about whether they were exposed to patriarchal pressure or not. All the participants are from Turkey where there is a widespread patriarchal culture that impacts these choices.

Before adding wage-gap information, all participants were asked to state whether they are content about their salary or not. Eventually, in order to receive the necessary information for the aim of this chapter wage-gap information was given to the participants Afterwards, they were asked whether they would choose a pink-collar job anyway, or not.

The next part of the survey had ten statements and the participants were expected to respond with one of the options.

The list of the statements:

- If my father asks me to quit my job, I will.
- If my mother asks me to quit my job, I will.
- If my partner asks me to quit my job, I will.
- Society will accept me if I choose a pink-collar job.
- If I find another job with better wage, I would quit my currently pink-collar job.
- I think in schools, enough information is given about jobs.
- If my boss wants me to lose weight, I would begin a diet.
- If my boss wants me to follow emotional display rules such as "always smiling", I do.
- It's inappropriate that the women who work in places that have more men workers It is inappropriate that pregnant women work.

The final part of the questionnaire had three statements which are:

- I follow socio-ethical norms and values when I have a conflict between those and my decisions.
- I have concerns about what people think about me.
- I think society's acceptance is more important than my thoughts and plans.

The survey questions can be seen in the Appendix.

RESULTS

Table 2 highlights the general characteristics of the participants. The highest proportion of female participants are women who had only high school degrees (38.00%, including currently under-graduate students), whereas males who had undergraduate degree are the largest proportion of the male samples (16.00%). The second-largest proportion of the male samples is high school graduates (14.00%, including currently undergraduate students), in contrast to women who had an undergraduate degree (24.00%).

Female participants who have never heard about the concept are the biggest proportion of the research (40.00%). On the other hand, male samples who have never heard about the concept are half of the percentage of the females (20.00%). Only 18.00% of female samples have already known about pink- collar jobs.

Table 2 also points out that the participants' occupations by their sex. The largest proportion of both males and females are students (25.00% and 55%, respectively). Teachers are the second largest proportion of females (4.00%) in contrast, the largest male proportion is the retired people (2.00%).

A closer look at the female occupations with age demographics (in Table 3) shows that; the third biggest proportion of the female occupants are teachers in their 50's (5.00%) who led by the female students between 19-25 years old (69.00%). The second-largest proportion was formed by the female students above 15 and under 18 years old (11.00%). The fourth row equally separated between three proportions which are retired females (3.00%), female students between 26-30 years old (3.00%), and female housewives who are in their 50's (%3.00) in a total of 9.00%.

As shown in Table 4, the largest proportion of the females who decided their profession themselves their department in college is high school degreed ones (31.00%). However, 5.00% of the females reported that their families or partners have involved in the decision process. 2.00% of the female participants, who are also in the high school degree graduate category, stated their families directly told them what profession they would choose.

Table 5 shows the results about knowledge of females about the pink-collar job concept. A bigger proportion belongs to females who do not agree with the concept (58.00%). 42.00% of the female participants chose the expression "Partially".

When the females who have heard about the pink-collar job concept were asked whether they agree with the brief explanation given, or not, the largest proportion of them chose "No" (90.00%). The ones who have agreed with the explanation (5.00%), and who has partially agreed with the explanation (5.00%) are equally separated, the sum of them which is 10.00% (Table 5)

Table 2. Participants' education status, occupations and pink-collar job concept awareness

Education	**Males**	**%**	**Females**	**%**	**Prefer not to say**	**%**
Primary School Degree	0	0%	0	0%	0	0%
High School Degree	16	14%	43	38%	1	1%
Undergraduate	18	16%	28	24%	0	0%
Graduate	2	2%	5	4%	0	0%
PhD and Above	0	0%	1	1%	0	0%
Total	36	32%	77	67%	1	1%
Occupation	Males	%	Females	%	Prefer not to say	%
Housewife	0	0%	3	3%	0	0%
Lawyer	0	0%	1	0.81%	0	0%
Medical Doctor	0	0%	1	0.81%	0	0%
Nurse	0	0%	1	0.81%	0	0%
Public Relations	0	0%	1	0.81%	0	0%
Retired	2	2%	2	2%	0	0%
Student	28	25%	63	55%	1	0.81%
Teacher	1	0.81%	5	4%	0	0%
Biologist	1	0.81%	0	0%	0	0%
Entrepreneurship	1	0.81%	0	0%	0	0%
Glass-worker	1	0.81%	0	0%	0	0%
Private Sector	1	0.81%	0	0%	0	0%
Private Driver	1	0.81%	0	0%	0	0%
Total	36	31.86%	77	67.24%	1	0.81%
Have you ever heard about the Pink-collar job concept?	Males	%	Females	%	Prefer not to say	%
Yes	10	9%	20	18%	1	1%
No	24	20%	45	40%	0	0%
I don't remember	2	2%	12	10%	0	0%
Total	36	31%	77	68%	1	1%

Table 3. Female sample occupations with age demographics

Occupation	Age 15-18	%	Age 19-25	%	Age 26-30	%	Age 31-49	%	Age 50-64	%	Age 65+	%
Housewife	0	0%	0	0%	0	0%	1	1%	2	3%	0	0%
Lawyer	0	0%	0	0%	0	0%	1	15	0	0%	0	0%
Medical Doctor	0	0%	0	0%	0	0%	0	0%	1	1%	0	0%
Nurse	0	0%	0	0%	0	0%	1	1%	0	0%	0	0%
Public Relations	0	0%	0	0%	0	0%	0	0%	1	1%	0	0%
Retired	0	0%	0	0%	0	0%	0	0%	2	3%	0	0%
Student	8	11%	53	69%	2	3%	0	0%	0	0%	0	0%
Teacher	0	0%	0	0%	0	0%	1	1%	4	5%	0	0%
Total	8	11%	53	69%	2	3%	4	4%	10	13%	0	0%

Table 4. Female participant response to decision process question with educational status

Decision Process	High School Degree	%	Undergraduate Degree	%	Graduate Degree	%	PhD and Above	%
I decided myself.	35	45%	26	34%	5	6%	1	1%
I decided with my family/partner.	6	8%	2	3%	0	0%	0	0%
My family told me what to choose.	2	3%	0	0%	0	0%	0	0%
My partner told me what to choose.	0	0%	0	0%	0	0%	0	0%
My friends helped me decide.	0	0%	0	0%	0	0%	0	0%
Total	43	56%	28	37%	5	6%	1	1%

Table 5. Females who do not remember if they heard about the pink-collar job concept

Do you agree with that concept?	Number	%	Number	%	Number	%
Yes	0	0%	3	7%	1	5%
No	7	58%	34	75%	18	90%
Partially	5	42%	8	18%	1	5%
Total	12	100%	45	100%	20	100%

Table 6. General participant responses to the question "It is a concept which describes jobs that con- sidered suitable for women by society. Being teacher, nurse, secretary, babysitter et cetera. Do you agree with that?"

It is a concept which describes jobes that considered suitable for women by society. Being teacher, nurse, secretary, babysitter et cetera. Do you agree with that?	**Total**	**%**
Yes	14	12%
No	82	72%
Partially	18	16%
Total	114	100%

The table also shows the group of females who have never heard about the pink-collar job concept before. The largest proportion of them chose the option "No" when they were asked about agreeing with the brief explanation given (75.00%), 18.00% of the females who are in this category partially agreed, and 7.00% of the females fully agreed.

Table 6 shows the percentages of the general participant responses to the question "It is a concept which describes jobs that considered suitable for women by society. Being teacher, nurse, secretary, babysitter et cetera. Do you agree with that?". The largest proportion of the participants chose "No" (72.00%). The second largest proportion is formed by the participants who chose "Partially" (16.00%), and the smallest proportion held by the participants who chose "Yes" (12.00%).

Table 7 shows that the 26% of the females that do not agree with the statement have high school degrees (26.00%, including current undergraduate student) when they were asked, "Do you feel happy about your wage?". The second biggest proportion who responded negatively to this question is the undergraduate female participants (18.00%), followed by the high school degreed female participants that responded positively (11.00%).

Table 7. Participants' responses to wage utility

	Female				**Male**				**Prefer not to say**	
Education Status	Yes	%	No	%	Yes	%	No	%	Yes	%
Graduate	2	2%	3	3%	0	0%	2	2%	0	0%
High School	13	11%	30	26%	4	3%	12	10%	1	1%
PhD and above	1	1%	0	0%	0	0%	0	0%	0	0%
Undergraduate	8	7%	20	18%	10	9%	8	7%	0	0%
Total	24	21%	53	47%	14	12%	22	19%	1	1%

Table 8. Sample responses when they were asked would they choose the pink-collar jobs anyway after the wage-gap information was given

	Female				**Male**		**Prefer not to say**			
	Yes		**No**		**Yes**	**No**				
Would you choose the pink-collar jobs anyways?	Number-	%	Number-	%	Number-	%	Number-	%	Number-	%
Yes	5	4%	18	16%	5	4%	7	6%	0	0%
No	19	17%	35	31%	9	8%	15	13% 1	1%	
Total	24	21%	53	47%	14	12% 22	19% 1	1%		

Table 8 states the responses of the participants when they were asked would they choose the pink-collar jobs anyway after the wage-gap information was given. The largest proportion is formed by the negative responses of the female participants who do not feel happy about their wage (31.00%) whereas 13% of the male participants who do not feel happy about their wage responded as "No" The second-largest proportion is the female participants who feel happy about their wage that responded "No" (17.00%), in contrast males who feel happy about their wage responded "No" is 8.00%. On the other hand, 16% of the female participants who do not feel happy about their wage gave a positive response to this statement.

Focus on female participant responses when they were given the expression "If my father asks me to quit my job, I will." can be seen in Table 9. 14.00% of the female respondents chose "I don't know". A bigger proportion is the response "No" which forms 33.00% of the given responses to the expression. The response "Never" is the largest proportion in the given category (39%). 9.00% of the female respondents chose "Maybe" and 4.00% of the female respondents chose "Yes" when they were asked to respond to the given expression. Only 1.00% of the female respondents chose "Definitely".

Table 9 shows female participants' answers when they were asked to respond to the expression "Society will accept me if I choose a pink-collar job.". The largest proportion of the respondents chose "I don't know" (23.00%), while 20% of them chose "No" followed by the ones who chose "Never" (18.00%), the sum of which is 38 per cent. The second to the smallest proportion is respondents who chose "Yes" (14.00%) followed by the smallest proportion which is respondents who chose "Definitely" (13.00%), the sum of which is 27 per cent.

Table 9. Female participant responses to the expressions "If my father asks me to quit my job, I will." and "Society will accept me if I choose a pink-collar job."

	If my father asks me to quit my job, I will		Society will accept me if I choose a pink-collar job	
Definitely	1	1%	10	13%
I don't know	11	14%	18	23%
Maybe	7	9%	9	12%
Never	30	39%	14	18%
No	25	33%	15	20%
Yes	3	4%	11	14%
Total	77	100%	77	100%

Table 10 highlights the various responses of the female samples who were asked to respond to the expressions "I think in schools, enough information is given about jobs.", and "If my boss wants me to follow emotional display rules such as "always smiling", I do.". 27% of the females gave a negative response to the first expression, while 25% of them gave a very strong negative response by saying "Never". As a result 52% of the females do not agree with this expression.

Table 10. Responses of the female samples who were asked to respond to the expression

Response	I think in schools, enough information is given about jobs		If my boss wants me to follow emotional display rules such as "always smiling," I do	
Definitely	5	7%	5	6%
I don't know	7	9%	17	22%
Maybe	17	22%	12	16%
Never	19	25%	19	25%
No	21	27%	16	21%
Yes	8	10%	8	10%
Total	77	100%	77	100%

Never was the most popular response of the females to the second expression (25%), which followed by "I do not know", and "No" (22%, and 21%, respectively). Only 6% of the females were very sure about their response, while 10% of them responded positively to this expression.

Figure 1 shows the general responses to the ten pregiven statements. When respondents were asked to respond the statement "It's inappropriate that the women

Figure 1. General responses to the given ten statements

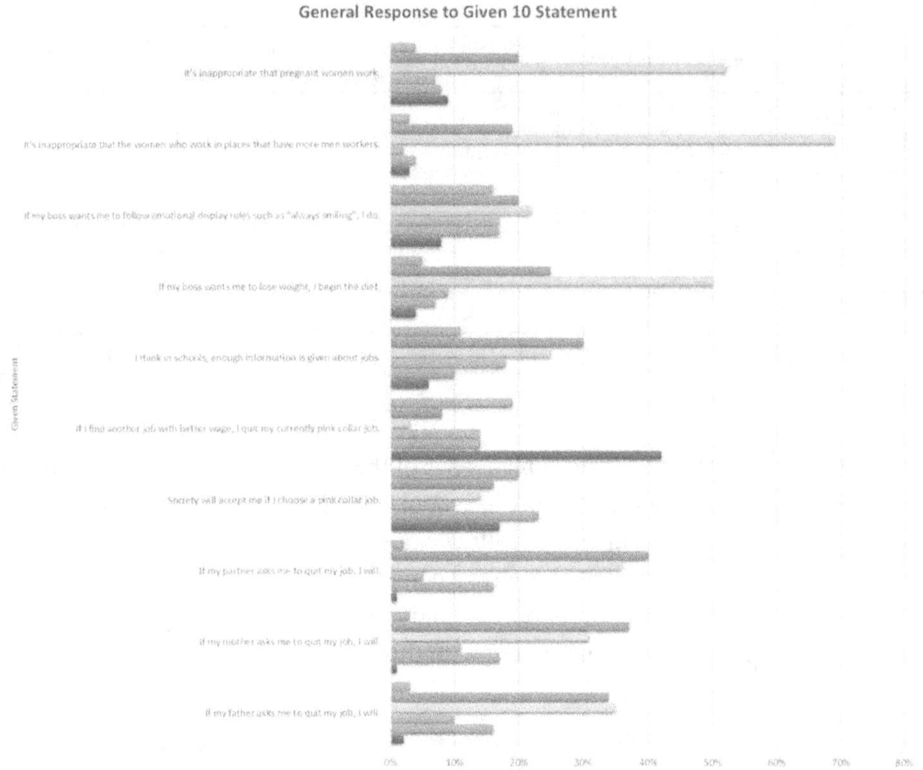

	If my father asks me to quit my job, I will.	If my mother asks me to quit my job, I will.	If my partner asks me to quit my job, I will.	Society will accept me if I choose a pink collar job.	If I find another job with better wage, I quit my currently pink collar job.	I think in schools, enough information is given about jobs.	If my boss wants me to lose weight, I begin the diet.	If my boss wants me to follow emotional display rules such as "always smiling", I do.	It's inappropriate that the women who work in places that have more men workers.	It's inappropriate that pregnant women work.
Yes	3%	3%	2%	20%	19%	11%	5%	16%	3%	4%
No	34%	37%	40%	16%	8%	30%	25%	20%	19%	20%
Never	35%	31%	36%	14%	3%	25%	50%	22%	69%	52%
Maybe	10%	11%	5%	10%	14%	18%	9%	17%	2%	7%
I don't know	16%	17%	16%	23%	14%	10%	7%	17%	4%	8%
Definitely	2%	1%	1%	17%	42%	6%	4%	8%	3%	9%

Percentage

Yes No Never Maybe I don't know Definitely

who work in places that have more men workers." 69.00% of them responded "Never" which is followed by the 19.00% who responded "No". When they were asked to respond the statement "It's inappropriate that pregnant women work.", 52.00% of them responded "Never" which is followed by 20.00% of them who responded "No". When they were asked to respond the statement "If my boss wants me to lose weight, I begin the diet.", 50% of the participants responded "Never", while 25% of them "No". The largest proportion of general participants responded when they were asked to respond the statement "If I find another job with better wage, I quit my currently pink-collar job." is "Definitely" (42.00%) followed by the ones who responded "Yes" (19.00%).

Figure 2 shows the general responses to the three pregiven statements. When participants were asked to respond the statement "I think society's acceptance is more important than my thoughts and plans." 61.00% of them responded "Never" followed by the 19.00% who responded "Rarely". 11.00% of them responded "Sometimes", 5.00% of them responded "Always", and 4.00% of them responded "Usually". When they were asked to respond the statement "I follow socio-ethical norms and values when I have a conflict between those and my decisions." 37.00% of them responded "sometimes" which is the largest proportion of that statement's responses followed by 21.00% of them who responded "Rarely". 17.00 percent of them responded "Usually", 15.00% of them responded "Never", and the 10.00% of them responded "Always".

When respondents were asked to respond the statement "I have concerns about what people think about me." the largest proportion formed by respondents who responded "Rarely" (33.00%), followed by samples who responded "Never" (29.00%). The third- largest proportion formed by participants who responded "Sometimes" (23.00%), followed by 10.00% of them who responded "Usually", and the smallest proportion formed by participants who responded "Always" (5.00%).

CONCLUSION

Participants with higher education are more likely to break the concept of pink-collar jobs and more likely to tend to look out for the jobs with the higher standards. It can be seen, even with a brief explanation of the concept female participants were more likely to deviate from their previous responses. Most of the women have never heard about pink-collar jobs and the majority of the women who attended this research believe that the schools do not educate them properly about jobs and labour concepts. It can be referred from collected data that the lack of access to information and poor quality of career education in schools cause more women to choose pink-collar jobs instead of white- and blue-collar jobs. However, this is less valid for the younger women than the elderly.

For inspection of the utility outcomes further research is needed but the interpretation of the data proves the fact that most of the participants in this research are not happy about or comfortable with their wage. Also, most of the women do not want to choose the pink-collar jobs after the given wage-gap information. As cited in the literature review, financial well-being is a strong factor which has a significant effect on the participants.

Figure 2. General responses to the given three statements

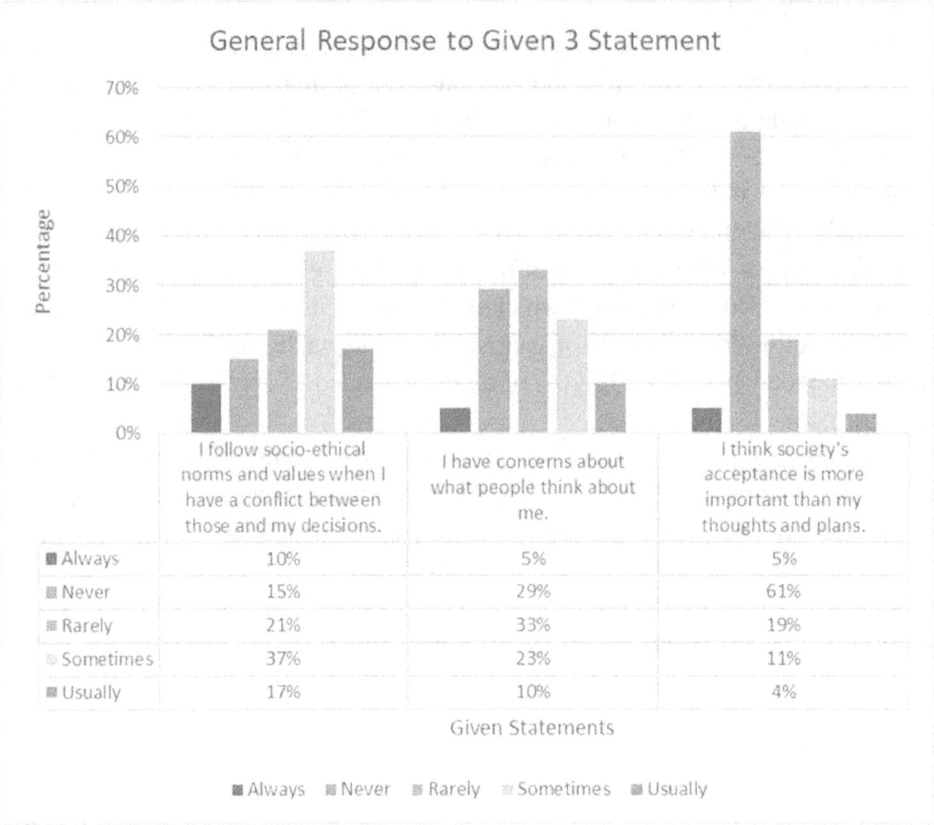

31.00% of the female respondents are candidates to quit their jobs if their father wants them to do so, and in addition 5.00% of them have no doubt. 23.00% of the female participants are hesitant about whether society accepts them or not if they choose a pink-collar job. 27.00% of the female respondents think they will be accepted by society if they choose a pink-collar job, which is a clear sign of the patriarchal pressure, yet 38.00% of the female respondents think they will not be accepted by society even when they choose one of the pink-collar jobs. These high percentages are really worrying.

Also, future research may be done about "why" the 38.00% of females think they will not be accepted by society even when they choose one of the pink-collar jobs. Causes might be the acknowledgement of the patriarchal structure, or it might be the learned helplessness that is imposed by a highly sex-polarized society like Turkey.

The majority of the women who were subject to this research do not think that they are going to follow EDR (46.00%). 54.00% of the females are candidates to follow EDR, and in addition 16.00% of them have no doubt which makes them a possible majority in this particular case. So, a proper approach could reveal what did the hesitant female samples consider when they were asked to respond to the EDR proposal.

The majority of participants were strongly polarized when they were asked to respond to the statement "If my boss wants me to lose weight, I begin the diet.". 75.00% of them responded that they would not do, but when it comes to quitting their jobs which is requested by a family member or their partner the percentages are not that strong enough to polarize the participants.

The general idea which they largely agreed on is that women can freely work in workplaces, where men are forming the majority (88.00%). However, among the participants 16.00% agreed partially, 12% agreed fully that women should work in jobs that fit into the pink-collar job concept.

To sum up, as the thesis statement of this chapter predicted, and the findings indicated, with proper career education in schools and providing accurate and safe information, women can break the glass ceiling, and they can be more than a pink-collar job occupant. It might cause the falling of the society's known foundations, which is built by patriarchal ideas, significantly by men.

FUTURE RESEARCH DIRECTIONS

Future research could add to the existing research about female pink-collar job occupant's further utility outcomes. One interesting area is the retirement benefits of the pink-collar labours. It would be interesting to explore further differences, if any, between how female pink-collar workers and white-collar workers earn their retirement benefits.

Another idea that is also interesting and deserves attention is breaking gender barriers in the pink- collar job concept. That could be done by investigating LGBTi+ individuals who are working as pink- collar labour. It would also be interesting to find out whether they are treated differently, or not in workplaces, and what are the positive and negative behaviours imposed on them different from their colleagues.

REFERENCES

Andersen, S., Ertac, S., Gneezy, U., List, J. A., & Maximiano, S. (2013). Gender, competitiveness, and socialization at a young age: Evidence from a matrilineal and a patriarchal society. *The Review of Economics and Statistics*, *95*(4), 1438–1443. doi:10.1162/REST_a_00312

Chun, H. R., Cho, I., Choi, Y., & Cho, S. I. (2020). Effects of emotional labor factors and working environment on the risk of depression in pink-collar workers. *International Journal of Environmental Research and Public Health, 17*(14), 5208. doi:10.3390/ijerph17145208 PMID:32707657

Green, M. (2005). *Job stress in the pink collar ghetto: clerical workers in the telecommunications industry*. Academic Press.

Gupta, N. (2019). *Perceived Quality of Work-Life in relation to Collar Jobs: Blue-Collar &amp*. Pink-Collar Workers.

Haj-Yahia, M. M. (2005). On the characteristics of patriarchal societies, gender inequality, and wife abuse: The case of Palestinian society. *Adalah's Newsletter, 20*, 1–6.

Hunt, G. (1993). Sex differences in a pink-collar occupation. *Relations Industrielles. Industrial Relations, 48*(3), 441–460. doi:10.7202/050872ar

Liben, L. S., Bigler, R. S., & Krogh, H. R. (2001). Pink and blue collar jobs: Children's judgments of job status and job aspirations in relation to sex of worker. *Journal of Experimental Child Psychology, 79*(4), 346–363. doi:10.1006/jecp.2000.2611 PMID:11511128

Mastracci, S. H. (2016). *Breaking out of the pink-collar ghetto. Policy solutions for non-college women*. Routledge. doi:10.4324/9781315497938

Organization, W. H. (2008). *The global burden of disease: 2004 update*. Author.

To, W. M., Gao, J. H., & Leung, E. Y. (2020). The Effects of Job Insecurity on Employees' Financial Well-Being and Work Satisfaction Among Chinese Pink-Collar Workers. *SAGE Open, 10*(4), 2158244020982993. doi:10.1177/2158244020982993

Uluköy, M., & Bayraktaroğlu, S. (2014). *A field research about oppression incurred of woman entrepreneurs in patriarchal societies*. Academic Press.

APPENDIX

The survey questions used in this research can be seen in figures 3 to 10.

Figure 3.

Pink-Collar Jobs

* Required

1. I acknowledge that the data provided are accurate, and I consent to the information provided may be used in academic research. *

   Check all that apply

   ☐ Yes

2. Name *

3. Surname *

4. Age *

   Mark only one oval.

   ◯ 15-18
   ◯ 19-25
   ◯ 26-30
   ◯ 31-49
   ◯ 50-64
   ◯ 65+

Figure 4.

5. Sex *

Mark only one oval.

- Male
- Female
- Prefer not to say

6. Employment Status *

Mark only one oval.

- Employed/Full-Time
- Employed/Part-Time
- Unemployed
- Not Seeking for a Job

7. Occupation *

8. Salary *

Mark only one oval.

- 0৳
- 0-1000৳
- 1000৳-2000৳
- 2000৳-3000৳
- 3000৳-5000৳
- 5000৳-7000৳
- 7000৳-10,000৳
- 10,000৳-15,000৳
- 15,000৳ +

Figure 5.

9. Education Status *

   Mark only one oval.

   - Primary School Degree
   - High School Degree
   - Undergraduate
   - Graduate
   - PhD and Above

10. Marital Status *

    Mark only one oval.

    - Married
    - Widowed
    - Single
    - Divorced
    - Engaged

11. Do you have any siblings ? *

    Mark only one oval.

    - Yes
    - No

12. How many siblings do you have ? *

    Mark only one oval.

    - 0
    - 1
    - 2
    - 3 and above

Figure 6.

13. Do you have any children ? *

Mark only one oval.

- 0
- 1
- 2
- 3 and above

14. Please choose the answer that fits you. *

Mark only one oval per row.

	Yes	No
Is your Father Alive ?		
Is your Mother Alive ?		
"I live with my family."		
"I live alone."		
"I live with my partner."		
"I live with my friends."		
" I live with my siblings."		
"I live in my own house."		
"I/We pay a rent for the house"		

15. Please say if anything you have different from the last question. *

Figure 7.

16. Have you ever heard about the Pink-collar job concept ? *

Mark only one oval.

- Yes
- No
- I don't remember

17. It is a concept which describes jobs that considered suitable for women by society. Being teacher, nurse, secretary, babysitter et cetera. Do you agree with that ? *

Mark only one oval.

- Yes
- No
- Partially
- Other:

18. How did you decide what to study at university or how to decide on your profession ? *

Mark only one oval.

- I decided myself.
- I decided with my family/partner.
- My family told me what to choose.
- My partner told me what to choose.
- My friends helped me to decide.

19. Do you feel happy about your wage ? *

Mark only one oval.

- Yes
- No

Figure 8.

20. Pink-collar job occupants are usually paid less rather than blue and white collar job occupants. Would you choose a pink collar job anyways ? *

Mark only one oval.

◯ Yes

◯ No

Figure 9.

21. Please choose the answer that fits you. *

Mark only one oval per row.

	Definitely	Yes	Maybe	I don't know	No	Never
"If my father asks me to quit my job, I will."						
"If my mother asks me to quit my job, I will."						
"If my partner asks me to quit my job, I will."						
"Society will accept me if I choose a pink collar job."						
"If I find another job with better wage, I quit my currently pink collar job."						
"I think in schools, enough information is given about jobs."						
"If my boss wants me to lose weight, I begin the diet."						
"If my boss wants me to follow emotional display rules such as "always smiling", I do."						
"It's inappropriate that the women who work in places that have more men workers."						
"It's inappropriate that pregnant women work."						

Figure 10.

22. Please choose the answer that fits you. *

Mark only one oval per row.

	Always	Usually	Sometimes	Rarely	Never
"I follow socio-ethical norms and values when I have a conflict between those and my decisions."	◯	◯	◯	◯	◯
"I have concerns about what people think about me."	◯	◯	◯	◯	◯
"I think society's acceptance is more important than my thoughts and plans."	◯	◯	◯	◯	◯

This content is neither created nor endorsed by Google.

Google Forms

Section 2

Eastern Women and Entrepreneurship

In the second section, five chapters are presented which that are by researchers from Morocco, Bangladesh, and Turkey. Each chapter focuses on female entrepreneurship with a specific viewpoint: women entrepreneurs and the challenges they face in Morocco; , how the female mind is enslaved by the patriarchal system; , the profile of women entrepreneurs in Antalya region in Turkey; , Generation X women entrepreneurs' social intelligence, and women entrepreneurs and the entrepreneurship ecosystem in Turkey. These studies contribute to the female entrepreneurship literature through providing insights from Turkey and Morocco and challenging the patriarchal system and understanding which that attempts to force women to stay behind in the entrepreneurial ecosystem.

Chapter 6
Women Entrepreneurs in the Eastern Region of Morocco:
Challenges and Opportunities

Soumia Boutkhil
Mohammed Premier University, Morocco

ABSTRACT

Despite the various reforms undertaken by the state, women entrepreneurship in Morocco barely constitutes 10% of all businesses in the country whereas the average in the rest of Africa is of 24%. Based on these figures, this chapter seeks to study the evolution and characteristics of female entrepreneurship in Morocco. It examines the motivation behind an entrepreneurial project as well as the environment around it and the struggle to adjust to a male-dominated ecosystem. By exploring a few examples from the eastern region of the country, the study shows that entrepreneurship in Morocco is mainly urban, non-innovative, and merely of a subsistent nature. Indeed, women entrepreneurs, mostly in socially conservative regions (as is the case of the region under study), show a great adaptability to their socio-economic context. While enhancing their leadership skills, autonomy, and self-confidence, the business models adopted by women entrepreneurs focus on their own well-being and that of their families and community. Therefore, the indicators of success are not the usual business and profit growth, but financial autonomy coupled with family responsibility and well-being.

DOI: 10.4018/978-1-7998-8742-3.ch006

INTRODUCTION

This chapter looks at specific cases of young women from diverse backgrounds who have embarked on entrepreneurial projects in the "Eastern Region" of Morocco. The author will start by giving a brief overview of the current state of entrepreneurship in Morocco in general, then will introduce the Eastern Region before looking at the stories of these women's experiences, and give some recommendations to improve their integration into the economic ecosystem.

However, before proceeding, it is necessary to point out that worldwide, women's entrepreneurship is encouraged as it is considered a driving force for socio-economic development (Jouiet, 2021; Conseil Economique Social et Environnemental (CESE), 2016). Most importantly, it has been demonstrated that the economic empowerment of women has a strong impact on the well-being of their immediate family, and significantly reduces poverty, social exclusion and violence (Crittenden et al., 2019; De Vita et al., 2014).

It is also important to note that in the current context of globalized trade and services, the economies of the world are constantly changing and the creation of wealth depends to a large extent on the capacity of States to guarantee the economic inclusion of the population despite the different challenges that may face such a policy. Thus, entrepreneurship and innovation have become watchwords especially in emerging countries where the liberalization of the labor market has often weakened the job prospects of young men and women (Mejjati-Alami, 2004).

Like several southern economies, Morocco has for the last decade strongly encouraged entrepreneurship in order to channel the increasingly important arrival of young men and women into the labor market (World Bank report, 2017). Indeed, more than 300,000 young people of working age enter the labor market each year and hope to get a job in the public service because of the stability and the security such jobs provide.

However, economic restructuring and the modernization of public administration have changed recruitment policy and the sector is no longer able to absorb the flow of job seekers. For example, the number of new positions itemized in the state budget for the year 2020-2021 hardly exceeded 21,256 positions across all ministries. Moreover, statistics of employment in the public service reveal the unequal access to those jobs between male and female citizens. Thus, the rate of feminization of the public service is 39.8%, according to Amina Lotfi member of the Democratic Association of Women of Morocco (ADFM). This figure hides other even more pronounced discriminations, such as that of the glass ceiling, so that in 2016, women represented only 22% of the total decision-making positions in the public service. Another consequence of the unequal access to the job market is that the significant drop in job creation in the public sector has a bigger impact on female graduates who find themselves particularly vulnerable to unemployment, (Haut-Commissariat Au Plan (HCP), 2013).

Statistics on the evolution of the labor market in Morocco reveal not only an alarming disparity between women and men in terms of access to employment, but also a very worrying decline in the employment of women in general. Indeed, the HCP study shows that the gap in employment rates between men and women is 49.5 points, respectively 71% and 21.5%, while the activity rate is even lower, barely reaching 18.6% compared to 65.5% for men (HCP, 2017). This took place despite the positive changes in favor of women in family law reform, and the 2011 constitution. Inequalities and symbolic institutional violence against women continue to take a multitude of appalling forms, defining the challenges women continue to face in Morocco today (Boutkhil, 2017). In addition, informal activity alone monopolizes the majority of existing jobs (80% of total employment in the country, for comparison, the figures for the informal sector are 67%, in the MENA region, and 86% in sub-Saharan Africa (Media24, 2021).

Therefore, it is clear that the decline in female activity has had a strong impact on the country's overall economy. The loss in growth has been stressed by numerous studies that show that the inclusion of women in the economy is capable of generating a Gross Domestic Product (GDP) increase of 35% (Ostry et al., 2018; Ferrant et al., 2016). And yet, stereotypes are tough and women struggle to find jobs, especially among graduates. The stark reality is that 78.5% of the female population of working age is outside the labor market, and more than six in ten employed women have no diploma (HCP, 2018). In other words, the more educated a woman is, the less likely she is to achieve financial independence.

In the face of such an adversity more and more Moroccan women are creating opportunities for self-employment either by starting or joining cooperatives, or through launching their own businesses. Indeed, 14% of the total cooperatives are exclusively founded and run by women (Azenfar et al., 2019). Although the number may seem low, it constitutes nonetheless a great cultural change as women are claiming management positions within these cooperatives, while in the past, those positions were always given to men because of their ability to strategize, find markets, do the bookkeeping and navigate the bureaucracy of public administration. The shift in women's attitudes within cooperatives shows that the figure of the submissive woman who is unable to challenge the gender and social norms is being challenged, and is being replaced by that of the determined businesswoman ready to defend her interests. Such a dynamic was thoroughly studied by Igamane (2020) who carried a qualitative survey among forty women members of different cooperatives in the country and noted a change in their dynamics, he concluded that market pressure and continued challenges create power conflicts between members of cooperatives resulting in managers tending to legitimize their empowerment within the structure and to serve their self-interest rather than the collective interest.

Social entrepreneurship/cooperative programs were very popular in the first decade of this century as the country launched a massive program to reduce poverty and social vulnerability. Labelled "The National Human Development Initiative" (INDH), the program was launched in 2005 with the objective of improving economic and social conditions of the poor. Multiple studies have praised the advantages of cooperatives as a lever for development, even in periods of economic recession as has been demonstrated by scholars (Bastida et al., 2020). The aforementioned study shows that this economic model (cooperatives) has experienced a significant increase after the 2008 crisis, and that it enabled a transformation of women's economic activity in Spain; "an increasing number of women are engaging in cooperatives, to the extent that the percentage of women in the workforce of these organizations surpasses by far that of women in the workforce as a whole" (Bastida 2020). This was corroborated by other scholars who also stressed the transformative power of social entrepreneurship enabling marginalized women to regain self-esteem empowering them economically, socially and domestically (Datta et al., 2012). However other studies go in an opposite direction highlighting the obstacles the cooperative and social entrepreneurship business model create for women in terms of equality in managerial matters. These studies have pointed out how structural and organizational issues such as the unequal distribution of tasks and the rate of personal investment in the service of the group, lead to unilateralism in decision-making and promotion of self-interest (Igamane, 2020, Guerin, 2011).

From the year 1990, and in order to get the country's economy out of its depression, Morocco shifted from state-run to market economy through joining the World Trade Organization (WTO) and the signing of free trade agreements with several countries (Binkkour, 2012). The state also encouraged business creation and self-employment to reduce the unemployment curve by setting up more than a dozen support programs for young entrepreneurs. Programs such as *Idmaj, Taeheel, Mouqawalati, Taatir, Moubadara, Istihaab, Tahfiz, Mouwakaba* and *Ilayki*, the latter being specifically aimed at women. Launched in 2013. More than half of entrepreneurs used it out of necessity and not out of choice (52.9% for men and 59.67% for women) Yet the labor market has remained non-inclusive, weakly evolving, and highly informal. (HCP & World Bank, 2017)

The periodic reports of the Global Entrepreneurship Monitor (GEM) show that although the culture of entrepreneurship is still slow to develop, it is progressing as indicated by the figures of the index of entrepreneurial activity going from 4.4% in 2015, to 5.6 in 2016, and 8.8 in 2017 (El Ouazzani, 2017.) However, several blocking factors persist, in particular the absence of an entrepreneurial culture, the weight of socio-cultural norms especially among women (Shinnar & al., 2018;

Benazzi et al., 2016; De Vita et al., 2014), and the lack of a spirit of innovation. Indeed, the motivation for most of those who embark on entrepreneurship remains the desire to create one's own job as an alternative to unemployment. It is therefore an entrepreneurship of necessity (Icart et al., 2013) and not an "entrepreneurial project" which is based on the broad philosophy of the concept: innovation and creativity. This trend is strongly observed among the unemployed for more than 12 months. (Laghzaoui et al., 2020; World Bank, 2005; OECD, 2004).

Thus, the number of women project leaders remains very low compared to that of men, as barely 0.8% of working women are entrepreneurs and 16.1% work as freelancers (CESE, 2014). Also, hardly 12% of businesses in the country are owned by women (HCP, 2012). This low inclusion is observed almost everywhere in the world (World Economic Forum, 2010). Multiple studies have looked at how gender intervenes in the context of entrepreneurship. Like all other spheres, the world of entrepreneurship is strongly marked by the patriarchal culture that prevails in the economic world. Thus, only a gender analysis of the contours of this eco-system is able to enlighten us on the causes of the gender gap in entrepreneurial activity. (Icart et al., 2013).

These differences are due to a multitude of factors, on the one hand the weight of culture which associates the image of the entrepreneur with the usual masculine personality traits (Gupta et al., 2009) such as competitiveness (Bridger et al., 1996; Kay, 2006) boldness, firmness and risk taking (Gupta et al., 2009). On the other hand, the context of the institutional anchoring of entrepreneurial behavior, which influences the nature, development and extent of entrepreneurship (Welter, 2011), as well as the patriarchal culture which confines women to the domestic sphere and to their "biological destiny". Indeed, the socialization of girls does not encourage risk-taking, self-confidence, or even autonomy, which are the pillars of the entrepreneurial spirit (Rachdi, 2006).

THE MOTIVATIONS BEHIND THE ENTREPRENEURIAL PROJECT

Like the profile of the entrepreneur, the motivations for embarking on a project with all the financial, social and sometimes even personal risks that this entails have been the subject of several studies (Goussaid et al., 2020; Laghzaoui et al., 2020; Dawson et al., 2012; Carsrud et al., 2009; Buttner et al., 1997). The motivation for the majority of women entrepreneurs varies between the desire to create their own project and to take advantage of what this offers in terms of flexibility and independence (Hart et al., 2003).

Two major theories seem to dominate the debate in this area of research, the "drive theory" (Carsrud et al., 2009) which assumes that some people are driven by an internal need, for example the desire to achieve a goal such as social success, or autonomy. This "drive" is capable of making them forget the difficulties and the stress that result from such an adventure. On the other hand, the "incentive theory" suggests that the entrepreneur is driven by a positive sense of action in the form of external rewards such as the freedom to manage his/her time, or prestige that come with success (Fayolle et al., 2014).

In their analysis of the entrepreneurial motivation of women, Patil and Deshpande (2019) note that there are positive and other negative factors that drive the decision to embark on an entrepreneurial project, among these attraction/positive factors is the "Pull factor" representing a person's passion, independence, availability of capital and self-growth. On the other hand, the "push factors" vary from economic necessity, difficult conditions of previous work, to job loss. While the motivation may be similar for male and female entrepreneurs, satisfaction, on the other hand, seems to follow a typical pattern for women.

Indeed, satisfaction for women entrepreneurs according to the study by Robichaud, Cachon & Haq, (2010) is not only linked to profit, but primarily and, respectively to the reputation of honesty, good customers service, rigorous work, friendliness, and charisma. Thus, success is not only linked to return on investment, but to a broad spectrum of criteria (Dej, 2010) which translate the need to flourish, assert and free oneself.

THE IMPACT OF THE STEREOTYPE ON WOMEN ENTREPRENEURS

As mentioned above, women entrepreneurs suffer from the weight of the patriarchal culture that pervades society. The will to be an entrepreneur is strongly impacted by the socio-cultural environment. In Morocco, tradition has maintained the debate on women's rights between two polarities: those of tradition and modernity; on the one hand the traditionalists justify the assumed superiority of men over women as being inscribed in the sacred texts, while the modernists reject such an assertion and plead for the full citizenship of women. (Boutkhil, 2016). It is true that the latter enjoy free access to public space, and the freedom to conduct business as guaranteed by the society's legal texts. However, their real inclusion in the economic fabric comes up against a cultural resistance strongly marked by the perception of the social roles pre-defined for women. The socialization of women is in fact governed in a hierarchical manner wherein women do not question the social order, but submit to it while seeking to find a balance between their own professional inclination and the needs of their families. (Bourquia, 2015) This pattern is confirmed by the study of the High Commission for Planning on the "Time Budget" (HCP, 2014) which underlines that the active, employed urban woman is not exempt from household and domestic activities. She is responsible for it at a rate of 97.5% against 98.9% for housewives whose main occupation remains household chores.

The unequal division of domestic labor leaves little time for women to undertake anything, or even to consider taking up decision-making positions. The career of the woman counts for little within the family, only that of the husband counts. In a social pattern so fixed on social roles, it is difficult to prepare women for entrepreneurship, which requires self-confidence, time dedication and risk taking. This, indeed, emerges in the interviews the author conducted with women entrepreneurs, who all complain about these personal obstacles that are difficult to overcome.

The first fear for any entrepreneur is the fear of failure, given the stakes of investment. Many studies seek to understand the sometimes-crippling relationship between fear of failure and entrepreneurship (Cacciotti et al., 2015; Cacciotti et al., 2016), some of which look at the possibility of the double effect of fear, of on the one hand, it influences the decisions and sometimes even on the ambition of the entrepreneur, and on the other hand, fear can have the opposite effect, it can act as a catalyst for growth. (Mitchell et al., 2011).

Women tend to doubt themselves more to the point of causing their own failure. This is the result of stereotyping, i.e. confining women to a limited set of pre-defined roles and character traits that may limit their performance. In this perspective, research on gender and academic or professional performance informs us about how stereotyping impacts its target group, in this case women in the business world. The fear of confirming all the negative stereotypes about them in terms of project creation and the ability to manage it, and make it profitable can create an additional stressful situation that disarms them in the face of obstacles and makes them unable to muster their resources for better performance. The threat of stereotyping in the business world has been the subject of several studies. Steel & al. for example, conclude that often the target of the stereotype disengages as a psychological defense mechanism to guard against evaluations and allows negatively stereotyped group members to avoid the possibility of confirming the stereotype (Steele et al., 2002).

It is obvious that such reactions end up demotivating the object of the stereotype. An environment riddled with negative stereotypes affects the ambitions of members of the target group. For example, exposure to television commercials depicting women in traditional roles influences the aspirations of study participants who only project themselves into the roles of perfect housewives (Geis et al., 1984). These same findings were confirmed by Davies, Spencer and Steele (2005) who observed that workingwomen exposed to gender stereotypical television commercials were less likely to choose a leadership role in their careers. The same stereotypical pattern of self-limitation is reproduced among women in the world of entrepreneurship which remains very weakly inclusive for women. (Gupta et al., 2008). In Morocco, as elsewhere, the different stereotypes about women influence the entrepreneurial intentions of the younger generations and can help explain the lack of confidence women have in their ability to start a business. (Asli et al., 2018).

Whether starting new businesses or running existing businesses, the aspirations and intentions of women are lower than those of their male counterparts, in part because of the threat of stereotyping.

In short, the multiple studies on the threat of the stereotype show us to what extent the stereotype has an impact on the entrepreneurial project. Women internalize their weaknesses and find themselves unable to overcome the image that society sends back to them.

WINNING THE LEGITIMACY CHALLENGE

What is legitimacy in the world of entrepreneurship? Do we really need it? Asking this kind of question proves that women are not within the legitimacy of the ecosystem. A healthy and inclusive entrepreneurial ecosystem requires four essential conditions: density, concerning the number and proportion of individuals engaged in entrepreneurship; fluidity, that of the population and of the labor market; connectivity, in particular the possibility of networking; and the diversity of opportunities (Bell-Masterson et al., 2015). From the outset, we can see that all four areas pose a problem for female entrepreneurship, which is relatively young, less established and weakly connected.

Legitimacy, as Suchman (1995) defines it, is "a generalized perception or assumption that the actions of an entity are desirable, proper and appropriate to the socially constructed system of norms, beliefs and definitions". Thus, it is assumed that there is a legitimate center around which women entrepreneurs revolve in search of legitimacy. In reality, there is more than one center, since women entrepreneurs must maintain their social legitimacy within the family (Eagly et al., 2000) while the legitimacy of the entrepreneur is achieved through networking with professional contacts. (De Clercq et al., 2009). The battle for legitimacy is cultural, since the peer network is built within a hierarchical social system in most cultures. (Mcadam et al., 2019) Thus, legitimacy is built in the temporality of the struggle to exist, wherein women entrepreneurs face various trials and build the capital of insertion in the circle of pairs.

Legitimacy is also linked to the cultural perception of the entrepreneur, which is challenged by newcomers to the field. In most cultures, the sector is entirely defined by values related to masculinity, courage, daring, steadfastness. It is therefore difficult for women to position themselves vis-à-vis peers, clients, families, financial institutions and others. Winning the legitimacy challenge is built over time, but once this step is taken, the project will have a good chance of survival.

PROFILES OF WOMEN ENTREPRENEURS

Several studies have looked at the profile of women entrepreneurs in order to understand what differentiates women from men in the field. In most of these studies, women entrepreneurs generally take longer to realize their projects, unlike men who quickly embark on "the adventure". "For men, getting their act together comes naturally. The women, for their part, think a lot and give their project a long time to mature. They want to make sure they're ready. "(Cisneros et al., 2020) Even well-trained women hesitate and calculate the risks while men" generally more impulsive and more pragmatic, go directly to a potential investor in order to launch their business project."

Regarding the age of female entrepreneurs, studies show that in general they are younger than their male counterparts, with an age between 30 and 59 years old (Channaje, 2021); (Benazzi et al., 2016); (Rachdi, 2016); (Ekpe, 2011); (Carrington, 2006) (Hisrich et al., 1999). This tendency is explained by the recourse to self-employment, especially of graduates (Kozubíková et al., 2016) who decide to go on their own after a period of unemployment or following frustration with working conditions at their place of employment. The education level of women entrepreneurs is generally higher than that of men, (Ahmadove et al., 2021). In Morocco, according to a study by the Association des Femmes Chefs d'Entreprises du Maroc (AFEM), two thirds of Moroccan women entrepreneurs have a university education. This trend is universal since 72% of women entrepreneurs in France have a Bac + 5 level, doctorate and MBA (Gousaid, 2020). Likewise, the family situation seems similar for most women entrepreneurs since 71% of them are married, the majority (77%) have young children. More than half of the companies are concentrated in the Casablanca Rabat axis (75%). Another characteristic of the female enterprise in Morocco is that it is overwhelmingly small in size, and very rarely employs more than a dozen mostly female employees; 41% of employees in female-run businesses are women (Sellam, 2019).

OBSTACLES TO FEMALE ENTREPRENEURSHIP

Any entrepreneurial project encounters obstacles at one time or another, but these difficulties are accentuated when it comes to women entrepreneurs, due to social patterns, which consider that entrepreneurship is a matter of men (Brush et al., 2009). Moreover, the name itself of "female entrepreneurship" or "female entrepreneur" carries a social and cultural burden for the subject who is not in her natural habitat, since except in comparison, the term male entrepreneurship is hardly ever used. The entrepreneur is universally assumed to mean "man," while the woman is assumed to the one who tries to intrude in His world and to clear a small path for herself. Several studies refute such assumptions and affirm indeed that the female entrepreneurship has always existed, but that it has been invisible in research as well as in the media (Ahl, 2006; Baker et al., 1997).

This socio-cultural red tape very quickly becomes a difficult obstacle for women to overcome since statistics show that female entrepreneurship constitutes only 10% of all entrepreneurs in Morocco (Oumerzoug, 2020). Women entrepreneurs are largely either discouraged from embarking on projects, or prefer to work in the informal sector, which penalizes them in terms of access to finance and condemns them to invisibility, lack of recognition and limits even the size of their business.

Indeed, access to funds remains a major obstacle for women entrepreneurs, (Laghzaoui et al., 2020); (Elotmani, 2020), thus, most of the women interviewed in the current study affirm that the launch of their projects was done with loans obtained from members of their families. Recourse to the family is often the first choice for women entrepreneurs (Logan, 2014) who do not wish to commit to a bank loan since this requires the presentation of guarantees, and entails fixed monthly payments and penalties in the event of late payment, whereas family loans, however small, are much more flexible. It is important to stress here that a good number of women entrepreneurs make the choice to never contract a loan from a bank because their approach differs entirely from the "normalized" approach of the entrepreneurial project which starts small and grows bigger. On the contrary, many women entrepreneurs are satisfied with their businesses remaining "small" and easier to manage.

Another major difficulty for women entrepreneurs is the recognition and viability of their businesses. As a general rule, it is assumed that family responsibilities, lack of experience and network as well as lack of funding will discourage women from entrepreneurship. Such assumptions influence the relationships institutions, clients and peers have with businesses started by women.

THE ORIENTAL REGION

Located in the northeast of the country, the Oriental region covers an area of 82,820 km^2, or 11.6% of the national territory, bordered by the Mediterranean coast to the north, Algeria to the east and the regions of Tangier-Tetouan-Al Hoceima and Fez-Meknes to the west.

The region counts 2.3 million inhabitants as per the General Population Census of 2014, representing 6.8% of the national population of which 50% are women and 44.6% of the whole population is under 25. The region contributes 6.5% of the national GDP, but has a fairly high unemployment rate of around 20.7% compared to the national average, which is 11.9%, in addition to a high migration rate as 30% of Moroccans abroad are from the Oriental region. The labor force participation rate for women is barely 15% compared to 75% for men. This glaring disparity is a sign of the economic fragility of women, as they cannot find work even when they are well trained and qualified. Nationally, the unemployment rate for women tends to increase with the level of education: where 3.1% of women without a degree are unemployed; those with a primary/secondary level represent 23.6%, whereas those with a higher education qualification are 28.5% of the unemployed (Manry, 2019). This is due to several factors including the mismatch between training and the needs of the labor market; the persistence of habits and customs that do not so much value female professional activity, but rather the security of marriage and children, in addition to the general national and international economy which fail to create sufficient employment opportunities to meet the expectations of job seekers.

Like all border regions, the economy of the East was cross border trade-oriented, so that for many decades there was little investment in industry and services. Since the border was closed, investments, especially by Moroccans living abroad, have turned to real estate, which is considered a safe bet, thus creating a surplus of investment and inflation in the area. All of this has contributed to the further weakening of the region's economy, which is still struggling to recover from the economic transition, and to create jobs.

Socio-culturally, the region is relatively conservative with variations from north to south. Women enjoy the rights guaranteed by the constitution, but the weight of culture remains very strong exerting pressure on them as evidenced by the unemployment rate of women of working age (26.6% against the national average of 14, 7%) (HCP, 2018). This high rate is largely explained by the unrecognized discrimination against women in employment. Socially and culturally, girls are encouraged to find employment with the state that not only provides guaranteed wages, but also fairly flexible working conditions and less risk of harassment. Also, women are conditioned to accept unemployment more easily than men because of the social division of labor. Indeed, an unemployed woman is always occupied with household chores and therefore tends to more or less accept the situation. (Shamir, 1986)

THE EXPERIENCES OF WOMEN ENTREPRENEURS

As mentioned above, the author decided to look at the experiences of women entrepreneurs from one of the most conservative regions of Morocco, it is a relevant choice since the success of these women in this type of context is a real feat, because it would mean succeeding in overcoming personal, institutional and cultural obstacles as can be seen below.

The author opted for semi-structured interviews and proceeded to the choice of respondents from three different avenues with the objective of widening the sampling as much as possible: The Regional Investment Center, entrepreneurship associations and finally personal contacts. The interviews took place between May 15 and May 30, 2021 using the same questions designed beforehand. The thirteen questions constituting the questionnaire aimed to inform about the motivations behind launching an entrepreneurial project, the sources of funding, the network on which they relied and the obstacles they faced.

The author made the choice not to include a question on the marital status because of the cultural charge of the married/unmarried status which would risk creating unnecessary blockages. While this variable could have given us more to analyze, it, however, runs the risk of raising resistance and even rejection for reasons of privacy. As Morse and Richards (2007) assert, qualitative research must be flexible and it is never certain of how many questions to ask, nor of the number of samples, as this becomes clearer over the course of the interview. The researcher must therefore be flexible to make it easier to decide even during the interview what to add or delete for good data collection. So, the author still kept thirteen variables and was quite flexible when discussing with the informants.

As can be seen in the table above, the entrepreneurs the author interviewed have diverse levels of study, from middle school certificate to college degrees (Bachelor, Master, and the Doctorate). These varied profiles have enabled her to understand that in most cases, except for the business consulting firm, entrepreneurship has emerged as the only alternative after a long or short period of unemployment, which vindicates the assertion above that unemployment in the region is quite high compared to the national average and that of women is even higher.

"I aimed for a position in higher education, after my studies in France, I was far from imagining that after such a long and hard journey, a focused research and an experience in higher education in France I did not expect that I wouldn't not find a place at the university in Morocco, especially since there is a terrible shortage of private law professors. But it seems that the scientific record is not the only criterion to get a job, you have to have the support of a strong network. » (Informant 1)

Informant 2 who obtained a master's degree in France advances the same reasons. "I decided to start my business because I did not find a job in my field of study. "

Table 1. Sampling description

Informants	Age	Level of study	Source of funding	Age of the business	Sector of activity	urban	rural	# of hours/ week
Inf. 1	35-45	Doctorate (International)	Personal savings	1-5 years	Legal Consulting	X		44-48h/s
Inf. 2	35-45	Master (International)	Family member	6 -10 years	Copy shop /bookstore	X		30-35h
Inf. 3	55-65	Master (International)	Corporate assistance	11-15 years	Counseling /business training	X		40h
Inf. 4	25-35	Bachelor	Parents (support)	1-5 years	Farming Cooperative		X	45h
Inf. 5	25-35	Bachelor	Small bank loan +family savings	1-5	Physical therapy	X		45h+
Inf. 6	35-45	2 year-college degree	Spouse (support)	6-10 years	Sewing & embroidery	X		45h
Inf. 7	35-45	Baccalaureate (high school degree)	Father (support)	6-10 years	Farming Cooperative (bee-keeping)		X	50h
Inf. 8	35-45	Baccalaureate	Family (loan from brother)	6-10 years	Beauty parlor	X		45-55h
Inf. 9	25-35	Baccalaureate	Micro-credit	1-5 years	Couture	X		30h
Inf. 10	35-45	Brevet	Family (support)	6-10 years	Farming Cooperative		X	35h
Inf. 11	25-35	Brevet	Personal savings	1-5 years	Farming Cooperative		X	20 -30h
Inf. 12	35-45	Brevet	Personal savings	6-10 years	Ready-made clothing (e-commerce)	X		30h
Inf. 13	35-45	Brevet	Family (support)	6-10 years	Handicraft Cooperative	X		40h +
Inf. 14	35-45	Brevet	Personal savings	1-5 years	Farming Cooperative		X	30h

As these two cases attest, unemployment of female graduates is on the rise, and in cities it is almost double that of men with 23.3% and 13.2% respectively. In fact, according to HCP statistics of 2020, more than 8 out of 10 unemployed women (82.6%) are university graduates. For more than 70% of the interviewed it is a question of push factor where entrepreneurship was not a career project but rather the solution to a more or less long unemployment, or to the difficulty of coming to an agreement with an employer who violates the rights of employees. "I decided to quit my job with an accountant who refused to declare me to the National Fund for Social Security, so I created my sales shop online... I didn't want to struggle anymore, or to be someone's employee. I wanted to be my own boss, to manage my time freely."

On the other hand, the pull factor accounts for less than a third of respondents' motivation to start a business; the vast majority of them are urban and their sector of activity is strongly favorable to entrepreneurship: (Physiotherapy, consulting firm, sewing and embroidery.)

When it comes to sources of funding, the vast majority of those interviewed raised personal funds (savings) or had recourse to help from a family member (father, sister) or an interest-free loan from a relative. Only two informants took a loan, one from a micro-credit organization and the other from a banking institution. The low recourse to credit for women entrepreneurs has many reasons, on the one hand, having no collateral to offer, women very rarely think that banks would grant them financing, on the other hand women entrepreneurs are generally not very well informed and nourish an exaggerated mistrust of financial institutions: "credits are conditional upon guarantees, I did not want to embark on this path, not having the certainty of being able to repay on time, that is why I started small."

Almost the majority of the informants did not learn enough about the government credit formulas and programs intended to promote female entrepreneurship. They spoke of guarantees as an obstacle to launching a project, while the CCG (Central Guarantee Fund) in such cases acts as guarantor to support women entrepreneurs through the *Ilayki* program launched in 2017 as well as through the *Intilaka* fund in 2020 which by the way does not require any guarantees. These two programs offer many advantages: a preferential rate of 2% over a period of seven years, the possibility of deferring reimbursements, personalized support and a short training module for capacity building by the public institutions such as the Office for Vocational Training and Work Promotion (OFPPT).

The interviewed entrepreneurs also complain about the difficulty of creating and/or belonging to a network capable of increasing the mutual performance of their companies. Most interviewees say they are trying to expand their network, but it is still fragile. Small businesses that suffer from competition are struggling to find a place:

" 'your brother in the business is your enemy' my mother always tells me, it is difficult to find a place when we have eyes fixed on us." (Informant 8).

While the network constitutes an intangible capital capable of ensuring the sustainability and survival of the business, it seems difficult to achieve, especially when the business is starting up or when there is a lot of competition. "Our work is quite distinct, we offer legal consulting, we do not infringe on the work of lawyers, notaries, or chartered accountants, but we work in parallel with them… and yet there was great mistrust towards us at the beginning, everyone watched us from afar ... but today, we manage to work together, they understood that we can be of use to them and it even happens that they ask us to outsource certain files for them » (Informant 1). The network is doubly more difficult to integrate when the female enterprise constitutes a competitor or an "invader" of a sector considered to be legitimately male (beekeeping cooperative, law or business consulting firm) but when it comes to the sector of activity deemed legitimately female, entrepreneurs usually get help from peers.

"The first obstacle I encountered was first of all my total ignorance of the sector in which I had started, I did not know who to ask for help or whom to go to. I had gone to see someone who had a bookstore and who gave me good advice. Then I did an internship for a few days in another bookstore and saw the services that can be offered to customers. » (Informant 2)

The importance of the network for the entrepreneur is no longer to be demonstrated, some interviewees invest in the communication and continuous networking of their company, while others are wary of contact with male partners. They apprehend situations of harassment and exert self-censorship in relations with partners:

"Being a woman is penalizing because the suppliers you talk to are almost always men, and so sometimes there is a certain behavior (harassment) that you have to turn a deaf ear to. But being a woman helps us in the sense that I think we are more patient and more courageous than men." (Informant 2)

Harassment in public places is very common even though Law 103-13 prescribes sanctions against perpetrators, but it is difficult to prove aggression.

The strong presence in the entrepreneurship ecosystem requires a strong communication strategy on the part of the entrepreneur to build strong relationships with the whole system around the company. However, in the absence of training, very few female entrepreneurs engage in this process and find themselves unable to break the domination of male culture in the business sphere. "A lot of business is done and decisions are made outside of official circuits/meetings, between decision-makers/influencers, in informal meetings in the evening. Since they are men, for socio-cultural considerations, no woman is invited, beyond the question of male/female, in these very closed circles all kinds of activities, (business, politics, lobbying) take place, and only "friends" are admitted " (Informant 3). Indeed, The Association of Female Entrepreneurs of Morocco (AFEM) has repeatedly denounced the exclusion of women entrepreneurs from public bids. The association advocates for the establishment of a quota for female enterprises when it comes to state tenders in order to guarantee equal access to women entrepreneurs.

Another factor of exclusion is the control the family exerts on the entrepreneurs, which does not allow them to evolve freely in the field: "Being a woman penalizes us, we cannot travel like men, attend meetings, trainings, participate in trade fairs because we are women" (Informant 11). These restrictions affect the development of the business and can sometimes lead to project failure. Upon returning to the family home, the entrepreneur is first a woman on whom the responsibilities of caring for the family rest, whether she is married or not. The interviews thus revealed that the unequal distribution of household chores weighs on the daily lives of women entrepreneurs.

"I spend the whole day with patients, but in the evening when I come home, I have to take care of the house, cook food, do the laundry, because I cannot afford a cleaning lady" (Informant 5).

CONCLUSION

This study allowed us to realize some positive points concerning female entrepreneurship in Morocco. What comes out of it is that the State has done a lot to promote entrepreneurship, that the economic environment is still favorable. The recommendation of all those interviewed to future young women entrepreneurs is to get started without further delay, as the entrepreneurial adventure allows them to gain self-esteem and nurture their leadership skills to confront society. Another positive point emerging from this study is the importance of family support for the start-up and survival of a project. Indeed, the constancy of family capital even with modest means allows the creation, monitoring and maintenance of the activity, and the project is no longer carried by one person, but by the whole family.

Morocco is part of the transnational tendency that aims to encourage female entrepreneurship. However, it would appear that the measures undertaken have failed to achieve the expected objectives. Female entrepreneurship remains largely a necessity, not an opportunity, which influences the opportunities, growth and even the survival of the business (Giacomin et al., 2016). This type of entrepreneurship generates very little growth and does not allow the desired economic trickle down one would expect, especially in countries with emerging economies. Also, the present study allowed the author to conclude that there are very strong geographical disparities when it comes to the locality of the entrepreneurial project, more than half of the companies are concentrated in the Casablanca-Rabat axis, which indicates that the State needs to come up with a strategy that covers the whole country, and more advantageous measures in the regions to allow more projects to take off.

In addition, pragmatic teaching curricula must be developed and integrated into all educational cycles in order to demystify, inform and encourage young people to undertake entrepreneurial projects. The study shows us also that even the most educated were unaware of important programs, especially those directed towards encouraging small business creation, as well as funding channels, market opportunities, networking and soft skills. The interviewees all learned for themselves, at different stages of their project, how to fill these gaps, which constitutes a colossal waste in terms of time and investment on their part. The study has also found that the biggest obstacle to female entrepreneurship is the socio-cultural factor. Girls' unemployment is socially more accepted than that of boys, the destiny of women is unfortunately still the domestic sphere, which constitutes a significant waste in terms of time, as the project is often initiated after a more or less long period of inactivity and isolation, especially in rural areas.

Finally, a transversal module of course on gender studies should be designed and implemented in colleges to demystify the foundations of male domination in the field of entrepreneurship, encourage young girls to seek opportunities other than in cooperatives, services and crafts, but invest in sectors dominated by men, in particular IT, industry, construction and logistics.

If the research paints a rather gloomy and bleak picture of the job marked for women in the Eastern Region of Morocco, it nevertheless reassures on the opportunities of success of the entrepreneurial project. It is certain that in terms of innovation, competitiveness, markets, size, profit and sector of activity women's businesses remain very modest. Yet, they constitute a source of economic empowerment far from the entrepreneurial logic defined by men where turnover remains the only indicator of success. Just as numerous studies have shown, non-economic outcomes such as self- esteem, empowerment, flexibility, networking, freedom, and work-life balance are far more important to women entrepreneurs than the economic ones (Carranza et al., 2018; Anna et al., 2000). Therefore, women entrepreneurs design business models where their own well-being and that of their families and community are the only indicators of success. They may be small scale enterprises, but they offer security, stability and retain the entrepreneurs in their social ecosystems where life most matters.

REFERENCES

Ahl, H. (2006). Why research on women entrepreneurs needs new directions. *Entrepreneurship Theory and Practice*, *30*(5), 595–621. doi:10.1111/j.1540-6520.2006.00138.x

Ahmadov, F., Zeynalova, U., Bayramova, U., & Mammadov, I. (2021). Analysis of Educational Impact on Women Entrepreneurs in Sustainable Social Business: The Case of Azerbaijan. *Turkish Journal of Computer and Mathematics Education*, *12*(6), 1847–1856.

Anna, A. L., Chandler, G. N., Jansen, E., & Mero, N. P. (2000). Women Business Owners in Traditional and Non-traditional Industries. *Journal of Business Venturing*, *15*(3), 279–303. doi:10.1016/S0883-9026(98)00012-3

Asli, A., & Bensassi, N. H. (2018). Female Entrepreneurship in Morocco, Obstacles and Ways to Overcome Them. In *6th International OFEL Conference on Governance, Management and Entrepreneurship. New Business Models and Institutional Entrepreneurs: Leading Disruptive Change.* Dubrovnik, Croatia: Governance Research and Development Centre (CIRU).

Azenfar, A., Elghiat, R., & Debbah, A. (2019). *Coopératives féminines au Maroc réalisations et ambitions.* http://www.socioeco.org/bdf_fiche-document-6602_en.html

Auger, C. (2020). *Dossier Femmes D'idées - Qui est la Femme Entrepreneure?* Gestion HEC Montréal. https://www.revuegestion.ca/dossier-femmes-didees-qui-est-la-femme-entrepreneure

Baker, T., Aldrich, H. E., & Liou, N. (1997). Invisible entrepreneurs: The neglect of women business owners by mass media and scholarly journals in the USA. *Entrepreneurship and Regional Development*, *9*(3), 221–238. doi:10.1080/08985629700000013

Banque mondiale. (2005). *Doing Business: Creating Jobs*. World Bank Publications.

Bastida, M., Pinto, L. H., Blanco, A. O., & Cancelo, M. (2020). Female Entrepreneurship: Can Cooperatives Contribute to Overcoming the Gender Gap? A Spanish First Step to Equality. *Sustainability*, *12*(6), 1–17. doi:10.3390u12062478

Bell-Masterson, J., & Stangler, D. (2015). *Measuring an Entrepreneurial Ecosystem*. Ewing Marion Kauffman Foundation. doi:10.2139srn.2580336

Benazzi, k., & Benazzi, L. (2017). L'entrepreneuriat féminin au Maroc: Réalité, freins et perspéctives de réussite. *Revue Marocaine de Gestion et d'Economie, 3*(7). https://revues.imist.ma/index.php/RMGE/article/view/7535

Berger, R., Benarousse, L., & El Kardi, R. (2020). *Accélérer la dynamique entrepreneuriale des femmes en Afrique*. Roland Berger gmbh.

Binkkour, M. (2012). *La promotion de l'entrepreneuriat au Maroc: Rôle de l'Etat et Perception des Entrepreneurs*. Conference: Business and Entrepreneurship in Africa Quebec – Canada.

Bourquia, R. (2015). Genre et reconfiguration de la société marocaine. In Le Maroc au Présent: D'une Epoque à l'Autre, une Société en Mutation. Centre Jacques-Berque. doi:10.4000/books.cjb.1041

Boutkhil, S. (2008). Moroccan Public Space: A Male Dominated Arena. In L. Touaf & S. Boutkhil (Eds.), *The World as A Global Agora: Critical Perspectives on Public Space*. Cambridge University Press.

Boutkhil, S. (2016). *The construction of the "other" Muslim February. Unpublished article read Guest speaker at the conference on The Culture of Islam and the question of gender. Organized by Laboratoire Langage et Société and the UNESCO Chair on Women and their rights*. Université Ibn Tofail Kénitra.

Boutkhil, S. (2017). Who's Under the Robe? On Women in the Judicial System in Morocco. In L. Touaf, S. Boutkhil, & C. Nasri (Eds.), *North African Women after the Arab Spring* (pp. 135–147). Palgrave Macmillan. doi:10.1007/978-3-319-49926-0_7

Bouzekraoui, H., & Ferhane, D. (2017). An Exploratory Study of Women's Entrepreneurship in Morocco. IBIMA Publishing. *Journal of Entrepreneurship: Research & Practice*.

Brush, C. G., De Bruin, A., & Welter, F. (2009). A Gender-aware Framework for Women's Entrepreneurship. *International Journal of Gender and Entrepreneurship, 1*(1), 8–24. doi:10.1108/17566260910942318

Cacciotti, G., & Hayton, J. C. (2015). Fear and Entrepreneurship: A Review and Research Agenda. *International Journal of Management Reviews, 17*(2), 165–190. doi:10.1111/ijmr.12052

Cacciotti, G., Hayton, J. C., Mitchell, J. R., & Giazitzoglu, A. (2016). A Reconceptualization of Fear of Failure in Entrepreneurship. *Journal of Business Venturing, 31*(3), 302–325. doi:10.1016/j.jbusvent.2016.02.002

Carranza, E., Dhakal, C., & Love, I. (2018). *Female Entrepreneurs: How and Why Are They Different?* Jobs Working Paper No. 20. World Bank. https://openknowledge.worldbank.org/handle/10986/31004

Carrington, C. (2006). *Small Business Financing Profiles.* SME Financing Data Initiative.

Carsrud, A. L., & Brännback, M. (2009). *Understanding the Entrepreneurial Mind.* Springer. doi:10.1007/978-1-4419-0443-0

Channaje, A. (2021, March 11). Création d'entreprises: Ces freins qui bloquent encore l'entreprenariat féminin au Maroc. *L'Opinion.* https://www.lopinion.ma/Creation-d-entreprises-Ces-freins-qui-bloquent-encore-l-entreprenariat-feminin-au-Maroc_a12540.html

Cisneros, L., Genin, E., Saba, T., & Gril, E. (2020). L'Escalier de Glace: La Dure Ascension des Femmes. *Gestion, 1*(45), 64–67. doi:10.3917/riges.451.0064

Conseil Economique, Social et Environnemental. (2016). L'auto-entreprise, levier de développement et d'intégration du secteur informel. *Auto – Saisine, 27.*

Conseil Economique, Social et Environnemental. (2014). Promotion de l'égalité entre les femmes et les hommes dans la vie économique, sociale, culturelle et politique Les discriminations à l'égard des femmes dans la vie économique: réalités et recommandations. *Auto-saisine, 18.*

Constantinidis, C., El Abboubi, M., Salman, N., & Cornet, A. (2017). L'Entrepreneuriat Féminin dans une Société en Transitions: Analyse de Trois Profils de Femmes Entrepreneures au Maroc. *Revue internationale P.M. E., 30*(3-4), 37–68. doi:10.7202/1042660ar

Victoria, L., Crittendena, V., Crittendenb, W. F., & Ajjan, H. (2019). Empowering Women Micro-Entrepreneurs in Emerging Economies: The role of Information Communications Technology. *Journal of Business Research, 98*, 191–203. doi:10.1016/j.jbusres.2019.01.045

Davies, P. G., Spencer, S. J., & Steele, C. M. (2005). Clearing the Air: Identity Safety Moderates the Effects of Stereotype Threat on Women's Leadership Aspirations. *Journal of Personality and Social Psychology, 88*(2), 276–287. doi:10.1037/0022-3514.88.2.276 PMID:15841859

Dawson, C., & Henley, A. (2012). "Push" versus "pull" Entrepreneurship: An Ambiguous Distinction? *International Journal of Entrepreneurial Behaviour & Research, 18*(6), 697–719. doi:10.1108/13552551211268139

Dej, D. (2010). Defining and Meausring Entrepreneurial Success. In Entrepreneurship: A Psychological Approach, (pp. 89-102). University of Economics Prague.

De Vita, L., Mari, M., & Poggesi, S. (2014). Women Entrepreneurs in and from Developing Countries: Evidences from the Literature. *European Management Journal, Elsevier, 32*(3), 451–460. doi:10.1016/j.emj.2013.07.009

De Clercq, D., & Voronov, M. (2009). Toward a Practice Perspective of Entrepreneurship: Entrepreneurial Legitimacy as Habitus. *International Small Business Journal, 27*(4), 395–419. doi:10.1177/0266242609334971

Datta, P. B., & Gailey, R. (2012). Empowering Women through Social Entrepreneurship: Case Study of a Women's Cooperative in India. *Entrepreneurship Theory and Practice, 36*(3), 569–587. doi:10.1111/j.1540-6520.2012.00505.x

Eagly, A. H., Wood, W., & Diekman, A. B. (2000). Social Role Theory of Sex Differences and Similarities: A Current Appraisal. In The Developmental Social Psychology of Gender, (pp. 123-174). Erlbaum.

Ekpe, I. (2011). Women Entrepreneurs and Economic Development in Nigeria: Characteristics for Success. *International Journal of Business and Social Science, 2*(1).

Elotmani, S. (2020 March 2-4). Les Déterminants du Succès Entrepreneurial des Femmes: Cas du Sénégal. In *Actes de la deuxième conférence internationale sur la Francophonie Economique L'Entrepreneuriat et L'insertion Professionnelle des Jeunes Et des Femmes en Afrique Francophone*. Université Mohammed V de Rabat.

El Ouazzani, K. (2017). *La Dynamique Entrepreneuriale au Maroc en 2017*. Editions Litograf.

Fayolle, A., Liñán, F., & Moriano, J. A. (2014). Beyond entrepreneurial intentions: Values and motivations in entrepreneurship. *The International Entrepreneurship and Management Journal, 10*(4), 679–689. doi:10.100711365-014-0306-7

Geis, F.L., & Brown, V., & Jennings, J. (1984). TV Commercials as Achievement Scripts for Women. *Sex Roles, 10*, 513–525. doi:10.1007/BF00287260

Giacomin, O., Janssen, F., & Guyot, J. (2016). Entrepreneurs de Nécessité et d'Opportunité: Quels comportements durant la phase de création? *Revue de l'Entrepreneuriat, 15*(3-4), 181–204. doi:10.3917/entre.153.0181

Gousaid, N., & Qanqom, A. (2020). Les Facteurs Expliquant la Motivation de L'entrepreneuriat chez la Femme Marocaine selon le Niveau d'Etudes. *In Actes de la deuxième conférence internationale sur la Francophonie Economique L'Entrepreneuriat et L'insertion Professionnelle des Jeunes Et des Femmes en Afrique Francophone*. Université Mohammed V de Rabat.

Greene, P., Hart, M. M., Gatewood, E., Brush, C., Carter, N., & Stein, G. (2003). Women Entrepreneurs: Moving Front and Center: An Overview of Research and Theory. *Semantic Scholar*. https://www.semanticscholar.org/paper/Women-Entrepreneurs%3A-Moving-Front-and-Center%3A-An-of-Greene-Hart/93f86a7c3bea663e620e07a7e57fed322082904a

Guerin, I., Hersent, M., & Fraisse, L. (2011). *Femmes, Economie et Développement. De la Résistance à la Justice Sociale*. IRD-ERES.

Gupta, V. K., Turban, D. B., & Bhawe, N. M. (2008). The Effect of Gender Stereotype Activation on Entrepreneurial Intentions. *The Journal of Applied Psychology*, *93*(5), 1053–1061. doi:10.1037/0021-9010.93.5.1053 PMID:18808225

Gupta, V. K., Turban, D. B., Wasti, S. A., & Sikdar, A. (2009). The Role of Gender Stereotypes in Perceptions of Entrepreneurs and Intentions to Become an Entrepreneur. *Entrepreneurship Theory and Practice*, *33*(2), 397–417. doi:10.1111/j.1540-6520.2009.00296.x

Haut Commissariat au Plan. (2020). *La Situation du Marché du Travail en 2020*. Publications du HCP.

Haut Commissariat au Plan. (2018). *La Femme Marocaine en Chiffres: Evolution des Caractéristiques Démographiques et Socioprofessionnelles*. Publications du HCP.

Haut Commissariat au Plan & la Banque Mondiale. (2017). *Le marché du travail au Maroc: Défis et opportunités*. Author.

Haut Commissariat au Plan. (2014). *Le Budget-Temps: les Emplois du Temps de la Femme au Maroc*. Publications du HCP.

Haut-Commissariat au Plan. (2013). *La Femme Marocaine en Chiffres: Tendances d'Evolution des Caractéristiques Démographiques et Socioprofessionnelles*. Direction de la statistique.

L'informel au Maroc représente 30% du PIB (Etude BAM). (2021 January 6). *Média 24*. https://www.medias24.com/2021/01/06/linformel-au-maroc-represente-30-du-pib-etude-bam/

Hisrich, R. D., & Öztürk, A. S. (1999). Women Entrepreneurs in a Developing Economy. *Journal of Management Development, 18*(2), 114–125. doi:10.1108/02621719910257639

Icart, I. B., & Pizzi, A. (2013). Effects of the sexual division of labor on self-employment creation in Spain. *Journal of Small Business and Entrepreneurship, 26*(2), 151–167. doi:10.1080/08276331.2013.771857

Igamane, S. (2020). Les inégalités de pouvoir au sein des coopératives de femmes au Maroc. *RECMA: Revue Internationale de l'Economie Sociale, 4*(358), 87–101. doi:10.3917/recma.358.0087

Jouiet, I. (2021). L'entreprenariat coopératif au Maroc: Une locomotive de développement socioéconomique. *Revue Internationale des Sciences de Gestion, 4*(1).

Kolev, A., & Ferrant, G. (2016). *Does gender discrimination in social institutions matter for long-term growth? Cross-country evidence. No 330*. OECD Publishing.

Kozubíková, L., Vojtovič, S., Rahman, A., & Smrčka, L. (2016). The Role of Entrepreneur's Gender, Age and Firm's Age in Autonomy. The Case Study from the Czech Republic. *Economia e Sociologia, 9*(2), 168–182. doi:10.14254/2071-789X.2016/9-2/12

Laghzaoui, S., Haoudi, K., Sliman, M., Decossa, J. J., & EL Otmani, S. (2020). *L'Entrepreneuriat des Jeunes au Maroc: Freins et Motivations.* DROFE no. 6. Observatoire de la Francophonie Economique. Université de Montréal.

Liu, Y., Schøtt, T., & Zhang, C. (2018). Women's Experiences of Legitimacy, Satisfaction and Commitment as Entrepreneurs: Embedded in Gender Hierarchy and Networks in Private and Business Spheres. Entrepreneurship & Regional Development, 31(3-4), 293-307.

Logan, J. (2014). An exploration of the Challenges Facing Women Starting Business at Fifty. *International Journal of Gender and Entrepreneurship, 6*(1), 83–96. doi:10.1108/IJGE-03-2013-0019

Manry, V. (2019). *Femmes et Entrepreneurs, la variable Inconnue*. Economia Research Center.

McAdam, M., Harrison, R. T., & Leitch, C. M. (2018). Stories from the Field: Women's Networking as Gender Capital in Entrepreneurial Ecosystems. *Small Business Economics*. Advance online publication. doi:10.100711187-018-9995-6

Mitchell, J. R., & Shepherd, D. (2011). Afraid of Opportunity: The Effects of Fear of Failure on Entrepreneurial Action. Frontiers of Entrepreneurship Research, 31.

Morse, J. M., & Richards, L. (2007). *Read Me First for A User's Guide to Qualitative Methods*. Sage Publications.

OCDE. (2004). *Entrepreneuriat féminin: questions et actions à mener.* 2e Conférence de l'OCDE des Ministres en charge des PME: promouvoir l'entreprenariat et les PME innovantes dans une économie mondiale, Istanbul, Turkey.

Ostry, J. D., & Lagarde, C. (2018). *Economic Gains from Gender Inclusion: Even Greater than You Thought*. IMFBlog. https://blogs.imf.org/2018/11/28/economic-gains-from-gender-inclusion-even-greater-than-you-thought/

Oumerzoug, S. (2020). *L'entrepreneuriat féminin, une évolution en dents de scie*. MAP Business.

Patil, P., & Deshpande, Y. (2019). Why Women enter into Entrepreneurship? An Exploratory Study. *Journal of Organizational Studies and Innovation*, *6*(2), 30–40.

Rachdi, F. Z. (2016). *L'Entrepreneuriat Feminin au Maroc: Une Approche par le Reseau Personnel* [Unpublished Doctoral Thesis]. Groupe Institut Supérieur de Commerce et D'administration des Entreprises Centre des Etudes Doctorales en Gestion.

Rachdi, F. Z. (2006). L'entrepreneuriat féminin au Maroc: une étude exploratoire. *8ème congrès international francophone en entrepreneuriat et PME.*

Sellam, M. (2019 March 10). L'entrepreneuriat féminin toujours à la traîne. *Le Matin*. https://lematin.ma/journal/2019/lentrepreneuriat-feminin-trai/312043.html

Shamir, B. (1986). Unemployment and Household Division of Labor. *Journal of Marriage and Family*, *48*(1), 195–206. doi:10.2307/352244

Shinnar, R. S., Hsu, D. K., Powell, B. C., & Zhou, H. (2018). Entrepreneurial Intentions and Start-ups: Are Women or Men More Likely to Enact their Intentions? *International Small Business Journal*, *36*(1), 60–80. doi:10.1177/0266242617704277

Suchman, M. C. (1995). Managing legitimacy: Strategies and institutional approaches. *Academy of Management Review*, *20*(3), 571–610. doi:10.2307/258788

Suchman, M. C. (1995). Managing legitimacy: Strategies and institutional approaches. *Academy of Management Review*, *20*(3), 571–610. doi:10.2307/258788

Steele, C. M., Spencer, S. J., & Aronson, J. (2002). Contending with Group Image: The Psychology of Stereotype and Social Identity Threat. *Advances in Experimental Social Psychology, 34*, 379–440. doi:10.1016/S0065-2601(02)80009-0

Suchman, M. (1995). Managing Legitimacy: Strategic and Institutional Approaches. *Academy of Management Review*, *20*(3), 571–610.

Welter, F., & Smallbone, D. (2011). Institutional Perspectives on Entrepreneurial Behavior in Challenging Environments. *Journal of Small Business Management*, *49*(1), 107–125.

World Economic Forum. (2010). *Global Competitiveness Report 2010-2011*. Author.

Chapter 7
Eastern Women's Entrepreneurship:
Liberating the Enslaved Mind Beyond the Patriarchal Gaze

Jannatul Akmam
Jamia Ahmadia Sunnia Mohila Fazil Madrasah, Bangladesh

ABSTRACT

The woman who fought for the liberation of women in the Indian subcontinent from the state of "other" is Rokeya Sakhawat Hossein (1880 – 1932). Another lady icon can be named in this occasion, Fatima al-Fihri, who, in the Moroccan city of Fez, founded a mosque that developed into the famous al-Qarawiyyin University, which has come to be recognized as the oldest existing university in the world. Many inspiring stories come along such as the one like Haya Faisal's from Pakistan who became a female cab driver for the sake of supporting her family. The issue of subversion or reversal of gaze is addressed by throwing light on Simone de Beauvoir's "Myth and Reality" and Michel Foucault's "Concept of Power" in The History of Sexuality. The chapter finally considers different endeavors of different Eastern women like Rokeya, Fatima, Haya, and the like to show women's participation or treatment of gender roles in organizational behavior, strategic management, and entrepreneurship.

DOI: 10.4018/978-1-7998-8742-3.ch007

INTRODUCTION

Our society undergoes a range of myths regarding gender roles and women are subjected to the mythical representation and its effect to a great extent. Women need to strive for establishing their rightful position in whatever endeavor they take. Likewise, entrepreneurial roles women play bring about many challenges faced by them along the way. From a distinctive literary perspective, the life and works (social and educational activism and the literature she produced) of Rokeya Sakhawat Hossain, the famous Bengali writer in the Indian subcontinent, can be studied from an entrepreneurial point of view as she worked as an agent of bringing social changes through her lifetime activities.

One of the tool for mythical representation is visual markings (that of marital, social, gender, religious and so on) which specify the identity of a person with particular symbols like hairstyle, clothing, tattoos, *sindoor* (vermilion), bangles, etc. These markings are gender specific and are mostly applied to women. This fact of gender specification encourages the "gaze" of the patriarchal society to operate which defines and redefines the identity of the woman - both her sexual and religious identity in a particular cultural scenario. The patriarchal gaze, working as a dominating apparatus, thus codifies women's identity by confining them to certain particulars, compelling them to be submissive to the patriarchal power system, and thereby, leaving little room of their own. Ultimately, it makes them "other" (most importantly, leading to be mentally marginalized). The woman who fought for the liberation of women in the Indian subcontinent from this state of "other" is Rokeya Sakhawat Hossain. Against the backdrop of patriarchal power, her social activism and every piece of her writings echo her longing for uplifting the womenfolk from the mental slavery. Her famous novella *Sultana's Dream* (1908) can be considered to be a classic piece of literature in its portrayal of a feminist utopia in which men are confined indoors and women take control over the public sphere, ending a war nonviolently and restoring peace, health and beauty to the kingdom. Women's participation or treatment of gender roles in organizational behavior, strategic management and entrepreneurship is evident in this exemplary piece of Rokeya's writings.

Through this utopian world, she subverts the idea of gaze exercised by patriarchy regarding the fixated or stereotyped role of women in a society. Portraying reversed sex-roles, Begum Rokeya inspires emancipation of women beyond the four walls of the "Zenana"[1] (Hossain, 2007, p. 377). The narrator dreams of her travel to a utopian Ladyland (Kingdom of Women - a peaceful and technologically advanced state ruled by women) where women –the previously marginalized – come to power at the centre, and men – the former patriarchal authority – are now in the margin or periphery. With the proceeding of the story, the mythical sex-roles are set in reverse in a manner that challenges the concept of patriarchal gaze. This metamorphosis is portrayed in the novel on different levels ranging from the private to the public sphere, including physical composition, household, brain power, purdah, religion, education, scientific endeavors, trade and politics. On the lexical level, giving an extra layer of meaning to words like "Zenana" (Stretching the four walls of the Zenana), coining words like "Murdana"[2] (Hossain, 2007, p. 383), and using words like "mannish" are bold and significant beyond words. Rokeya aspires to make women dream through her dream story, to have strong faith on their true caliber and to liberate them from the condition of mental enslavement, so that they will dynamically partake in all spheres of life. Another lady icon can be named on this occasion, Fatima al-Fihri, who remained famous as the founder of the oldest existing university in the world. Besides, many inspiring stories come along such as that of Haya Faisal from Pakistan who became a female cab driver against the mythical gender roles set for women. These women entrepreneurs exemplify the idea of subversion of gaze regarding gender roles as portrayed in Rokeya's *Sultana's Dream*.

The issue of subversion or reversal of gaze necessitates to throw light on Simone de Beauvoir's "Myth and Reality" from *The Second Sex* (1949) and Michel Foucault's Concept of Power in *The History of Sexuality* (first publish in English in 1978). This paper also refers to her other thematically related essays and stories, and brings about examples of real-life women who themselves challenged and went beyond the fixating gaze and now works for the emancipation of others. To explore Rokeya's dream identity of women free from mental enslavement and having their own space, this paper zeroes in on the different levels in which Rokeya subverts the gaze of patriarchy in constructing the women identity in her utopian world and liberating women from the mental slavery throwing light on the theoretical approaches mentioned. Through this discussion, the paper analyzes different endeavors of Eastern women like Rokeya, Fatima, Haya and the like to demonstrate women's entrepreneurial faculty defying their mythical representation.

In studying the issue, this paper adopts the process of theoretical analysis. It is a qualitative analytical research in the field of gender studies. The paper reads Rokeya's life and works, and a number of critical essays regarding the topic taken from both the electronic media and printed materials. The data collected from the sources are then given a critical reading to develop a framework which explains Rokeya's contribution as an entrepreneur and illustrates how she worked towards breaking patriarchal norms. The paper starts with the analysis of the concept of "gaze" and how it constructs female identity as stereotyped. Then, the paper moves to the discussion of the process how the stereotypes regarding women lead to the creation of "other" i.e. women being enslaved in their own mindset illustrating with examples from Rokeys's works. It further explains how the gender roles can be reversed through the analysis of *Sultana's Dream* to prove that breaking stereotypes, women can become global leaders. Moreover, the paper exemplifies Rokeya's entrepreneurial ability and leadership quality and concludes with an overview of how women's entrepreneurship can liberate them from the shackles of mental slavery and social stigmas.

THE PATRIARCHAL GAZE AND STEREOTYPED FEMALE

The challenges for women stars with their subjugation within the patriarchy and their stereotypical representation. The origin of the term "the patriarchal gaze" can be traced back to Laura Mulvey and her essay "Visual Pleasure and Narrative Cinema" which was published in 1975 (Leitch, 2010, p. 2181). "Gaze", originally a psychoanalytical term, is put into much popular use by Laura Mulvey in this essay. According to Mulvey, as she states in her essay, women are objectified (as an erotic object) on the screen in classic Hollywood films by the heterosexual men as they control the camera (Camera – Eye – Gaze). This objectification works on two different levels: for the directors and the characters in the film, and the spectator watching it as well. This male gaze is both voyeuristic[3] and fetishistic[4]. Besides, the audience gets narcissistic pleasure when they identify themselves with the protagonist in the film.

The term "gaze" has gradually got other implications outside of the framework that Mulvey initially imagined. Putting this concept of "gaze" into the scenario of patriarchal dominance over women, the active gaze from the men (powered by the patriarchy) compels the women to be submissive as they are on the screen of the film. This subjugation of women makes them an object for male dominance. For Simone de Beauvoir, this sense of domination lets men to view women as "Other" – ". . . patriarchy constructs woman as immanence and man as transcendence" (Leitch, 2010, p.1404). On the whole, the power of the gaze of the patriarchy defines women in terms of its own set of concepts and values. Accordingly, there arises the stereotyped image and mythical representation of women – submissive, dutiful and subjected to the patriarchal structure of the society. Patriarchal gaze initiates a line of "processes through which women internalize the ideologies of otherness that regulate them to immanence and to the position of being man's Other" (Leitch, 2010, p.1404).

The process of stereotyping is severely criticized in the chapter "Myth and Reality" in the classical book *The Second Sex* by Simone de Beauvoir. According to her, this process of stereotyping is typical to society, where the group higher in the hierarchy stereotype the lower one based on several categories - race, class, religion sex and so on. But it is more evident in case of sex than others when men, to organize and maintain the patriarchal society, stereotype women and make them "Other" (Leitch, 2010, p.1413).

Regarding the treatment of myth of women in "Myth and Reality", De Beauvoir discusses various mythical representations of women and examines the two levels of stereotypes about women. On the first level, she demonstrates how these myths fixate the role of women in the society, "The paternalism that claims woman for hearth and home defines her as sentimental, inwardness, immanence[5]" (Leitch 2010, p.1408). For example, in *Sultana's Dream*, while the students of the girls' universities in Ladyland are busy with extensive scientific experiments, the males are engaged in expanding military power. They stereotyped the endeavor of the female scientists and "... they only laughed at the members of the Universities and called the whole thing 'a sentimental nightmare'!" (Hossain, 2007, p.381). Secondly, Beauvoir uses the term "Other" (Leitch, 2010, p.1404, 1411, 1413) throughout *The Second Sex* to diagnose the female's secondary position in society as well as within her own patterns of thought i.e., mental slavery. In Rokeya's novella, "I was feeling very shy, thinking I was walking in the street in broad daylight" (Hossain, 2007, p.376) – this was the reaction of Sultana when she goes out with Sister Sara in her dream. "[A] t the moment when man asserts himself as subject and free being, the idea of the 'Other' arises," Beauvoir states in her essay. Myth of woman denies the position of woman as a "subject" or essential entity and makes her the "other".

Even if we put aside the general, oppressed, marginalized womenfolk and put the successful, powerful women into focus, we find to our utter surprise that they are not beyond certain stereotyping. In the article "The 10 Worst Stereotypes About Powerful Women", Jenna Goudreau, a Forbes Staff, talks about stereotype of powerful women as "Ice-Queen", "Single and Lonely", "Tough", "Masculine", "A Token", "A Cheerleader" (Goudreau, 2011) and so on. This is because through such roles the myth of women is shattered and Beauvoir provides the reason behind this at its best, "It may be disturbing to contemplate woman as at once a social personage and carnal prey ... For a woman to hold some "man's position" and be desirable at the same time has long been a subject for more or less ribald joking" (Leitch, 2010, p.1414). However, when the stereotyped females internalize certain stereotypes or set pattern of images within their own selves i.e. thought process, the minds become enslaved.

THE ENSLAVED MIND

To grab an idea of the enslaved mind, this paper needs to discuss how power works. Michel Foucault's concept of Power in *The History of Sexuality* (1978) includes the presence of power in multiple social relations and how individuals experience and exercise power. According to Foucault, power is exercised generally through a net-like organization, that is, in different social levels power acts like a net and individuals move inside the threads of this power structure. With reference to this concept of power which Foucault brings forth, in case of patriarchal power structure, the centre-periphery relationship is defined in a way where the patriarchy is in the centre, and it controls and dominates the women within the periphery drawn by the stereotyped roles. In *Sultana's Dream*, Sultana focuses on this subjugated position of women in contemporary Indian society characterized by the power of patriarchy: "We have no hand or voice in the management of our social affairs. In India man is lord and master. He has taken to himself all powers and privileges and shut up the women in the zenana" (Hossain, 2007, p.378). Patriarchy, holding the centre of the power structure, exercises dominance on women, and at certain point, women become subjugated in their own thought patterns. Thus the power structure with center-periphery relationship paves the mind (that of women and society on a larger scale) to be enslaved. As women in Rokeya's society were marginalized and doubly colonized because of their gender, Rokeya, like many other women writers of colonial India, "was doubly 'Other' – as woman and as colonized person" (Tharu and Lalita, "Preface" xvii). Against this backdrop, Rokeya had to work on three frontlines concurrently: literary, political and educational. Provided that such an obnoxious culture of neglecting women persisted in the colonial Bengal, Rokeya made extraordinary contribution to the enrichment of women.

Creation of the Enslaved Mind

Education is one of those decisive forces which play a great role to condition us to accept certain ideas. The primer in Toni Morrison's famous novel *The Bluest Eye* (1979) portrays the picture of a happy white world. When the black children read it at school, they gradually develop an idea of a sense of deprivation, start to accept the white world as the model of "perfection" and become psychologically colonized ("Other"). Through the memorizing process in which we memorize something from books, words on the pages of books get inscribed on the brains and thought processes of children. When indoctrination is completed, the words become a part of their psyche and children are not ready to accept anything contradictory to that. Famous post-structuralist theorist Judith Butler in her influential work *Gender Trouble: Feminism and the Subversion of Identity* (1990) proposes us to understand the term "citational repetitions" (Leitch, 2010, p.2486). We as individuals are conditioned from our childhood to understand certain ideas and meanings constructed and reconstructed by certain powerful social forces and cultural discourses. That is why the little boys in the particular scenario of certain cultures learns that crying is a "girlish" activity and it is the symbol of weakness, thereby something NOT masculine. In the same way, the little girls are taught to certain attributes pertaining to their gender roles. So, when the patriarchal societal force codifies the "girl" or "woman" they become the "Other" in the power structure. Thus, the power functions are oft repeated and some particular ideas go ingrained in their minds. Ultimately, fixation mechanism of gaze is completed when, thus, the enslaved mind is born.

In many of Rokeya's writings other than *Sultana's Dream,* the enslaved state of women is vividly portrayed. *Oborodhbashini* i.e., *The Secluded Women* (1931) portrays the women of the Indian subcontinent, especially Muslim women, in their most oppressed state. While presenting some personal stories regarding the secluded state of women (both Muslim and Hindu), she states that they are made to be accustomed to this seclusion and at one point they even forget to complain, because they lack the perception that there is anything to complain. Palanquin (a closed carrier generally on the shoulders of four bearers) (Hossain, 2007, p.294, 296, 308, 311, 318) is mentioned several times in the stories, which both physically and symbolically stands for the confined, secluded condition of women in this subcontinent.

Rokeya marks the difference between seclusion and *purdah* (veil) in several different pieces of her writing. The "seclusion" practiced among the women of the subcontinent at that time (as pictured in *Oborodhbashini*) is different from the "purdah" they are supposed to maintain as women as per Islam. Very often society puts pressure on women over and over again to maintain "purdah" while according to Islamic sharia, it is mandatory (a farz) for both men and women to follow the rules of veil. In her essay "Burkah", Rokeya differentiates the custom of "purdah" from that of seclusion. Women lack the proper education regarding their particular roles according to Islam; this fact cultures their brain and mind, and thus, they are segregated and made to live in seclusion masquerading "purdah". Rokeya herself maintained "purdah" and was immensely praised for delivering her speech in *burkah* (Hossain, 2007, p.509) at "All India Mohamedan Educational Conference" celebrating the Golden Jubilee of Aligarh University in 1925. In her speech at Bengali Women Education Council she compared the custom of seclusion with the deadly Carbolic acid (Hossain, 2007, p.464). Just like the gas from this acid causes immediate and painless death, the secluding custom works in that very way. Women, who are affected, are already dead (mentally until they meet their physical death) before they even know it.

In the same speech at Bengali Women Education Council (Hossain 2007, p.460, 464), Rokeya criticizes the tendency of parents to spend less in their daughter's education. This is still relevant to today's society. Often the education of the son of a family is much more emphasized than that of the daughter. If the family is not well off, only the male child is given the privilege of education. In many other cases, the family gives the better opportunity to the male child. But they fail to see the negative consequences. The female child suffers in her every way of life in the subsequent days. She fails to play the roles she needs to perform-even as a mother. That's why Rokeya showed in her essay "Ardhangee" (Hossain 2007, p.30) that when the mother is not educated enough, "the mind of the male child is confined within the hearth with his mother" (Hossain 2007, p.33), that is, his mind is not free from certain biases and prejudices. In the same essay, comparing the role of husband and wife to the wheels of a car, she depicted the disfigured portrayal of a family. She compared them with the two wheels of a car (Hossain 2007, p.32) of which one is big and the other is small according to their calibre. As a result, the car fails to have a proper movement and only gets a circular motion which definitely hampers the proper management of a family. To move out of this terrible situation, Rokeya puts emphasis on the rights of education for the girls just like their male counterparts. She also focuses on the need of studying the holy Quran to know about the rights of women in Islam bestowed by the Almighty. Through education, women can be aware of their rightful position in the world, widen the horizon of their thought process by breaking the shackles of the enslaved mind and perform their proper roles beyond any stereotypes.

THINKING GLOBALLY, ACTING GLOBALLY

Focusing on mythical representation of women in Sultana's India, Rokeya portrays in her utopian world the reversal of roles through subverting the gaze. This subversion works in several spheres within the novella which include physical composition, household, brain power, *purdah*, religion, education, scientific endeavor, trade and politics. In case of every sphere mentioned, Rokeya presents the gaze or stereotypes regarding the females and then, subverts it.

There are many socio-cultural factors which manufacture the idea of women's inferior position in society on the logic of men being physically stronger than women. At the beginning of the novella, Rokeya mentions that the "logic" of a "stronger" physical composition of men to dominate women is overruled in Ladyland. Sister Sara says that "A lion is stronger than a man, but it does not enable him to dominate the human race" (Hossain, 2007, p.378).

On the contrary, women take control of the public sphere and men are confined in the household. Gender role is subverted here when women are depicted as multitaskers – both doing the official jobs and household chores. On the other hand, men cannot be trusted neither with the public sphere (as corruption prevailed there earlier) nor with the household, as Sister Sara says, "We do not trust our 'zenana' members with embroidery! . . . As a man has not patience enough to pass the thread through a needle hole even!" (Hossain, 2007, p.379). Likewise, numerous examples of women can be given from today's world who are performing their roles both within and beyond the domestic periphery.

According to Sister Sara, Bengali women have "neglected the duty [they] owe yourselves and lost [their] natural rights by shutting [their] eyes to [their] own interest" (Hossain, 2007, p.378). Such an idea was revolutionary and very much unfamiliar as presented to them. Having been brought up to believe as Sultana has, that "men have larger brains" (Hossain 2007, p.381), Bengali women got accustomed to the mythical representation of themselves as the weaker sex. Rokeya reverses this idea saying the following statement through the voice of Sister Sara: "An elephant also has got a bigger and heavier brain than a man has. Yet man can enchain elephants and employ them, according to their own wishes" (Hossain, 2007, p.381). Again, during the war when the military of the country fails to save the country, the Queen focuses on the brain power of the womenfolk, "If you cannot save your country for lack of physical strength, try to do so by brain power" (Hossain, 2007, p.382). Thus, Rokeya reverses the myth of "man-having bigger brain" with woman's brain power exemplifying with the entrepreneurial skills of the female university students.

Here is an interesting and inspiring story to share. In the 1940s, Albert Einstein received a letter from a young South African girl named Tyfanny, who wanted to build up her career in science and technology. The letter was full of self-doubt that have for so long confused women having higher ambitions at that social scenario. Later, she sent Einstein another letter telling that she forgot something about her to mention which she thought as "a potentially damaging detail about herself". That detail was that she was a "girl" which the society had always made her regret a great deal about. BUT Einstein's response to this young scientist has become an everlasting lesson, "I do not mind that you are a girl, but the main thing is that you yourself do not mind" (Polo, 2012). The point to bring up the story is that the girl in the story was confined in a set of stereotypes just because of being a girl. In other words, this is how an enslaved mind is created. Most importantly, Einstein encouraged her to go beyond such set ups and according to him, the first step must come from the girl herself.

This fact can be further exemplified by the numerous famous women working in difference sectors of education, research, scientific, social, economic and political arena. If we consider examples of female scientists, who worked and are still working in diverse fields of science, the list will be a never-ending one. There was a famous chemist and physicist, Marie Curie, who was the first person in the history to receive two Nobel Prizes in diverse fields of science (chemistry and physics). There is also Maria Mayer, the American physicist, who received Nobel Prize for suggesting the nuclear shell model of the atomic nucleus). The other examples are Rachel Carson (American marine biologist and conservationist whose work revolutionized the global environmental movement.), Barbara McClintock (American scientist receiving Nobel Prize in 1983 for the discovery of genetic transposition.), Rita Levi-Montalcini (Italian neurologist receiving Nobel Prize in 1986 for the discovery of Nerve Growth Factor), Elizabeth Blackwell (American physician who was the first woman to become a medical doctor in the United States) and many more, who made and changed history to a great extent.

Moving on further with the discussion of subverting roles, Rokeya's novella extraordinarily examines and questions *purdah* by turning the issue into a "dream" sequence (in a place where the men are in purdah!). Men are kept in confinement in that cherished Lady-land to safeguard society from crimes like theft, murder, arson, rape, plunder, burglary and so many other evils. Just as in Bengal women belong in *purdah*, in Lady-land men are "in their proper places" (Hossain, 2007, p.377). Furthermore, when the country is about to go to war against invaders, the Lady Principal of the university insists that ". . . before we go out the men must enter the zenanas…for the sake of purdah" (Hossain, 2007, p.382). The statement is effective - endorsing the "entrapment" of men for the sake of "freedom" of women, two contradictory terms. The point is that Bengali men have done precisely this; in a similarly absurd configuration, they have entrapped women into symbolizing the nation's honor and true spiritual essence. Thus, the novella offers a critique of the values of its patriarchal society, demonstrates how ridiculous these are and shows the total deconstruction of power structure. It is through this satirical representation that Rokeya gives the rationale for the Murdana, "They are accustomed to the purdah system and have ceased to grumble at their seclusion, we call the system 'Murdana'" (Hossain, 2007, p.383). This is her own coinage which comes from the Urdu word "Mard", meaning "man". Thus, along with the reversal portrayed in the power structure, Rokeya reverses the gender role by deconstructing the language itself.

"I see purity itself reigns over your land" (Hossain, 2007, p.385) – Sultana tells Sister Sara regarding the prevailing peaceful condition of Lady-land. Here comes another reversal of gaze in case of religion as Sara says, "Our religion is based on Love and Truth. It is our religious duty to love one another and to be truthful" (Hossain, 2007, p.385). Rokeya attacks the patriarchal misinterpretation of religion which subjugates women for the sake of domination only.

In conceiving the dream world of Sultana, Rokeya should be seen as a contemporary of the feminist writers of utopias who place women in a scientifically advanced and peaceful world. In Lady-land, since "our good Queen liked science very much… she circulated an order that all the women in her country should be educated" (Hossain, 2007, p.380). The importance of science to the Queen, both literally and syntactically, leads directly to women being educated. Accordingly, a number of girls' schools are founded and "education was spread far and wide among women" (Hossain, 2007, p.380). Proper patronization is given for scientific researches and innovations, which results in the victory with the enemy in the war. When man's military power fails, the intellect and brain power of the female students of the universities wins in turning down the gaze, as their endeavor was previously called to be "a sentimental nightmare" (Hossain, 2007, p.381). This myth is torn down by the statement, "Women's brains are somewhat quicker than men's" (Hossain, 2007, p.381). Thus, Rokeya demonstrates the value of women's work and intelligence compared to that of men.

Regarding their trade strategy, the Queen of Lady-land says, "Men, we find, are rather of lower morals and so we do not like dealing with them" (Hossain, 2007, p.386). So, this is another sphere where Rokeya subverts the gaze by emphasizing on women's ability to trade which is far beyond imagination in Sultana's Bengal.

One of the most significant features of this fantasy world is women's behavior in the utopian society of Lady-land. The absence of men merely means more time for the pursuit of arts, science and gardening. Similarly, Rokeya familiarizes her female readers with the idea of engaging in traditionally male disciplines. In Lady-land, women are scientists inventing air-cars, heating, showers and electricity for farming and cooking, using the concentrated sun-light in war and so on (Hossain, 2007, p.384, 385,383). Rokeya describes how women in Lady-land are able to complete office work in only two hours (Hossain 2007, p.379), which takes men days. Now they are able enough to control both the public and private spheres while playing roles as multitaskers. This utopian state of affairs is achieved because unlike in Sultana's Bengal, education is geared towards making women well-rounded citizens rather than only homemakers. By highlighting the constructed nature of gender, Rokeya demonstrates that women should not be confined to a set model of womanhood. Thus, Rokeya de-familiarizes the gender roles Bengali women consider "normal".

As "... tables are turned" (Hossain 2007, p.380) in the Lady-land, the reversal of gaze draws attention to Rokeya's utopian feminist ideology. Women in Lady-land are powerful, but to portray a society where women are in a position of power, Rokeya did not find it necessary to divorce men from woman's world. She does not desire for the exclusion of men from their world as it is not practically feasible. Indeed, Rokeya's yearning is for liberty and equality; the domination of either sex is disagreeable. Here lies her concept of gender equality and utopian feminist ideology. Rokeya addresses the responsibility of the male folk in this regard. She herself was educated, inspired and helped by her elder brother and her husband that paved the way for her to be the woman who made and changed history. For her, man and woman (especially husband and wife as it is referred in the essay "Ardhangee") are like the two wheels of a car (Hossain, 2007, p.31). If both the wheels are not equal, the car will merely continue to move into a circle losing its usual pace and movement forward. Regarding gender equality, Rokeya says in "Arghangee":

We are not halves to the Almighty and mother compared to our brothers. If that was so then it would have been the rule that the girl would remain in mother's womb for five months while the son for ten. The production and supply of mother's milk would also be divided into half in case of the baby girl. But that is not the case. (Hossain, 2007, p.35).

She emphasizes on the fact that similar care should be taken and similar amount of money should be spent on both the male and female children (Hossain 2007, p.26).

For Rokeya, equality does not mean identicality; thereby, gender equality means freeing men too, from certain prescribed prejudices. Men need to change a great deal for ensuring gender equality. Unless men are changed, unless they recognize the worth of women, the world cannot be a thriving one. Similar resonance can be found in Beauvoir, "Man would have nothing to lose, quite the contrary, if he gave up disguising woman as a symbol … To recognize in woman a human being is not to impoverish man's experience: this would lose none of its (experience as a human being) diversity, its richness, or its intensity if it were to occur between two subjectivities" (Leitch, 2010, p.1413). Moreover, Beauvoir sets a line of expectation for all, "What must be hoped for is that the men for their part will unreservedly accept the situation that is coming into existence; only then will women be able to live in that situation without anguish" (Leitch, 2010, p.1414).

Significant number of examples can be found of women including Muslim women playing the roles in familial, social and global levels as depicted in *Sultana's Dream*. They are playing important roles as presidents, prime ministers, scientists, politicians, teachers, researchers and so on, and marking significant changes in the course of history. Rokeya herself is a great example from the early decades of 20th century. As from today's world, Yemeni journalist, politician and the Nobel Peace Laureate in 2011 Tawakkol Karman is an inspiring figure to name for all women and particularly Muslim women. Another lady icon can be named on this occasion, Fatima al-Fihri, who, in the Moroccan city of Fez, instituted a mosque which developed to be the famous Al-Qarawiyyin University. Eventually, it became to be the oldest existing university in the world. "The University of al-Qarawyyin is considered the most ancient university in the world still operating, preceding the first European universities. This is according to UNESCO and Guinness World Records. The date of reference is the year al-Qarawiyyin was founded as a mosque, which implies that its educational character goes back to its beginnings. In this sense, it precedes the Sankore Mosque in Timbuktu (founded in 989 A.D.) by more than a century and the University of Bologna (1088 A.D.) by more than two centuries" (Ilham, 2020) Besides, many inspiring stories come along such as the one like Haya Faisal's. In Pakistan, women are often discriminated against when they enter the workforce to support their household needs. No matter how skilled and confident they are, there comes a point where they get criticism from patriarchy. However, things have improved drastically in Pakistan. Recently, a woman named Haya Faisal became a female cab driver for the sake of supporting her family. A small yet significant portion of society does encourage women empowerment. Such appreciation encourages those women that have to financially support their family. Among those inspirational women that are working tirelessly to support their family is Haya Faisal.

Over and over again, Rokeya describes the sectors where Muslim Women are given rights by the Holy Scripture Al-Quran (Hossain, 2007, p.464), e.g. education, property, marriage, job. That's why she gives an alarm to women, "If the Almighty asks you, 'Have you properly used your mind, e.g. intellect, brain, eyes', what will you answer?" (Hossain, 2007, p.22). All that she has emphasized on is that women should know about their rights. This will establish their voice and make them free of their enslaved state.

STORIES OF APORAJITA (THE UNBEATEN)

Numerous examples are set by Rokeya's writing that women can be unbeaten when they can establish their own position. In *Padmarag* (1924), Siddika, along with other major characters, can be a great example. Rokeya tells the story of several women crowded together at Tarini Bhaban – a community entrepreneurship in contemporary Bengal built and supervised by only females. They are women from diverse backgrounds of racial and ethnic groups and religions, who are here to lead a new life leaving behind a life of oppression and slavery.

As the narrative of the novella unfolds, we come across a series of personal narratives of the women gathered in Tarini Bhavan. All the women share a past of sufferings in marriage and family life. Gradually, Siddika starts to develop bondage of shared feelings. Siddika puts some fundamental questions: "Is there no medicine to cure these running sores of society? To stay bound to a madman all one's life, to be abandoned without reason, to be forcibly sent to live with a drunken husband and a co-wife by one's brother even when one expresses unwillingness.... Is there no remedy for this?"[6] (Hossain, 2007, p.234) Then comes the bold answer from Saudamini: "There is! That remedy is the 'Society for the Alleviation of Women's Suffering' in Tarini Bhavan. Come, all women who are abandoned, pauperized, neglected, helpless and oppressed—come all. Then we declare war against society. And Tarini Bhavan is our fortress." (Hossain, 2007, p.234)

Through the storyline, Rokeya shows Siddika's self-development and maturation of her personality and Siddika develops a ardent quest for a vocation that will benefit others by the end of the novella. Most of the inhabitants of Tarini Bhavan foresee a reunion of Siddika and Latif while Siddika is unwavering in her resolution to devote her life to other women and the welfare of society as well.

Apart from fictional characters, to exert examples from real life, Rokeya herself is a great inspiration who had to fight a twofold struggle for the emancipation of women: to free the women from mental slavery and to take steps to educate them for that purpose. Rokeya also mentioned her elder sister, Korimunnessa Begum in the essay "Lukano Roton" ("Hidden Treasure" as the author translates) (Hossain, 2007, p.466) as her great inspiration who herself could not manage to bloom fully but never lost hope and quitted. Besides, on another note, Rokeya struggled to change men's attitude towards women so that a society based on equity can be ensured. In all of her activities, Rokeya shares qualities or characteristics of an entrepreneur. She initiated and set up a school for girls' education in 1909 named as Shakhawat Memorial Girls' School. She had to cross a long arduous path to establish girls' right for education and overcame many challenges of the society. She hoped for the profit of her ardent work which is depicted through the "dream" of Sultana in her novella *Sultana's Dream* i.e. if women are properly nurtured and get proper opportunities, they can contribute to build the family and society. As an entrepreneur would do, Rokeya promoted her ideals through her writings and social activism till her last breath.

THE DREAM: THE FIRE

To fight for their rights through entrepreneurial skills, women must recognize the voice inside, hear it and let it be heard. Thus, the "Dream" of Rokeya will be fulfilled as portrayed through her life's works and entrepreneurship. As the forerunner of Muslim women's awakening and women's liberation movement, she does not merely present the ills and ordeals of women in many of her essays but facilitates the ways to place them in power from margin to centre. *Sultana's Dream* is a wonderful satirical work set in Lady-land, which as she portrays, is a constant destabilization of gender roles fixated by the gaze of the patriarchy. This is a call for women to "rise" like the idea of "rise" depicted in Maya Angelou's poem "Still I Rise",

Leaving behind nights of terror and fear
I rise
Into a daybreak that's wondrously clear
I rise
(Line – 35-38)

In one of her essays titled "Nareepuja" (Hossain 2007, p.441) ("Female Worship" as the author translates), Rokeya describes a conversation of several women about women's condition in Indian subcontinent at that time and one of the participants equals the suffering of women to fire as she says, "Who counts the numerous flames of that fire!" (Hossain, 2007, p.443). This fire of suffering is still not less dominant and in many cases is still ablaze with new and newer flames. Just like Sultana's dream remains unfulfilled or like the unfinished last essay of Rokeya that she wrote on the night before her death, "Nareer Adhikar" (The Rights of Women), Rokeya's dream about women's emancipation is still unaccomplished. Nevertheless, progress is there, however slow its pace is.

Through the examples of Rokeya Shakhawat Hossain and other eastern women, it is evident that women entrepreneurship can be a powerful tool to combat the mythical representation of women in the society and to establish their rightful positions in the world.

REFERENCES

Angelou, M. (n.d.). *Still I Rise*. www.youtube.com/watch?v=7HiE4lt_DUY

Bagchi, B. (2003-4). *Inside Tarini Bhavan: Rokeya Sakhawat Hossain's Padmarag and the Richness of South Asian Feminism in Furthering Unsectarian, Gender-Just Human Development*. http://www.igidr.ac.in/pdf/publication/WP-2003-004

Beauvoir, S. (2010). The Second Sex Chapter XI. Myth and Reality. In V. B. Leitch (Ed.), The Norton Anthology of Theory and Criticism. W.W. Norton & Co. (Original work published 1949)

Butler, J. (2010). Preface to Gender Trouble: Feminism and the Subversion of Identity. In V. B. Leitch (Ed.), The Norton Anthology of Theory and Criticism. W.W. Norton & Co. (Original work published 1990)

Foucault, M. (2010). The Incitement to Discourse. In V. B. Leitch (Ed.), The Norton Anthology of Theory and Criticism. New York: W.W. Norton & Co. (Original work published 1978)

Goudreau, J. (2011). *The 10 Worst Stereotypes about Powerful Women*. https://www.forbes.com/sites/jennagoudreau/2011/10/24/worst-stereotypes-powerful-women-christine-lagarde-hillary-clinton/

Hasan, M. M. (2013). Commemorating Rokeya Sakhawat Hossain and Contextualising her Work in South Asian Muslim Feminism. *Asiatic, 7*(2). https://www.researchgate.net/publication/273898717_Commemorating_Rokeya_Sakhawat_Hossain_and_Contextualising_her_Work_in_South_Asian_Muslim_Feminism

Henderson, A. (1994). Power and knowledge in nursing practice: The contribution of Foucault. *Journal of Advanced Nursing*, *20*(5), 935–939. doi:10.1046/j.1365-2648.1994.20050935.x PMID:7745186

Hossain, R. S. (2007). *Rochonashomogro [The Complete Works]*. Jhinuk Prakashoni.

Ilham, T. (2020). *African Roots*. https://www.dw.com/en/fatima-al-fihri-founder-of-the-worlds-oldest-university/a-53371150

Jahan, R. (1998). *Editor's Introduction: "Sultana's Dream: Purdah Reversed"*. Feminist Press. https://www.barnesandnoble.com/w/sultanas-dream-rokeya-sakhawat-hossain/1122980437

Leitch, V. B. (2010). *The Norton Anthology of Theory and Criticism*. W.W. Norton & Co.

Morrison, T. (1979). *The Bluest Eye*. Chatto and Windus.

Mulvey, L. (1975). Visual Pleasure and Narrative Cinema. In V. B. Leitch (Ed.), The Norton Anthology of Theory and Criticism. W.W. Norton & Co. doi:10.1007/978-1-349-14428-0_27

Polo, S. (2012). *Albert Einstein's Letter to a Little Girl Who Loved Science and Hated Being a Girl*. https://www.themarysue.com/albert-einstein-little-girl/

Tharu, S., & Lalita, K. (1993). Preface. In S. Tharu & K. Lalilta (Eds.), *Women Writing in India: 600 B.C. to the Present* (Vol. 2). Pandora.

ENDNOTES

1. Aka "Purdah", the gender-segregated system for women in Indian subcontinent.
2. Counter term of "Zenana", a coinage by Rokeya; comes from the Urdu word "Mard", meaning "man".
3. Relating to activities through which people get sexual gratification from other's sexual behaviour.
4. Relating to sexual arousal or gratification resulting from handling a fetish (organs other than sexual ones and different objects).
5. Term associated with existential philosophy, means stagnation and subjugation to given conditions; thereby, refers to women. Transcendence, being the counter term, means a mode of activity that leads to liberty; thereby, refers to men.
6. translated by Barnita Bagchi in the essay "Inside Tarini Bhavan: Rokeya Sakhawat Hossain's Padmarag and the Richness of South Asian Feminism in Furthering Unsectarian, Gender-Just Human Development"

Chapter 8
The Profile of Women Entrepreneurs:
A Contextual Analysis From a Developing Country

Nuray Atsan
Akdeniz University, Turkey

ABSTRACT

This chapter focuses on motivations, problems, and future needs of Turkish women entrepreneurs. The study uses a quantitative research methodology. A self-administered questionnaire is applied to a randomly selected group of urban women entrepreneurs in Antalya region, Turkey. One hundred and nineteen responses are statistically analyzed. Findings indicate that women entrepreneurs are driven mostly by psychological and economic motivators such as working independently, achieving economic independence, and doing the job she wants which suited her abilities. Obtaining capital is the primary problem they faced. In addition, the majority of women entrepreneurs need support in marketing and branding.

INTRODUCTION

As the number of working women increase, the role women entrepreneurs play in modernizing developing economies is of increasing importance. Accordingly, studies of women entrepreneurs in developing countries are rising dramatically (Minniti and Naude, 2010; Yadav and Unni, 2016). As a developing country, studies on women entrepreneurship have gained momentum in Turkey since 1990s. However,

DOI: 10.4018/978-1-7998-8742-3.ch008

researchers still have no reliable data of how well Turkey is doing at empowering women's entrepreneurship. Growing rapidly, these studies are focused on analyzing women entrepreneurship in different aspects, such as work and family balance, factors related to work life, socio-demographic factors, patterns and characteristics of women entrepreneurs (Hisrich and Öztürk, 1999; Ufuk and Özgen, 2001; Çakıcı, 2006; Ecevit, 2007; Ökten, 2015; Cebeci, 2015; Fis et al., 2019).

Meanwhile, there has been an intense effort to create entrepreneurship awareness with the newly enacted laws of the state, entrepreneurship programs added to the curricula of universities and incubation centers and technology transfer offices opened by the private sector, innovative business idea programs and competitions in order to spread the entrepreneurship culture in Turkey for a decade. On the other hand, the state's development of financial support for women entrepreneurs and the establishment of public policies supporting women, especially in child care, are also important developments. This effort lead to an increase in the number of women entrepreneurs in the last decade. The number of women entrepreneurs was 41 thousand in 2000, it was 125 thousand in 2017 and approximately 142 thousand in 2018 (TURKSTAT, 2019). However, the share of women entrepreneurs in the total number is still very low. Intense efforts to create an entrepreneurial culture in the country from the recent past have also changed the contextual characteristics of women entrepreneurs. Past and current motivations for being an entrepreneur and the nature of the problems may differ. Therefore, this study aims to provide an overview of current women's entrepreneurship in Turkey before stepping into the 2020s and to investigate its nature and scope based on statistical and survey data.

Regarding the impact of women entrepreneurship on the growth and stability of Turkish economy, this study examines the motivations, problems and expectations facing women entrepreneurs in Antalya region in Turkey. There are three main research questions of the study. These are:

- What factors do motivate women entrepreneurs to establish their businesses?
- What challenges do women entrepreneurs face in the startup phase of their entrepreneurial activity?
- What are the main areas women entrepreneurs need support to conduct their businesses?

The study focuses on women entrepreneurs around Antalya region. Antalya city is the locomotive of Turkey's tourism sector, tourism-related service sectors and agriculture sector. It is Turkey's fifth largest city. Moreover, it is the 6th province of the country in total gross product. While the 2019 population was two million five hundred eleven thousand, 49% of this was women. Statistical data reveals that the rate of women employees in Antalya is higher than the average of

Turkey. For example it is between 41- 45% on the average and is higher than the Turkey average of 30-36% in between 20-54 age groups (TURKSTAT, Regional Statistics, 2019). As of 2019, the number of women employees was 84,899, while the number of women employers was 9121. Although Antalya is one of the top 5 cities contributing to national economy, the number of studies focusing on women employees and entrepreneurs in the city is almost non-existent. Considering that the economic and sociological differences among regions have a great influence on women entrepreneurship, this region specific study can contribute to building a better understanding of women entrepreneurship dynamics in Turkey. As Kibler et al. (2014) emphasized, regional socio-economic characteristics significantly affect the emergence of business startup behavior.

After this introductory section, the conceptual framework and the current state of women's entrepreneurship in Turkey will be discussed followed by the research methodology and findings of the study. The study concludes with the discussion, limitations and recommendations for future research sections.

THEORETICAL FRAMEWORK AND RELATED CONCEPTS

Women Entrepreneurship: Conceptual Framework

Since this study will discuss women entrepreneurs from a broad perspective- their motivations that lead them to become entrepreneurs, the obstacles they face, and their future expectations-, the definition of women entrepreneur needs to be a more integrated rather than a short-sighted one. The definition of Ecevit (1993) which is adopted for this study, conveys such an holistic approach; "woman entrepreneur is the one who sees an opportunity and thinks of a business idea, initiates her enterprise, organises and combines the resources, operates the enterprise and undertakes risks and handles economic uncertainty involved in running a business enterprise".

Women entrepreneurs have been recognized as untapped sources of economic growth. Indeed, women have the potential to contribute to economy as much as men. There is evidence to support the fact that women entrepreneurs can have a positive impact on economic prosperity (Ganesan et al., 2002). With unique characteristics, they create new ideas and jobs, employ labor, bring practical solutions to problems and fair approaches to business management. Participation of women in the industrial development not only results in the productive use of the labour, but also improves quality of life (Ufuk ve Özgen, 2001). A particularly important point is that the development of women entrepreneurship diversifies the income streams of families. Moreoever, they become role models for young women and promote gender equality in society. In addition to their contribution to employment creation and economic growth, they lead the diversity of entrepreneurship in the economic process (Verhul et al., 2006).

Despite the economic importance of women entrepreneurs, the level of women involvement in entrepreneurial activity is still significantly lower than that of men. Men are about twice as likely to be involved in entrepreneurial activity than women (Reynolds et al.,2002; Kim et al., 2006). Women's participation in entrepreneurship is lower than that of men in all over the world. Global Entrepreneurship Monitor (GEM) 2018 data also confirms this status. Moreover, the ratio of female and male entrepreneurs in developing countries differs more than in developed countries. Women entrepreneurship in developing countries is more challenging because of the lack of adequate opportunities, resource constraints, and the challenges inherent in such societies (Panda, 2018).

It can be observed that the factors that motivate women to become entrepreneurs are often discussed as a "push and pull" framework, especially in the literature of developing countries (Buttner and Moore, 1997; Yetim, 2002; Özdemir, 2010; Poggesi 2015). Necessity entrepreneurship refers to negative factors that force individuals to become entrepreneurs. Opportunity entrepreneurship refers to positive factors that attract individuals to entrepreneurship. "Necessity driven factors" include basically the overall unemployment situation in the country and unfavorable working conditions, job dissatisfaction, and gender discrimination. On the other hand, being independent, self-actualization, being the boss of your own business and being a role model to other women rank among the "opportunity driven factors" (Ganesan et al., 2002; Yetim, 2008). There are also studies in the literature that classify motivational factors as economic and non-economic factors. The work of Cromie (1987) is the well-known among them. He examined the differences between the male and female entrepreneurial motivations based on twelve socio-economic factors such as autonomy, achievement, career dissatisfaction, job dissatisfaction, money expected to be earned, child-rearing opportunity, inheritance opportunity, providing employment opportunity to others, enjoying greater social status in self-employment.

Women entrepreneurs have an important role in economic growth, particularly in developing countries. Yet many of them struggle with a variety of problems which cause their businesses to fail. The main problems of women detected in Panda's (2018) study, which analyzed 35 studies examining the problems of women entrepreneurs in 90 developing countries were gender discrimination, work-family conflict, financial constraints, lack of infrastructural support, unfavourable business, economic and political environments, lack of entrepreneurship-related training and personality-based constraints. It can be seen that the problems faced by women entrepreneurs in these countries are mostly caused by traditional division of labor and strict gender roles (Ganesan et al., 2002). The male-dominated social structure restricts women's participation in economic and social life outside home and considers it worthless

(Maden, 2015; Tüzün ve Takay, 2017). For example, since the current position of a woman in a patriarchal society is her home, and her main responsibilities are limited to her family, it is impossible for women to work and start a business without the permission of her spouse or family members. This traditional social structure poses a big barrier for women's entrepreneurial activities. Limited access to finance, inability to get support from financial institutions, lack of marketing skills were also found to be problematic areas for women entrepreneurs (Ganesan et al. 2002; Santoni and Barth, 2014).

A large number of studies on the traits of women entrepreneurs are found in the relevant literature. Looking at the general patterns of these studies, it can be observed that education is important in the entrepreneurial process (Arthur et al., 2012; Bhardwaj, 2013). Minniti and Naude (2010) also emphasize that entrepreneurship skills are influenced by the level of education and experience, and formal and vocational education is important for developing entrepreneurial skills, especially in developing countries. On the other hand, it is claimed that married women and women with children may have a higher tendency to become entrepreneurs than single women because self-employment gives the former groups more time flexibility (Minniti and Naude, 2010; EDGE Project, 2018).

Women Entrepreneurship in Turkey: Facts and Figures

To create economic growth, a sustainable understanding of business and ultimately, development and prosperity of the society, women entrepreneurs and employees are needed in Turkey. Since the 1980s, as in many developed and developing countries, the number of women who joined working life and who tended to be entrepreneurs has started to increase in Turkey (Hisrich and Öztürk, 1999, Tüzün and Takay, 2017). Correspondingly, governmental policies were developed to support women entrepreneurs. For example, Turkey's 2015-2018 Entrepreneurship Strategy and Action Plan included strategic goals and action plans specific to women entrepreneurs. The plan aims to analyze educational needs for women entrepreneurs, conduct research on their problems, develop and implement a sustainable support system. Despite those developments, the number of women entrepreneurs in Turkey has always been less than male entrepreneurs.

According to 2018 TURKSTAT household labor force survey, Turkey's total population was 73.7 million, and 49.8% of its population was women. The labor force participation rate was 72.1% for men and 33.8% for women. The majority of economically active women work in agriculture (56.8% of women vs. 25.2% of men), while many fewer work in industry (14.4% of women, 29.5% of men) and services (28.8% of women, 45.3% of men) (TURKSTAT, Labor Force Survey Results, 2000).

Table 1. Distribution of working women according to 2000-2007-2017 data

Working position	2000 data		2010 data		2017 data	
	Number of Working Women	Percent (%)	Number of Working Women	Percent (%)	Number of Working Women	Percent (%)
Unpaid family worker	3.028	52.2	2.262	35.2	2.142	24.1
Own account worker	684	11.8	822	12.8	829	9.3
Employer	41	0.7	84	1.3	125	1.4
Paid employee	2.048	35.3	3.257	50.7	5.808	65.2
Total	5.801	100	6.425	100	8.904	100

Source: TURKSTAT, 2000, 2007, 2017

There is also a large informal sector in Turkey in which a sizable number of women work (e.g. waged domestic household helpers).

As it can be seen from Table 1, although there has been a regular increase in women employment and the number of women employers since 2000, the rate of women entrepreneurs in the country is still at a very low level. According to 2017 data, the rate of employers among women in Turkey was only 1.4%. The ratio of women employers to total employers in Turkey was 8%. It was 6.2% in 2007 (TURKSTAT, 2007, 2017). When compared with EU level, it can be said that the rate of women employers in Turkey is considerably lower than the EU average which is 27% (TURKONFED Report, 2017). By the same token, "Global Entrepreneurship and Development Index (GEDI) Women Entrepreneurship Research (2014)" demonstrates that Turkey is the 18th among 30 countries in the ranking of innovative, global market-oriented women entrepreneurs.

On the other hand, total entrepreneurial activity (TEA) of women corresponds to 8.4 percent while the TEA of men is 20 percent. The gender gap in TEA is as much as 60% in Turkey (2018/2019 GEM Women report). This continuous gap requires socio-cultural analysis beyond economic explanations. Despite the changing social, economic and cultural factors in Turkey, traditional view of women determines all social relations. A very strong patriarchal family structure and gender discrimination in society determine the roles that apply to women. Marriage and family are of indispensable importance in this social structure (Arat, 1995). The heavy load of women's responsibilities in the family, the gender roles of men and women segregated by sharp boundaries and social pressures keep women away from social and working life (Aycan, 2004).

In terms of technological entrepreneurship, the rate of women entrepreneurs in technology field in Turkey is 15.4%. It is only two percentage below the world average of 17% (Crunchbase 2017 Report). Between the years 2010 and 2017, it is observed that women entrepreneurs in technology entrepreneurship most often started enterprises in e-commerce, marketplace, biotechnology, baby and parent related issues in Turkey (Startups.watch, 2019). The number of entrepreneurs carrying out a social entrepreneurship mission is also quite high. According to the British Council's "Status of Social Entrepreneurs in the Turkey" Report (2019), the number of social entrepreneurs in Turkey has reached 9000 and 55% of them are women.

In terms of demographics such as age, education, marital status and the sector information, it is seen that women entrepreneurs primarily operate in the service and trade sectors rather than in the manufacturing sector (Yetim, 2002; Boudet and Agar, 2014; Ecevit and Yüksel, 2015). The major reasons are that entry into these sectors is easier and requires less capital. In addition, it is possible to be more flexible in establishing a balance of work and private life (Yetim, 2002).

The finding that women entrepreneurs are mostly highly educated has been included in the results of many studies (Hisrich and Öztürk, 1999; Boudet and Agar, 2014; Ecevit and Yüksel, 2015). Again, it is observed that women who think of being an entrepreneur are mostly middle-aged (Ufuk and Özgen, 2001). It is stated that they can take a step into entrepreneurial life after the age of 30 when their familial roles especially the responsibilities of children lessen (Yetim, 2002; Ecevit ve Yüksel, 2015).

Among the motivational factors for urban women entrepreneurs, push factors such as being independent, taking advantage of business opportunities, gaining success and realizing a dream are more common (Hisrich and Öztürk, 1999; Ufuk and Ozgen, 2001; Cetindamar, 2005; Çakıcı, 2006; Tuzun and Takay, 2017). Also, the findings of the "GEM 2010 Report on Turkey" indicate that as the level of education increases, people are more likely to become opportunity-driven entrepreneurs (Karadeniz, 2010). On the other hand, women entrepreneurs of rural origin and less educated people are guided by the necessity-driven factors to increase family income (Yetim, 2002; Tüzün and Takay, 2017).

As with all women entrepreneurs in the world, Turkish women entrepreneurs experience many difficulties in starting and running a business. Majority of these problems fundamentally related to the community's view of a woman's place in society. It was found that traditional gender and family roles (such as wife, mother, housewife) are one of the biggest challenges of women entrepreneurs (Ufuk and Özgen, 2001; Boudet and Ağar, 2014; Tüzün and Takay, 2017). Other problems include mainly financial problems - access to capital comes first-, bureaucratic procedures in public offices, municipalities and customs and managerial and marketing issues (Hisrich and Öztürk, 1999; Çetindamar, 2005; Boudet and Ağar, 2014; Ecevit and Yüksel, 2015; Tüzün and Takay, 2017).

RESEARCH METHODOLOGY

This study aims to define the current situation of women entrepreneurs in Antalya, Turkey by focusing on the following issues:

- Profile of women entrepreneurs and their enterprises
- Key economic, psychological and social drivers to establish their own businesses
- Problems they face when setting and running their business
- Future needs to develop their businesses.

The research was carried out among the members of The Union of Chambers and Commodity Exchanges of Turkey (TOBB) Antalya Women Entrepreneurs Council (Antalya KGK), Antalya Industrialist and Business People Association (ANSIAD) and Antalya Business Women Association (ANTİKAD) in Antalya region. Antalya KGK is a consultative body within TOBB that develops general policies on women's entrepreneurship and provides training and capacity development support for current and potential women entrepreneurs. ANSIAD and ANTIKAD are NGOs with a focus on business and entrepreneurship, of which women entrepreneurs in the region are members. A self-administered questionnaire was used to collect the data. The initial version of the questionnaire was pre-tested with three women entrepreneurs and appropriate modifications were made. A total of 200 questionnaires were applied to randomly selected participants via e-mail or face-to-face. After a reminder e-mail, 119 responses were received which refers to a 59 percent response rate.

The questionnaire was developed by using the relevant literature and previous studies (Hisrich and Öztürk, 1999; Boudet and Agar, 2014). It consisted of two sections. The first section included the demographic variables about women entrepreneurs and their businesses. The second section included the items about the motivations why women entrepreneurs start a business, the difficulties they face when starting their businesses, and where they want to see their businesses in the future.

RESEARCH FINDINGS

Profile of the Women Entrepreneurs

The demographic characteristics of women entrepreneurs are presented in Table 2. According to the table, the mean age of women entrepreneurs is 38. Of the 119 women, 67% has a university degree, followed by post-graduate degree (17%) and high school (16%). Regarding marital status, 85 women are married, 28 of them single and the rest are divorced or widowed. The majority of women entrepreneurs have either 2 children (55%) or 1 (37%) child.

70% of the women entrepreneurs operate in the service sector (health, consulting, education, etc.) while the others (30%) are operating in the manufacturing sector (agriculture, construction materials, textile, etc.). 63% of the women established their businesses on their own, while the rest with partners or took over from someone. The enterprises have an average size of 9 employees and average age of 8 years. 15% of women entrepreneurs have previous entrepreneurial experience. In terms of financing options in the startup phase, 45% of the participants used their own savings when starting their own business, and 33% received support from their families. It is presumed that the remaining individuals obtained capital from institutional mechanisms mostly from banks.

Motivations, Problems, and Future Needs of Women Entrepreneurs

Motivational factors to become entrepreneurs and start a business were asked under 3 headings: economic, psychological and social. According to the Table 3, *gaining economic independence* (57%) is the most stated factor among the economic factors which is followed by the *desire to have a better life* and *create employment* factors. Out of 7 psychological factors, the factors that women entrepreneurs found most important were the factors of *working without depending on someone else* (58%), *doing the job I wanted which is well suited to my abilities* (54%) and *realizing my ideal* (53%). Among the social factors, the most influential factors are the *support of my family* (37%) and the *effect of the education I received* (36%). The factors that motivate women to become entrepreneurs constitute a complex system of factors that interact with each other. In assessing what is the most important thing that motivates women to become an entrepreneur, it could be argued that it is more a combination of pull and push factors in such a way that women are "pulled" than "pushed" to create their business. In particular, it has been observed that the importance of psychological factors is relatively greater than economic and social factors.

Another aim of the study is to identify the problems that women entrepreneurs face while establishing their businesses. As seen in Table 4, the most emphasized problems are *obtaining capital* (52%), *failing to establish the right business contacts* (36%) and *lack of financial support channels* (30%). Meanwhile, nineteen participants stated that they did not experience any problems in the process of establishing a business.

With respect to support mechanisms needed, responses showed that the majority of women entrepreneurs need support in *marketing and branding* (57%). Apart from that, it is seen that a significant number of women entrepreneurs emphasized the

Table 2. Demographic characteristics of women entrepreneurs and their firms

Demographics	Frequency	(%)
Age(years)		
< 20	0	-
20-29	19	16
30-39	55	47
40-49	35	29
>50	10	8
Education level		
High school	19	16
Bachelor	80	67
Graduate degree	20	17
Marital Status		
Married	85	71
Single	28	24
Divorced/widow	6	5
Number of children		
None	5	4
1	44	37
2	65	55
3	5	4
>3	0	-
Age of venture		
<5	49	42
5-10	30	25
11-20	23	19
>20	17	14

need for *improvement opportunities in terms of managerial skills* (42%), *financial literacy* (42%) and *personal development* (40%) (Table 5).

As a final question, women entrepreneurs were asked where and how they see their business 10 years later? This was an open ended question. The majority of the participants stated their expectations for a market growth, having branch offices and institualization. However, there is also a small group of participants who wish that their current activities and earnings will remain the same due to the unfavorable conditions in the economy.

Table 3. Motivators for entrepreneurship

Motivators	Frequency	%
Economic		
Gaining economic independence	68	57
Having a better life	59	49
The desire to create employment	39	30
Meeting family needs	33	27
Seeing a business opportunity with commercial potential	24	20
Doing my profession	20	16
Having economic resources	20	15
Contribution to the national economy	15	12
Taking advantage of entrepreneurship support	9	7
Psychological		
Working without being dependent on someone else	70	58
Doing the job I want that suites my abilities	65	54
Realizing an ideal	64	53
Self actualization	52	43
Personal responsibility and willingness to take initiative	56	47
Gaining social status and respectability	40	33
The desire to bring solutions to the problems seen	39	32
Social		
Support and encouragement of the family	45	37
The effect of the education	43	36
Being from a family with entrepreneurial experience	36	30
Support and encouragement of friends	21	17
The impact of the environment	15	12
Being influenced by successful entrepreneurs in the media	10	8
Guidance of career counseling institutions	4	3

DISCUSSION

This study is a followup study to analyze the current situation of women entrepreneurs in Turkey. Its aim is to identify the basic characteristics, motivations, problems and areas that women entrepreneurs need support. The study was conducted with women entrepreneurs who are active in various NGOs to develop women entrepreneurship in Antalya region.

Table 4. Problems of women entrepreneurs

Problems	Frequency	%
Obtaning capital	63	52
Failing to make right business contacts	44	36
Lack of financial support channels	36	30
Work-family imbalance	32	26
Lack of mentors	25	21
Gender discrimination	22	18
Lack of managerial skills	19	15
Lack of entrepreneurial skills	17	14
Negative attitude of surroundings	16	13
Lack of knowledge and experience	13	10
Lack of foreign languages and intercultural skills	5	4

The results on the age of women entrepreneurs show that their average age is 38, and almost half of the participants are in their 30s. The majority of women entrepreneurs' firms are young and small sized enterprises. These findings are consistent with the results of previous studies (Çakıcı, 2006; Cebeci, 2015; Sallan Gül and Altındal, 2016). It has been confirmed once again that women in the country step into entrepreneurship mostly in their middle age. Likewise, this study shows that as the level of education increases, the tendency of women to become entrepreneurs also increases. Therefore, it can be said that higher education reduces gender gap in entrepreneurship in Turkey (Ökten, 2015). In addition, as women's access to educational opportunities increases, women's place in society becomes

Table 5. Areas Support Needed

Areas	Frequency	%
Marketing and branding	69	57
Managerial skills	51	42
Financial literacy	50	42
Personal development	48	40
Mentoring	44	36
Professional support center in the region	23	19
Design and development	20	16
Strategic development	20	16

stronger and social pressure on women decreases. It points to the need for policies to support higher education attainment for women.

It is seen that women entrepreneurs generally carry out entrepreneurial activities in the service and trade sectors which supports previous findings (Sallan Gül and Altındal, 2016). In manufacturing sectors, women entrepreneurs are in the minority, as it is difficult to maintain family related social roles in these sectors. Other factors that make manufacturing sectors less appealing to women are high level of barriers to entry to the market and higher demands for experience, knowledge and capital. In addition, traditionally industrial and engineering jobs in Turkey are known as men's jobs. For this reason, these sectors are found to be dominated by men (Maden, 2015).

Among the economic motivations that influence women's decision to become entrepreneurs, it is seen that economic independence and the desire to build a better life are mentioned by half of the participants. Again, a significant part of women entrepreneurs have emphasized working without being dependent on someone else, doing a job that suits their abilities, and realizing their ideal as psychological factors. Both the economic and psychological motivations can be classified as the "pull factors" that attract women to entrepreneurship. Moreover, psychological factors seem to have had more impact on the decision of women entrepreneurs compared to economic factors. Although family support and education seem to be effective among the social factors, it has been determined that the social motivations are not as effective as psychological and economic motivations. In previous studies, it was shown that factors such as desire for independence, self-actualization, achievement, being productive, having one's own business affect the decision of Turkish women entrepreneurs to become entrepreneurs (Hisrich and Öztürk, 1999; Maden, 2015; Tüzün and Takay, 2017). In sum, it can be said that entrepreneurship is not the result of a necessity for urban women anymore. It has increasingly become focused on taking advantage of individual preferences and opportunities.

Women entrepreneurs in Turkey face multidimensional problems. Obtaining capital seems to be the most common problem. In addition, lack of financial support channels is one of the most mentioned problems. The existence of financial barriers is a common finding in all studies conducted on women entrepreneurs (Hisrich and Öztürk, 199; Ufuk and Özgen, 2001; Maden, 2015). The findings of this study also point to the persistence of this problem. Women benefit more from their own savings and the savings of their spouses and families than from institutional support mechanisms especially in the startup phase. Moreover, women entrepreneurs are discriminated against when trying to secure loans or credit for their businesses, and still face barriers based on gender stereotypes which indicate gender discrimination barriers.

It is understood that women entrepreneurs have also problems in accessing the right connections that they will benefit from. Empirical studies have revealed the importance of social networks in establishing and growing new businesses (Atsan, 2019). Social networks allow entrepreneurship opportunities to be seen and facilitate access to resources such as physical assets, information, advice, implicit knowledge, especially capital and financial resources. The greatest strength of social networks in being successful is that, they provide resources more cheaply than from markets and secure resources such as reputation and customer connections that are impossible to find in markets (Witt, 2004). Thus, personal networks are the most valuable asset of an enterprise (Johannisson, 2000). However, in Panda's (2018) study, it was pointed out that women experience stress in managing their home and work lives together, and therefore they cannot allocate time for work-related activities such as networking and mentoring. In fact, there is a widely accepted belief that women are generally better than men at developing and maintaining relationships. But as found in this study, many women seem unable to transfer those skills into the business life.

Some other problems women entrepreneurs encounter are socio-cultural issues embedded in the society. A significant part of the participants talked about the role dilemma between their private and business life. Entrepreneurial women have difficulties in balancing work and family responsibilities due to their traditional social roles. In previous qualitative studies, it was found that being an entrepreneur brought women to a better level in social, personal and economic terms, but negatively affected their family life (Maden, 2015; Tüzün & Takay, 2017). Being an entrepreneur does not change women's social responsibilities, it even increases their burden twice (Ufuk and Özgen, 2001). As Ahl (2006) points out, it is impossible for a woman to take on both household and work responsibilities together and to compete on equal terms in the same field of work. This claim of double responsibility is definitely confirmed for women in Turkey. It has become an endemic social and cultural problem (Seçkin Halaç and Seçkin Çelik, 2019); it creates work-family balance barrier for women entrepreneurs.

On the other hand, in the ranking of areas where women entrepreneurs think they need support, more than half of the participants stated that they need support in marketing and branding. It is included in the previous study findings that women do not have sufficient knowledge about modern marketing methods such as using technological tools and e-commerce (Sallan Gül and Altındal, 2016). However, for the continuity of the enterprises, it is necessary to successfully carry out marketing activities. Thanks to branding efforts, it becomes easier for companies to compete with their competitors and long-term success can be achieved by achieving differentiation. In order to survive in today's intense competitive context, entrepreneurs who want to brand themselves need to carry out this process strategically.

Developing managerial skills and the level of financial literacy are other important areas of support that women entrepreneurs find important. The success of women in entrepreneurship is enhanced by managerial skills. In addition, there is a relationship between managerial competency level and perception of financial and bureaucratic differences. Their relationship could be explained by the fact that women with greater managerial skills have much more administrative savy and in general a better awareness of the problems faced when starting up a company (Huarng et al., 2012). Thus, acquiring managerial skills seems to be important for entrepreneurial success.

The contribution of this study to the relevant literature emerge in multiple ways. First, by adding new contextual information to the existing domestic studies, evidence has been produced for the generalizability of some of the findings and some of the results have been opened to be tested by further studies. Secondly, by producing quantitative results from a developing country, contributions were made to the international literature. Thirdly, a framework has been provided that will benefit policymakers in producing policies for women entrepreneurs and practitioners in evaluating their entrepreneurship profiles as well.

LIMITATIONS AND FUTURE RESEARCH DIRECTIONS

As with any research, this study also has some limitations. First, urban women entrepreneurs who have attained a certain level of education and have a high awareness of entrepreneurship and business development participated in the study. However, not all women entrepreneurs in Turkey conform to this profile (see Sefer, 2020). Therefore, in future studies, comparative studies are needed for women with different backgrounds, lifestyles and sectors. Especially comparisons between rural and urban women entrepreneurs will provide valuable insights. Secondly, although our study was conducted in one of the largest cities in Turkey, the manufacturing industry is not very developed in Antalya. Instead tourism and agriculture sectors are strong in the city. Therefore, the service sector has created a more dominant picture in the sectoral distribution of women entrepreneurs. An important issue for future research is the use of qualitative and innovative methods such as in-depth interviews, life history, discourse analysis, and case studies. This can strengthen the findings by bringing methodological richness. In the study, women entrepreneurs were considered as an independent construct and the comparison of male-female entrepreneurs was avoided as much as possible. Assuming that women entrepreneurship has its own patterns, not a counterpart of male entrepreneurship, will facilitate the development of theoretical models specific to women entrepreneurship.

It is to say that research on women entrepreneurship is also increasing regularly in Turkish literature. It is clear that this academic interest is a parallel development with the increase in the number of women entrepreneurs in the economic system. However, the expansion of the range of topics on which the studies are focused, as well as the use of multidisciplinary approaches, will make it easier to present a wide-ranging picture of women's entrepreneurship. In addition, there is no doubt that the effects of the pandemic have deeply affected the business lives of women entrepreneurs (Manolova, 2020). Pandemic changed and transformed the needs of women entrepreneurs. Therefore, pandemic-oriented local research is also needed to evaluate recent dynamics.

REFERENCES

Ahl, H. (2006). Why research on women entrepreneurs needs new directions. *Entrepreneurship Theory and Practice*, *30*(September), 595–621. doi:10.1111/j.1540-6520.2006.00138.x

Arat, N. (1995). *Turkiye'de Kadın Olgusu*. Say Yayınları.

Arthur, S. J., Hisrich, R. D., & Cabrera, A. (2012). The importance of education in the entrepreneurial process: A world view. *Journal of Small Business and Enterprise Development*, *19*(3), 500–514. doi:10.1108/14626001211250180

Atsan, N. (2019). Utilizing Social Networks in Social Entrepreneurship. In N. Iyigun (Ed.), *Creating Business Value and Competitive Advantage With Social Entrepreneurship* (pp. 232–250). IGI Global. doi:10.4018/978-1-5225-5687-9.ch011

Aycan, Z. (2004). Key Success Factors for Women in Management in Turkey. *Applied Psychology*, *53*(3), 453–477. doi:10.1111/j.1464-0597.2004.00180.x

Bedük, A. (2005). Türkiye'de Çalışan Kadın ve Kadın Girişimciliği. *Elektronik Sosyal Bilimler Dergisi*, *3*(12), 106–117.

Bhardwaj, R. B. (2014). Impact of education and training on performance of women entrepreneurs: A study in emerging market context. *Journal of Entrepreneurship in Emerging Economies*, *6*(1), 38–52. doi:10.1108/JEEE-05-2013-0014

Boudet, A. M. M., & Agar, M. (2014). *Female Entrepreneurship in Turkey*. The World Bank. Retrieved from https://betam.bahcesehir.edu.tr/wp-content/uploads/2014/06/Female-Entrepreneurship-in-Turkey1.pdf

British Council. Turkey/ (2019). *The State of Social Enterprise in Turkey*. Available at: https: //britishcouncil.org.tr/programmes/education/social-enterprise-research

Buttner, H., & Moore, D. P. (1997). Women's Organizational Exodus to Entrepreneurship: Self Reported Motivations and Correlations with Success. *Journal of Small Business Management*, *35*(1), 34–46.

Çakıcı, A. (2006). Mersin'deki kadın girişimcilerin iş yaşamını etkileyen faktörler. *Dokuz Eylül Üniversitesi Sosyal Bilimler Enstitüsü Dergisi*, *8*(4), 54–78.

Cebeci, T. (2015). *Performance of Female Employers in Turkey*. The World Bank Report. Retrieved from https://kadininstatusu.aile.gov.tr/data/54296a4b369dc32358ee2c3d/4.pdf

Çetindamar, D. (2005). Policy Issues for Turkish Entrepreneurs. *International Journal of Entrepreneurship and Innovation Management*, *5*(314), 187–205. doi:10.1504/IJEIM.2005.006525

Cromie, S. (1987). Motivations of aspiring male and female entrepreneurs. *Journal of Organizational Behavior*, *8*(3), 251–261. doi:10.1002/job.4030080306

Ecevit, Y. (1993). Kadın Girişimciliğinin Yaygınlaştırılmasına Yönelik Bir Model Önerisi, Der. A. Altınel, Kadını Girişimciliğe Özendirme ve Destekleme Paneli: Bildiriler ve Tartışmalar. *KSSGM, Ankara*, *74*, 15–34.

Ecevit, Y. (2007). *A critical approach to women's entrepreneurship in Turkey*. International Labour Office.

Ecevit, Y., & Yüksel-Kaptanoğlu, İ. (2015). *Kadın Girişimciler Araştırması*. Retrieved from www.garanti.com.tr./.../us201_garanti_kadin_girisimciler_rapor_201506

EDGE Project. (2018). *United Nations, Department of Economic and Social Affairs, Statistics Division Technical Report on Measuring Entrepreneurship: Lessons Learned from the EDGE Project*. United Nations.

Fis, A. M., Ozturkcan, S., & Gur, F. (2019). Being a Woman Entrepreneur in Turkey: Life Role Expectations and Entrepreneurial Self-Efficacy. *SAGE Open*, *9*(April). Advance online publication. doi:10.1177/2158244019846192

Ganesan, R., Dilbagh, K., & Maheshwari, R. C. (2002). Women Entrepreneurs: Problems and Prospects. *The Journal of Entrepreneurship*, *11*(75), 75–93. doi:10.1177/097135570201100105

GEDI. (2014). *Country Excepts Turkey*. http://cepp.gmu.edu/wpcontent/uploads/2012/02/Turkey_ 2014.pdf

GEM Report. (2018/2019). Retrieved from https://www.gemconsortium.org/report/gem-2018-2019-global-report

Hisrich, R., & Öztürk, S. A. (1999). Women Entrepreneurs in a Developing Economy. *Journal of Management Development*, *18*(2), 347–364. doi:10.1108/02621719910257639

Huarng, K. H., Mas-Tur, A., & Hui-Kuang Yu, T. (2012). Factors affecting the success of women entrepreneurs. *The International Entrepreneurship and Management Journal, 8*(4), 487–497. doi:10.100711365-012-0233-4

Johannisson, B. (2000). Networking and entrepreneurial growth. In D. L. Sexton & H. Landström (Eds.), *The Blackwell Handbook of Entrepreneurship* (pp. 368–386). Blackwell Publishers.

Karadeniz, E. (2010). *Entrepreneurship in Turkey 2010*. The Global Entrepreneurship Monitor (GEM). Retrieved from https://mobil.tobb.org.tr/HaberResimleri/724-8.pdf

Karadeniz, O., & Yılmaz, H.H. (2017). *Turkonfed İş Dunyasında Kadın Raporu*. Academic Press.

Kibler, E., Kautonen, T., & Fink, M. (2014). Regional social legitimacy of entrepreneurship: Implications for entrepreneurial intention and start-up behaviour. *Regional Studies, 48*(6), 995–1015. doi:10.1080/00343404.2013.851373

Kim, P. H., Aldrich, H. E., & Keister, L. A. (2006). Access (Not) Denied: The Impact of Financial, Human, and Cultural Capital on Entrepreneurial Entry in the United States. *Small Business Economics, 27*(1), 5–22. doi:10.100711187-006-0007-x

Maden, C. (2015). A gendered lens on entreprenership: Women entrepreneurship in Turkey. *Gender in Management, 30*(4), 312–331. doi:10.1108/GM-11-2013-0131

Manolova, T. S., Brush, C. G., Edelman, L. F., & Elam, A. (2020). Pivoting to stay the course: How women entrepreneurs take advantage of opportunities created by the COVID-19 pandemic. *International Small Business Journal: Researching Entrepreneurship, 38*(6), 481–491. doi:10.1177/0266242620949136

Minniti, M. (2010). Female Entrepreneurship and Economic Activity. *European Journal of Development Research, 22*(3), 294–312. doi:10.1057/ejdr.2010.18

Minniti, M., & Naude, W. (2010). What Do We Know about the Patterns and Determinants of Female Entrepreneurship across Countries? *European Journal of Development Research, 22*(3), 277–293. doi:10.1057/ejdr.2010.17

Ökten, Ç. (2015). *Female Entrepreneurship in Turkey: patterns, Characteristics and Trends*. The World Bank Report, 102013-TR, 1-36. Retrieved from https://openknowledge.worldbank.org/handle/10986/25410

Orhan, M., & Scott, D. (2001). Why Women Enter into Entrepreneurship: An Explanatory Model. *Women in Management Review, 16*(5), 232–247. doi:10.1108/09649420110395719

Özdemir, A. (2010). Potansiyel Girişimci Olan Kadınların Motivasyon Faktörleri ve Eskişehir'de Bir Araştırma. *Ege Akademik Bakış*, *10*(1), 117–139. doi:10.21121/eab.2010119651

Panda, S. (2018). Constraints faced by women entrepreneurs in developing countries: Review and ranking. *Gender in Management*, *33*(4), 315–331. doi:10.1108/GM-01-2017-0003

Poggesi, S., Mari, M., & De Vita, L. (2016). What's new in female entrepreneurship research? Answers from the literature. *The International Entrepreneurship and Management Journal*, *12*(3), 735–764. doi:10.100711365-015-0364-5

Reynolds, P. D., Bygrave, W. D., Autio, E., Cox, L. W., & Hay, M. (2002). *Global Entrepreneurship Monitor, 2002 Executive Report*. Babson College, London Business School and Kauffman Foundation.

Sallan Gül, S., & Altındal, Y. (2016). The Adventure of Woman Enterpreneurship in Turkey: Is Succes Possible? *Süleyman Demirel Üniversitesi İktisadi ve İdari Bilimler Fakültesi Dergisi*, *21*(4), 1361–1377.

Seckin Halac, D., & Seckin Celik, T. (2019). A Qualitative Look into Gendered Entrepreneurship in Turkey. *Istanbul Business Research*, *47*(2), 105–123.

Sefer, B. K. (2020). A gender- and class-sensitive explanatory model for rural women entrepreneurship in Turkey. *International Journal of Gender and Entrepreneurship*, *12*(2), 191–210. doi:10.1108/IJGE-07-2019-0113

Startups.watch. (2019). *Reports*. Retrieved from https://startups.watch/reports?page=5&view_mode=list

Turkey Entrepreneurship Strategy and Action Plan. (2015-2018). Retrieved from http://www.sp.gov.tr/tr/temelbelge/s/122/Turkiye+Girisimcilik+Stratejisi+ve+Eylem+Plani+_2015-2018

TURKSTAT. (n.d.). *2000, 2007, 2017, 2019, 2020 Labor Force Survey Results*. Author.

Tüzün, I. K., & Takay, A. B. (2017). Patterns of female entrepreneurial activities in Turkey. *Gender in Management*, *32*(3), 166–182. doi:10.1108/GM-05-2016-0102

Ufuk, H., & Özgen, Ö. (2001). Interaction Between the Business and Family Lives of Women Entrepreneurs in Turkey. *Journal of Business Ethics*, *31*(2), 95–106. doi:10.1023/A:1010712023858

Verheul, I., Van Stel, A., & Thurik, R. (2006). Explaining female and male entrepreneurship at the country level. *Entrepreneurship and Regional Development, 18*(2), 151–183. doi:10.1080/08985620500532053

Witt, P. (2004). Entrepreneurs' networks and the success of start-ups. *Entrepreneurship and Regional Development, 16*(5), 391–412. doi:10.1080/0898562042000188423

Yadav, V., & Unni, J. (2016). Women entrepreneurship: A research review and future directions. *Journal of Global Entrepreneurship Research, 6*(12), 1–18. doi:10.118640497-016-0055-x

Yetim, N. (2002). Sosyal Sermaye Olarak Kadın Girişimciler: Mersin Örneği. *Ege Akademik Bakış, 2*(2), 79–92.

ADDITIONAL READING

Amit, R., & Muller, E. (1995). "Push" and "Pull" Entrepreneurship. *Journal of Small Business and Entrepreneurship, 12*(4), 64–80. doi:10.1080/08276331.1995.10600505

Cardella, G. M., Hernández-Sánchez, B. R., & Sánchez-García, J. C. (2020). Women Entrepreneurship: A Systematic Review to Outline the Boundaries of Scientific Literature. *Frontiers in Psychology, 11*, 1557–1774. doi:10.3389/fpsyg.2020.01557 PMID:32765357

De Vita, L., Mari, M., & Poggesi, S. (2014). Women entrepreneurs in and from developing countries: Evidences from the literature. *European Management Journal, 32*(3), 451–460. doi:10.1016/j.emj.2013.07.009

Gartner, W. (1985). A conceptual framework for describing the phenomenon of new venture creation. *Academy of Management Review, 10*(4), 696–706. doi:10.5465/amr.1985.4279094

Gupta, V. K., Turban, D. B. S., Wasti, S. A., & Sikdar, A. (2009). The role of gender stereotypes in perceptions of entrepreneurs and intentions to become an entrepreneur. *Entrepreneurship Theory and Practice, 33*(2), 397–417. doi:10.1111/j.1540-6520.2009.00296.x

Poggesi, S., Mari, M., & De Vita, L. (2016). What's new in female entrepreneurship research? Answers from the literature. *The International Entrepreneurship and Management Journal, 12*(3), 735–764. doi:10.100711365-015-0364-5

KEY TERMS AND DEFINITIONS

Pull Factors: Factors that draw people to start businesses such as seeing an opportunity or desire to become independent.

Push Factors: Factors that force people to start businesses such as unemployment or dissatisfaction.

Social Network: Network of resources or social relationships surrounding individuals, groups, and organizations and the qualities of the connections in these networks.

Women Entrepreneurship: Entrepreneurial process where women create and lead businesses.

Chapter 9
Exploring the Social Intelligence Impact on Job Engagement:
A Research Study on Generation X Women Entrepreneurs at TR62 Region

Ibrahim Inan
https://orcid.org/0000-0003-3986-2890
Cukurova University, Turkey

ABSTRACT

Social intelligence has been recognized as a remarkable factor affecting individuals' success and performance on the job with intent engagement. This research explores the social intelligence's impact on job engagement of Generation X women entrepreneurs who operate in the TR62 region, covering Adana and Mersin provinces. Business scholars and industry leaders have widely recognized the importance of women's entrepreneurship. Thus, research aimed to shed light on women entrepreneurship in the Turkish business ecosystem. Social intelligence can have a catalyst role on job engagement to advance entrepreneurship skills. As a part of social intelligence, there was a moderate relationship between the social information process and social awareness. Social intelligence had a moderate correlation with emotional and cognitive job engagement. Also, there was a moderate relationship between social information processing and physical job engagement being collaborated with emotional job engagement on account of Generation X women entrepreneurs' active role in a social and business environments.

DOI: 10.4018/978-1-7998-8742-3.ch009

INTRODUCTION

The rapid changes in technology, economy, and the new opportunities they offer have shaped human desires & needs, their way of life, and personal traits (O'Halloran, 2015). When generations are examined, it remains obvious how they have evolved and how those evolutions are reflected within their businesses (Ensari, 2017). Generation X women (born between 1965-1980), who show great progress especially in recent years in Europe and America, high-value training and autonomy (Lub, et al., 2016) make people observe their importance in business life. Especially in the last decade, women entrepreneurs initiate their own businesses by using their personal savings, family supports, or getting into debt as having the desire to use innovative skills, run their own businesses, and obtain flexible working hours (Rahim et al., & Sung, 2017). The main purpose of why Generation X is preferred in this study is that Generation X individuals are looking for better career opportunities, are sensitive to social problems, and have high work motivations (Aydın & Başol, 2014), and perceiving digital tools for social and commercial purposes (Levickaite, 2010). Generation X women have embraced an active role in both social and business life as they have been pursuing an intention to expand knowledge and practices through business models (Berkup, 2014). It is succinctly documented that women entrepreneurs contribute exponential growth to the economic wealth of states (Ambepitiya, 2016). Therefore, the conceptual framework of this study entails the definition and description of entrepreneurship in detail to comprehend the abilities of Generation X women in business life, with focus on factors such as social intelligence and job engagement that empower entrepreneurship skills. Recent research has proven that entrepreneurial behavior is mostly emphasized considering the individuals' intentions (Esfandiar et al., 2019). Although success is related to general environment of the individual, the entrepreneurial performance depends on the characteristics of each entrepreneur (Chavez, 2016). Entrepreneurship is also related to the individual's ability to use their business knowledge and skills to meet the requirements of the business development process and achieve creative solutions for problems (Aaboen et al., 2017). On the other hand, social intelligence is a mechanism for entrepreneurs who require effective communication among team members.

Women's extensive participation in business life has to trigger untapped potential (Estrin et al., 2019). Women have been working hard to advance their living standards and support their family members financially (Neneh, 2017). It is necessary to determine which mechanisms prevent Generation X women from handling entrepreneurship activities in developing economies (Rashid & Ratten, 2020). Especially in fragile economies (e.g., Brazil, Turkey, Greece, and Egypt), it is essential to remember that encouraging women's entrepreneurial activities is the key to growing the economy and ensuring society's wealth (Marques et al., 2021).

In this context, it can be necessary to designate policies and programs that support women entrepreneurs and lead women to acknowledge their power to motivate their potential in economic and social life (Yenilmez, 2018). Generation X women entrepreneurs have a different perspective than other generations in many areas due to the social relationships, in balancing personal and work-life factors, which is becoming a priority mainly for working women (Cabrera et al., 2019).

Generation X women entrepreneurs are a social entity that leads us to investigate the compatibility between their social intelligence and job engagement. The research takes place around issues such as improving Generation X women entrepreneurs' status in society and improving their economic success. Furthermore, Generation X women's entrepreneurship is important in regional development. This research will help Generation X women entrepreneurs make significant decisions as they move forward to improve their efforts by understanding how to succeed in business. With respect to entrepreneurship in all aspects of business life, it is essential to explore how social intelligence impacts Generation X women's job engagement when they focus on new potential business ideas. The search fills a remarkable gap in the literature by systematically reviewing the extant literature on women entrepreneurship in Turkey. This research will also explore other areas essential to the overall topic of Generation X women entrepreneurs for the future of business growth.

THEORETICAL BACKGROUND

Entrepreneurship is the source of economic and social indicators that many states aim to reinforce critical drivers to enhance prosperity through sustainable growth, social development, and social welfare (Crecente-Romero et al., 2016). Entrepreneurship is considered an essential factor that provides economic growth as it leads to increased income locally & internationally and facilitates economic progression (Du & O'Connor, 2018). Entrepreneurship emphasizes growing income sizes, advancing the living standards of the people and, economic freedom (Cebula et al., 2016). Moreover, collaboration with the new technological improvements accelerates production, health infrastructure, and safety environment in developing and developed countries (Tosunoğlu, 2014). Entrepreneurship is a phenomenon formed by a combination of socioeconomic (Giacomin et al., & Lohest, 2017), cultural-political factors in which other external-environmental conditions reveal the individual characteristics and potential of the entrepreneur (Gómez-Gras et al., 2010). Entrepreneurship can be defined as continuous monitoring and evaluation of opportunities through creative activities in an uncertain environment with limited resources (Nga & Shamuganathan, 2010).

Although the success of entrepreneurship depends on many factors, the essential determinant is the individuals themselves and their skills required for various stages (Chatterjee et al., & Srivastava, 2019). An entrepreneur must know their strengths & weaknesses because entrepreneurship is the ability to build a resourceful team (Olakitan & Ayobami, 2011). Entrepreneurs can have a creative personality, and proactive personality that create new business opportunities (Hu et al., 2018). Entrepreneurs are people who evaluate opportunities, make great efforts to turn possibilities into benefits, take and manage risks well (Filion, 2021). Koh (1996) noted that the personality traits of entrepreneurs are people who need to succeed, take risks, have tolerance for uncertainty, have self-confidence, and are innovative (Başar et al., 2013). Being proactive, business skills, self-sufficient, tolerant, independent, and socially competent can be added to these characteristics (Luca & Robu, 2016).

As women entrepreneurship is one of the crucial factors of economic growth of a country, it has attracted the attention of scholars (Aaboen et al., 2017). Entrepreneurship has developed rapidly since the 1980s (Jing et al., 2015). It has attracted women as much as men and turned women into essential elements of business life in this process (Truman, 2016). Studies on women entrepreneurship witnessed rapid growth over the past 30 years. However, the field is still in its initial phase, with many journal articles, research projects, and books being published on women entrepreneurs (Yadav & Unni, 2016).

The report "The Missing Entrepreneurs 2017: Policies for Inclusive Entrepreneurship" of the "Organisation for Economic Co-operation and Development" (OECD) indicates that in 2016 men were on average 1.7 times more likely to be self-employed than women. Moreover, self-employed women tend to run smaller businesses than men (Halabisky, 2017). However, as Carter & Shaw (2006) pointed out, entrepreneurship research focuses on how gender makes a difference, rather than looking at whether or not gender makes a difference. Despite the growing interest in the issue and the radical acceleration of the number of women entrepreneurs in recent years (Sarfaraz et al., 2014), a male-centric business environment has dominated the globe for many years (Goffee & Scase, 2015). However, research into female entrepreneurs reveals that entrepreneurial activities can be based on families (Bettinelli et al., 2014). In OECD (Organisation for Economic Co-operation and Development) economies, one in ten employed women is self-employed. During the past ten years, however, the gap between men's and women's self-employment rates has decreased in almost every country, particularly in Iceland, New Zealand, and Turkey (OECD, 2017). More Turkish women are involved in necessity-based entrepreneurship rather than opportunity-based entrepreneurship (Tuzun & Takay, 2017). The potential for women's entrepreneurship has just begun to be realize in Turkey (Maden, 2015). "Turkish Industry and Business Association" (TUSİAD) as an NGO has been influential in supporting, popularizing, and spreading the number of women entrepreneurs in Turkey (Alkan, 2019). The first studies on women entrepreneurs in Turkey were conducted in the 1990s (Maden, 2015).

According to Turkish Statistical Institute Labour Force (TUIK, 2019), 31.075.000 women are in the range of working age. Only 9 million of them can work in Turkey, which means the women's participation in employment remains low (28.9%). According to Startup Heatmap's latest research on Women Entrepreneurs in Europe (Startup Heatmap Europe, 2020), the rate of female entrepreneurs is around 8% which is relatively low in our country, compared to Europe (15.5%). The importance of female entrepreneurship for economic development is widely recognized (TerjeSen, 2016). There is a positive impact of female entrepreneurs on economic growth and development and sustainable & durable peace as long as entrepreneurship is considered one of the key drivers of economic development (Okeke-Uzodike et al., 2018). Turkey has a noticeable gender gap among efficiency-driven economies, which presents difficulties for women when starting and continuing their business (Tuzun & Takay, 2017). In Turkey, female entrepreneurs cope with many difficulties in starting up and maintaining their businesses (Hisrich & Öztürk, 1999). An entrepreneurial role tends to be perceived as stereotypically masculine in Turkish society, which causes women to suffer from both open and hidden discrimination. (Panda, 2018). The results have revealed significant similarities among Turkish women entrepreneurs concerning their personality traits or characteristics (Özsungur, 2019). In Turkey, successful women entrepreneurs were described as being persistent and determined, patient, mentally strong and visionary, and innovative (Maden, 2015). Developing countries have made several reforms to empower women economically (Buvinic & O'Donnell, 2016). However, women's participation in economic life is still not at the expected level in Turkey (İlkkaracan, 2012).

Today's workforce is categorized into five generations known as Traditionalists, Baby Boomers, Generation X, Generation Y, and Generation Z (Sainger, 2019). Because mainly the three generations (Baby Boomers, Generation X, and Y) are working together and considering their differences in today's business environment, it would be appropriate to give a little information about the basic characteristics of these groups. Baby Boomers (1946-1964) refer to individuals born during the population boom that occurred immediately following World War II. Baby boomers are also the first generation to regularly question authority in the workplace (Myers, 2020). Generation X (1965-1979) denotes technological developments in this period of economic straits. Whereas the workplace was no longer considered a second home, establishing a balance of business, private life became important, and skill development is important to this generation (Beutell & Wittig-Berman, 2008). Generation Y (1980-1999) is called in different ways: Millennial, Next Generation, Digital Generation, Echo Boomers, and Nexters (Morgan, 2011).

People belonging to Generation X are skilled and confident in their structures, workaholic, and have high egos. One of the reasons for this is that they grew up with less parental attention (Berkup, 2014). Generation X individuals are compelled to be alone, which facilitates obtaining great responsibility at early ages. In contrast, Baby Boomers (parents of Generation X) spent a greater majority of time outside on any given day (Bristow, 2015). Thus, responsibilities acquired by teen Generation X lead them to have skills that can be useful in business environments, including entrepreneurship adaptation and resilience (Scheef & Thielfoldt, 2004). Generation X is motivated by the challenges they face and the feedback they obtain from personal development programs and opportunities in business life (Berkup, 2014). Representatives of this generation have active role in social and business life today. One of the great advantages of Generation X is being open to change in business life (Berkup, 2014). Generation X is the first generation with a global perspective that thinks any place is accessible with the ability to be open to change and adapt quickly to new platforms (McHenry & Ash, 2013). The essential goal of Generation X, whose motto in their business is "living for work," is to develop their careers (Özcan & Bayarçelik, 2019).

Intelligence means acquiring the habits of basic knowledge in new situations (Breakspear, 2013). Intelligence is defined as the ability to explain the causes of observed events, actions, and attributes that interpret symbols to provide an understanding of relationships (Goldstein et al., 2015). According to Buzan (2002), social intelligence has eight important factors as following; (1) Perceiving the people' intentions and attitudes (accurately understand the verbal and nonverbal messages of the people whom one is in contact with) (2) Dynamic Communication (ability to listen effectively and react accordingly) (3) Social Integration (4) Ability to convince people to have an impact (5) Influencing how other people think (6) Ability to discuss, and solve social problems (7) Encouragement (influencing people) (8) Knowing how to act in different social fields (Dogan & Cetin, 2009). According to Thorndike, intelligence is social and mechanical, and abstract. Much research has been carried out for more than ten decades. However, the problems that were addressed in the research into social intelligence related to the definition of social intelligence. Thorndike (1920) stated that social intelligence is (1) the ability to understand and manage people and (2) the ability to act wisely in human relations. This definition has been expanded and developed in the years that have followed. Although researchers have put forward various definitions in different disciplines, according to Marlowe (1986), Social intelligence or social competence is the ability to understand feelings, thoughts, and behaviors. Social intelligence has distinctive and essential factors such as solving and discussing social problems, persuading people to make a positive impact, and knowing what to do when circumstances become clear (Bar-On, 2006). According to Walker & Foley (1973), social intelligence can be described as recognizing and managing people's behavior & attitudes by anticipating their feelings & thoughts and obtaining an accurate perception regarding their intentions, moods, and motivation.

With the increasing importance of positive psychology, which emphasizes the positive aspects of organizational arrangements, the number of studies on the concept of job engagement has increased in recent years (Attridge, 2009). Job engagement is currently attracting the attention of academics and practitioners and has itself become a topic (Christian et al., 2011). Studies on job engagement up to date have made efforts to unearth the main principles of job engagement (Gupta, 2015). To exemplify, (Schaufeli, 2013) notes that job resources appraised as motivators end in job engagement, where interested employees demonstrate favorable job attitudes, refer to positive mental health, and show better performance than those who are less interested and engaged. Kahn (1990) addresses and focuses on the engagement concept. Later Rich et al., (2010) articulate that the triggering factors of job engagement are value coherence, recognized organizational support, and core self-evaluation. As Kahn (1990) states, employees bring a wide range of cognitive, emotional, and physical energies to work roles that come together to discern the experience of being engaged. The investment of cognitive, affective, and behavioral energies is understood as an indicator of the individual performance representative of motivation (Shuck et al., 2014).

Job engagement is a significant term with a unique theoretical framework and definitional content (Rich et al., 2010). Job engagement is a complex form that is considered a positive factor that affects emotional motivation, which increases commitment to work and provides strong participation in work (Schaufeli & Bakker, 2010). Job engagement is not a substitute for organizational commitment or intellectual & social engagement (Schaufeli, 2013). However, scholars have contrary perspectives on the relationship between these two concepts. While some studies have examined job engagement as a driving component for ensuring organizational commitment, others have scrutinized job engagement as an outcome of the organizational commitment (Kim et al., & Lim, 2017). Job engagement increases positive emotions among employees which can be seen in productivity and proactive behaviors as well as improved job satisfaction (Bakker et al., 2011). Job engagement helps companies to survive in economic downswings (Schaufeli, 2018). Therefore, these Generation X entrepreneurs are supposed to prioritize certain principles, such as using a participatory approach and developing critical thinking skills to significantly contribute to their business setting. In this respect, job engagement has become a far more critical issue due to the active participation of Generation X women entrepreneurs in business life.

RESEARCH METHODOLOGY

This study was implemented to explore the relationship between social intelligence and job engagement levels of Generation X women entrepreneurs who have a considerable role in the Turkish entrepreneurship ecosystem. Turkey has several prominent trade zones that provide financial and non-financial opportunities and benefits to businesses and individuals (Sevil & Gültekin-Karakaş, 2017). The TR62, a term coined by the Turkish Republic, is a trade zone composed of Adana and Mersin provinces where a broad range of industries (e.g., agricultural, textile, automotive, chemical, packaging) have existed in global competition. Local associations regarding women's entrepreneurship can encourage and support entrepreneurs and candidate entrepreneurs by generating new ideas to manage and execute steps in a company. Additionally, these associations can provide some funds through angel investors, economic development agencies, and industry & business networks at local zones (Darmawan & Yeşilbaş, 2016). When considering the logistics centers, inter-connectivity with other trade zones, and plenty of raw materials that provide valuable opportunities for entrepreneurship, this study was held in the so-called TR62 region (a trade sub-region including Adana & Mersin cities), located in the southern part of Turkey.

The participants of the study were selected only from local entrepreneurship associations. The scales were composed with the contributions of the women members of GIŞKAD (Entrepreneurial Businesswomen Association) operating in Mersin city (71), and İŞKAD (Businesswomen Association) members (63), AGIAD (22) female members (Adana Young Businessmen Association), and CUGIAD (24) female members (Çukurova Young Businessmen Association) operating in Adana city. The scales were conducted online due to Covid-19.

The criteria for selecting the appropriate participants were year of birth (1965-1980), educational level, and the membership of the local entrepreneurship association. There were, randomly selected, 180 participants who were voluntarily involved in sharing coherence with the purpose of the research study. As part of quantitative research methodology, the conducted research study was designed regarding a correlation research model that investigates relationships between variables through statistics (Creswell & Creswell, 2017). In the following Figure 1, the research model aims to find possible correlations (dash lines) and regression (solid line) among variables which are described through hypothetical reasoning in the introduction section.

Social life includes establishing communication, interaction, and carrying out activities among people. In this respect, social life is a complex structure that covers different cases and issues based on the axis of human life. Awareness of the social life process requires analysing rich information in daily and business lives. Social information processing, a part of social intelligence, can help a person evaluate and analyse their social outcomes, evaluate and form expectations of others, and make decisions involving others (Silvera et al., 2001). X-generation women entrepreneurs can listen effectively to the people they communicate with, understand their attitude, be aware of their wishes, and the use of body language in communication gives them the ability to behave in accordance with their environmental conditions. Therefore, the generation X women entrepreneurs with social consciousness should also have high social information processing skills.

H1: Social Information Processing has a positive relationship with Social Awareness.

Figure 1. The research model
(Source: Author)

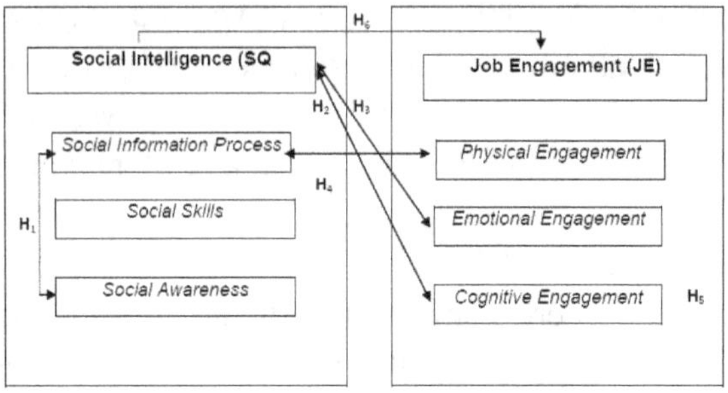

Social intelligence is the set of abilities and skills that people use to manage and maintain their social relationships (Lau, 2016). Social intelligence is an essential skill for comprehending what other people consider and perceive regarding their intentions, emotions, and feelings. In addition, many people with high social intelligence are more successful in challenging situations such as predicting what other people may do next and deciding how to act accordingly. Cognitive engagement refers to the individual's state of being healthy in terms of positive psychology, reflecting their energy to work and self-actualization (Leiter & Bakker, 2010). The brain manages different cognitive mechanisms such as learning, attention, memory, language, decision making and involves observing, analysing, assimilating, and processing messages from sources (perception, experience, beliefs) to turn them into information (Smith et al., 2020). The cognitive functions possess an observable role in these processes: perception, attention, memory, and reasoning that work together to incorporate new information and understanding of the world around them. Unless a social situation is adopted cognitively, it is not appropriate to talk about the effectiveness of social intelligence, as the sub-factors of social intelligence are a part of intelligence and lead people to think. Cognitive engagement means cooperation, joining a group, emotional support, interest, reliable collaboration. Thus, cognitive engagement has a positive effect on social intelligence for Generation X women entrepreneurs.

H2: Social Intelligence has a positive relationship with Cognitive Engagement.

Emotional engagement can be positive or negative. Positive emotional engagement such as enjoyment, gratitude, peace, interest, hope, inspiration, or negative emotional engagement such as loneliness, boredom, and sadness affect one's "Social Information Process," "Social Skills," and "Social Awareness" pain (Boniwell & Tunariu, 2019). People process positive social information from an optimistic perspective, while those who are depressed may focus on more undesired outcomes. When people are emotionally very comfortable, their social skills increase, and they communicate comfortably. Most likely, aggressive people cannot maintain their social relations well enough to create beneficial solutions for life problems. For this reason, when the level of the emotional engagement of generation X women entrepreneurs increases, social intelligence tends to be affected positively.

H3: Social Intelligence has a positive relationship with Emotional Engagement.

Businesswomen, who are assigned many responsibilities, do their jobs lovingly and willingly, which is related to the level of satisfaction that they get from their jobs. According to Macey & Schneider (2008), to understand the situation of job engagement, it is necessary to evaluate the work conditions and individual characteristics together and decisively examine the harmony between them. Physical engagement refers to the energy and mobility of the individuals while performing their job roles. Physical engagement examines whether people work in empathy and harmony with their colleagues, customers, and other business stakeholders in the work environment. People who are willing to listen and understand others, have a balanced ego and can develop empathy, may understand the emotional states of their stakeholders more easily, and realize their needs more quickly. Furthermore, management skills and previous work experiences can support their success. Thus, Generation X women entrepreneurs' ability to openly express their feelings and thoughts to their colleagues can relate to their social information processes.

H4: Social Information Processing has a positive relationship with Physical Engagement.

There is a direct and positive relationship between emotional engagement and cognitive engagement. Emotions and cognitive processes are connected. If a person is depressed or faced with anxiety, their cognitive processes do not work efficiently and become passive. In contrast, if cognitive processes are positive, job satisfaction and happiness increase. The positive relationship between emotional engagement and cognitive engagement supports the continuity of job engagement. Businesswomen expect to have a reward for their effort into fulfilling their job roles. It mainly depends on the right attitude, the proper behavior, and the positive relationship and healthy communication that they develop with their colleagues. The studies show that the high perception of job engagement has positive results for individuals and organizations (Hernandez & Guarana, 2018). In this context, the perception of psychological security, which expresses the emotion felt by individuals, and the compatibility of an individual's role and personal values motivate people (Brown & Leigh, 1996). Women entrepreneurs feel positive feelings towards their job when it covers a good working group, an efficient working environment and as long as their emotional and cognitive engagement are balanced.

H5: Emotional Engagement has a positive relationship with Cognitive Engagement.

Recently, Generation X women entrepreneurs have coped with social problems that mainly resulted from family relationships that may have an adverse impact on their business performance and job engagement levels. In particular, individuals possessing multiple responsibilities may influence their business performance at varying degrees when they are engaged in their jobs (Poggesi et al., 2019). Deficiencies in social relations that might decrease business performance often result in low job engagement levels. Therefore, social intelligence can positively affect the job engagement levels of Generation X women entrepreneurs.

H6: The degree of social intelligence has a positive effect on job engagement level.

In the light of assertions made by previous studies, research questions were hypothesized to investigate possible relationships among two mechanisms such as social intelligence and job engagement of Generation X women entrepreneurs, including sub-dimensions of each mechanism.

The Job Engagement Scale (JES) and Tromso Social Intelligence Scale (TSIS) were preferred to analyze Generation X women's remarks, perceptions, attitudes, and behaviors on the whole. The JES scale was developed by Rich (2006) and was composed of 18 items with a 5-point Likert type to observe job engagement levels of individuals through physical, emotional, and cognitive engagement factors in full work performance (Drake, 2012). The JES measures three factors: cognitive, physical, and emotional engagement (Rich et al., 2010; Shuck et al., 2014). Cognitive engagement measures the intensity of mental focus expressed toward positive organizational outcomes. Based on Kahn's (1990) conceptualization, cognitive engagement characterizes the direction of an employee's cognitive engagement, focus on work-related tasks, and concentration toward work. Emotional engagement describes an employee's intensity and willingness to invest emotionality toward positive organizational outcomes and demonstrates a deep, active, and emotional connection to the active working experience. Behavioral engagement represents a psychological state and is not yet an action-related attitude. Employees see themselves as more willing to work with high enthusiasm if they are behaviorally engaged.

The Tromso Social Intelligence Scale (TSIS), improved by Silvera et al., (2001) has been used to determine the levels of social intelligence. The TSIS is used in this study measures these three dimensions (Silvera et al., 2001): (1) Social Information Processing: includes competencies such as understanding the feelings and thoughts of the individual and other individuals, and understanding the desires and expectations of others in relationships. (2) Social Skills: related to the performance dimension of social intelligence. A person with a high level of social skills can easily be found in social environments, has no difficulty in getting along with other people, and easily adapts to social environments. (3) Social Awareness: describes the ability of an individual to behave in coherence with the social environment and conditions in which he or she resides. Individuals with high social awareness are very successful in displaying behaviors appropriate to the social environment in which they are located, giving appropriate responses to these behaviors, and giving feedback.

RESULTS

Before examining the scales used in the study, observing the demographic variables of Generation X Women Entrepreneurs can be helpful to have brief information about their educational levels, marital status, and age intervals. The age ranges of participants was in three groups. As shown below, 40 to 44 years, 44 to 49 years, and 50 to 54 years. Their educational levels differed in five distinct levels composed of high school (12%), pre-graduate (6%), bachelor's (47%), master's (28%), and Ph.D. degree (8%). Additionally, (57%) of participants were married, (24%) were single, and (19%) were divorced. Table 1, as follows, represents the demographic variables within three different sub-groups in frequency and percentage in total.

The research study was applied to use the JES and TSIS scales for determining the social intelligence and job engagement levels of Generation X women. Firstly, the internal validity of scales was verified, and descriptive statistics of variables were analyzed to decide which correlation and regression analysis can be used. As recorded in Table 2, the Cronbach's alpha values indicated that scales were responded to by the participants coherently. It could be said that answers did not lead to any misunderstandings among the participants. The Cronbach's alpha values ranged from .81 to .94, proving that the participants properly responded to scales and their sub-factors. On the other side, Skewness & Kurtosis values, which should be in an interval between -1.5 and +1.5, verified scales' normality and factors (Tabachnick & Fidel, 2007). Observations indicated that both the JES and TSIS scales and their factors had normality distribution. Besides, the mean value of each scale and its factor was above 4.00. The standard deviation value was in a range of 36 to 54, which showed that differentiation between the participants was not remarkably high. On the other side, factor analysis was applied to examine the factor structure of each scale depending on participants' responses. Each scale had three factors to observe the job engagement and social intelligence levels of the individuals. When factor analysis was implemented through AMOS 26 Software, results indicated that the JES (x2 / df: 2.44; CFI: .92; GFI: .88; NFI: .89; RMSEA: 0.046) and TSIS scale (x2 / df: 2.67; CFI: .91; GFI: .87; NFI: .85; RMSEA: 0.054), which included appropriate results for a good model-fit (Brown & Moore, 2012), were compatible with factor structure as claimed by Rich (2006) and Silvera et al., (2001).

Table 1. Demographic values of Generation X women entrepreneurs

Demographic Variables	Frequency	Percentage (%)
Age Intervals		
40-44 Years	126	70%
44-49 Years	16	9%
50-54 Years	38	21%
Educational Level		
High School Degree	22	12%
Pre-Graduate Degree	10	6%
Bachelor's Degree	84	47%
Master's Degree	50	28%
Ph.D.	14	8%
Marital Status		
Single	44	24%
Married	102	57%
Divorced	34	19%

Table 2. Descriptive statistics of scales and sub-factors

Scales & Sub-Factors	Mean	SD	Skewness	Kurtosis	Cronbach's Alpha
TSIS	4.19	.3673	-.167	-.685	.86
Social Information Processing	4.13	.4502	.063	-.956	.81
Social Skills	4.30	.5185	-.332	-.954	.83
Social Awareness	4.12	.4709	-.124	-.793	.84
JES	4.42	.4532	-.539	-.516	.93
Physical Engagement	4.38	.4998	-.497	-.457	.87
Emotional Engagement	4.51	.5468	-.766	-.621	.91
Cognitive Engagement	4.37	.5600	-.329	-1.071	.94

This research aims to find possible correlations and regression among variables placed in the hypothesis claimed by the researchers. Therefore, the correlation analysis was conducted to observe the significance of the relationship among the variables such as social information processing, social awareness, social intelligence, and emotional, cognitive, physical engagement as indicated Table 3. Furthermore, the regression analysis was used to observe the effect of social intelligence on participants' job engagement levels.

Table 3. Correlations between scales and sub-factors

Scales & Sub-Factors	1	2	3	4	5	6	7	8
TSIS (1)	-	.781	.749	.769	.578	.367	.514	.576
Social Information Processing (2)	.781	-	.357	.479	.448	.426	.300	.414
Social Skills (3)	.749	.357	-	.310	.479	.246	.445	.510
Social Awareness (4)	.769	.479	.310	-	.398	.180	.426	.390
JES (5)	.578	.448	.479	.398	-	.806	.839	.889
Physical Engagement (6)	.367	.426	.246	.180	.806	-	.474	.601
Emotional Engagement (7)	.514	.300	.445	.426	.839	.474	-	.638
Cognitive Engagement (8)	.576	.414	.510	.390	.889	.601	.638	-

Hence, the correlation between social information processing and social awareness was moderate and significant, enabling us to accept hypothesis 1 (r: .479; p<0.05). Social intelligence had a moderate and significant correlation with emotional and cognitive job engagement which enables us to accept hypotheses 2 and 3 (r: .514; p<0.05; r: 576, p<0.05). A moderate and significant correlation between social information processing and physical job engagement enabled us to accept hypothesis 4 (r: .426; p<0.05). Also, a moderate and significant correlation between emotional job engagement and physical job engagement allowed us to accept hypothesis 5 (r: .638; p<0.05).

Table 4. The effect of social intelligence on job engagement

Variables	**β**	**t**	**Sig.**
Job Engagement *	-	4.511	0.00*
Social Intelligence	.578	9.460	0.00*

Besides, Table 4 indicates the general effect of social intelligence on the job engagement level of the individual was moderate and significant (b: .578, t: 9.460 p<0.05) with a significant correlation (r: .578) that permitted us to accept hypothesis 6. Overall, the correlation results among sub-factors and the regression results observing the impact of social intelligence on job engagement indicated that all hypotheses claimed by researchers were accepted with moderate significance.

DISCUSSION

In this research, the significance of the relationship between social intelligence and job engagement levels of Generation X women entrepreneurs was examined using TSIS developed by Tromso (2001), and JES developed by Rich (2006). Likewise, the validity of scales was tested in many different sample groups. The possible relationship between their social intelligence levels and their job engagement to work contributes a different feature to the study. There is a noticeable relationship between the sub-dimensions of social intelligence and job engagement of Generation X women entrepreneurs due to women's intention to be successful in business and social life. The information obtained in this framework will help Generation X women entrepreneurs to enhance their efforts to know themselves better. Thus, it should be borne in mind that being an effective and successful entrepreneur entails using and improving social intelligence.

Social intelligence is the ability of Generation X women entrepreneurs to communicate with their team, encourage and motivate them with their abilities, attitudes, and behavior (Marecki, 2014). For keeping the balance between business and social life, it is pivotal to focus on work, improve job performance, advance enthusiasm, and use the emotional, cognitive and physical engagement of the environment and time as well as empathy, active listening, and appropriate attitude towards others (Oludayo & Omonijo, 2020). Social intelligence has distinctive and necessary factors which regulate behaviors under the mechanisms such as reading, listening, social interactions, ability to convince people to have a positive impact, and knowing what to do when the conditions are clear (Bar-On, 2006). Individuals with high social awareness are very successful in displaying appropriate behaviors to the social environment in which they live, giving beneficial responses and feedback (Joseph & Lakshmi, 2010). In this direction, with the active participation of female employees in business life, job engagement has become a much more critical issue. It can be concluded that entrepreneurship is so closely related to social intelligence that there is a definite effect on job engagement.

Entrepreneurship is considered a critical factor for the economy of any country and the engine of economic growth since it leads to generating income locally or internationally and finally facilitates economic progression (Du & O'Connor, 2018). Comprehensive studies on women entrepreneurs reveal that women entrepreneurs who play an active role in business life are low. There is significant growth potential in this field in developing countries (Urbano & Noguera, 2020). Globally, women entrepreneurs have become a key player in sustaining social development and economic growth (Hart, 2003). The results have revealed significant similarities among Turkish women entrepreneurs concerning their personality traits or characteristics (Boz & Ergeneli, 2014). In Turkey, successful women entrepreneurs were described as being persistent and determined, patient, mentally strong and visionary, and innovative (Maden, 2015). Although many countries have made a series of reforms to empower women economically, women's participation in economic life in Turkey is still not at the expected level as women entrepreneurs in Turkey have to deal with many difficulties while establishing and maintaining their businesses.

This generation has a self-directed characteristic, they desire to master knowledge by studying and reading by themselves (Liddell, 2008). Most women of this age have graduated, gained momentum in their careers, had a family, and most importantly, understand themselves more clearly (Erickson, 2010). As women entrepreneurship is one of the crucial factors of economic growth of a country, it has attracted the attention of scholars (De Silva & Wijewardene, 2019). Women of this age manage many responsibilities (Green, 2011). Despite the social problems that women have been experiencing in recent decades, they have adopted new strategies and ideas to keep up with modern life changes and accomplish their aims in business life.

Generation X women respond quickly to innovations and changes and attract the entrepreneurial world's attention with these characteristics. (Bova & Kroth, 2001). For women seeking innovation and pursuing it, this role will be more central and crucial in the future (Nissan et al., 2012). From this point of view, the possibilities of accessing information for Generation X women should be increased and facilitated (Bova & Kroth, 2001). However, specific problems have confronted them and thus need to be resolved to provide space and platforms for them (Wube, 2010). Insufficient female role models in the business sector, inadequate effectiveness of business-oriented networks in their communities, lack of capital and assets, lower status in society, and lack of confidence in their ability to be successful in business life can prevent women from the success of their entrepreneurship (Berkup, 2014). It would not be possible for women entrepreneurs to achieve success without efficient work, high morale, and the ability to face challenges (Nair, 2016). Therefore, the state of women on a social, cultural, and economic level should be taken into consideration if the business world aims to involve them in business life as promising or successful entrepreneurs (Poggesi, 2016). The most important factors behind the decisions of Turkish Generation X women entrepreneurs to become entrepreneurs are to evaluate unique opportunities in the business environment, to work for the benefit of society, and to be independent in their decisions and actions.

One of the findings revealed a significant relationship between the social information process and social awareness. The social information process includes competencies such as understanding the feelings and thoughts of an individual and other people, reading their body language, and understanding the wishes and expectations of others (Silvera et al., 2001). The dimension of social awareness refers to a person's ability to behave under the social environment and conditions in which they are located (Silman & Dogan, 2013). A person with high social awareness is successful in showing behaviors appropriate to the situation in social settings, giving appropriate responses to behaviors directed at them, and giving feedback (Joseph & Lakshmi, 2010). In other words, they know when to talk, how to behave, how to influence people to balance their behaviors in front of others (Albrecht, 2006). Social skill, on the other hand, is related to the performance dimension of social intelligence. In other words, it is the skillful behavior of the individual in human relations (Lievens & Chan, 2010). A person with a high level of social skills can quickly enter social environments, have no difficulty getting along with other people, and comfortably adapt to social environments.

People with high social intelligence can understand other people's wishes, joys, anger, volatility in emotions, adjust their behavior accordingly and have the ability to get along well with others and communicate well (Joseph & Lakshmi, 2010). They recognize interactions within the group and better understand the people's expectations (Elenkov & Pimentel, 2015). People with high social intelligence can easily empathize, influence, and direct their intentions, desires, and thoughts, although they may not show them. Thus, it should be considered to distinguish the characteristics of each person.

On the other hand, job engagement, which can also be defined as the reflection of internal potential to the outside world, has received more attention in recent years (Shuck et al., 2017). Job engagement is a multidimensional motivation that reflects the simultaneous investment of an individual's physical, cognitive, and emotional engagement and total performance (Schaufeli et al., 2002). Accordingly, the relationship between the social intelligence of the Generation X women entrepreneurs and their emotional job engagement is high. There was a significant relationship between social intelligence and integration with emotional and cognitive job engagement.

This research focused on a scale composed of three subfactors: cognitive, emotional, and behavioral. Cognitively engaged employees are attentive and concentrated in their workplace and distribute mental focus expressed toward work-related activities (Ferguson & Carstairs, 2007). A cognitively engaged employee would be proportionately concentrated, focused, and attentive toward work-related experiences (Sharoni et al., 2015). The sub-dimension of emotional engagement is defined as an employee's intensity and willingness that contains positive organizational outcomes (Macey & Schneider, 2008). Concretely, emotional engagement is related to being connected on an emotional level, resources which are personalized with the examples of believing in, feeling a sense of personal meaning toward, and being emotionally connected, to a specific condition, individual, or a given context incorporating experience in business life (Schaufeli, W. B. (2013). This sub-dimension demonstrates a deep, active, and emotional connection to the active working experience (Özer et al., 2017). Emotionally engaged employees express an effect directed toward various work-focused targets that relate to the present momentary experience (Shuck et al., 2017). For example, emotionally engaged employees would say they believe in the mission and purpose of their organization and that the organization attaches personal meaning to them considerably. The sub-dimension of behavioral engagement is defined as the psychological state of the intention to behave in a manner that positively affects performance (Macey & Schneider, 2008; Rich et al., 2010). Tangibly, behaviorally engaged employees are eager to make extra efforts, labor harder for their team and organization, and do more than is expected (Bakker, 2010). Behavioral engagement represents a psychological state and is not yet action-related behavior.

CONCLUSION

According to the labor force participation and employment figures in Turkey, women entrepreneur's roles result in fewer opportunities due to their social position and society's value judgments. The active participation of businesswomen in the labor market may allow them to stand on their own feet by gaining their economic freedom and independence from their family or spouse, and reinforcing their position in the given society.

Generation X women entrepreneurs constantly facing different challenges have striven to solve problems to balance work and social lives. In this sense, they play a significant role in the growth of future business in the world and particularly Turkey. Therefore, this study examined whether the job engagement level of Generation X women affects their social intelligence in the business environment. The results imply that social intelligence is an essential skill that facilitates Generation X women entrepreneurs' communication with their employees and encourages and motivates them to take advantage of being a woman possessing powerful intuition and feelings. This result may also help Generation X women entrepreneurs make decisions when they try to conceptualize how to succeed considering the current and future business growth and regional development. Briefly, almost all the Generation X women entrepreneurs who participated in the study have family businesses. Applying and advancing social intelligence in this framework may enhance their efforts to be successful in business and social life.

Practical and Academic Implications

The social self-development of women and the acquisition of new skills influence the development of the region and the country directly. Therefore, the increasing interest in supporting women's entrepreneurship in the coming years may provide regional balance and help them set new employment targets.

It is crucial to support women entrepreneurs seeking new job opportunities, facilitate their process in finding loans for the capital needed, and provide the necessary training for entrepreneurship tactics in management, finance, marketing, and communication. Because their business performance has decreased due to their multiple roles, such as being a spouse, and a business partner, taking part in entrepreneurship training may increase women's self-confidence and enhance their awareness of different business opportunities. Public institutions, local administrations, professional organizations, women's organizations, and other NGOs can help women entrepreneurs with regard to these issues.

The interested parties, such as policymakers, should create a properly devised economic, social, political, cultural, and legal environment for women entrepreneurs so that they can willingly gain access to and run businesses.

Limitations and Recommendations

The scales were conducted online due to Covid-19 with the support of active members of the association of women entrepreneurs such as GIŞKAD (The Association of enterprising businesswomen, founded in March 2006) and NGO organizations operating in Mersin & Adana cities. In future studies, scales could be more appropriate if carried out face-to-face, and passive association members should also be included in the sample. In this research, generations were classified according to period, not according to social structure. Since the vast majority (99%) of Generation X women entrepreneurs participating in the survey own family businesses, future research can examine the dynamics of the family business and how they affect the firm's performance. As another area of future research, the impact of changes in lifestyles and culture on Generation X women entrepreneurs can be examined. Women deserve and should be provided social justice and equality and encouraged and motivated to be actively involved in business life to augment their state and status in society. In addition, training regarding the importance of social intelligence should also be available for women. Therefore, they can develop better social relations, practical communication skills, and efficient interactive abilities.

Further research should focus on women's entrepreneurship skills as an emerging area by observing next generations' entrepreneurship abilities considering their mental orientation, perception, and psychological well-being. In this respect, it may be helpful to examine the relationship between "Social Intelligence" and "Job Engagement" of young women entrepreneurs by using interaction styles among different ethnic origins and socioeconomic backgrounds.

REFERENCES

Aaboen, L., La Rocca, A., Lind, F., Perna, A., & Shih, T. (2017). Introduction: Starting Up in Business Networks—Why Relationships Matter in Entrepreneurship. In Starting Up in Business Networks (pp. 1-16). Palgrave Macmillan.

Albrecht, K. (2006). *Social intelligence: The new science of success*. John Wiley & Sons.

Alkan, D. P. (2019). Women Entrepreneurship in Turkey as an Emerging Economy. *Women Entrepreneurs and Strategic Decision Making in the Global Economy, 40.*

Ambepitiya, K. R. (2016). The role of women entrepreneurs in establishing sustainable development in developing nations. *World Review of Business Research, 6*(1), 161–178.

Attridge, M. (2009). Measuring and managing employee work engagement: A review of the research and business literature. *Journal of Workplace Behavioral Health, 24*(4), 383–398. doi:10.1080/15555240903188398

Aydın, G. Ç., & Başol, O. (2014). X ve Y Kuşağı: Çalışmanın Anlamında Bir Değişme Var mı? *Ejovoc, 4*(4), 1–15.

Bakker, A. B. (2010). Engagement and "job crafting": Engaged employees create their own great place to work. In *Handbook of employee engagement*. Edward Elgar Publishing. doi:10.4337/9781849806374.00027

Bakker, A. B., Albrecht, S. L., & Leiter, M. P. (2011). Key questions regarding work engagement. *European Journal of Work and Organizational Psychology, 20*(1), 4–28. doi:10.1080/1359432X.2010.485352

Bar-On, R. (2006). The Bar-On model of emotional-social intelligence (ESI) 1. *Psicothema*, 13–25. PMID:17295953

Başar, M., Ürper, Y., & Tosunoğlu, B. T. (2013). *Girişimcilik*. Anadolu Üniversitesi.

Berkup, S. B. (2014). Working with generations X and Y in generation Z period: Management of different generations in business life. *Mediterranean Journal of Social Sciences, 5*(19), 218–218. doi:10.5901/mjss.2014.v5n19p218

Bettinelli, C., Fayolle, A., & Randerson, K. (2014). Family entrepreneurship: A developing field. Now Publishers.

Beutell, N. J., & Wittig-Berman, U. (2008). Work-family conflict and work-family synergy for generation X, baby boomers, and matures: Generational differences, predictors, and satisfaction outcomes. *Journal of Managerial Psychology.*

Boniwell, I., & Tunariu, A. D. (2019). *Positive Psychology: Theory, Research, and Applications*. McGraw-Hill Education.

Bova, B., & Kroth, M. (2001). Workplace learning and Generation X. *Journal of Workplace Learning*.

Boz, A., & Ergeneli, A. (2014). Women entrepreneurs' personality characteristics and parents' parenting style profile in Turkey. *Procedia: Social and Behavioral Sciences, 109*, 92–97. doi:10.1016/j.sbspro.2013.12.425

Breakspear, A. (2013). A new definition of intelligence. *Intelligence and National Security*, *28*(5), 678–693. doi:10.1080/02684527.2012.699285

Bristow, J. (2015). *Baby boomers and generational conflict*. Springer. doi:10.1057/9781137454737

Brown, S. P., & Leigh, T. W. (1996). A new look at psychological climate and its relationship to job involvement, effort, and performance. *The Journal of Applied Psychology*, *81*(4), 358–368. doi:10.1037/0021-9010.81.4.358 PMID:8751453

Brown, T. A., & Moore, M. T. (2012). Confirmatory factor analysis. Handbook of structural equation modeling, 361-379.

Buvinic, M., & O'Donnell, M. (2016). *Revisiting what works: women, economic empowerment and smart design. Center for Global Development review*. Published November.

Cabrera, G. A., Conde, C. A. C. L., & Ingles, K. A. S. (2019). Difficulties on Work-Life Balance of Married Career Women: The Case of Generation X. Asia Pacific Journal of Academic Research in Business Administration, 5.

Carter, S. L., & Shaw, E. (2006). *Women's business ownership: Recent research and policy developments*. Academic Press.

Cebula, R., Rossi, F., & Clark, J. (2016). The impact of higher quality government regulation of business and greater economic freedom on living standards: Evidence from OECD nations. *Journal of Entrepreneurship and Public Policy.*

Chatterjee, N., Das, N., & Srivastava, N. K. (2019). A structural model assessing key factors affecting women's entrepreneurial success. *Journal of Entrepreneurship in Emerging Economies.*

Chavez, J. (2016). *The personality characteristics of an entrepreneur and their effects on the performance of a new business venture*. Academic Press.

Christian, M. S., Garza, A. S., & Slaughter, J. E. (2011). Work engagement: A quantitative review and test of its relations with task and contextual performance. *Personnel Psychology*, *64*(1), 89–136. doi:10.1111/j.1744-6570.2010.01203.x

Crecente-Romero, F., Giménez-Baldazo, M., & Rivera-Galicia, L. F. (2016). Subjective perception of entrepreneurship. Differences among countries. *Journal of Business Research*, *69*(11), 5158–5162. doi:10.1016/j.jbusres.2016.04.097

Creswell, J. W., & Creswell, J. D. (2017). *Research design: Qualitative, quantitative, and mixed methods approaches*. Sage Publications.

Darmawan, A. (2016). Regional Development Agencies as Actors of Local Economic Development in Turkey. Academic Press.

De Silva, D. C. H., & Wijewardene, L. (2019). *A literature review on individual factors affecting the business performance of women entrepreneurs in Sri Lanka*. Academic Press.

Drake, T. J. (2012). *Assessing employee engagement: A comparison of the job engagement scale and the Utrecht Work Engagement Scale* (Doctoral dissertation). Colorado State University.

Du, K., & O'Connor, A. (2018). Entrepreneurship and advancing national level economic efficiency. *Small Business Economics*, *50*(1), 91–111. doi:10.100711187-017-9904-4

Elenkov, D. S., & Pimentel, J. R. (2015). Social intelligence, emotional intelligence, and cultural intelligence. Handbook of Cultural Intelligence, 289-305.

Ensari, M. S. (2017). A study on the differences of entrepreneurship potential among generations. *Research Journal of Business and Management*, *4*(1), 52–62. doi:10.17261/Pressacademia.2017.370

Erickson, T. J. (2010). *Keeping up, moving ahead, and getting the career you want*. Harvard Business Press.

Esfandiar, K., Sharifi-Tehrani, M., Pratt, S., & Altinay, L. (2019). Understanding entrepreneurial intentions: A developed integrated structural model approach. *Journal of Business Research*, *94*, 172–182. doi:10.1016/j.jbusres.2017.10.045

Estrin, S., Mickiewicz, T., Stephan, U., & Wright, M. (2019). Entrepreneurship in emerging markets. The Oxford Handbook of Management in Emerging Markets, 457.

Ferguson, A., & Carstairs, J. (2007). Employee engagement: Does it exist, and if so, how does it relate to performance, other constructs and individual differences. *Industrial and Organizational Psychology: Perspectives on Science and Practice*, *23*, 133–147.

Filion, L. J. (2021). Defining the entrepreneur. In *World encyclopedia of entrepreneurship*. Edward Elgar Publishing. doi:10.4337/9781839104145.00015

Giacomin, O., Janssen, F., Guyot, J. L., & Lohest, O. (2011). *Opportunity and/or necessity entrepreneurship? The impact of the socio-economic characteristics of entrepreneurs*. Academic Press.

Goffee, R., & Scase, R. (2015). *Women in charge: The experiences of female entrepreneurs*. Routledge. doi:10.4324/9781315708751

Goldstein, S., Princiotta, D., & Naglieri, J. A. (2015). Handbook of intelligence. Evolutionary theory, historical perspective, and current concepts. doi:10.1007/978-1-4939-1562-0

Gómez-Gras, J. M., Mira-Solves, I., & Martinez-Mateo, J. (2010). Determinants of entrepreneurship: An overview. *International Journal of Business Environment*, *3*(1), 1–14. doi:10.1504/IJBE.2010.031267

Green, M. T. (2011). Comfortable Gen X. In Inside the Multi-Generational Family Business (pp. 139-153). Palgrave Macmillan.

Gupta, A. S. B. (2015). Job involvement, organizational commitment, professional commitment, and team commitment: A study of generational diversity. *Benchmarking*, *22*(7).

Halabisky, D. (2017). Five ways that policy could close the gender gap in entrepreneurship. In *International Trade Forum* (No. 4, pp. 10-11). International Trade Centre. 10.18356/15645304-2017-4-4

Hart, D. (2003). Entrepreneurship policy: What it is and where it came from. *The emergence of entrepreneurship policy. Governance, start-ups and growth in the US knowledge economy*, 3-19.

Hernandez, M., & Guarana, C. L. (2018). An examination of the temporal intricacies of job engagement. *Journal of Management*, *44*(5), 1711–1735. doi:10.1177/0149206315622573

Hisrich, R. D., & Öztürk, S. A. (1999). Women entrepreneurs in a developing economy. *Journal of Management Development*, *18*(2), 114–125. doi:10.1108/02621719910257639

Hu, R., Wang, L., Zhang, W., & Bin, P. (2018). Creativity, proactive personality, and entrepreneurial intention: The role of entrepreneurial alertness. *Frontiers in Psychology*, *9*, 951. doi:10.3389/fpsyg.2018.00951 PMID:29962985

İlkkaracan, İ. (2012). Why so few women in the labor market in Turkey? *Feminist Economics*, *18*(1), 1–37. doi:10.1080/13545701.2011.649358

Jing, S., Qinghua, Z., & Landström, H. (2015). Entrepreneurship research in three regions-the USA, Europe and China. *The International Entrepreneurship and Management Journal*, *11*(4), 861–890. doi:10.100711365-014-0315-6

Joseph, C., & Lakshmi, S. S. (2010). Social Intelligence, a Key to Success. *The IUP Journal of Soft Skills*, *4*(3).

Kahn, W. A. (1990). Psychological conditions of personal engagement and disengagement at work. *Academy of Management Journal*, *33*(4), 692–724.

Kim, W., Kim, J., Woo, H., Park, J., Jo, J., Park, S. H., & Lim, S. Y. (2017). The relationship between work engagement and organizational commitment: Proposing research agendas through a review of empirical literature. *Human Resource Development Review*, *16*(4), 350–376. doi:10.1177/1534484317725967

Koh, H. C. (1996). Testing hypotheses of entrepreneurial characteristics. *Journal of Managerial Psychology*, *11*(3), 12–25. doi:10.1108/02683949610113566

Lau, J. (2016). *Social intelligence and the next generation*. National Service Citizen.

Leiter, M. P., & Bakker, A. B. (2010). Work engagement: introduction. Work engagement: A handbook of essential theory and research, 1-9.

Levickaite, R. (2010). Generations X, Y, Z: How social networks form the concept of the world without borders (the case of Lithuania). LIMES. *Cultural Regionalistics*, *3*(2), 170–183.

Liddell, T. N. (2008). Executive women's self-directed learning and leading in charitable foundations. *International Journal of Self-Directed Learning*, *5*(1), 15–29.

Lievens, F., & Chan, D. (2010). *Practical intelligence, emotional intelligence, and social intelligence*. Academic Press.

Lub, X. D., Bal, P. M., Blomme, R. J., & Schalk, R. (2016). One job, one deal or not: Do generations respond differently to psychological contract fulfilment? *International Journal of Human Resource Management*, *27*(6), 653–680. doi:10.1080/09585192.2015.1035304

Luca, M. R., & Robu, A. (2016). Personality Traits in Entrepreneurs and Self-Employed. *Bulletin of the Transilvania University of Braşov. Series VII. Social Sciences*, *9*(58), 115–138.

Macey, W. H., & Schneider, B. (2008). The meaning of employee engagement. *Industrial and Organizational Psychology: Perspectives on Science and Practice*, *1*(1), 3–30. doi:10.1111/j.1754-9434.2007.0002.x

Maden, C. (2015). A gendered lens on entrepreneurship: Women entrepreneurship in Turkey. *Gender in Management*, *30*(4), 312–331. doi:10.1108/GM-11-2013-0131

Marecki, J. (2014). *The importance of social intelligence for entrepreneurial leaders* (Bachelor's thesis). University of Twente.

Marlowe, H. A. (1986). Social intelligence: Evidence for multidimensionality and construct independence. *Journal of Educational Psychology, 78*(1), 52–58. doi:10.1037/0022-0663.78.1.52

Marques, D. H. F., de Souza, N. R. M., & Rezaei, S. (2021). Female Entrepreneurship à Brasileira: Entrepreneurship by Choice or Entrepreneurship by Force. In *The Emerald Handbook of Women and Entrepreneurship in Developing Economies*. Emerald Publishing Limited. doi:10.1108/978-1-80071-326-020211011

McHenry, W. K., & Ash, S. R. (2013). Knowledge management and collaboration: Generation x vs. generation Y. *International Journal of Business and Social Science, 4*(12).

Morgan, C. (2011). Generational Differences in the Workplace. Academic Press.

Myers, J. (2020). The Value of the Mature Worker: Knowledge Management/Transfer in the 21st century. In Strategies for Attracting, Maintaining, and Balancing a Mature Workforce (pp. 62-84). IGI Global.

Nair, S. R. (2016). Women entrepreneurship across nations: Opportunities and challenges. Handbook of research on entrepreneurship in the contemporary knowledge-based global economy, 189-216.

Neneh, B. N. (2017). Family support and performance of women-owned enterprises: The mediating effect of family-to-work enrichment. *The Journal of Entrepreneurship, 26*(2), 196–219. doi:10.1177/0971355717716762

Nga, J. K. H., & Shamuganathan, G. (2010). The influence of personality traits and demographic factors on social entrepreneurship start up intentions. *Journal of Business Ethics, 95*(2), 259–282. doi:10.100710551-009-0358-8

Nissan, E., Carrasco, I., & Castaño, M. S. (2012). Women entrepreneurship, innovation, and internationalization. In *Women's entrepreneurship and economics* (pp. 125–142). Springer. doi:10.1007/978-1-4614-1293-9_9

O'Halloran, D. (2015). How technology will change the way we work. In *World Economic Forum* (*Vol. 13*). Academic Press.

Okeke-Uzodike, O. E., Okeke-Uzodike, U., & Ndinda, C. (2018). Women entrepreneurship in Kwazulu-Natal: A critical review of government intervention politics and programs. *Journal of International Women's Studies, 19*(5), 147–164.

Olakitan, O. O., & Ayobami, A. P. (2011). An investigation of personality on entrepreneurial success. *Journal of Emerging Trends in Economics and Management Science*, *2*(2), 95–103.

Oludayo, A. O., & Omonijo, D. O. (2020). Work-life Balance: Relevance of Social Support. *Academy of Strategic Management Journal*, *9*(3), 1–10.

Organisation for Economic Co-operation and Development. (2017). *Entrepreneurship at a Glance 2017*. OECD Publishing.

Özcan, A. H., & Bayarçelik, E. B. (2019). *Kuşaklara Göre İş Tatmini, Tükenmişlik ve İş Yaşam Dengesi* (Doctoral dissertation). Yüksek Lisans Tezi, Bahçeşehir Üniversitesi.

Özer, Ö., Uğurluoğlu, Ö., & Saygılı, M. (2017). Effect of organizational justice on work engagement in healthcare sector of Turkey. *Journal of Health Management*, *19*(1), 73–83. doi:10.1177/0972063416682562

Özsungur, F. (2019, May). A research on women's entrepreneurship motivation: Sample of Adana Province. *Women's Studies International Forum*, *74*, 114–126. doi:10.1016/j.wsif.2019.03.006

Panda, S. (2018). Constraints faced by women entrepreneurs in developing countries: Review and ranking. *Gender in Management*, *33*(4), 315–331. doi:10.1108/GM-01-2017-0003

Poggesi, S., Mari, M., & De Vita, L. (2016). What's new in female entrepreneurship research? Answers from the literature. *The International Entrepreneurship and Management Journal*, *12*(3), 735–764. doi:10.100711365-015-0364-5

Poggesi, S., Mari, M., & De Vita, L. (2019). Women entrepreneurs and work-family conflict: An analysis of the antecedents. *The International Entrepreneurship and Management Journal*, *15*(2), 431–454. doi:10.100711365-017-0484-1

Rahim, I. H. A., Fabeil, N. F., & Sung, T. P. (2017). Motivator and challenges of women entrepreneurs. *Journal of Global Business and Social Entrepreneurship*, *1*(3), 115.

Rashid, S., & Ratten, V. (2020). A systematic literature review on women entrepreneurship in emerging economies while reflecting specifically on SAARC countries. *Entrepreneurship and Organizational Change*, 37-88.

Rich, B. L., Lepine, J. A., & Crawford, E. R. (2010). Job engagement: Antecedents and effects on job performance. *Academy of Management Journal*, *53*(3), 617–635. doi:10.5465/amj.2010.51468988

Sainger, G. (2019). Multigenerations and world of work: Managing clash at work. JIMS8M. *The Journal of Indian Management & Strategy*, *24*(1), 57–62. doi:10.5958/0973-9343.2019.00005.X

Sarfaraz, L., Faghih, N., & Majd, A. A. (2014). The relationship between women entrepreneurship and gender equality. *Journal of Global Entrepreneurship Research*, *4*(1), 1–11. doi:10.1186/2251-7316-2-6

Schaufeli, W. B. (2013). What is engagement? In *Employee engagement in theory and practice* (pp. 29–49). Routledge.

Schaufeli, W. B. (2018). Work engagement in Europe. *Organizational Dynamics*, *47*(2), 99–106. doi:10.1016/j.orgdyn.2018.01.003

Schaufeli, W. B., & Bakker, A. B. (2010). Defining and measuring work engagement: Bringing clarity to the concept. Work Engagement: A Handbook of Essential Theory and Research, 12, 10-24.

Schaufeli, W. B., Salanova, M., González-Romá, V., & Bakker, A. B. (2002). The measurement of engagement and burnout: A two sample confirmatory factor analytic approach. *Journal of Happiness Studies*, *3*(1), 71–92. doi:10.1023/A:1015630930326

Scheef, D., & Thielfoldt, D. (2004). What you need to know about mentoring the new generations. In *Article adapted from workshop* (pp. 5–7). Engaging the Generations.

Sevil, A. C. A. R., & Gültekin-Karakaş, D. (2017). Free zones in the world and in Turkey. *Marmara Journal of Economics*, *1*(1), 21–35.

Sharoni, G., Shkoler, O., & Tziner, A. (2015). Job engagement: Antecedents and outcomes. *Journal of Organizational Psychology*, *15*(1).

Shuck, B., Adelson, J. L., & Reio, T. G. Jr. (2017). The employee engagement scale: Initial evidence for construct validity and implications for theory and practice. *Human Resource Management*, *56*(6), 953–977. doi:10.1002/hrm.21811

Shuck, B., & Reio, T. G. Jr. (2014). Employee engagement and well-being: A moderation model and implications for practice. *Journal of Leadership & Organizational Studies*, *21*(1), 43–58. doi:10.1177/1548051813494240

Silman, F., & Dogan, T. (2013). Social intelligence as a predictor of loneliness in the workplace. *The Spanish Journal of Psychology*, *16*, 16. doi:10.1017jp.2013.21 PMID:23866231

Silvera, D., Martinussen, M., & Dahl, T. I. (2001). The Tromsø Social Intelligence Scale, a self-report measure of social intelligence. *Scandinavian Journal of Psychology*, *42*(4), 313–319. doi:10.1111/1467-9450.00242 PMID:11547906

Smith, E. B., Brands, R. A., Brashears, M. E., & Kleinbaum, A. M. (2020). Social networks and cognition. *Annual Review of Sociology*, *46*(1), 159–174. doi:10.1146/annurev-soc-121919-054736

Startups & Places. (2020, November 20). *Report on Women Entrepreneurs in Europe*. https://startupsandplaces.com/startup-heatmap-europe-report-on-women-entrepreneurs-in-europe/

Tabachnick, B. G., & Fidel, L. S. (2007). *Using Multivariate Statistics*. Person Education Inc.

TerjeSen, S. A. (2016). Conditions for high-potential female entrepreneurship. *IZA World of Labor: Evidence-Based Policy Making*.

Thorndike, E. L. (1920). Intelligence and its uses. *Harper's Magazine*.

Tosunoğlu, B. T. (2014). *Girişimcilik ve Türkiye'nin ekonomik gelişme sürecinde girişimciliğin yeri* (Doctoral dissertation). Anadolu University, Turkey.

Truman, C. (2016). Women and men entrepreneurs: life strategies, business strategies. In *Women in Business* (pp. 13–25). Routledge.

TUIK. (2019). *Turkish Statistics Institute Database*. Author.

Tuzun, I. K., & Takay, B. A. (2017). Patterns of female entrepreneurial activities in Turkey. *Gender in Management*.

Urbano, D., Audretsch, D., Aparicio, S., & Noguera, M. (2020). Does entrepreneurial activity matter for economic growth in developing countries? The role of the institutional environment. *The International Entrepreneurship and Management Journal*, *16*(3), 1065–1099. doi:10.100711365-019-00621-5

Walker, R. E., & Foley, J. M. (1973). Social intelligence: Its history and measurement. *Psychological Reports*, *33*(3), 839–864. doi:10.2466/pr0.1973.33.3.839

Wube, M. C. (2010). *Factors affecting the performance of women entrepreneurs in micro and small enterprises*. Academic Press.

Yadav, V., & Unni, J. (2016). Women entrepreneurship: Research review and future directions. *Journal of Global Entrepreneurship Research*, *6*(1), 1–18. doi:10.118640497-016-0055-x

Yenilmez, M. I. (2018). An inquiry into improving women participation in entrepreneurship in Turkey. *International Journal of Entrepreneurship*, *22*(3), 1–15.

Chapter 10
Critical Conceptualization of Women's Entrepreneurship:
Reflections on the Turkish Entrepreneurship Ecosystem

Duygu Seckin-Halac
https://orcid.org/0000-0002-1956-7563
Yaşar University, Turkey

Seray Begum Samur-Teraman
Istanbul Kültür University, Turkey

ABSTRACT

While women's entrepreneurship preserves its traditional entrepreneurial mission from a neo-liberal perspective, it has also been accepted as an essential tool in ensuring equality and empowering women with a gender perspective. It is seen that supranational institutions are trying to realize these two perspectives together, at least working in this direction. This study aims to conceptualize "women's entrepreneurship" and bring it to the agenda in Turkey form a gender perspective. Evaluating the literature on women's entrepreneurship from a historical perspective and examining the fundamental inequalities embedded in entrepreneurship, especially in a developing economy such as Turkey that still has structural gaps, is the study's main contribution.

DOI: 10.4018/978-1-7998-8742-3.ch010

INTRODUCTION

Globalization and economic and social change have brought about a severe change in the definition and scope of the concept of entrepreneurship today (Seckin-Halac, 2017, pp. 4). Gartner (1989) opposed the description of the entrepreneur with individual/psychological characteristics and emphasized that the entrepreneur should be considered something that the individual does rather than something they are. While entrepreneurship is viewed as an umbrella concept, entrepreneurship studies are regarded as only one of the dimensions of entrepreneurship that continues grounded on growth and employment (Haas & Hwang, 2010). In addition, it has begun to be widely accepted that different goals, motivations, and obligations expand the definitions of entrepreneurship.

Entrepreneurship is today considered a field of research that seeks answers to the following questions (Shane & Venkatraman, 2000): How and why some (as an individual or a group) may recognize opportunities and decide that it is doable and turn it to their advantage (profit), while others do not? Furthermore, how do these opportunities ultimately reach the point of product, firm, industry, or wealth creation? However, in today's conditions, the idea that entrepreneurship does not only emerge with opportunities but rather that necessity pushes people to become entrepreneurs is also accepted in many countries.

Women's entrepreneurship has emerged and been widely supported in many countries within the framework of neo-liberal approaches, such as economic growth, employment increase, and poverty reduction. Furthermore, women are not the real subject of those discussions (Ecevit, 2007, pp. 47). On the other hand, women's entrepreneurship is supported within the empowerment approach by aiming to raise awareness beyond economic empowerment, political organization, and closing gender inequality (Bölükbaş 2006, pp. viii). Regardless of which perspective it focuses on, the common goal has become to increase women's entrepreneurship. It has been understood that more comprehensive studies are needed on the factors determining women's entrepreneurship, how women's entrepreneurship should be supported, and comparisons between countries in order to make detailed analyzes in the global competitive environment.

BACKGROUND

Critical Discussion on Women Entrepreneurship: Historical Perspective

In the early 1970s, when women were also oriented towards entrepreneurship, entrepreneurship was handled as a gender-neutral concept in America. In this environment, some studies have been carried out to remove the inequalities experienced by women in accessing resources while they are inclined to entrepreneurial activities. Accordingly, a series of programs were enacted in the mid-1970s to meet women's need for equal economic opportunities and financing. The concept gained popularity with a report on female entrepreneurship published by the American Department of Commerce in 1979 (Minniti, 2009, pp. 505).

Policy implementations for women entrepreneurs and the movement in the market also found an echo in the academy. Considering its historical emergence and development, the milestones in women's entrepreneurship, which is a relatively new field of study, can be summarized as follows: 1976- the first academic research article; 1979- first policy report; 1981- first conference presentation; 1985- first academic-oriented book; 1986- first literature review; 1989- first edited book series; 1997- first academic journal special issue; 1998- first policy-oriented conference; 2003- first academic conference; 2007- first awareness award; 2009- the first academic journal dedicated to the subject (Brush & Cooper, 2012; Jennings & Brush, 2013).

With the first academic research article on women's entrepreneurship in the last 50 years (See Schwartz, 1976 for more detail), women have started to find a new place in the entrepreneurship literature. The studies of women entrepreneurship, which followed the traditional entrepreneurship literature, either handled gender as a 'variable' and made comparisons with the characteristics of male entrepreneurs-where men were accepted as the "norm" until the 1990s-; or focused on personal aspect and sought an answer to the question of who a female entrepreneur is (Foss, 2010; Ahl, Berglung, Petterson & Tillmar, 2016).

Women's empowerment, both in the political sense and in the job markets, has brought a gender perspective and women's entrepreneurship studies in the context of feminist theories in academia (Minniti, 2009 pp. 507-508). In other words, the feminist movement has started to put forward its counter-entrepreneurship arguments against the traditional entrepreneurship arguments.

Different feminist views naturally led to varying interpretations of women's entrepreneurship (Eddleston &Powell, 2012). In this context, Ahl (2006) classified feminist theories under three different views: liberal feminist theories, social/radical feminist theories, and social constructivist (post-structuralist) feminist theories. Liberal feminist theories advocating equality between women and men explain women's secondary status with structural barriers (e.g., inequality in education) and discrimination (such as being stuck in a glass ceiling at work). While social/radical feminist theories discuss the advantages of being a woman, social constructivist feminist theories are concerned with how femininity and masculinity are constructed and expressed in the social structure. Although they examine different fields and have different views, these feminist theories argue that mainstream entrepreneurship is based on masculine norms and that women's characteristics should be considered when defining and discussing entrepreneurship (Ahl, 2006).

In the social constructivist view, entrepreneurship is constructed with social norms, ideologies, and beliefs like gender. This shared memory is embedded in social structures and social relations networks. Therefore, all cultural variables are influential on entrepreneurship (Amanda et al., pp.56). Moreover, traditional entrepreneurship literature assumes that entrepreneurship is a gender-neutral concept. Since the definitions are originated from traditional entrepreneurship, the entrepreneurial characteristics are given as adjectives describing successful entrepreneurs, and the dominant norms in the society are accepted as the same for each gender. Therefore, it is not considered that women may have different needs and expectations than men. However, social expectations and culture also cause different needs and desires for different genders (De Bruin et al., 2006). Therefore, Jennings and Brush (2013) oppose the evaluation of the concept of mainstream entrepreneurship separately from the context of gender and family.

Entrepreneurship Sociology: Embedded Inequality

Gender is the transformation of biological sex acquired at birth into behavioral patterns/expectations that reflect common beliefs and values transmitted socially and culturally during socialization processes. In other words, gender, as a culture-based phenomenon, is a set of beliefs that are difficult to change and transferred from generation to generation (Seçkin-Halaç & Takımcı, 2018, pp.510-511). There can be differences in the meanings that each culture and sub-culture socially ascribe to genders. In other words, the meanings attributed to being a woman/man, or a family can vary from country to country, as well as in different economic and cultural environments within the same country (Brandth & Kvande, 1998; Çarkoğlu & Kalaycıoğlu, 2012). Indeed, some other specific determinants such as legal regulations in society, norms related to social life, the general socio-economic structure of the society, and the level of cultural development are essential factors in determining the general behavior patterns of individuals (Almqvist, 2008). For example, in our world where fathers are given the role of " breadwinning" and mothers the role of "caring," society- consciously or not - pressures both parents to meet this expectation. In the end, these expectations are not only affecting family dynamics but also affecting the labor market.

The concept of gender is also theoretically relational; that is, men and women are not considered separately (Almqvist, 2008; Almqvist, Sandberg, & Dahlgren, 2011). For example, for women to stand out more in social life and reduce their domestic responsibilities, men need to take more domestic responsibilities and be more involved in the care of their children (Haas and Hwang, 2010). For this reason, to understand women's entrepreneurship, it is necessary to grasp the gendered structure of traditional entrepreneurship literature.

In this context, Ahl (2006), in his study comparing the words associated with masculinity and entrepreneurship, revealed that the traditional image of entrepreneurship, which is claimed to be gender-neutral, reflects the completely male-dominated perspective of entrepreneurship. Adjectives describe entrepreneurship (e.g., independent, ready to fight, successful-oriented), and adjectives denoting masculinity (e.g., individualistic/independent, competitive, ambitious) overlap one-to-one in the context of the BEM femininity-masculinity index. Also, any adjective associated with femininity does not correspond to entrepreneurship (Ahl, 2006). Therefore, entrepreneurship should be considered as a socially constructed gendered concept.

De Bruin, Brush, and Welter (2006) also argue that the gendered nature of the concept should not be ignored in the discussion of entrepreneurship. These researchers argue that traditional entrepreneurship theories, shaped by the concepts of money, market, and management, called 3M (Money, Market, Management), should be expanded in this context. In addition, they suggest that women can also be represented in their proposed model, which they call "5M", including motherhood/ family responsibility and the meso/macro environment.

Entrepreneurship is culturally seen as a 'male job' in some regions, indicating that entrepreneurship is a gendered concept (Shinnar, Giacomin, & Janssen, 2012). For example, with their study conducted in America, India, and Turkey, Gupta et al. (2009) found that entrepreneurship is seen as a male job in these three cultures. In addition, Seckin-Halac (2017), who modified Ahl's (2006) study and placed adjectives used to describe men in studies conducted in Turkey, also revealed that entrepreneurship is seen as a job associated with men in Turkey.

In addition to these, Stevenson (1990) determined that the measurement tools used in research to measure entrepreneurial performances and identify successful entrepreneurs are non-objective tools that reflect male-dominated norms. Similarly, Hurley (1999) states that entrepreneurship theories were put forward by men on samples of men, with measurement techniques developed by men. Therefore, these male-oriented traditional entrepreneurship criteria, created by evaluating men's motivations and perceptions of success based on 3M, and described as successful entrepreneurial characteristics even in textbooks for years, show women as unsuccessful counterparts. So, it should be seen as a measurement error that women do not meet these expected criteria and are evaluated as lower performing, less ambitious, and unsuccessful entrepreneurs (Stevenson, 1990). In addition, due to cultural perceptions such as women's responsibilities related to housework in the family, entrepreneurship is seen and reflected as a male job, creating an image that women are less competent than men in entrepreneurship (DeBruin et al., 2006).

Thus, women are constantly evaluated according to men's rules and ways of doing business in the male-dominated business world (Hurley, 1999). Consequently, they are accused of failing when they try to show themselves in ways that do not conform to the traditional understanding. However, women and men have been raised quite differently throughout their lives, starting from even before birth. Their families and society have different expectations from them. Therefore, they have different motivations for entrepreneurship (Cromie, 1987). Ahl and Marlow (2012) also criticize the mainstream entrepreneurship literature for several reasons: (1) producing dominant masculine discourses that say who can be an entrepreneur with whatever characteristics, and (2) trying to fit different types of entrepreneurs, such as women entrepreneurs, who do not fit these definitions. Therefore, to fit the mold has become the general effort for women entrepreneurs.

It is stated that women entrepreneurs, who are evaluated by comparing them with men over traditional entrepreneurship norms, take less risk, are less energetic, and are less autonomous (Sexton & Bowman-Upton, 1990). Similarly, it is emphasized that their jobs are less profitable, relatively small in size (Fasci & Valdez, 1998), usually home-based and part-time jobs (Marlow et al., 2012). However, women, who have different expectations from men due to their socialization styles, are prosecuted for not complying with social norms and contradicting traditional gender roles, even if they have traditional entrepreneurial characteristics and achieve success (Glick &Fiske, 1996; Heilman, 2001). For example, if women entrepreneurs are not divorced or single in the general profile, earning money is not a critical success criterion (De Martino & Barbato, 2003), but they are characterized as low performing. However, even if a woman works as much as men's working hours in male norms and earns high profits, it is possible to be judged as a woman who neglects her motherhood responsibilities, leaving her home and children. Therefore, this dilemma created by social expectations can also put women at a dead end. On the other hand, entrepreneurship can be the only job opportunity for women living in societies where patriarchy is at the forefront. For women living in low-income families, where spouses do not allow women to work, entrepreneurial activities by working at home can emerge as a way where they can earn money, share their identities and express themselves (Al-Dajani & Marlow, 2013).

Considering the reports of EUROSTAT's *"profile of successful entrepreneur"* research, it is seen that the top three motivations for both women and men are the same: Being one's own boss, earning more money, and finding a new occupation. However, these three are not the only motivations cited in the study. While women stated that they turned to entrepreneurship for other reasons such as not being unemployed, regulating work-life balance, and having children at a young age, men generally did not report reasons related to their home and family responsibilities (Schrör, 2006). In parallel, GEM's 2013 Women's Report revealed that the foremost essential reasons women become entrepreneurs are domestic roles such as creating enough time to take care of their children or family elders. While such care-related duties may be delegated to various care centers, they may remain on women due to economic difficulties. Even if they do not experience any difficulties economically, women may feel hesitant about going into business life due to the social pressures (Kelly et al., 2013, pp. 6).

It is thought that, above all, women have domestic responsibilities; their career goals are usually shaped by their household responsibilities. Moreover, even if they are successful when considered with male norms, their work always comes second (Bögenhold & Klinglmair, 2015; Mehtap et al., 2019). Women who are socially given responsibility for "care" feel all responsibility for the home and children due to the socialization process that lasts for years (Drew & Humbert, 2012). For example, studies show that mothers who returned to work full-time after giving birth felt guilty (Ekinsmtyh, 2011, Surgevil-Dalkilic, 2015, pp.438). Those mothers stated that they are intensely worried about not being able to devote enough time to their children and constantly worried about not being a good mother. In parallel, fathers describe their decision to use parental leave (which is provided to both mothers and fathers in European countries) as a "choice," while mothers state that it is their "responsibility" (Almqvist, Sandberg and Dahlgren, 2011; Braun, Vincent, and Ball, 2011).

The entrepreneurial structure based on male-dominated norms, the features that attribute to entrepreneurs, and the definitions that deepen the gendered division of labor pushes women away from entrepreneurship. When the entrepreneurial characteristics that fit men exactly leave women out, the remaining jobs such as housework and childcare will be automatically transferred to women, resulting in a gendered division of labor (Ahl, 2004, pp. 59). Therefore, it would be beneficial to pay special attention to this issue while preparing state policies regarding entrepreneurship in underdeveloped or developing patriarchal societies not to reinforce gender inequality.

Women Entrepreneurship in Turkish Literature

In line with world trends, women's entrepreneurship studies in Turkey started in the early 1990s, with the publicizing that it was a way to provide women with economic freedom. However, since the mid-1990s, women's entrepreneurship has reduced high unemployment rates and poverty among low-income families in cities. Therefore, the focus of women's entrepreneurship shifted from women to households (Ecevit, 2007, pp. 47). Due to its contributions to the country's economy, women's entrepreneurship has been at the center of attention in academic literature since the 1990s. In most of the studies conducted in the field of women's entrepreneurship in Turkey, women, that is, gender, have been considered as a variable, and entrepreneurship has been evaluated as a gender-neutral concept in such studies (for example, Yılmaz et al., 2012; Sönmez &Toksoy, 2014).

Again, similar to global trends, entrepreneurship in Turkey has been considered as the locomotive of the economy and has been associated with growth/regional development. The male-dominated characteristics and characters attributed to the entrepreneur and entrepreneurship were accepted as the norm and developed within how far women are from these norms. On the other hand, due to Turkey's status as a candidate country to the European Union in 1999, policies and public initiatives imposed on the government came to the fore within the scope of European Union harmonization policies. However, all these initiatives have been limited to the economic dimension of women's entrepreneurship, such as employment, poverty, and income generation, by ignoring labor market analyses to reduce/eliminate the gender gap and power relations at home and work (Gül and Altındal, 2016).

In Turkey, one of the most extensive field studies was carried out in 1995 with the female and male owners of small-scale companies by the Department of the Status of Women under the Ministry of Family and Social Policies. Accordingly, being unmarried is one of the most compelling motivations to participate in the job market. While flexible working hours make entrepreneurship attractive for women, it is seen that women with work experience before birth or after their children start school tends to entrepreneurship as a home-based source of secondary income for the household.

Another study presents the profile of women entrepreneurs between the ages of 36-45, live in the cities, at least high school graduates, are married, and with children (Yetim, 2008). The studies of Ufuk and Özgen (2001) show that women entrepreneurs are over the age of 38, at least high school graduate, have previous work experience, have been married for over 17 years on average, and have an average of 5 years of entrepreneurship experience with two children aged between 13 and 18. The same study also lists the entrepreneurial motivations of women, who are generally in the service sector, as follows: (1) meeting family needs, (2) providing social relations,

(3) self-actualization. Half of these women state that there is no change in their domestic workload and therefore, they cannot spare any time for themselves, and it is very stressful to balance their home and work life. In other words, they state that their responsibilities have increased even more when they become an entrepreneur and are still a wife, a mother, and a housewife.

Another study indicates that the women who have been awarded as the "most successful women entrepreneurs" are in the service sector, over the age of 41 on average, have 18 years of work experience, and are generally university graduates (Maden, 2015). While half of the participants are sole proprietorships and 9-year-old business owners with an average of 34 employees, they often talk about their determination, patience, mental strength, foresight, and vision. These "successful" women entrepreneurs, who state their motivation to be an entrepreneur as creating job opportunities, catching new opportunities, and trying new things; list the problems they face as (1) finding capital, (2) lack of social support, (3) male dominance in the sector. However, the point that should not be forgotten here is these women, attributed as successful, were again evaluated according to the dominant male norms. Therefore, it should not be surprising that they show a profile very close to the traditionally accepted male entrepreneurial characteristics. It should be emphasized that it does not reflect the female entrepreneur profile in Turkey in general.

Findings of the "Research on Women Entrepreneurs" (Ecevit & Yüksel-Kaptanoğlu, 2015) published in 2015 indicate the profile of women entrepreneurs: most of them having less than ten employees, aged 26 and over, embarking on entrepreneurship in the service sector, at least a bachelor's degree graduate, married, past job experience, whose capital is primarily provided by their own means, and who plan to expand their business even though they faced some difficulties during the establishment phase. These women describe themselves as (1) independent, determined and ambitious, (2) highly self-confident, and (3) passionate, hardworking and disciplined, respectively. In addition, growing a business is for them (1) to be recognized in the market through the brand they created, (2) to diversify products and services, (3) to expand the workplace physically, (4) to increase the business volume, (5) to employ more employees, (6) to increase profits in male-dominated areas. 42% of those who do not want to expand their business say they are satisfied with the current situation, and 13% say they cannot spare time for themselves or their family. The biggest problem encountered is the problems in establishing a work-life balance, which includes taking care of children (48%), while some state that they postpone marriage. In addition, others state that they postpone their dreams of entrepreneurship until the children start school. Although some may delegate childcare responsibilities to family members, workplaces are generally close to homes, and children are moved to the workplace when necessary (Ecevit & Yüksel-Kaptanoğlu, 2015).

As a result of content analysis, it was found that, unlike men, women's entrepreneurial motivation was driven by family situations (83.33%), which generally refers to the child, and freedom/flexibility (60%) focused on providing work-life balance (Seckin-Halac & Seckin-Celik, 2018). Therefore, it is seen that the dominant social roles attributed to women, such as motherhood, housewifery, and being a wife, are behind these women's entrepreneurship. Seckin-Halac and Halac (2019), based on how gender-centered variables originating from the family structure affect women's entrepreneurship in the country, analyzed Turkey using OECD data for the years 2006-2017. This study has determined that gender perceptions and social roles attributed to individuals are among the determinants of the number of women entrepreneurs in Turkey. The findings of this study showed that the most important determinant of women's entrepreneurship is divorce, and financial aid to the family reduces women's entrepreneurship. In addition, although the gender inequality variable does not have a powerful effect, it has also been observed that it has a reducing effect on women's entrepreneurship.

Contextual Indicators on Women Entrepreneurship: Turkey

According to the 2017 report of the International Monetary Fund (IMF), Turkey cannot use its female workforce potential because women do not participate in the workforce. For this reason, it is the second country (after Israel) with the highest loss in entrepreneurship in the world, with 25% in per capita income. If Turkey can eliminate gender-based inequality in the labor market and use all of its existing female labor potentials, it will be able to increase its per capita gross domestic product by 50%; able to eliminate gender inequality in entrepreneurship (Kochhar, Jain-Chandra & Newiak, 2016, pp. 37).

Beyond the economic indicators, within a simple calculation, it can be determined that almost half of Turkey's population is women. However, even these women play a minor role in employment, a considerable percentage of them are not even looking for a job. Therefore, the main issue is the strategies and action plans on how this potential can be unleashed and how women can contribute to the country's economy. However, it should not be overlooked at this point: (1) not to consider women only as an "input-labor force" within the economy-oriented perspective of neo-liberal discourse, and (2) to include regulations that will provide humane living and working conditions within the social structure.

In 2009, a detailed report on women's labor force participation in Turkey was prepared in partnership with the State Planning Organization (DPT) and the World Bank (WB). According to this report, the labor force participation rate of women with low education levels is relatively low in cities. It has been stated that there are both economic and cultural reasons behind this. Low wages, long working hours, high informality, economic crises, low education level, and expensive child care services constitute the economic reasons. Spouse or father not allowed to work, doubting safety away from home, "what the others think about us" mentality, child/elderly care, and domestic workload are the cultural reasons (State Planning Organization & World Bank, 2009, pp.21-23). TurkStat Family Structure Survey 2016 shows that mothers (86%) take care of children aged 0-5 during the daytime working hours in Turkey (TurkStat, January 18, 2017). The same research shows that women do most housework such as cooking (91.2%), dishes, laundry, and ironing at home in Turkey. It also shows that men mainly undertake to pay the bills with works such as repair and paint-whitewashing (80.4%) (TurkStat, March 2 2017). Therefore, the inequality in the domestic division of labor is parallel to the inequality in the labor market (Baxter, 1997). The Turkey Demographic and Health Survey 2018 indicates that the two main reasons women are not working are taking care of children (21%) and being a housewife (20%). In addition, 11% of the women participating in the study said that their spouses or families do not allow them to work (Hacettepe University Institute of Population Studies, 2019, pp. 181). The Turkey Demographic and Health Survey 2014 report revealed that women, who were previously in the labor force but did not work during the research period, state that the main reason for leaving the job was marriage (25%), and the second reason is pregnancy or child care (14%) (as cited in Kapucugil-İkiz, 2015).

While increasing women's employment is one of the most discussed topics within the scope of women-themed social policies, women's entrepreneurship and empowerment appear as the first solutions and policy suggestions that come to mind.

The number of women entrepreneurs in Turkey cannot be known precisely due to the problems related to data collection and some situations encountered in practice. Here are three main reasons (Çivici, October 15, 2007, pp. 5): The first of these is due to errors caused by data collection. Secondly, it has been observed that although those who appear as "female partners" are not real entrepreneurs who undertake the business, but women whose names are stated as partners simply because they are family members or spouses. Thirdly, while many women are not actively involved in the labor market, they are shown as women entrepreneurs to benefit from the health system and retirement rights for social security purposes. Therefore, even when we think with the official figures we accept, women's employment and entrepreneurship have not been raised to the desired levels at the point reached today.

According to the Global Entrepreneurship Monitoring Women's Report 2015 data, Turkey has the highest inequality in entrepreneurial activities among 83 countries with "3 female entrepreneurs for every ten male entrepreneurs" (Kelly et al., 2015, p.8). Furthermore, according to the research data repeated in the Global Entrepreneurship Monitoring Women's Report 2018/19, Turkey is one of the five countries with the highest inequality in entrepreneurial activities, along with Sweden, Slovenia, Greece, and Egypt (Amanda et al., 2019, pp. 21).

Following the establishment of the Republic and the sanctions brought by the EU harmonization process, women gained several rights in the historical process, and all necessary legal arrangements have been made in the name of gender equality in Turkey. However, in practice and labor markets, it is seen that this equality is still not achieved based on culture. As stated in the detailed report on women's labor force participation in Turkey prepared in partnership with the State Planning Organization (SPO) and the World Bank (WB) in 2009, the labor force participation rate of women with low levels of education in cities is relatively low. It has been stated that there are both economic and cultural reasons behind this.

In order to evaluate women's entrepreneurship in Turkey more accurately, it is also necessary to examine the variables of gender that have possible effects on women's employment and, more specifically, on entrepreneurial activities. The 2018 Global Gender Gap Report of the World Economic Forum shows that Turkey ranks 130th among the 149 participating countries in the general ranking. When these reports are followed, Turkey emerges as a country where the gender gap is seriously experienced, and this gap is following an increasing trend.

In the 2013 report of the Commission on Equal Opportunities for Men and Women, established within the Turkish Grand National Assembly, the leading causes of gender-based inequality in the labor market are, without specifying the order of importance, (1) low education level among women, (2) domestic responsibilities and childcare due to the traditional division of labor, (3) the inadequacy of mechanisms to reconcile work and family life (Metin & Kariman, 2013).

DISCUSSION AND CONCLUSION

According to 2018 data in Turkey, women constitute 49.8% of the population (TurkStat, March 6, 2019). When women's policies in Turkey are examined, it is seen that the studies are generally handled with the economic dimension within the framework of neoliberal discourse (Seckin-Halac & Mese, 2021). The Ministry of Development (2014, pp. 76) considers this data as the inactivity of great economic potential apart from half of the population staying away from social life. Entrepreneurship is accepted as a powerful tool in attracting women to employment. Therefore, country-level targets to increase the number of women entrepreneurs have been determined in the strategic plans of institutions such as KOSGEB (e.g., KOSGEB, 2018), which are particularly interested in entrepreneurship. In addition, the Development Plans (e.g., 10th Development Plan- Ministry of Development, 2014, pp. 89) also heavily depend on entrepreneurship. While these strategies focus on the number of women entrepreneurs by supporting new/potential entrepreneurs, they ignore the initiatives of women entrepreneurs that are currently established (Ecevit, 2007, pp. 53). As a result of this, it is seen that Turkey has the lowest survival rates, with Iran, Egypt, and Palestine, in enterprises 3.5 years or more (Kelly et al., 2012, pp.17).

Another shortcoming of the policies is that they are insufficient to develop policies specific to groups with different needs and characteristics, such as potential women entrepreneurs living in rural and urban areas, by considering women as a homogeneous group (Ecevit, 2007, pp. 51).Similarly, there is a need to produce policies specific to mother entrepreneurs-a group that emerges with motherhood and is considered as a new type of entrepreneurship (Seckin-Halac, 2015). Also, Hughes et al. (2012) suggest that there should be different support mechanisms for women (1) belonging to different ethnic groups, (2) who were unemployed because they did not have good management and business experience/knowledge, and (3) who have the desire and competence to start a business in fields where men dominate such as STEM.

In a nutshell, research in women's entrepreneurship in Turkey needs to be expanded into particular themes such as: (1) not being able to use the female workforce potential, (2) cultural variables, (3) as a political intervention tool, (4) disinformation/data access difficulties in detecting the current situation, and (5) gender inequality both in a general sense and in entrepreneurship activities. There is a need to regulate the economic-oriented approach of women's entrepreneurship in Turkey in a way that includes the gender-oriented approach. However, identifying women entrepreneur groups with different support needs and providing the necessary support to these groups in the establishment and ongoing survival and growth processes can be considered the essential steps related to women's entrepreneurship.

ACKNOWLEDGMENT

This study is mostly based on Duygu Seckin-Halac's study entitled "A Qualitative Look at the Gender Structure of Women's Entrepreneurship with OECD Data: An International Effectiveness Analysis".

This research received no specific grant from any funding agency in the public, commercial, or not-for-profit sectors.

REFERENCES

Ahl, H. (2004). *The scientific reproduction of gender inequality: A discourse analysis of research texts on women's entrepreneurship*. Copenhagen Business School Press.

Ahl, H. (2006). Why research on women entrepreneurs needs new directions. *Entrepreneurship Theory and Practice, 30*(5), 595–621. doi:10.1111/j.1540-6520.2006.00138.x

Ahl, H., Berglund, K., Pettersson, K., & Tillmar, M. (2016). From Feminism to FemInc.ism: On the uneasy relationship between feminism, entrepreneurship and the Nordic welfare state. *The International Entrepreneurship and Management Journal, 12*(2), 369–392. doi:10.100711365-014-0341-4

Ahl, H., & Marlow, S. (2012). Exploring the dynamics of gender, feminism and entrepreneurship: Advancing debate to escape a dead end? *Organization, 19*(5), 543–562. doi:10.1177/1350508412448695

Al-Dajani, H., & Marlow, S. (2013). Empowerment and entrepreneurship: A theoretical framework. *International Journal of Entrepreneurial Behaviour & Research, 19*(5), 503–524. doi:10.1108/IJEBR-10-2011-0138

Almqvist, A. L. (2008). Why most Swedish fathers and few French fathers use paid parental leave: An exploratory qualitative study of parents. *Fathering, 6*(2), 192–200. doi:10.3149/fth.0602.192

Almqvist, A. L., Sandberg, A., & Dahlgren, L. (2011). Parental leave in Sweden: Motives, experiences, and gender equality amongst parents. *Fathering, 9*(2), 189–206. doi:10.3149/fth.0902.189

Bögenhold, D., & Klinglmair, A. (2015). Female solo self-employment – Features of gendered entrepreneurship. *International Review of Entrepreneurship, 13*(1), 47–58.

Brandth, B., & Kvande, E. (1998). Masculinity and childcare: The reconstruction of fathering. *The Sociological Review, 46*(2), 293–313. doi:10.1111/1467-954X.00120

Brush, C. G. (1992). Research on women business owners: Past trends, a new perspective and future directions. *Entrepreneurship Theory and Practice, 16*(4), 5–31. doi:10.1177/104225879201600401

Çarkoğlu, A., & Kalaycıoğlu, E. (2012). *Türkiye'de Aile, İş ve Toplumsal Cinsiyet*. Koç Üniversitesi ve Sabancı Üniversitesi İstanbul Politikalar Merkezi.

Çetindamar, D., Gupta, V. K., Karadeniz, E. E., & Eğrican, N. (2012). What the numbers tell: The impact of human, family and financial capital on women and men's entry into entrepreneurship in Turkey. *Entrepreneurship and Regional Development, 24*(1-2), 29–51. doi:10.1080/08985626.2012.637348

Çivici, Ş. (2007). *Türkiye'de Kadın Girişimci- 2007 Durum Raporu, Kayseri Ticaret Odası Raporu.* Retrieved November, 2014 from http://www.kayserito.org.tr/web2/media/kadingirisimci_tr.doc

Cromie, S. (1987). Motivations of aspiring male and female entrepreneurs. *Journal of Occupational Behaviour, 8*(3), 251–261. doi:10.1002/job.4030080306

DeBruin, A., Brush, C. G., & Welter, F. (2006). Introduction to the special issue: Towards building cumulative knowledge on women's entrepreneurship. *Entrepreneurship Theory and Practice, 30*(5), 585–593. doi:10.1111/j.1540-6520.2006.00137.x

DeMartino, R., & Barbato, R. (2003). Differences between women and men MBA entrepreneurs: Exploring family flexibility and wealth creation as career motivators. *Journal of Business Venturing, 18*(6), 815–832. doi:10.1016/S0883-9026(03)00003-X

Drew, E., & Humbert, A. L. (2012). 'Men Have Careers, Women Have Babies': Unequal Parental Care Among Irish Entrepreneurs. *Community Work & Family, 15*(1), 49–67. doi:10.1080/13668803.2011.580128

Ecevit, Y. (2007). Türkiye'de Kadın Girişimciliğine Eleştirel Bir Yaklaşım. Uluslararası Çalışma Örgütü (ILO) Yayınları.

Ecevit, Y., & Yüksel-Kaptanoğlu, I. (2015). Research on women entrepreneurs. Proje Report, Garanti Bankası Yayınları, Istanbul.

Eddleston, K. A., & Powell, G. N. (2012). Nurturing entrepreneurs' work–family balance: A gendered perspective. *Entrepreneurship Theory and Practice, 36*(3), 513–541. doi:10.1111/j.1540-6520.2012.00506.x

Ekinsmyth, C. (2011). Challenging the boundaries of entrepreneurship: The spatialities and practices of UK mumpreneurs. *Geoforum, 42*(1), 104–114. doi:10.1016/j.geoforum.2010.10.005

Elam, A. B., Brush, C. G., Greene, P. G., Baumer, B., Dean, M., & Heavlow, R. (2019). *Women's Entrepreneurship Report 2018/2019.* Babson College: Smith College and the Global Entrepreneurship Research Association (GERA). https://scholarworks.smith.edu/conway_research/4

Fasci, M. A., & Valdez, J. (1998). Performance contrast of male- and female-owned small accounting practices. *Journal of Small Business Management*, *36*(3), 1–7. https://www.proquest.com/scholarly-journals/performance-contrast-male-female-owned-small/docview/220956847/se-2?accountid=10527

Foss, L. (2010). Research on entrepreneur networks: The case for a constructionist feminist theory perspective. *International Journal of Gender and Entrepreneurship*, *2*(1), 83–102. doi:10.1108/17566261011026565

Glick, P., & Fiske, S. T. (1996). The ambivalent sexism inventory: Differentiating hostile and benevolent sexism. *Journal of Personality and Social Psychology*, *70*(3), 491–512. doi:10.1037/0022-3514.70.3.491

Gül, S. S., & Altındal, Y. (2016). Türkiye'de kadın girişimciliğin serüveni: Başarı mümkün mü? *Süleyman Demirel Üniversitesi IIBF Dergisi*, *21*(4), 1361-1377. Retrieved from https://dergipark.org.tr/en/pub/sduiibfd/issue/52991/701828

Gupta, V. K., Turban, D. B., Wasti, S. A., & Sikdar, A. (2009). The role of gender stereotypes in perceptions of entrepreneurs and intentions to become an entrepreneur. *Entrepreneurship Theory and Practice*, *33*(2), 397–417. doi:10.1111/j.1540-6520.2009.00296.x

Heilman, M. E. (2001). Description and prescription: How gender stereotypes prevent women's ascent up the organizational ladder. *The Journal of Social Issues*, *57*(4), 657–674. doi:10.1111/0022-4537.00234

Hurley, A. E. (1999). Incorporating feminist theories into sociological theories of entrepreneurship. *Women in Management Review*, *14*(2), 54-62.

Jennings, J. E., & Brush, C. G. (2013). Research on women entrepreneurs: Challenges to (and from) the broader entrepreneurship literature? *The Academy of Management Annals*, *7*(1), 663–715. doi:10.5465/19416520.2013.782190

Kelly, D. J., Brush, C., Greene, P. G., Herrington, M., Ali, A., & Kew, P. (2015). *Global Entrepreneurship Monitor (GEM) 2015 Women's Report. Global Entrepreneurship Research Association*. GERA.

Kelly, D. J., Brush, C. G., Greene, P. G., & Litovsky, Y. (2013). *Global Entrepreneurship Monitor (GEM) 2013 Women's Report. Global Entrepreneurship Research Association*. GERA.

Kochhar, K., Jain-Chandra, S., & Newiak, M. (Eds.). (2016). Women, work, and economic growth: Leveling the playing field. International Monetary Fund.

Marlow, S., Hart, M., Levie, J., & Shamsul, M. K. (2012). *Women in enterprise: A different perspective*. RBS Group Report, University of Strathclyde. https://www.rbs.com/content/dam/rbs/Documents/Sustainability/Women-in-Enterprise.pdf

Mehtap, S., Ozmenekse, L., & Caputa, A. (2019). "I'm a stay at home businesswoman": An insight into informal entrepreneurship in Jordan. *Journal of Entrepreneurship in Emerging Economies*, *11*(1), 44–65. doi:10.1108/JEEE-10-2017-0080

Metin, Ş., & Kariman, R. A. (2013). *TBMM Kadın Erkek Fırsat Eşitliği Komisyonu Yayınları* (No. 12). http://www.tbmm.gov.tr/komisyon/kefe/docs/komisyon_raporu_2014_1.pdf

Schrör, H. (2006). *The profile of successful entrepreneur.* EUROSTAT report. https://ec.europa.eu/eurostat/documents/3433488/5443129/KS-NP-06-029-EN.PDF/22202ac8-b984-4b87-9f72-7e774e80a1ac?version=1.0

Schwartz, E. B. (1976). Entrepreneurship, a new female frontier. *Journal of Contemporary Business*, *5*(1), 47–76.

Seçkin-Halaç, D., & Halaç, U. (2019). *Türkiye'de Kadın Girişimciliğinin Cinsiyetçi Yapısına OECD Verileriyle Nicel Bir Bakış*, [Conference presentation]. 10th International Entrepreneurship Congress, Manisa Celal Bayar Üniversitesi.

Seçkin-Halaç, D. (2017). Değişen babalık ve girişimcilik kavramları çerçevesinde 'yeni/modern' babalar ve girişimcilik. In O. Sürgevil (Ed.), *ÇalışBabamÇalış: Baba olmak ve baba olmanın çalışma yaşamına yansımaları* (pp. 289–320). Nobel Akademik Yayıncılık.

Seçkin Halaç, D., & Meşe, G. (2021). Toplumsal Cinsiyet Bakış Açısından Türkiye'de Kadın Girişimciliğinin Durumu. *Dumlupınar Üniversitesi Sosyal Bilimler Dergisi*, (68), 255–270. doi:10.51290/dpusbe.838567

Seçkin-Halaç, D., & Seçkin-Çelik, T. (2018). A qualitative look into gendered entrepreneurship in Turkey. *Istanbul Business Research*, *47*(2), 105-123. Retrieved from https://dergipark.org.tr/en/pub/ibr/issue/44184/550011

Seçkin-Halaç, D., & Takımcı, D. (2018). Yerli çizgi dizi Niloya'da annelik ve babalık temsilleri. In A. Altay (Ed.), *Aile Araştırmaları* (pp. 495–522). Ekin Yayınevi.

Sexton, D. L., & Bowman-Upton, N. (1990). Female and male entrepreneurs: Psychological characteristics and their role in gender-related discrimination. *Journal of Business Venturing*, *5*(1), 29–36. doi:10.1016/0883-9026(90)90024-N

Shinnar, R. S., Giacomin, O., & Janssen, F. (2012). Entrepreneurial perceptions and intentions: The role of gender and culture. *Entrepreneurship Theory and Practice, 36*(3), 465–493. doi:10.1111/j.1540-6520.2012.00509.x

Sönmez, A., & Toksoy, A. (2014). Türkiye'de girisimcilik ve Türk girişimci profili üzerine bir analiz. *Yönetim ve Ekonomi, 21*(2), 41–58. doi:10.18657/yecbu.26416

Stevenson, L. (1990). Some methodological problems associated with researching women entrepreneurs. *Journal of Business Ethics, 9*(4-5), 439–446. doi:10.1007/BF00380343

Sürgevil-Dalkılıç, O. (2015). Annelerin öykülerinden açığa çıkanlar: Annelik ve çalışan anneliğe yüklenen anlamlar, çalışma hayatından örnek olaylar, ihtiyaçlar ve beklentiler. In O. Sürgevil-Dalkılıç (Ed.), *ÇalışAnne: Kadın Akademisyenlerin Kaleminden Çalışma Yaşamında Annelik* (pp. 407–466). Nobel Akademik Yayıncılık.

TurkStat. (March 2, 2017). Women with Statistics, 2016 [Bullet in], retrieved from http://www.tuik.gov.tr/PreHaberBultenleri.do?id=24643

TurkStat. (2017, January 18). Family [Bullet in] [, Retrieved from http://www.tuik.gov.tr/PreHaberBultenleri.do?id=21869]. *Structural Survey, 2016*, •••.

TurkStat. (March 6, 2019). Women with Statistics, 2018 [Bullet in], Retrieved from http://www.tuik.gov.tr/PreHaberBultenleri.do?id=30707

Ufuk, H., & Ozgen, O. (2001). Interaction between the business and family lives of women entrepreneurs in Turkey. *Journal of Business Ethics, 31*(2), 95–106. doi:10.1023/A:1010712023858

World Economic Forum. (2018). *The Global Gender Gap Report*. https://www3.weforum.org/docs/WEF_GGGR_2018.pdf

Yetim, N. (2008). Social capital in female entrepreneurship. *International Sociology, 23*(6), 864–885. doi:10.1177/0268580908095913

Yılmaz, E., Özdemir, G., & Oraman, Y. (2012). Women entrepreneurs: Their problems and entrepreneurial ideas. *African Journal of Business Management, 6*(26), 7896–7904. doi:10.5897/AJBM12.081

KEY TERMS AND DEFINITIONS

Female Entrepreneurship: Indicates a type of entrepreneurial activity that is engaged by women through organizing and managing an enterprise.

Gender: Implies socially constructed phenomena not residing inside the human as being a man or women, rather bringing about redefinitions of subjectivities and subject positions over time.

Gender Equality: Refers the state of having the same rights, status, and opportunities as others, regardless of one's gender therefore considered necessary foundation for a peaceful, prosperous and sustainable world by UN (https://www.un.org/sustainabledevelopment/gender-equality/).

Gender Gap: Refers a relative gap in any area between women and men in terms of their levels of participation, access, rights, remuneration or benefits in society.

Organization for Economic Co-operation and Development (OECD): Is an international organization with an aim of bringing prosperity, equality, opportunity, and well-being around the world through building better policies.

Social Constructivism: Is epistemological perspective argues that reality is not a phenomenon waiting to be discovered but is created in a meaningful social interaction.

Social Role: Are a socially established pattern of behavior that is required of people in certain social positions or from certain social groups https://link.springer.com/referenceworkentry/10.1007%2F978-3-319-16999-6_2469-1).

Work-Life Balance: Is a phenomenon used to describe a balanced division between working and non-working activities.

Conclusion

As you turned the pages of this book, you witnessed the experiences, reflections, problems and struggles of Eastern working women and the conditions they are subject to. Bounded by culture, religion, systems and structures, these women struggle to continue their pursuit of an independent, fulfilling and satisfying life.

The contributing authors promoted our understanding of being "an Eastern working women" from different perspectives.

- The first chapter provided us a portrayal of how gender is experienced and work is positioned by male and female employees from different occupations in Turkey. The study showed that women perceive work as a collective experience which involves other people. But for men, work is an individual experience.
- The second chapter presented a holistic perspective to female body and dress in the workplace. It stated that women's dresses reflect and shape their professional identities in organizational settings. While they are trying to communicate their independent identities, they also seek to get social approval with their dresses and adornments.
- The third chapter told us what it is to be a woman in the academia in Turkey. It presented experiences of female academicians and shed light to the discrimination and mobbing they were subjected to. They not only have to meet the legal and academic criteria but also have to satisfy the totally subjective and personal requirements of their professors to proceed in their careers.
- The forth chapter presented the experiences of token women from male dominated industries in Turkey. These women encountered differential treatment, lack of support and instruction in their workplaces. Their colleagues and superiors were hostile and resistant and they were subjected to punitive supervision and stereotyping.
- The fifth chapter submitted people's perceptions of and knowledge about pink collar jobs in Turkey. The results showed that most women have never heard about the concept and as the education level increased the likelihood of choosing professions which are not labelled as pink-collar also increased. Other

findings included a significant percentage of female participants thinking they would not be approved by the society even if they selected a pink-collar job.

- The sixth chapter provided us with a thorough profile of female entrepreneurship in Morocco. Even though the state has done a lot to support women entrepreneurs, the unfavorable atmosphere prevails. The eighth, ninth and tenth chapters studied female entrepreneurship and characteristics of female entrepreneurs in Turkey and they presented the nature and dynamics of the entrepreneurial ecosystem.
- The seventh chapter examined the influential and historical literary texts of Rokeya Sakhawat Hossain from an entrepreneurial perspective. The study argued that women must recognize their voices so that they can fight for their rights in the entrepreneurship ecosystem.

Each chapter leads the reader to spend time for reflection and thinking on how the findings can be of use in creating difference in women's lives. The world as we know it has never been fair. Women have been punished for being women all throughout the history. They were deprived of the chances of being the masters of their own destiny. They were treated as second class citizens, subordinate and inferior people. They were forced to do things they never chose to do or they were prevented from doing the things they wanted to. The system was designed and maintained in a way that it benefited men.

It is time for women to have their rights and realize their potentials. This can only be actualized by identifying the barriers and working together to remove them. This is where social sciences contribute to the cause. Knowledge makes us see things clearer so that we can find ways out.

In the name of the contributing authors I sincerely hope this book makes even a tiny contribution to the cumulative knowledge and help paving the way for equal opportunities.

Ela Burcu Uçel

Compilation of References

Acker, J. (1990). Hierarchies, Jobs, Bodies: A Theory of Gendered Organizations. *Gender & Society*, *4*(2), 139–158. doi:10.1177/089124390004002002

Acker, J. (1992). From sex roles to gendered institutions. *Contemporary Sociology*, *21*(5), 565–569. doi:10.2307/2075528

Ahl, H. (2004). *The scientific reproduction of gender inequality: A discourse analysis of research texts on women's entrepreneurship*. Copenhagen Business School Press.

Ahl, H. (2006). Why research on women entrepreneurs needs new directions. *Entrepreneurship Theory and Practice*, *30*(5), 595–621. doi:10.1111/j.1540-6520.2006.00138.x

Ahl, H., Berglund, K., Pettersson, K., & Tillmar, M. (2016). From Feminism to FemInc.ism: On the uneasy relationship between feminism, entrepreneurship and the Nordic welfare state. *The International Entrepreneurship and Management Journal*, *12*(2), 369–392. doi:10.100711365-014-0341-4

Ahl, H., & Marlow, S. (2012). Exploring the dynamics of gender, feminism and entrepreneurship: Advancing debate to escape a dead end? *Organization*, *19*(5), 543–562. doi:10.1177/1350508412448695

Ahmadov, F., Zeynalova, U., Bayramova, U., & Mammadov, I. (2021). Analysis of Educational Impact on Women Entrepreneurs in Sustainable Social Business: The Case of Azerbaijan. *Turkish Journal of Computer and Mathematics Education*, *12*(6), 1847–1856.

Akdemir, N. (2018). Visible Expression of Social Identity: The Clothing and Fashion. *Gaziantep University Journal of Social Sciences*, *17*(4), 1389–1397. doi:10.21547/jss.411181

Akehurst, G., Simarro, E., & Mas-Tur, A. (2012). Women entrepreneurship in small service firms: Motivations, barriers and performance. *Service Industries Journal*, *32*(15), 2489–2505. doi:10.1080/02642069.2012.677834

Al-Dajani, H., & Marlow, S. (2013). Empowerment and entrepreneurship: A theoretical framework. *International Journal of Entrepreneurial Behaviour & Research*, *19*(5), 503–524. doi:10.1108/IJEBR-10-2011-0138

Almqvist, A. L. (2008). Why most Swedish fathers and few French fathers use paid parental leave: An exploratory qualitative study of parents. *Fathering*, *6*(2), 192–200. doi:10.3149/fth.0602.192

Almqvist, A. L., Sandberg, A., & Dahlgren, L. (2011). Parental leave in Sweden: Motives, experiences, and gender equality amongst parents. *Fathering*, *9*(2), 189–206. doi:10.3149/fth.0902.189

Altınoluk, D. (2018). Kadın olmak mı, akademisyen olmak mı?: İşte bütün mesele bu. *Fe Dergi*, *10*(1), 57–66.

Alvesson, M., & Karreman, D. (2000). Taking the linguistic turn in organizational research: Challenges, responses, consequences. *The Journal of Applied Behavioral Science*, *36*(2), 136–158. doi:10.1177/0021886300362002

Andersen, S., Ertac, S., Gneezy, U., List, J. A., & Maximiano, S. (2013). Gender, competitiveness, and socialization at a young age: Evidence from a matrilineal and a patriarchal society. *The Review of Economics and Statistics*, *95*(4), 1438–1443. doi:10.1162/REST_a_00312

Angelou, M. (n.d.). *Still I Rise*. www.youtube.com/watch?v=7HiE4lt_DUY

Angouri, J. (2011). 'We are in a masculine profession…': Constructing gender identities in a consortium of two multinational engineering companies. *Gender and Language*, *5*(2), 373–404. doi:10.1558/genl.v5i2.373

Angouri, J., & Bargiela-Chiappini, F. (2011). 'So what problems bother you and you are not speeding up your work?' Problem solving at work. *Discourse & Communication*, *5*(3), 209–229. doi:10.1177/1750481311405589

Anna, A. L., Chandler, G. N., Jansen, E., & Mero, N. P. (2000). Women Business Owners in Traditional and Non-traditional Industries. *Journal of Business Venturing*, *15*(3), 279–303. doi:10.1016/S0883-9026(98)00012-3

Arat, N. (1995). *Turkiye'de Kadın Olgusu*. Say Yayınları.

Arifeen, S. R., & Gatrell, C. (2020). Those glass chains that bind you: How British Muslim women professionals experience career, faith and family. *British Journal of Management*, *31*(1), 221–236. doi:10.1111/1467-8551.12387

Arthur, S. J., Hisrich, R. D., & Cabrera, A. (2012). The importance of education in the entrepreneurial process: A world view. *Journal of Small Business and Enterprise Development*, *19*(3), 500–514. doi:10.1108/14626001211250180

Asli, A., & Bensassi, N. H. (2018). Female Entrepreneurship in Morocco, Obstacles and Ways to Overcome Them. In *6th International OFEL Conference on Governance, Management and Entrepreneurship. New Business Models and Institutional Entrepreneurs: Leading Disruptive Change*. Dubrovnik, Croatia: Governance Research and Development Centre (CIRU).

Atsan, N. (2019). Utilizing Social Networks in Social Entrepreneurship. In N. Iyigun (Ed.), *Creating Business Value and Competitive Advantage With Social Entrepreneurship* (pp. 232–250). IGI Global. doi:10.4018/978-1-5225-5687-9.ch011

Auger, C. (2020). *Dossier Femmes D'idées - Qui est la Femme Entrepreneure?* Gestion HEC Montréal. https://www.revuegestion.ca/dossier-femmes-didees-qui-est-la-femme-entrepreneure

Aycan, Z. (2004). Key Success Factors for Women in Management in Turkey. *Applied Psychology*, *53*(3), 453–477. doi:10.1111/j.1464-0597.2004.00180.x

Azenfar, A., Elghiat, R., & Debbah, A. (2019). *Coopératives féminines au Maroc réalisations et ambitions.* http://www.socioeco.org/bdf_fiche-document-6602_en.html

Bagchi, B. (2003-4). *Inside Tarini Bhavan: Rokeya Sakhawat Hossain's Padmarag and the Richness of South Asian Feminism in Furthering Unsectarian, Gender-Just Human Development.* http://www.igidr.ac.in/pdf/publication/WP-2003-004

Baker, T., Aldrich, H. E., & Liou, N. (1997). Invisible entrepreneurs: The neglect of women business owners by mass media and scholarly journals in the USA. *Entrepreneurship and Regional Development*, *9*(3), 221–238. doi:10.1080/08985629700000013

Banque mondiale. (2005). *Doing Business: Creating Jobs.* World Bank Publications.

Barthes, R. (1983). *The Fashion System.* Hill and Wang. (Original work published 1967)

Bastida, M., Pinto, L. H., Blanco, A. O., & Cancelo, M. (2020). Female Entrepreneurship: Can Cooperatives Contribute to Overcoming the Gender Gap? A Spanish First Step to Equality. *Sustainability*, *12*(6), 1–17. doi:10.3390u12062478

Baxter, J. (2010). *The Language of Female Leadership.* Palgrave Macmillan. doi:10.1057/9780230277915

Baxter, J. (2012). Survival or success? A critical exploration of the use of 'double-voiced discourse' by women business leaders in the UK. *Discourse & Communication*, *5*(3), 231–245. doi:10.1177/1750481311405590

Beauvoir, S. (2010). The Second Sex Chapter XI. Myth and Reality. In V. B. Leitch (Ed.), The Norton Anthology of Theory and Criticism. W.W. Norton & Co. (Original work published 1949)

Becker, G. S. (1964). *Human capital.* National Bureau of Economic Research.

Bedük, A. (2005). Türkiye'de Çalışan Kadın ve Kadın Girişimciliği. *Elektronik Sosyal Bilimler Dergisi*, *3*(12), 106–117.

Beham, B., Drobnic, S., Präg, P., Baierl, A., & Lewis, S. (2020). Work-to-family enrichment and gender inequalities in eight European countries. *International Journal of Human Resource Management*, *31*(5), 589–610. doi:10.1080/09585192.2017.1355837

Bell-Masterson, J., & Stangler, D. (2015). *Measuring an Entrepreneurial Ecosystem.* Ewing Marion Kauffman Foundation. doi:10.2139srn.2580336

Benazzi, k., & Benazzi, L. (2017). L'entrepreneuriat féminin au Maroc: Réalité, freins et perspéctives de réussite. *Revue Marocaine de Gestion et d'Economie, 3*(7). https://revues.imist.ma/index.php/RMGE/article/view/7535

Benn, J. (2004). Consumer Education between 'Consumership' and Citizenship: Experiences from Studies of Young People. *International Journal of Consumer Studies*, *28*(2), 108–116. doi:10.1111/j.1470-6431.2003.00364.x

Benson, M. B. (1929). Labor turnover of working women. *The Annals of the American Academy of Political and Social Science*, *143*(1), 109–119. doi:10.1177/000271622914300113

Berger, R., Benarousse, L., & El Kardi, R. (2020). *Accélérer la dynamique entrepreneuriale des femmes en Afrique*. Roland Berger gmbh.

Bhardwaj, R. B. (2014). Impact of education and training on performance of women entrepreneurs: A study in emerging market context. *Journal of Entrepreneurship in Emerging Economies*, *6*(1), 38–52. doi:10.1108/JEEE-05-2013-0014

Binkkour, M. (2012). *La promotion de l'entrepreneuriat au Maroc: Rôle de l'Etat et Perception des Entrepreneurs*. Conference: Business and Entrepreneurship in Africa Quebec – Canada.

Blau, F., Ferber, M., & Winkler, A. (2002). *The economics of women, men and work*. Prentice-Hall.

Blauner, R. (1964). *Alienation and freedom: The factory worker and his industry*. The University of Chicago Press.

Boden, S. (2006). Dedicated Followers of Fashion? The Influence of Popular Culture on Children's Social Identities. *Media Culture & Society*, *28*(2), 289–298. doi:10.1177/0163443706061690

Bögenhold, D., & Klinglmair, A. (2015). Female solo self-employment – Features of gendered entrepreneurship. *International Review of Entrepreneurship*, *13*(1), 47–58.

Bordo, S. R. (1993). *Unbearable Weight: Feminism, Western Culture, and the Body*. University of California Press.

Boudet, A. M. M., & Agar, M. (2014). *Female Entrepreneurship in Turkey*. The World Bank. Retrieved from https://betam.bahcesehir.edu.tr/wp-content/uploads/2014/06/Female-Entrepreneurship-in-Turkey1.pdf

Bourquia, R. (2015). Genre et reconfiguration de la société marocaine. In Le Maroc au Présent: D'une Epoque à l'Autre, une Société en Mutation. Centre Jacques-Berque. doi:10.4000/books.cjb.1041

Boutkhil, S. (2008). Moroccan Public Space: A Male Dominated Arena. In L. Touaf & S. Boutkhil (Eds.), *The World as A Global Agora: Critical Perspectives on Public Space*. Cambridge University Press.

Boutkhil, S. (2016). *The construction of the "other" Muslim February. Unpublished article read Guest speaker at the conference on The Culture of Islam and the question of gender. Organized by Laboratoire Langage et Société and the UNESCO Chair on Women and their rights.* Université Ibn Tofail Kénitra.

Boutkhil, S. (2017). Who's Under the Robe? On Women in the Judicial System in Morocco. In L. Touaf, S. Boutkhil, & C. Nasri (Eds.), *North African Women after the Arab Spring* (pp. 135–147). Palgrave Macmillan. doi:10.1007/978-3-319-49926-0_7

Bouzekraoui, H., & Ferhane, D. (2017). An Exploratory Study of Women's Entrepreneurship in Morocco. IBIMA Publishing. *Journal of Entrepreneurship: Research & Practice.*

Boydell, C. (2004). Review: Fashioning Identities: Gender, Class and the Self. *Journal of Contemporary History, 39*(1), 137–146. doi:10.1177/0022009404039889

Brandth, B., & Kvande, E. (1998). Masculinity and childcare: The reconstruction of fathering. *The Sociological Review, 46*(2), 293–313. doi:10.1111/1467-954X.00120

Brannigan, M. (2021). *The Psychology of Post-Pandemic Dressing*. https://fashionista.com/2021/05/covid-19-pandemic-fashion-psychology

Brewis, J. (2014). The ethics of researching friends: On convenience sampling in qualitative management and organization studies. *British Journal of Management, 25*(4), 849–862. doi:10.1111/1467-8551.12064

Brewis, J., & Warren, S. (2001). Pregnancy as project: Organizing reproduction. *Administrative Theory & Praxis, 23*(3), 383–406. doi:10.1080/10841806.2001.11643533

Brindley, C. (2005). Barriers to women achieving their entrepreneurial potential. *International Journal of Entrepreneurial Behaviour & Research, 11*(2), 144–161. doi:10.1108/13552550510590554

Brinton, M. C., Lee, Y. J., & Parish, W. L. (1995). Married women's employment in rapidly industrializing societies: Examples from East Asia. *American Journal of Sociology, 100*(5), 1099–1130. doi:10.1086/230633

British Council. Turkey/ (2019). *The State of Social Enterprise in Turkey*. Available at: https: // britishcouncil.org.tr/programmes/education/social-enterprise-research

Bruner, J. (1987). Life as narrative. *Social Research, 54*(1), 11–32.

Brush, C. G. (1992). Research on women business owners: Past trends, a new perspective and future directions. *Entrepreneurship Theory and Practice, 16*(4), 5–31. doi:10.1177/104225879201600401

Brush, C. G., De Bruin, A., & Welter, F. (2009). A Gender-aware Framework for Women's Entrepreneurship. *International Journal of Gender and Entrepreneurship, 1*(1), 8–24. doi:10.1108/17566260910942318

Burke, S., & Collins, M. K. (2001). Gender differences in leadership styles and management skills. *Women in Management Review, 16*(5), 244–256. doi:10.1108/09649420110395728

Butler, J. (2010). Preface to Gender Trouble: Feminism and the Subversion of Identity. In V. B. Leitch (Ed.), The Norton Anthology of Theory and Criticism. W.W. Norton & Co. (Original work published 1990)

Buttner, H., & Moore, D. P. (1997). Women's Organizational Exodus to Entrepreneurship: Self Reported Motivations and Correlations with Success. *Journal of Small Business Management*, *35*(1), 34–46.

Byrne, J., Fattoum, S., & Diaz Garcia, M. C. (2019). Role models and women entrepreneurs: Entrepreneurial superwoman has her say. *Journal of Small Business Management*, *57*(1), 154–184. doi:10.1111/jsbm.12426

Cacciotti, G., & Hayton, J. C. (2015). Fear and Entrepreneurship: A Review and Research Agenda. *International Journal of Management Reviews*, *17*(2), 165–190. doi:10.1111/ijmr.12052

Cacciotti, G., Hayton, J. C., Mitchell, J. R., & Giazitzoglu, A. (2016). A Reconceptualization of Fear of Failure in Entrepreneurship. *Journal of Business Venturing*, *31*(3), 302–325. doi:10.1016/j.jbusvent.2016.02.002

Cagan, E. (1978). The selling of the Women's Movement. *Social Policy*, (May/June), 4–12.

Çakıcı, A. (2006). Mersin'deki kadın girişimcilerin iş yaşamını etkileyen faktörler. *Dokuz Eylül Üniversitesi Sosyal Bilimler Enstitüsü Dergisi*, *8*(4), 54–78.

Carey, A. (1967). The Hawthorne Studies: A radical criticism. *American Sociological Review*, *32*(3), 403–416. doi:10.2307/2091087

Çarkoğlu, A., & Kalaycıoğlu, E. (2012). *Türkiye'de Aile, İş ve Toplumsal Cinsiyet*. Koç Üniversitesi ve Sabancı Üniversitesi İstanbul Politikalar Merkezi.

Carolan, S. M. (2005). The Conspicuous Body: Capitalism, Consumerism, Class and Consumption. *Worldviews: Global Religions, Culture, and Ecology*, *9*(1), 82–111. doi:10.1163/1568535053628436

Carranza, E., Dhakal, C., & Love, I. (2018). *Female Entrepreneurs: How and Why Are They Different?* Jobs Working Paper No. 20. World Bank. https://openknowledge.worldbank.org/handle/10986/31004

Carrington, C. (2006). *Small Business Financing Profiles*. SME Financing Data Initiative.

Carsrud, A. L., & Brännback, M. (2009). *Understanding the Entrepreneurial Mind*. Springer. doi:10.1007/978-1-4419-0443-0

Cebeci, T. (2015). *Performance of Female Employers in Turkey*. The World Bank Report. Retrieved from https://kadininstatusu.aile.gov.tr/data/54296a4b369dc32358ee2c3d/4.pdf

Çetindamar, D. (2005). Policy Issues for Turkish Entrepreneurs. *International Journal of Entrepreneurship and Innovation Management*, *5*(314), 187–205. doi:10.1504/IJEIM.2005.006525

Çetindamar, D., Gupta, V. K., Karadeniz, E. E., & Eğrican, N. (2012). What the numbers tell: The impact of human, family and financial capital on women and men's entry into entrepreneurship in Turkey. *Entrepreneurship and Regional Development*, *24*(1-2), 29–51. doi:10.1080/08985626.2012.637348

Channaje, A. (2021, March 11). Création d'entreprises: Ces freins qui bloquent encore l'entreprenariat féminin au Maroc. *L'Opinion.* https://www.lopinion.ma/Creation-d-entreprises-Ces-freins-qui-bloquent-encore-l-entreprenariat-feminin-au-Maroc_a12540.html

Chun, H. R., Cho, I., Choi, Y., & Cho, S. I. (2020). Effects of emotional labor factors and working environment on the risk of depression in pink-collar workers. *International Journal of Environmental Research and Public Health*, *17*(14), 5208. doi:10.3390/ijerph17145208 PMID:32707657

Cisneros, L., Genin, E., Saba, T., & Gril, E. (2020). L'Escalier de Glace: La Dure Ascension des Femmes. *Gestion*, *1*(45), 64–67. doi:10.3917/riges.451.0064

Çivici, Ş. (2007). *Türkiye'de Kadın Girişimci- 2007 Durum Raporu, Kayseri Ticaret Odası Raporu.* Retrieved November, 2014 from http://www.kayserito.org.tr/web2/media/kadingirisimci_tr.doc

Clark, A. E. (1997). Job satisfaction and gender: Why are women so happy at work? *Labour Economics*, *4*(4), 341–372. doi:10.1016/S0927-5371(97)00010-9

Cochran, L. (1990). Narrative as a paradigm for career research. In R. A. Young & W. A. Borgen (Eds.), *Methodological approaches to the study of career* (pp. 71–86). Greenwood Publishing.

Cohen, L. L., & Swim, J. K. (1995). The differential ımpact of gender ratios on women and men: Tokenism, self-confidence, and expectations. *Personality and Social Psychology Bulletin*, *21*(9), 876–884. doi:10.1177/0146167295219001

Collins, P. H. (1986). Learning from the outsider within: The sociological significance of Black feminist thought. *Social Problems*, *33*(6), S14–S32. doi:10.2307/800672

Conseil Economique, Social et Environnemental. (2014). Promotion de l'égalité entre les femmes et les hommes dans la vie économique, sociale, culturelle et politique Les discriminations à l'égard des femmes dans la vie économique: réalités et recommandations. *Auto-saisine, 18.*

Conseil Economique, Social et Environnemental. (2016). L'auto-entreprise, levier de développement et d'intégration du secteur informel. *Auto – Saisine, 27.*

Constantinidis, C., El Abboubi, M., Salman, N., & Cornet, A. (2017). L'Entrepreneuriat Féminin dans une Société en Transitions: Analyse de Trois Profils de Femmes Entrepreneures au Maroc. *Revue internationale P.M. E.*, *30*(3-4), 37–68. doi:10.7202/1042660ar

Cook, D. T., & Kaiser, S. B. (2004). Betwixt and be Tween: Age Ambiguity and the Sexualization of the Female Consuming Subject. *Journal of Consumer Culture*, *4*(2), 203–227. doi:10.1177/1469540504043682

Cooke, F. L. (2010). Women's participation in employment in Asia: A comparative analysis of China, India, Japan and South Korea. *International Journal of Human Resource Management, 21*(12), 2249–2270. doi:10.1080/09585192.2010.509627

Coser, R. L. (1981). *Women of a Certain Age: The Midlife Search for Self.* Academic Press.

Crane, D. (2000). *Fashion and Its Social Agendas: Class, Gender and Identity in Clothing*. The University of Chicago Press. doi:10.7208/chicago/9780226924830.001.0001

Creswell, J. W. (2013). *Nitel Araştırma Yöntemleri.* Siyasal Kitabevi.

Cromie, S. (1987). Motivations of aspiring male and female entrepreneurs. *Journal of Organizational Behavior, 8*(3), 251–261. doi:10.1002/job.4030080306

Dale, A. (2005). Combining family and employment: evidence from Pakistani and Bangladeshi women. In D. M. Houston (Ed.), *Work–life balance in the 21st century* (pp. 230–245). Palgrave Macmillan. doi:10.1057/9780230373594_12

Datta, P. B., & Gailey, R. (2012). Empowering Women through Social Entrepreneurship: Case Study of a Women's Cooperative in India. *Entrepreneurship Theory and Practice, 36*(3), 569–587. doi:10.1111/j.1540-6520.2012.00505.x

Davies, P. G., Spencer, S. J., & Steele, C. M. (2005). Clearing the Air: Identity Safety Moderates the Effects of Stereotype Threat on Women's Leadership Aspirations. *Journal of Personality and Social Psychology, 88*(2), 276–287. doi:10.1037/0022-3514.88.2.276 PMID:15841859

Davis, K. (2021). *How the pandemic changed what it means to look 'professional' at work.* https://www.fastcompany.com/90618736/how-the-pandemic-changed-what-it-means-to-look-professional-at-work

Davis, F. (1992). *Fashion, Culture, and Identity.* The University of Chicago Press. doi:10.7208/chicago/9780226167954.001.0001

Dawson, C., & Henley, A. (2012). "Push" versus "pull" Entrepreneurship: An Ambiguous Distinction? *International Journal of Entrepreneurial Behaviour & Research, 18*(6), 697–719. doi:10.1108/13552551211268139

Day, D. R., & Stogdill, R. M. (1972). Leader behavior of male and female supervisors: A comparative study. *Personnel Psychology, 25*(2), 353–360. doi:10.1111/j.1744-6570.1972.tb01110.x

De Clercq, D., & Voronov, M. (2009). Toward a Practice Perspective of Entrepreneurship: Entrepreneurial Legitimacy as Habitus. *International Small Business Journal, 27*(4), 395–419. doi:10.1177/0266242609334971

De Vita, L., Mari, M., & Poggesi, S. (2014). Women Entrepreneurs in and from Developing Countries: Evidences from the Literature. *European Management Journal, Elsevier, 32*(3), 451–460. doi:10.1016/j.emj.2013.07.009

DeBruin, A., Brush, C. G., & Welter, F. (2006). Introduction to the special issue: Towards building cumulative knowledge on women's entrepreneurship. *Entrepreneurship Theory and Practice*, *30*(5), 585–593. doi:10.1111/j.1540-6520.2006.00137.x

Dej, D. (2010). Defining and Meausring Entrepreneurial Success. In Entrepreneurship: A Psychological Approach, (pp. 89-102). University of Economics Prague.

DeMartino, R., & Barbato, R. (2003). Differences between women and men MBA entrepreneurs: Exploring family flexibility and wealth creation as career motivators. *Journal of Business Venturing*, *18*(6), 815–832. doi:10.1016/S0883-9026(03)00003-X

Dennis, N., Henriques, F., & Slaughter, C. (1969). *Coal Is Our Life*. Tavistock Publications. (Original work published 1956)

Dingley, J., & Catterall, P. (2020). Language, religion and ethno-national identity: The role of knowledge, culture and communication. *Ethnic and Racial Studies*, *43*(2), 410–429. doi:10.1080/01419870.2019.1587309

Drew, E., & Humbert, A. L. (2012). 'Men Have Careers, Women Have Babies': Unequal Parental Care Among Irish Entrepreneurs. *Community Work & Family*, *15*(1), 49–67. doi:10.1080/13668803.2011.580128

due Billing, Y. (2011). Are Women in Management Victims of the Phantom of the Male Norm? *Gender, Work and Organization, 18*(3), 298-317.

Durbin, S. (2015). *Women who succeed: Strangers in paradise*. Palgrave Macmillan.

Eagly, A. H., Wood, W., & Diekman, A. B. (2000). Social Role Theory of Sex Differences and Similarities: A Current Appraisal. In The Developmental Social Psychology of Gender, (pp. 123-174). Erlbaum.

Ecevit, Y. (2007). Türkiye'de Kadın Girişimciliğine Eleştirel Bir Yaklaşım. Uluslararası Çalışma Örgütü (ILO) Yayınları.

Ecevit, Y., & Yüksel-Kaptanoğlu, İ. (2015). *Kadın Girişimciler Araştırması*. Retrieved from www.garanti.com.tr./…/us201_garanti_kadin_girisimciler_rapor_201506

Ecevit, Y., & Yüksel-Kaptanoğlu, I. (2015). Research on women entrepreneurs. Proje Report, Garanti Bankası Yayınları, Istanbul.

Ecevit, Y. (1993). Kadın Girişimciliğinin Yaygınlaştırılmasına Yönelik Bir Model Önerisi, Der. A. Altınel, Kadını Girişimciliğe Özendirme ve Destekleme Paneli: Bildiriler ve Tartışmalar. *KSSGM, Ankara*, *74*, 15–34.

Ecevit, Y. (2007). *A critical approach to women's entrepreneurship in Turkey*. International Labour Office.

Eddleston, K. A., & Powell, G. N. (2012). Nurturing entrepreneurs' work–family balance: A gendered perspective. *Entrepreneurship Theory and Practice*, *36*(3), 513–541. doi:10.1111/j.1540-6520.2012.00506.x

EDGE Project. (2018). *United Nations, Department of Economic and Social Affairs, Statistics Division Technical Report on Measuring Entrepreneurship: Lessons Learned from the EDGE Project*. United Nations.

Ekinsmyth, C. (2011). Challenging the boundaries of entrepreneurship: The spatialities and practices of UK mumpreneurs. *Geoforum*, *42*(1), 104–114. doi:10.1016/j.geoforum.2010.10.005

Ekpe, I. (2011). Women Entrepreneurs and Economic Development in Nigeria: Characteristics for Success. *International Journal of Business and Social Science*, *2*(1).

El Ouazzani, K. (2017). *La Dynamique Entrepreneuriale au Maroc en 2017*. Editions Litograf.

Elam, A. B., Brush, C. G., Greene, P. G., Baumer, B., Dean, M., & Heavlow, R. (2019). *Women's Entrepreneurship Report 2018/2019*. Babson College: Smith College and the Global Entrepreneurship Research Association (GERA). https://scholarworks.smith.edu/conway_research/4

Elan, P. (2020). *'The Zoom shirt': How the pandemic changed work dress codes*. https://www.theguardian.com/business/2020/jul/20/the-zoom-shirt-how-the-pandemic-changed-work-dress-codes

Elan, P. (2021). *'Hate-wear' and 'sadwear': fashion's new names for lockdown dressing*. https://www.theguardian.com/fashion/2021/jan/17/hate-wear-and-sadwear-fashion-new-names-for-covid-lockdown-dressing

Elotmani, S. (2020 March 2-4). Les Déterminants du Succès Entrepreneurial des Femmes: Cas du Sénégal. In *Actes de la deuxième conférence internationale sur la Francophonie Economique L'Entrepreneuriat et L'insertion Professionnelle des Jeunes Et des Femmes en Afrique Francophone*. Université Mohammed V de Rabat.

Engels, F. (1892). *The condition of the working-Class in England in 1844*. Swan Sonnenschein & Co. (Original work published 1844)

Entwistle, J. (2000). *The Fashioned Body: Fashion, Dress and Modern Social Theory*. Polity Press.

Entwistle, J. (2007). *'Power Dressing' and the Construction of the Career Woman*. Routledge.

Fasci, M. A., & Valdez, J. (1998). Performance contrast of male- and female-owned small accounting practices. *Journal of Small Business Management*, *36*(3), 1–7. https://www.proquest.com/scholarly-journals/performance-contrast-male-female-owned-small/docview/220956847/se-2?accountid=10527

Fayolle, A., Liñán, F., & Moriano, J. A. (2014). Beyond entrepreneurial intentions: Values and motivations in entrepreneurship. *The International Entrepreneurship and Management Journal*, *10*(4), 679–689. doi:10.100711365-014-0306-7

Featherstone, M. (1991). The Body in Consumer Culture. In M. Featherstone, M. Hepworth, & B. S. Turner (Eds.), *The Body: Social Process and Cultural Theory*. Sage.

Featherstone, M. (2010). Body, Image and Affect in Consumer Culture. *Body & Society*, *16*(1), 193–221.

Feldman, J. (2020). *What People Wore to Work Before the Pandemic vs. Now.* https://www.huffpost.com/entry/work-from-home-outfits_l_5f96feeac5b646c70e9b3475

Finlay, L. (2003). Through the looking glass: Intersubjectivity and hermeneutic reflection. In L. Finlay & B. Gough (Eds.), *Reflexivity: A practical guide for Researchers in health and social sciences*. Blackwell Publishing. doi:10.1002/9780470776094.ch8

Firat, A. F., & Dholakia, N. (2003). *Consuming People from Political Economy to Theaters of Consumption*. Routledge.

Fis, A. M., Ozturkcan, S., & Gur, F. (2019). Being a Woman Entrepreneur in Turkey: Life Role Expectations and Entrepreneurial Self-Efficacy. *SAGE Open*, *9*(April). Advance online publication. doi:10.1177/2158244019846192

Foss, L. (2010). Research on entrepreneur networks: The case for a constructionist feminist theory perspective. *International Journal of Gender and Entrepreneurship*, *2*(1), 83–102. doi:10.1108/17566261011026565

Foucault, M. (2010). The Incitement to Discourse. In V. B. Leitch (Ed.), The Norton Anthology of Theory and Criticism. New York: W.W. Norton & Co. (Original work published 1978)

Foucault, M. (1979). *Discipline and Punish: The Birth of the Prison*. Vintage.

Ganesan, R., Dilbagh, K., & Maheshwari, R. C. (2002). Women Entrepreneurs: Problems and Prospects. *The Journal of Entrepreneurship*, *11*(75), 75–93. doi:10.1177/097135570201100105

Gannon, M. J., & Pillai, R. (2010). Understanding global cultures: Metaphorical journeys through 29 nations, clusters of nations, continents, and diversity. *Sage (Atlanta, Ga.)*. Advance online publication. doi:10.4135/9781452224886

Gannon, M. J., & Pillai, R. (2013). Understanding global cultures: Metaphorical journeys through 31 nations, continents, and diversity. *Sage (Atlanta, Ga.)*.

Gatrell, C. (2010). Who rules the game? An investigation of sex-work, gender, agency and the body. *Gender in Management*, *25*(3), 208–226. doi:10.1108/17542411011036419

Gatrell, C. (2013). Maternal bodywork: How women managers and professionals negotiate pregnancy and new motherhood at work. *Human Relations*, *66*(5), 621–644. doi:10.1177/0018726712467380

Gavis, Y., Shoham, A., & Ruvio, A. (2008). A Qualitative Study of Mother-Adolescent Daughter: Vicarious Role Model Consumption Interactions. *Advances in Consumer Research. Association for Consumer Research (U. S.)*, *35*, 732–734.

GEDI. (2014). *Country Excepts Turkey.* http://cepp.gmu.edu/wpcontent/uploads /2012/02/ Turkey_ 2014.pdf

Geis, F.L., & Brown, V., & Jennings, J. (1984). TV Commercials as Achievement Scripts for Women. *Sex Roles, 10*, 513–525. doi:10.1007/BF00287260

GEM Report. (2018/2019). Retrieved from https://www.gemconsortium.org/report/gem-2018-2019-global-report

Gerber, G. L. (1996). Status in same-gender and mixed-gender police dyads: Effects on personality attributions. *Social Psychology Quarterly*, 350–363.

Gergen, K. J. (1985). Social constructionist inquiry: Context and implications. In K. J. Gergen & K. E. Davis (Eds.), *The social construction of the person* (pp. 3–18). Springer. doi:10.1007/978-1-4612-5076-0_1

Gergen, K. J. (1999). An invitation to social construction. *Sage (Atlanta, Ga.)*.

Gherardi, S. (1994). The gender we think, the gender we do in our everyday organizational lives. *Human Relations, 47*(6), 591–610. doi:10.1177/001872679404700602

Gherardi, S. (1995). Gender, symbolism and organizational cultures. *Sage (Atlanta, Ga.)*.

Gherardi, S., & Poggio, B. (2001). Creating and recreating gender order in organizations. *Journal of World Business, 36*(3), 245–259. doi:10.1016/S1090-9516(01)00054-2

Giacomin, O., Janssen, F., & Guyot, J. (2016). Entrepreneurs de Nécessité et d'Opportunité: Quels comportements durant la phase de création? *Revue de l'Entrepreneuriat, 15*(3-4), 181–204. doi:10.3917/entre.153.0181

Giddens, A. (1979). *Central problems in social theory: Action, structure, and contradiction in social analysis.* University of California Press. doi:10.1007/978-1-349-16161-4

Glick, P., & Fiske, S. T. (1996). The ambivalent sexism inventory: Differentiating hostile and benevolent sexism. *Journal of Personality and Social Psychology, 70*(3), 491–512. doi:10.1037/0022-3514.70.3.491

Goffman, E. (1956). *The presentation of self in everyday life.* Doubleday.

Goffman, E. (1959). *The Presentation of Self in Everyday Life.* Doubleday.

Goldthorpe, J. H., Lockwood, D., Bechhofer, F., & Platt, J. (1968). *The affluent worker: Industrial attitudes and behaviour.* Cambridge University Press.

Goodman, J., Knotts, G., & Jackson, J. (2007). Doing Dress and the Construction of Women's Gender Identity. *Journal of Occupational Science, 14*(2), 100–107.

Goudreau, J. (2011). *The 10 Worst Stereotypes about Powerful Women.* https://www.forbes.com/sites/jennagoudreau/2011/10/24/worst-stereotypes-powerful-women-christine-lagarde-hillary-clinton/

Gousaid, N., & Qanqom, A. (2020). Les Facteurs Expliquant la Motivation de L'entrepreneuriat chez la Femme Marocaine selon le Niveau d'Etudes. *In Actes de la deuxième conférence internationale sur la Francophonie Economique L'Entrepreneuriat et L'insertion Professionnelle des Jeunes Et des Femmes en Afrique Francophone*. Université Mohammed V de Rabat.

Grant, D., Hardy, C., Oswick, C., & Putnam, L. (2004). *Handbook of Organizational Discourse*. Sage.

Green, M. (2005). *Job stress in the pink collar ghetto: clerical workers in the telecommunications industry*. Academic Press.

Greenberg, D., Ladge, J., & Clair, J. (2009). Negotiating pregnancy at work: Public and private conflicts. *Negotiation and Conflict Management Research, 2*(1), 42–56. doi:10.1111/j.1750-4716.2008.00027.x

Greene, P., Hart, M. M., Gatewood, E., Brush, C., Carter, N., & Stein, G. (2003). Women Entrepreneurs: Moving Front and Center: An Overview of Research and Theory. *Semantic Scholar*. https://www.semanticscholar.org/paper/Women-Entrepreneurs%3A-Moving-Front-and-Center%3A-An-of-Greene-Hart/93f86a7c3bea663e620e07a7e57fed322082904a

Gruber, J. E., & Bjorn, L. (1982). Blue-collar blues: The sexual harassment of women autoworkers. *Work and Occupations, 9*(3), 271–298.

Guerin, I., Hersent, M., & Fraisse, L. (2011). *Femmes, Economie et Développement. De la Résistance à la Justice Sociale*. IRD-ERES.

Guillemin, M., & Gillam, L. (2004). Ethics, reflexivity, and "ethically important moments" in research. *Qualitative Inquiry, 10*(2), 261–280. doi:10.1177/1077800403262360

Gül, S. S., & Altındal, Y. (2016). Türkiye'de kadın girişimciliğin serüveni: Başarı mümkün mü? *Süleyman Demirel Üniversitesi IIBF Dergisi, 21*(4), 1361-1377. Retrieved from https://dergipark.org.tr/en/pub/sduiibfd/issue/52991/701828

Gummer, B. (1998). In the Eye of the Beholder. *Administration in Social Work, 22*(4), 75–90.

Gupta, N. (2019). *Perceived Quality of Work-Life in relation to Collar Jobs: Blue-Collar &amp*. Pink-Collar Workers.

Gupta, V. K., Turban, D. B., & Bhawe, N. M. (2008). The Effect of Gender Stereotype Activation on Entrepreneurial Intentions. *The Journal of Applied Psychology, 93*(5), 1053–1061. doi:10.1037/0021-9010.93.5.1053 PMID:18808225

Gupta, V. K., Turban, D. B., Wasti, S. A., & Sikdar, A. (2009). The Role of Gender Stereotypes in Perceptions of Entrepreneurs and Intentions to Become an Entrepreneur. *Entrepreneurship Theory and Practice, 33*(2), 397–417. doi:10.1111/j.1540-6520.2009.00296.x

Haber, T. R. T. (2020). *İhracat takım elbisede azaldı, eşofmanda arttı* [Export of suits decreased and sweats increased]. https://www.trthaber.com/foto-galeri/ihracat-takim-elbisede-azaldi-esofmanda-artti/31582/sayfa-1.html

Hagen, R. L., & Kahn, A. (1975). Discrimination Against Competent Women 1. *Journal of Applied Social Psychology*, *5*(4), 362–376. doi:10.1111/j.1559-1816.1975.tb00688.x

Haj-Yahia, M. M. (2005). On the characteristics of patriarchal societies, gender inequality, and wife abuse: The case of Palestinian society. *Adalah's Newsletter*, *20*, 1–6.

Hardy, L. (2010). *From One Worried Mother, a Passionate Call to Arms... It's Time to Stop the Fashion Industry Dressing Girls of Ten Like This.* http://www.dailymail.co.uk/femail/article-1249538/from-worried-mother-passionate-arms--its-time-stop-fashion-industry-dressing-girls-like-this.html.

Harris, O. (2007). What makes people work? In R. Astuti, J. Parry, & C. Stafford (Eds.), Questions of anthropology. Berg.

Hasan, M. M. (2013). Commemorating Rokeya Sakhawat Hossain and Contextualising her Work in South Asian Muslim Feminism. *Asiatic, 7*(2). https://www.researchgate.net/publication/273898717_Commemorating_Rokeya_Sakhawat_Hossain_and_Contextualising_her_Work_in_South_Asian_Muslim_Feminism

Hassard, J. (2012). Rethinking the Hawthorne Studies: The Western Electric research in its social, political and historical context. *Human Relations*, *65*(11), 1431–1461. doi:10.1177/0018726712452168

Haut Commissariat au Plan & la Banque Mondiale. (2017). *Le marché du travail au Maroc: Défis et opportunités.* Author.

Haut Commissariat au Plan. (2014). *Le Budget-Temps: les Emplois du Temps de la Femme au Maroc*. Publications du HCP.

Haut Commissariat au Plan. (2018). *La Femme Marocaine en Chiffres: Evolution des Caractéristiques Démographiques et Socioprofessionnelles*. Publications du HCP.

Haut Commissariat au Plan. (2020). *La Situation du Marché du Travail en 2020*. Publications du HCP.

Haut-Commissariat au Plan. (2013). *La Femme Marocaine en Chiffres: Tendances d'Evolution des Caractéristiques Démographiques et Socioprofessionnelles*. Direction de la statistique.

Healy, G., Özbilgin, M., & Aliefendioğlu, H. (2005). Academic employment and gender: A Turkish challenge to vertical sex segregation. *European Journal of Industrial Relations*, *11*(2), 247–264. doi:10.1177/0959680105053966

Heilman, M. E. (1983). Sex bias in work settings: The lack of fit model. Journal of Nursing Management, 13(2), 137–46.

Heilman, M. E. (2001). Description and prescription: How gender stereotypes prevent women's ascent up the organizational ladder. *The Journal of Social Issues*, *57*(4), 657–674. doi:10.1111/0022-4537.00234

Henderson, A. (1994). Power and knowledge in nursing practice: The contribution of Foucault. *Journal of Advanced Nursing*, *20*(5), 935–939. doi:10.1046/j.1365-2648.1994.20050935.x PMID:7745186

Hisrich, R. D., & Öztürk, A. S. (1999). Women Entrepreneurs in a Developing Economy. *Journal of Management Development*, *18*(2), 114–125. doi:10.1108/02621719910257639

Hoffman, L. (1992). A reflexive stance for family therapists. In S. McNamee & K. Gergen (Eds.), *Therapy as a social construction* (pp. 7–24). Sage.

Hofstede, G. (1984). *Culture's consequences: International differences in work-related values* (Vol. 5). Sage.

Hofstede, G. (1984). Culture's consequences: International differences in work-related values. *Sage (Atlanta, Ga.)*.

Holmes, J. (2006). *Gendered Talk atWork: Constructing Social Identity through Work Place Interaction*. Blackwell Publishing. doi:10.1002/9780470754863

Hossain, R. S. (2007). *Rochonashomogro [The Complete Works]*. Jhinuk Prakashoni.

House, R. J., Hanges, P. J., Javidan, M., Dorfman, P. W., & Gupta, V. (Eds.). (2004). *Culture, leadership, and organizations: The GLOBE study of 62 societies*. Sage publications.

Huarng, K. H., Mas-Tur, A., & Hui-Kuang Yu, T. (2012). Factors affecting the success of women entrepreneurs. *The International Entrepreneurship and Management Journal*, *8*(4), 487–497. doi:10.100711365-012-0233-4

Humphreys, M., & Brown, A. D. (2002). Dress And Identity: A Turkish Case Study. *Journal of Management Studies*, *39*(7), 927–952.

Hunt, G. (1993). Sex differences in a pink-collar occupation. *Relations Industrielles. Industrial Relations*, *48*(3), 441–460. doi:10.7202/050872ar

Hurley, A. E. (1999). Incorporating feminist theories into sociological theories of entrepreneurship. *Women in Management Review*, *14*(2), 54-62.

Icart, I. B., & Pizzi, A. (2013). Effects of the sexual division of labor on self-employment creation in Spain. *Journal of Small Business and Entrepreneurship*, *26*(2), 151–167. doi:10.1080/08276331.2013.771857

Igamane, S. (2020). Les inégalités de pouvoir au sein des coopératives de femmes au Maroc. *RECMA: Revue Internationale de l'Economie Sociale*, *4*(358), 87–101. doi:10.3917/recma.358.0087

Ilham, T. (2020). *African Roots*. https://www.dw.com/en/fatima-al-fihri-founder-of-the-worlds-oldest-university/a-53371150

ILO. (2012). *International Standard Classification of Occupations: Structure, group definitions and correspondence tables*. International Labour Organization. https://www.ilo.org/wcmsp5/groups/public/---dgreports/---dcomm/---publ/documents/publication/wcms_172572.pdf

ILO. (2018). *Global Wage Report 2018/19*. International Labor Organization.

ILO. (2019). *Maternity Protection and Work-Family Policies (The Care Economy)*. Retrieved from https://www.ilo.org/global/topics/care-economy/parental-leave/lang-- en/index.htm

Jacobs, J. E., Chhin, C. S., & Bleeker, M. M. (2006). Enduring links: Parents' expectations and their young adult children's gender-typed occupational choices. *Educational Research and Evaluation*, *12*(4), 395–407.

Jahan, R. (1998). *Editor's Introduction: "Sultana's Dream: Purdah Reversed"*. Feminist Press. https://www.barnesandnoble.com/w/sultanas-dream-rokeya-sakhawat-hossain/1122980437

Jennings, J. E., & Brush, C. G. (2013). Research on women entrepreneurs: Challenges to (and from) the broader entrepreneurship literature? *The Academy of Management Annals*, *7*(1), 663–715. doi:10.5465/19416520.2013.782190

Johannisson, B. (2000). Networking and entrepreneurial growth. In D. L. Sexton & H. Landström (Eds.), *The Blackwell Handbook of Entrepreneurship* (pp. 368–386). Blackwell Publishers.

Josselson, R. (2011). "Bet you think this song is about you": Whose narrative is it in narrative research? *Narrative Works*, *1*(1), 33–51.

Jouiet, I. (2021). L'entreprenariat coopératif au Maroc: Une locomotive de développement socioéconomique. *Revue Internationale des Sciences de Gestion*, *4*(1).

Jurik, N. C. (1985). An officer and a lady: Organizational barriers to women working as correctional officers in men's prisons. *Social Problems*, *32*(4), 375–388.

Kabasakal, H., & Bodur, M. (2002). Arabic cluster: A bridge between East and West. *Journal of World Business*, *37*(1), 40–54. doi:10.1016/S1090-9516(01)00073-6

Kanter, R. (1977). *Men and women of the corporation*. Basic Books.

Kanter, R. M. (1976). The ımpact of hierarchical structures on the work behavior of women and men. *Social Problems*, *23*(4), 415–430.

Kanter, R. M. (1977). *Men and Women of the Corporation*. Basic Books.

Kanter, R. M. (1977b). *Some effects of proportions on group life, the gender gap ın psychotherapy*. Springer.

Kanter, R. M. (1987). Men and women of the corporation revisited: Interview with rosabeth moss kanter. *Human Resource Management*, *26*(2), 257–263.

Kanter, R. M. (1994). Change ın the global economy: An ınterview with rosabeth moss kanter. *European Management Journal*, *12*(1), 1–9.

Karadeniz, E. (2010). *Entrepreneurship in Turkey 2010*. The Global Entrepreneurship Monitor (GEM). Retrieved from https://mobil.tobb.org.tr/HaberResimleri/724-8.pdf

Karadeniz, O., & Yılmaz, H.H. (2017). *Turkonfed İş Dunyasında Kadın Raporu*. Academic Press.

Karasar, N. (1998). *Bilimsel Araştırma Yöntemi*. Nobel Yayın Dağıtım.

Katrinli, A. (Ed.). (2008). *Real life stories of how people feel and behave in organizations*. BookSurge Publishing.

Kaushik, N., Sharma, A., & Kumar Kaushik, V. (2014). Equality in the workplace: A study of gender issues in Indian organisations. *Journal of Management Development*, *33*(2), 90–106. doi:10.1108/JMD-11-2013-0140

Keashly, L. (2001). Interpersonal and systemic aspects of emotional abuse at work: The target's perspective. *Violence and Victims*, *16*(3), 233–268. doi:10.1891/0886-6708.16.3.233 PMID:11437116

Kelan, E. K. (2010). Gender logic and (un) doing gender at work. *Gender, Work and Organization*, *17*(2), 174–194.

Kelly, D. J., Brush, C. G., Greene, P. G., & Litovsky, Y. (2013). *Global Entrepreneurship Monitor (GEM) 2013 Women's Report. Global Entrepreneurship Research Association*. GERA.

Kelly, D. J., Brush, C., Greene, P. G., Herrington, M., Ali, A., & Kew, P. (2015). *Global Entrepreneurship Monitor (GEM) 2015 Women's Report. Global Entrepreneurship Research Association*. GERA.

Kessler-Harris, A. (1981). *A woman has always worked: a concise story*. University of Illinois Press.

Kibler, E., Kautonen, T., & Fink, M. (2014). Regional social legitimacy of entrepreneurship: Implications for entrepreneurial intention and start-up behaviour. *Regional Studies*, *48*(6), 995–1015. doi:10.1080/00343404.2013.851373

Kimosop, J., Korir, M., & White, M. (2016). The moderating effect of demographic characteristics on the relationship between strategic capabilities and firm performance in women-owned entrepreneurial ventures in Nairobi, Kenya. *Canadian Journal of Administrative Sciences*, *33*(3), 242–256. doi:10.1002/cjas.1399

Kim, P. H., Aldrich, H. E., & Keister, L. A. (2006). Access (Not) Denied: The Impact of Financial, Human, and Cultural Capital on Entrepreneurial Entry in the United States. *Small Business Economics*, *27*(1), 5–22. doi:10.100711187-006-0007-x

Klepp, I. G., & Storm-Mathisen, A. (2005). Reading Fashion as Age: Teenage Girls' and Grown Women's Accounts of Clothing as Body and Social Status. *Fashion Theory*, *9*(3), 323–342.

Kochhar, K., Jain-Chandra, S., & Newiak, M. (Eds.). (2016). Women, work, and economic growth: Leveling the playing field. International Monetary Fund.

Kolev, A., & Ferrant, G. (2016). *Does gender discrimination in social institutions matter for long-term growth? Cross-country evidence. No 330*. OECD Publishing.

Kozubíková, L., Vojtovič, S., Rahman, A., & Smrčka, L. (2016). The Role of Entrepreneur's Gender, Age and Firm's Age in Autonomy. The Case Study from the Czech Republic. *Economia e Sociologia*, *9*(2), 168–182. doi:10.14254/2071-789X.2016/9-2/12

Ku, M. C. (2011). When does gender matter? Gender differences in speciality choice among physicians. *Work and Occupations*, *38*, 221–262.

L'informel au Maroc représente 30% du PIB (Etude BAM). (2021 January 6). *Média 24*. https://www.medias24.com/2021/01/06/linformel-au-maroc-represente-30-du-pib-etude-bam/

Laghzaoui, S., Haoudi, K., Sliman, M., Decossa, J. J., & EL Otmani, S. (2020). *L'Entrepreneuriat des Jeunes au Maroc: Freins et Motivations*. DROFE no. 6. Observatoire de la Francophonie Economique. Université de Montréal.

Larty, J., & Hamilton, E. (2011). Structural approaches to narrative analysis in entrepreneurship research: Exemplars from two researchers. *International Small Business Journal*, *29*(3), 220–237. doi:10.1177/0266242611401796

Leeuwena, M. H. D., & Zijdemanb, R. L. (2014). Digital humanities and the history of working women: A cascade. *The History of the Family*, *19*(4), 411–425. doi:10.1080/1081602X.2014.955517

Leitch, V. B. (2010). *The Norton Anthology of Theory and Criticism*. W.W. Norton & Co.

Lewis, P., Simpson, R., & Sealy, R. (2010). Meritocracy, difference and choice: Women's experiences of advantage and disadvantage at work. *Gender in Management*, *25*(3), 165–169. doi:10.1108/17542411011036374

Liben, L. S., Bigler, R. S., & Krogh, H. R. (2001). Pink and blue collar jobs: Children's judgments of job status and job aspirations in relation to sex of worker. *Journal of Experimental Child Psychology*, *79*(4), 346–363. doi:10.1006/jecp.2000.2611 PMID:11511128

Lieblich, A., Tuval-Mashiach, R., & Zilber, T. (1998). Narrative research: Reading, analysis, and interpretation. *Sage (Atlanta, Ga.)*.

Lincoln, Y. S., & Guba, E. G. (1985). *Naturalistic inquiry*. Sage. doi:10.1016/0147-1767(85)90062-8

Liu, Y., Schøtt, T., & Zhang, C. (2018). Women's Experiences of Legitimacy, Satisfaction and Commitment as Entrepreneurs: Embedded in Gender Hierarchy and Networks in Private and Business Spheres. Entrepreneurship & Regional Development, 31(3-4), 293-307.

Logan, J. (2014). An exploration of the Challenges Facing Women Starting Business at Fifty. *International Journal of Gender and Entrepreneurship*, *6*(1), 83–96. doi:10.1108/IJGE-03-2013-0019

Lorber, J., & Farrell, S. A. (Eds.). (1991). *The social construction of gender*. Sage.

Lupton, B. (2000). Maintaining masculinity: Men who do women's work. *British Journal of Management*, *11*(s1), 33–48.

Maden, C. (2015). A gendered lens on entreprenership: Women entrepreneurship in Turkey. *Gender in Management*, *30*(4), 312–331. doi:10.1108/GM-11-2013-0131

Manolova, T. S., Brush, C. G., Edelman, L. F., & Elam, A. (2020). Pivoting to stay the course: How women entrepreneurs take advantage of opportunities created by the COVID-19 pandemic. *International Small Business Journal: Researching Entrepreneurship*, *38*(6), 481–491. doi:10.1177/0266242620949136

Manry, V. (2019). *Femmes et Entrepreneurs, la variable Inconnue*. Economia Research Center.

Marlow, S., Hart, M., Levie, J., & Shamsul, M. K. (2012). *Women in enterprise: A different perspective*. RBS Group Report, University of Strathclyde. https://www.rbs.com/content/dam/rbs/Documents/Sustainability/Women-in-Enterprise.pdf

Martin, K. A. (1998). Becoming a Gendered Body: Practices of Preschools. *American Sociological Review*, *63*(4), 494–511.

Martin, S. E. (1994). "Outsider within" the station house: The impact of race and gender on Black women police. *Social Problems*, *41*(3), 383–400.

Mastracci, S. H. (2016). *Breaking out of the pink-collar ghetto. Policy solutions for non-college women*. Routledge. doi:10.4324/9781315497938

Mas-Tur, A., Pinazo, P., Tur-Porcar, A. M., & Sánchez-Masferrer, M. (2015). What to avoid to succeed as an entrepreneur. *Journal of Business Research*, *68*(11), 2279–2284. doi:10.1016/j.jbusres.2015.06.011

Mau, W. C. (2003). Factors that influence persistence in science and engineering career aspirations. *The Career Development Quarterly*, *51*(3), 234–243.

McAdam, M., Harrison, R. T., & Leitch, C. M. (2018). Stories from the Field: Women's Networking as Gender Capital in Entrepreneurial Ecosystems. *Small Business Economics*. Advance online publication. doi:10.100711187-018-9995-6

McCrone, D. (1994). Getting by and making out in Kirkcaldy. In M. Anderson, F. Bechofer, & J. Gershuny (Eds.), The Social and Political Economy of the Household (pp. 68–99). Oxford University Press.

McDowell, J., & Schaffner, S. (2011). Football, it's a man's game: Insult and gendered discourse in The Gender Bowl. *Discourse & Society*, *22*(5), 547–564.

Mehtap, S., Ozmenekse, L., & Caputa, A. (2019). "I'm a stay at home businesswoman": An insight into informal entrepreneurship in Jordan. *Journal of Entrepreneurship in Emerging Economies*, *11*(1), 44–65. doi:10.1108/JEEE-10-2017-0080

Metcalfe, B. (2008). Women, management and globalization. *Journal of Business Ethics*, *83*(1), 85–100. doi:10.100710551-007-9654-3

Metin, Ş., & Kariman, R. A. (2013). *TBMM Kadın Erkek Fırsat Eşitliği Komisyonu Yayınları* (No. 12). http://www.tbmm.gov.tr/komisyon/kefe/docs/komisyon_raporu_2014_1.pdf

Meyer, Z. (2020). *Do you show your face in Zoom meetings? Your gender may play a role.* https://www.fastcompany.com/90514033/do-you-show-your-face-in-zoom-meetings-your-gender-may-play-a-role

Miles, M. B., & Huberman, A. M. (1984). Qualitative data analysis: An expanded sourcebook. *Sage (Atlanta, Ga.).*

Milkman, R. (2016). On gender, labor and equality. University of Illinois Press.

Miller, T. (2017). *Making sense of parenthood: Caring, gender and family lives.* Cambridge University Press. doi:10.1017/9781316219270

Minniti, M. (2010). Female Entrepreneurship and Economic Activity. *European Journal of Development Research, 22*(3), 294–312. doi:10.1057/ejdr.2010.18

Minniti, M., & Naude, W. (2010). What Do We Know about the Patterns and Determinants of Female Entrepreneurship across Countries? *European Journal of Development Research, 22*(3), 277–293. doi:10.1057/ejdr.2010.17

Mitchell, J. R., & Shepherd, D. (2011). Afraid of Opportunity: The Effects of Fear of Failure on Entrepreneurial Action. Frontiers of Entrepreneurship Research, 31.

Molloy, J. T. (1976). *Dress for Success.* Grand Central Pub.

Morrison, T. (1979). *The Bluest Eye.* Chatto and Windus.

Morris-Roberts, K. (2004). Girls' Friendships, 'Distinctive Individuality' and Socio-spatial Practices of (Dis)identification. *Children's Geographies, 2*(2), 237–255.

Morse, J. M., & Richards, L. (2007). *Read Me First for A User's Guide to Qualitative Methods.* Sage Publications.

Mull, A. (2020). *After the Pandemic, the Office Dress Code Should Never Come Back.* https://www.theatlantic.com/magazine/archive/2020/05/kill-the-office-dress-code/609070/

Mulvey, L. (1975). Visual Pleasure and Narrative Cinema. In V. B. Leitch (Ed.), The Norton Anthology of Theory and Criticism. W.W. Norton & Co. doi:10.1007/978-1-349-14428-0_27

Neale, J., & Özkanlı, O. (2010). Organisational barriers for women in senior management: A comparison of Turkish and New Zealand universities. *Gender and Education, 22*(5), 547–563. doi:10.1080/09540250903524113

Neumeyer, X., Santos, S. C., Caetano, A., & Kalbfleisch, P. (2019). Entrepreneurship ecosystems and women entrepreneurs: A social capital and network approach. *Small Business Economics, 53*(2), 475–489. doi:10.100711187-018-9996-5

Niessen, S. (2016). Afterword: Fashion's Fallacy. In M. A. Jansen & J. Craik (Eds.), *Modern Fashion Traditions: Negotiating Tradition and Modernity through Fashion* (pp. 209–217). Bloomsbury Academic.

Nilsson, K., & Larsson, S. U. (2005). Conceptions of gender: A study of female and male head nurses' statements. *Journal of Nursing Management, 13*(2), 179–186.

OCDE. (2004). *Entrepreneuriat féminin: questions et actions à mener.* 2e Conférence de l'OCDE des Ministres en charge des PME: promouvoir l'entreprenariat et les PME innovantes dans une économie mondiale, Istanbul, Turkey.

Ökten, Ç. (2015). *Female Entrepreneurship in Turkey: patterns, Characteristics and Trends.* The World Bank Report, 102013-TR, 1-36. Retrieved from https://openknowledge.worldbank.org/handle/10986/25410

Oliver, K. (2017). The male gaze is more relevant, and more dangerous, than ever. *New Review of Film and Television Studies, 15*(4), 451–455.

Onedio (2020). *Gelecek Yılın Yepyeni Moda Trendleri Belli Oldu: Pandemi Dönemi Bittiğinde En Çok Neler Giyeceğiz*? [Fashion Trends for next year seems obvious: What will we wear the most after the post-pandemic period?]. https://onedio.com/haber/gelecek-yilin-yepyeni-moda-trendleri-belli-oldu-pandemi-donemi-bittiginde-en-cok-neler-giyecegiz-926956

Orchard, T., & Burke, S. (2020). *On Zoom, men don't like feeling watched and judged — but women are used to it.* https://theconversation.com/on-zoom-men-dont-like-feeling-watched-and-judged-but-women-are-used-to-it-150594

Organization, W. H. (2008). *The global burden of disease: 2004 update*. Author.

Orhan, M., & Scott, D. (2001). Why Women Enter into Entrepreneurship: An Explanatory Model. *Women in Management Review, 16*(5), 232–247. doi:10.1108/09649420110395719

Orser, B. J., Riding, A. L., & Manley, K. (2006). Women entrepreneurs and financial capital. *Entrepreneurship Theory and Practice, 30*(5), 643–665. doi:10.1111/j.1540-6520.2006.00140.x

Ostry, J. D., & Lagarde, C. (2018). *Economic Gains from Gender Inclusion: Even Greater than You Thought.* IMFBlog. https://blogs.imf.org/2018/11/28/economic-gains-from-gender-inclusion-even-greater-than-you-thought/

Ott, E. M. (1989). Effects of the male-female ratio at work: Policewomen and male nurses. *Psychology of Women Quarterly, 13*(1), 41–57.

Oumerzoug, S. (2020). *L'entrepreneuriat féminin, une évolution en dents de scie*. MAP Business.

Özbilgin, M., & Healy, G. (2004). The gendered nature of career development of university professors: The case of Turkey. *Journal of Vocational Behavior, 64*(2), 358–371. doi:10.1016/j.jvb.2002.09.001

Ozdamar Ertekin, Z., Ucel, E. B., Oflac, B. S., and Dalkilic, O. S. (2021, June). *Dress and Professional Identity: Changing Wardrobes of Women in the Pandemic-era)* [Paper presentation]. Fashion Tales 2020+1 Conference, Università Cattolica del Sacro Cuore.

Ozdamar Ertekin, Z. (2019). Linda Welters and Abby Lillethun, Fashion History: A Global View (2018). *Markets, Globalization &. Developmental Review*, *4*(1), 6.

Ozdamar Ertekin, Z., & Atik, D. (2015). Aging of Youth through Fashion: Influential Dynamics and Societal Implications. In *Proceedings of the 40th Annual Macromarketing Conference* (pp. 38-53). The Macromarketing Society, Inc.

Özdemir, A. (2010). Potansiyel Girişimci Olan Kadınların Motivasyon Faktörleri ve Eskişehir'de Bir Araştırma. *Ege Akademik Bakış*, *10*(1), 117–139. doi:10.21121/eab.2010119651

Panda, S. (2018). Constraints faced by women entrepreneurs in developing countries: Review and ranking. *Gender in Management*, *33*(4), 315–331. doi:10.1108/GM-01-2017-0003

Parker, L. D., & Warren, S. (2017). The presentation of the self and professional identity: Countering the accountant's stereotype. *Accounting, Auditing & Accountability Journal*, *30*(8), 1895–1924.

Patil, P., & Deshpande, Y. (2019). Why Women enter into Entrepreneurship? An Exploratory Study. *Journal of Organizational Studies and Innovation*, *6*(2), 30–40.

Patterson, J. B. (1975). *Occupational Training for Mature Women: A Survey of the Enrollment of Women Over Age 35 in Proprietary Institutions in Cuyahoga County, Spring 1974*. Academic Press.

Pearce, S. C. (2012). The "Turkish model" of sociology: East-west science, state formation, and the post-secular. *The American Sociologist*, *43*(4), 406–427. doi:10.100712108-012-9163-4

Plummer, K. (2001). The call of life stories in ethnographic research. In P. Atkinson, A. Coffey, S. Delamont, J. Lofland, & L. Lofland (Eds.), *Handbook of Ethnography* (pp. 395–406). Sage. doi:10.4135/9781848608337.n27

Poggesi, S., Mari, M., & De Vita, L. (2016). What's new in female entrepreneurship research? Answers from the literature. *The International Entrepreneurship and Management Journal*, *12*(3), 735–764. doi:10.100711365-015-0364-5

Polo, S. (2012). *Albert Einstein's Letter to a Little Girl Who Loved Science and Hated Being a Girl*. https://www.themarysue.com/albert-einstein-little-girl/

Pratt, M. G., & an, d Rafaeli, A. (1997). Organizational Dress as a Symbol of Multilayered Social Identities. *Academy of Management Journal*, *40*(4), 862–898.

Rachdi, F. Z. (2006). L'entrepreneuriat féminin au Maroc: une étude exploratoire. *8ème congrès international francophone en entrepreneuriat et PME.*

Rachdi, F. Z. (2016). *L'Entrepreneuriat Feminin au Maroc: Une Approche par le Reseau Personnel* [Unpublished Doctoral Thesis]. Groupe Institut Supérieur de Commerce et D'administration des Entreprises Centre des Etudes Doctorales en Gestion.

Rafaeli, A., Button, J., Harquail, C. V., & Mackie-Lewis, S. (1997). Navigating by attire: The use of dress by female administrative employees. *Academy of Management Journal*, *40*(1), 9–45.

Rafaeli, A., & Pratt, M. G. (1993). Tailored Meanings: On the Meaning and Impact of Organizational Dress. *Academy of Management Review*, *18*(1), 32–55.

Rawlins, E. (2006). Mother Knows Best? Intergenerational Notions of Fashion and Identity. *Children's Geographies*, *4*(3), 359–377.

Reskin, B. F. (1988). Bringing the men back in: Sex differentiation and the devaluation of women's work. *Gender & Society*, *2*(1), 58–81.

Reynolds, P. D., Bygrave, W. D., Autio, E., Cox, L. W., & Hay, M. (2002). *Global Entrepreneurship Monitor, 2002 Executive Report*. Babson College, London Business School and Kauffman Foundation.

Riessman, C. K. (1993). Narrative analysis. *Sage (Atlanta, Ga.)*.

Riessman, C. K. (2008). Narrative methods for the human sciences. *Sage (Atlanta, Ga.)*.

Roach-Higgins, M. E., & Eicher, J. B. (1992). Dress and Identity. *Clothing & Textiles Research Journal*, *10*(4), 1–8.

Robinson, O. C. (2014). Sampling in interview-based qualitative research: A theoretical and practical guide. *Qualitative Research in Psychology*, *11*(1), 25–41. doi:10.1080/14780887.2013.801543

Rumens, N. (2017). Postfeminism, men, masculinities and work: A research agenda for gender and organization studies scholars. *Gender, Work and Organization*, *24*(3), 245–259. doi:10.1111/gwao.12138

Russell, R., & Tyler, M. (2002). Thank Heaven for Little Girls: 'Girl Heaven' and the Commercial Context of Feminine Childhood. *Sociology*, *36*(3), 619–637.

Rustad, M. L. (1982). *Women in Khaki: The American Enlisted Woman*. Praeger Publishers.

Sackett, P. R., Dubois, C. L., & Noe, A. W. (1991). Tokenism ın performance evaluation: The effects of work group representation on male-female and white-black differences ın performance ratings. *The Journal of Applied Psychology*, *76*(2), 263.

Sallan Gül, S., & Altındal, Y. (2016). The Adventure of Woman Enterpreneurship in Turkey: Is Succes Possible? *Süleyman Demirel Üniversitesi İktisadi ve İdari Bilimler Fakültesi Dergisi*, *21*(4), 1361–1377.

Sarwari, K. (2020). *Will the Covid-19 Pandemic Change How People Dress for Work in the Future?* https://news.northeastern.edu/2020/12/14/will-the-covid-19-pandemic-change-how-people-dress-for-work-in-the-future/

Schrör, H. (2006). *The profile of successful entrepreneur*. EUROSTAT report. https://ec.europa.eu/eurostat/documents/3433488/5443129/KS-NP-06-029-EN.PDF/22202ac8-b984-4b87-9f72-7e774e80a1ac?version=1.0

Schwartz, E. B. (1976). Entrepreneurship, a new female frontier. *Journal of Contemporary Business*, *5*(1), 47–76.

Scott, L. M. (2005). *Fresh Lipstick: Redressing Fashion and Feminism*. Palgrave Macmillan.

Seçkin Halaç, D., & Meşe, G. (2021). Toplumsal Cinsiyet Bakış Açısından Türkiye'de Kadın Girişimciliğinin Durumu. *Dumlupınar Üniversitesi Sosyal Bilimler Dergisi*, (68), 255–270. doi:10.51290/dpusbe.838567

Seckin Halac, D., & Seckin Celik, T. (2019). A Qualitative Look into Gendered Entrepreneurship in Turkey. *Istanbul Business Research*, *47*(2), 105–123.

Seçkin-Halaç, D., & Halaç, U. (2019). *Türkiye'de Kadın Girişimciliğinin Cinsiyetçi Yapısına OECD Verileriyle Nicel Bir Bakış*, [Conference presentation]. 10th International Entrepreneurship Congress, Manisa Celal Bayar Üniversitesi.

Seçkin-Halaç, D., & Seçkin-Çelik, T. (2018). A qualitative look into gendered entrepreneurship in Turkey. *Istanbul Business Research*, *47*(2), 105-123. Retrieved from https://dergipark.org.tr/en/pub/ibr/issue/44184/550011

Seçkin-Halaç, D. (2017). Değişen babalık ve girişimcilik kavramları çerçevesinde 'yeni/modern' babalar ve girişimcilik. In O. Sürgevil (Ed.), *ÇalışBabamÇalış: Baba olmak ve baba olmanın çalışma yaşamına yansımaları* (pp. 289–320). Nobel Akademik Yayıncılık.

Seçkin-Halaç, D., & Takımcı, D. (2018). Yerli çizgi dizi Niloya'da annelik ve babalık temsilleri. In A. Altay (Ed.), *Aile Araştırmaları* (pp. 495–522). Ekin Yayınevi.

Sefer, B. K. (2020). A gender- and class-sensitive explanatory model for rural women entrepreneurship in Turkey. *International Journal of Gender and Entrepreneurship*, *12*(2), 191–210. doi:10.1108/IJGE-07-2019-0113

Sellam, M. (2019 March 10). L'entrepreneuriat féminin toujours à la traîne. *Le Matin*. https://lematin.ma/journal/2019/lentrepreneuriat-feminin-trai/312043.html

Sen, A. (2000). *Development as freedom / Amartya Sen*. Anchor Book.

Şentürk, B. (2015). Çokuz ama yokuz: türkiye'deki akademisyen kadinlar üzerine bir analiz. *ViraVerita E-Dergi*, (2), 1–22.

Sexton, D. L., & Bowman-Upton, N. (1990). Female and male entrepreneurs: Psychological characteristics and their role in gender-related discrimination. *Journal of Business Venturing*, *5*(1), 29–36. doi:10.1016/0883-9026(90)90024-N

Shamir, B. (1986). Unemployment and Household Division of Labor. *Journal of Marriage and Family*, *48*(1), 195–206. doi:10.2307/352244

Shinnar, R. S., Giacomin, O., & Janssen, F. (2012). Entrepreneurial perceptions and intentions: The role of gender and culture. *Entrepreneurship Theory and Practice*, *36*(3), 465–493. doi:10.1111/j.1540-6520.2012.00509.x

Shinnar, R. S., Hsu, D. K., Powell, B. C., & Zhou, H. (2018). Entrepreneurial Intentions and Start-ups: Are Women or Men More Likely to Enact their Intentions? *International Small Business Journal*, *36*(1), 60–80. doi:10.1177/0266242617704277

Sky news. (2020). *Coronavirus: Women Told to Dress 'Sexier' When Working from Home, Survey Finds.* https://news.sky.com/story/coronavirus-women-told-to-dress-sexier-when-working-from-home-survey-finds-12034520

Smith, A. (2020). *Dress-Code Policies Reconsidered in the Pandemic.* https://www.shrm.org/resourcesandtools/legal-and-compliance/employment-law/pages/coronavirus-dress-code-policies.aspx

Solomon, M. R. (2018). *Consumer Behavior: Buying, Having, and Being.* Pearson Education Limited.

Sönmez, A., & Toksoy, A. (2014). Türkiye'de girisimcilik ve Türk girişimci profili üzerine bir analiz. *Yönetim ve Ekonomi*, *21*(2), 41–58. doi:10.18657/yecbu.26416

Spangler, E., Gordon, M. A., & Pipkin, R. M. (1978). Token women: An empirical test of Kanter's hypothesis. *American Journal of Sociology*, *84*(1), 160–170.

Startups.watch. (2019). *Reports.* Retrieved from https://startups.watch/reports?page=5&view_mode=list

Steele, C. M., Spencer, S. J., & Aronson, J. (2002). Contending with Group Image: The Psychology of Stereotype and Social Identity Threat. *Advances in Experimental Social Psychology, 34*, 379–440. doi:10.1016/S0065-2601(02)80009-0

Stevenson, L. (1990). Some methodological problems associated with researching women entrepreneurs. *Journal of Business Ethics*, *9*(4-5), 439–446. doi:10.1007/BF00380343

Stone, G. P. (1962). Appearance and the Self. In A. M. Rose (Ed.), *Human Behavior and Social Processes: An Interactionist Approach* (pp. 86–118). Houghton-Mifflin.

Strauss, A., & Corbin, J. (1998). Basics of qualitative research techniques. *Sage (Atlanta, Ga.).*

Strazzeri, V. (2015). Max Weber and the 'labour question': An initial appraisal. *Max Weber Studies*, *15*(1), 69–100. doi:10.15543/MWS/2015/1/5

Suchman, M. (1995). Managing Legitimacy: Strategic and Institutional Approaches. *Academy of Management Review*, *20*(3), 571–610.

Suchman, M. C. (1995). Managing legitimacy: Strategies and institutional approaches. *Academy of Management Review*, *20*(3), 571–610. doi:10.2307/258788

Sürgevil-Dalkılıç, O. (2015). Annelerin öykülerinden açığa çıkanlar: Annelik ve çalışan anneliğe yüklenen anlamlar, çalışma hayatından örnek olaylar, ihtiyaçlar ve beklentiler. In O. Sürgevil-Dalkılıç (Ed.), *ÇalışAnne: Kadın Akademisyenlerin Kaleminden Çalışma Yaşamında Annelik* (pp. 407–466). Nobel Akademik Yayıncılık.

Swerdlow, M. (1989). Men's accommodations to women entering a nontraditional occupation: A case of rapid transit operatives. *Gender & Society*, *3*(3), 373–387.

Tastad, C., & Deanna, B. (2020). *The route to true gender equality? Fix the system, not the women.* https://www.weforum.org/agenda/2020/01/gender-gap-equality-income-wages-solution/

Tatarlar, C. D. (2019). *Contamination at workplace* [Unpublished doctoral dissertation]. Izmir University of Economics, Izmir, Turkey.

Terborg, J. R. (1977). Women ın management: A research review. *The Journal of Applied Psychology*, *62*(6), 647.

Terborg, J. R., Peters, L. H., Ilgen, D. R., & Smith, F. (1977). Organizational and personal correlates of attitudes toward women as managers. *Academy of Management Journal*, *20*(1), 89–100.

Tharu, S., & Lalita, K. (1993). Preface. In S. Tharu & K. Lalilta (Eds.), *Women Writing in India: 600 B.C. to the Present* (Vol. 2). Pandora.

Thomas, L. (2007). *Why Do We Dress Children Like Tarts*? http://www.telegraph.co.uk/comment/personal-view/3640879 /why-do-we-dress-children-like-tarts.html

Thompson, J. C., & Hirschman, C. E. (1995). Understanding the Socialized Body: A Poststructuralist Analysis of Consumers' Self-conceptions, Body Images, and Self-care Practices. *The Journal of Consumer Research*, *22*(2), 139–153.

Toffoletti, K., & Starr, K. (2016). Women academics and work-life balance: Gendered discourses of work and care. *Gender, Work and Organization*, *23*(5), 489–504. doi:10.1111/gwao.12133

Tomlinson, J. (2007). Employment regulation, welfare and gender regimes: A comparative analysis of women's working-time patterns and work–life balance in the UK and the US. *International Journal of Human Resource Management*, *18*(3), 401–415. doi:10.1080/09585190601167466

Took, J. (2020). *10 big changes to business casual you will see in the post-pandemic workplace.* https://www.theladders.com/career-advice/10-big-changes-to-business-casual-you-will-see-in-the-post-pandemic-workplace

Toren, N., & Kraus, V. (1987). The effects of minority size on women's position in academia. *Social Forces*, *65*(4), 1090–1100. doi:10.2307/2579024

To, W. M., Gao, J. H., & Leung, E. Y. (2020). The Effects of Job Insecurity on Employees' Financial Well-Being and Work Satisfaction Among Chinese Pink-Collar Workers. *SAGE Open*, *10*(4), 2158244020982993. doi:10.1177/2158244020982993

Trauth, M. E. (2002). Odd girl out: An individual differences perspective on women in the IT profession. *Information Technology & People*, *15*(2), 96–118.

Tuncer, S. (2019). Cinsiyetlendirilmiş bir kurum olarak akademi: Türkiye'de akademinin cinsiyet kültürüne bakmak. *Kültür ve İletişim*, (44), 173–208. doi:10.18691/kulturveiletisim.629082

Turkey Entrepreneurship Strategy and Action Plan. (2015-2018). Retrieved from http://www.sp.gov.tr/tr/temelbelge/s/122/Turkiye+Girisimcilik+Stratejisi+ve+Eylem+Plani+_2015-2018

TURKSTAT. (n.d.). *2000, 2007, 2017, 2019, 2020 Labor Force Survey Results*. Author.

Tüzün, I. K., & Takay, A. B. (2017). Patterns of female entrepreneurial activities in Turkey. *Gender in Management, 32*(3), 166–182. doi:10.1108/GM-05-2016-0102

Twigg, J. (2007). Clothing, Age and the Body: A Critical Review. *Ageing and Society, 27*, 285–305.

Ufuk, H., & Özgen, Ö. (2001). Interaction Between the Business and Family Lives of Women Entrepreneurs in Turkey. *Journal of Business Ethics, 31*(2), 95–106. doi:10.1023/A:1010712023858

Uluköy, M., & Bayraktaroğlu, S. (2014). *A field research about oppression incurred of woman entrepreneurs in patriarchal societies*. Academic Press.

Verheul, I., Van Stel, A., & Thurik, R. (2006). Explaining female and male entrepreneurship at the country level. *Entrepreneurship and Regional Development, 18*(2), 151–183. doi:10.1080/08985620500532053

Victoria, L., Crittendena, V., Crittendenb, W. F., & Ajjan, H. (2019). Empowering Women Micro-Entrepreneurs in Emerging Economies: The role of Information Communications Technology. *Journal of Business Research, 98*, 191–203. doi:10.1016/j.jbusres.2019.01.045

Vinnicombe, S. (2000). The position of women in management in Europe. In M. J. Davidson & R. J. Burke (Eds.), *Women in management: Current research issues* (Vol. 2). Sage.

Wade, L. (2012). *Waxing for Girls 15 and Younger*. https://thesocietypages.org/socimages/2012/07/25/waxing-for-girls-15-and-younger

Warhurst, C., & Nickson, D. (2020). *Lookism: beauty still trumps brains in too many workplaces*. https://theconversation.com/lookism-beauty-still-trumps-brains-in-too-many-workplaces-148278

Warner, W. L., & Lunt, P. S. (1941). *The social life of a modern community* (Vol. 1). Yale University Press.

Warren, S., & Parker, L. D. (2009). Bean counters or bright young things? Towards the visual study of identity construction among professional accountants. *Qualitative Research in Accounting & Management, 6*(4), 205–223.

Watt, H. M. (2010). Gender and occupational choice. In *Handbook of gender research in psychology* (pp. 379–400). Springer.

Welsh, D. H. B., Kaciak, E., & Shamah, R. (2018). Determinants of women entrepreneurs' firm performance in a hostile environment. *Journal of Business Research, 88*, 481–491. doi:10.1016/j.jbusres.2017.12.015

Welter, F., & Smallbone, D. (2011). Institutional Perspectives on Entrepreneurial Behavior in Challenging Environments. *Journal of Small Business Management, 49*(1), 107–125.

Welters, L., & Lillethun, A. (2018). *Fashion History: A Global View (Dress, Body, Culture).* Bloomsbury Academic.

Williams, L. C. (1995). *Still a Man's World: Men who Do 'Women's Work.* University of California Press.

Wilson, E. (1985). *Adorned in Dreams: Fashion and Modernity.* I.B. Tauris.

Wimmer, D. D., & Dominick, J. R. (2000). *Mass Media Research: An Indroduction.* Wadsworth Publishing Company.

Witt, P. (2004). Entrepreneurs' networks and the success of start-ups. *Entrepreneurship and Regional Development, 16*(5), 391–412. doi:10.1080/0898562042000188423

Wolkowitz, C. (2006). *Bodies at Work.* SAGE Publications Ltd.

World bank gender data portal. (2020). *World Bank.* https://blogs.worldbank.org/opendata/women-entrepreneurs-needed-stat

World Bank. The global gender gap report 2018. (2018). World Bank.

World Economic Forum. (2010). *Global Competitiveness Report 2010-2011.* Author.

World Economic Forum. (2018). *The Global Gender Gap Report.* https://www3.weforum.org/docs/WEF_GGGR_2018.pdf

Yadav, V., & Unni, J. (2016). Women entrepreneurship: A research review and future directions. *Journal of Global Entrepreneurship Research, 6*(12), 1–18. doi:10.118640497-016-0055-x

Yetim, N. (2002). Sosyal Sermaye Olarak Kadın Girişimciler: Mersin Örneği. *Ege Akademik Bakış, 2*(2), 79–92.

Yetim, N. (2008). Social capital in female entrepreneurship. *International Sociology, 23*(6), 864–885. doi:10.1177/0268580908095913

Yılmaz, E., Özdemir, G., & Oraman, Y. (2012). Women entrepreneurs: Their problems and entrepreneurial ideas. *African Journal of Business Management, 6*(26), 7896–7904. doi:10.5897/AJBM12.081

Yoder, J. D., Aniakudo, P., & Berendsen, L. (1996). Looking Beyond Gender: The Effects Of Racial Differences On Tokenism Perceptions Of Women. *Sex Roles, 35*(7-8), 389-400.

Yoder, J. D. (1983). Another Look At Women In The Army: A Comment On Woelfel's Article. *Sex Roles, 9*(3), 285–288.

Yoder, J. D. (1983). Another look at women ın the army: A comment on woelfel's article. *Sex Roles, 9*(3), 285–288.

Yoder, J. D. (1992). Rethinking Tokenism: Looking Beyond Numbers. *Gender & Society, 5*(2), 178–192.

Yoder, J. D. (1994). Looking Beyond Numbers: The Effects Of Gender Status, Job Prestige, And Occupational Gendertyping On Tokenism Processes. *Social Psychology Quarterly*, *57*, 150–159.

Yoder, J. D. (2002). 2001 Division 35 Presidential Address: Context Matters: Understanding Tokenism Processes And Their Impact On Women's Work. *Psychology of Women Quarterly*, *26*(1), 1–8.

Yoder, J. D., Adams, J., & Prince, H. T. (1983). The price of a token. *Journal of Political and Military Sociology*, 325–337.

Yoder, J. D., & Schleicher, T. L. (1996). Undergraduates Regard Deviation From Occupational Gender Stereotypes As Costly For Women. *Sex Roles*, *34*(3-4), 171–188.

Yoder, J. D., Schleicher, T. L., & Mcdonald, T. W. (1998). Empowering Token Women Leaders: The Importance Of Organizationally Legitimated Credibility. *Psychology of Women Quarterly*, *22*(2), 209–222.

Yoder, J. D., & Sinnett, L. M. (1985). Is It All In The Numbers? A Case Study Of Tokenism. *Psychology of Women Quarterly*, *9*(3), 413–418.

Young, C. J., MacKenzie, D. L., & Sherif, C. W. (1980). In search of token women in academia. *Psychology of Women Quarterly*, *4*(4), 508–525.

Zimmer, L.(1988). Tokenism And Women In The Workplace: The Limits Of Gender-Theory. Social Problems, 35(1), 64–77.

Zimmer, L. (1987). How women reshape the prison guard role. *Gender & Society*, *1*(4), 415–431.

Related References

To continue our tradition of advancing academic research, we have compiled a list of recommended IGI Global readings. These references will provide additional information and guidance to further enrich your knowledge and assist you with your own research and future publications.

Ababio, G. K. (2018). Nutraceuticals: The Dose Makes the Difference – It's All in the Dose. In A. Verma, K. Srivastava, S. Singh, & H. Singh (Eds.), *Nutraceuticals and Innovative Food Products for Healthy Living and Preventive Care* (pp. 24–47). Hershey, PA: IGI Global. doi:10.4018/978-1-5225-2970-5.ch002

Adams, M. G. (2018). Systematically Investigating Instructor Impact on Student Satisfaction in Graduate Programs. In D. Polly, M. Putman, T. Petty, & A. Good (Eds.), *Innovative Practices in Teacher Preparation and Graduate-Level Teacher Education Programs* (pp. 200–214). Hershey, PA: IGI Global. doi:10.4018/978-1-5225-3068-8.ch012

Akgül, Y., & Tunca, M. Z. (2018). Proliferating View of Knowledge Management and Balanced Scorecard Outcome Linkage. In N. Baporikar (Ed.), *Global Practices in Knowledge Management for Societal and Organizational Development* (pp. 168–193). Hershey, PA: IGI Global. doi:10.4018/978-1-5225-3009-1.ch008

Alcaraz-Valencia, P. A., Gaytán-Lugo, L. S., & Gallardo, S. C. (2018). An Exploratory Study on the Interaction Beyond Virtual Environments to Improve Listening Ability When Learning English as a Second Language. In F. Cipolla-Ficarra (Ed.), *Optimizing Human-Computer Interaction With Emerging Technologies* (pp. 306–331). Hershey, PA: IGI Global. doi:10.4018/978-1-5225-2616-2.ch013

Altıntaş, F. Ç., & Kavurmacı, C. (2018). Value Statements in Web Pages of Turkish State Universities: A Basic Classification. In U. Thomas (Ed.), *Advocacy in Academia and the Role of Teacher Preparation Programs* (pp. 302–316). Hershey, PA: IGI Global. doi:10.4018/978-1-5225-2906-4.ch017

Amoroso, D. L. (2018). The Importance of Advocacy on Reputation and Loyalty: Comparison of Japanese, Chinese, and the Filipino Consumers. In P. Ordóñez de Pablos (Ed.), *Management Strategies and Technology Fluidity in the Asian Business Sector* (pp. 114–125). Hershey, PA: IGI Global. doi:10.4018/978-1-5225-4056-4.ch007

Atiku, S. O., & Fields, Z. (2018). Organisational Learning Dimensions and Talent Retention Strategies for the Service Industries. In N. Baporikar (Ed.), *Global Practices in Knowledge Management for Societal and Organizational Development* (pp. 358–381). Hershey, PA: IGI Global. doi:10.4018/978-1-5225-3009-1.ch017

Ayoola-Amale, A. (2018). Women in Leadership: Why We Need More Women Leaders. In B. Cook (Ed.), *Handbook of Research on Examining Global Peacemaking in the Digital Age* (pp. 211–222). Hershey, PA: IGI Global. doi:10.4018/978-1-5225-3032-9.ch015

Baran, A. G. (2018). Through the Syrians Refuge in Turkey Towards the Creation of the War Migration Theory. In Ş. Erçetin (Ed.), *Social Considerations of Migration Movements and Immigration Policies* (pp. 178–196). Hershey, PA: IGI Global. doi:10.4018/978-1-5225-3322-1.ch011

Beckett-Camarata, J. (2018). Public Choice and Financing Local Government Fiscal Reform in Albania. In H. Levine & K. Moreno (Eds.), *Positioning Markets and Governments in Public Management* (pp. 197–208). Hershey, PA: IGI Global. doi:10.4018/978-1-5225-4177-6.ch015

Bedford, D. A. (2018). Sustainable Knowledge Management Strategies: Aligning Business Capabilities and Knowledge Management Goals. In N. Baporikar (Ed.), *Global Practices in Knowledge Management for Societal and Organizational Development* (pp. 46–73). Hershey, PA: IGI Global. doi:10.4018/978-1-5225-3009-1.ch003

Benaouda, A., & García-Peñalvo, F. J. (2018). Towards an Intelligent System for the Territorial Planning: Agricultural Case. In F. García-Peñalvo (Ed.), *Global Implications of Emerging Technology Trends* (pp. 158–178). Hershey, PA: IGI Global. doi:10.4018/978-1-5225-4944-4.ch010

Beneventi, P. (2018). When Technology Becomes Popular: A Multimedia, Shared Production for the Information Age. In *Technology and the New Generation of Active Citizens: Emerging Research and Opportunities* (pp. 23–44). Hershey, PA: IGI Global. doi:10.4018/978-1-5225-3770-0.ch002

Bernal, L. D., & Cusi, M. L. (2018). Corporate Entrepreneurship in Colombia: Contrast Cases of Two Colombian Manufacturing SMEs. In R. Perez-Uribe, C. Salcedo-Perez, & D. Ocampo-Guzman (Eds.), *Handbook of Research on Intrapreneurship and Organizational Sustainability in SMEs* (pp. 368–390). Hershey, PA: IGI Global. doi:10.4018/978-1-5225-3543-0.ch017

Berning, S. C., & Ambrosius, J. (2018). How the Human Resource Practices of Chinese MNEs in Africa Create Economic Growth and Livelihood Options. In S. Hipsher (Ed.), *Examining the Private Sector's Role in Wealth Creation and Poverty Reduction* (pp. 85–109). Hershey, PA: IGI Global. doi:10.4018/978-1-5225-3117-3.ch005

Bharti, A., & Mittal, A. (2018). Perishable Goods Supply Cold Chain Management in India. In A. Kumar & S. Saurav (Eds.), *Supply Chain Management Strategies and Risk Assessment in Retail Environments* (pp. 232–246). Hershey, PA: IGI Global. doi:10.4018/978-1-5225-3056-5.ch013

Bhattacharya, S., Kumar, R. V., & Dutta, A. (2018). Exploring Kapferer's Brand Identity Prism Applicability in Indian Political Marketing Aspect With Special Focus to Youth Voters. In Rajagopal, & R. Behl (Eds.), Start-Up Enterprises and Contemporary Innovation Strategies in the Global Marketplace (pp. 136-152). Hershey, PA: IGI Global. doi:10.4018/978-1-5225-4831-7.ch010

Bhattarai, R. K. (2018). Enterprise Immune System. In *Enterprise Resiliency in the Continuum of Change: Emerging Research and Opportunities* (pp. 88–111). Hershey, PA: IGI Global. doi:10.4018/978-1-5225-2627-8.ch003

Bhattarai, R. K. (2018). Enterprise Philosophy. In *Enterprise Resiliency in the Continuum of Change: Emerging Research and Opportunities* (pp. 1–43). Hershey, PA: IGI Global. doi:10.4018/978-1-5225-2627-8.ch001

Bhattarai, R. K. (2018). Enterprise Resiliency. In *Enterprise Resiliency in the Continuum of Change: Emerging Research and Opportunities* (pp. 112–137). Hershey, PA: IGI Global. doi:10.4018/978-1-5225-2627-8.ch004

Bisen, S. S., & Deshpande, Y. (2018). The Impact of the Internet in Twenty-First Century Addictions: An Overview. In B. Bozoglan (Ed.), *Psychological, Social, and Cultural Aspects of Internet Addiction* (pp. 1–19). Hershey, PA: IGI Global. doi:10.4018/978-1-5225-3477-8.ch001

Biswal, S. K. (2018). Branding Culture: A Study of Telugu Film Industry. In S. Dasgupta, S. Biswal, & M. Ramesh (Eds.), *Holistic Approaches to Brand Culture and Communication Across Industries* (pp. 1–23). Hershey, PA: IGI Global. doi:10.4018/978-1-5225-3150-0.ch001

Blake, S., & Burkett, C. M. (2018). Individual Creativity: Predictors and Characteristics. In *Creativity in Workforce Development and Innovation: Emerging Research and Opportunities* (pp. 88–104). Hershey, PA: IGI Global. doi:10.4018/978-1-5225-4952-9.ch005

Blomeley, S., & Hamilton, A. H. (2018). Writing Partners: Bridging the Personal and Social in the Service-Learning Classroom. In O. Delano-Oriaran, M. Penick-Parks, & S. Fondrie (Eds.), *Culturally Engaging Service-Learning With Diverse Communities* (pp. 202–222). Hershey, PA: IGI Global. doi:10.4018/978-1-5225-2900-2.ch012

Bohra, M., & Visen, A. (2018). Nutraceutical Properties in Flowers. In A. Verma, K. Srivastava, S. Singh, & H. Singh (Eds.), *Nutraceuticals and Innovative Food Products for Healthy Living and Preventive Care* (pp. 217–235). Hershey, PA: IGI Global. doi:10.4018/978-1-5225-2970-5.ch010

Boyd, L. N. (2018). Fortifying Parent Partnerships Through the Black Church Space. In K. Norris & S. Collier (Eds.), *Social Justice and Parent Partnerships in Multicultural Education Contexts* (pp. 118–137). Hershey, PA: IGI Global. doi:10.4018/978-1-5225-3943-8.ch007

Bozoglan, B. (2018). The Role of Family Factors in Internet Addiction Among Children and Adolescents: An Overview. In B. Bozoglan (Ed.), *Psychological, Social, and Cultural Aspects of Internet Addiction* (pp. 146–168). Hershey, PA: IGI Global. doi:10.4018/978-1-5225-3477-8.ch008

Briz-Ponce, L., Juanes-Méndez, J. A., & García-Peñalvo, F. J. (2018). Current Situation and Appraisal Tendencies of M-Learning. In F. García-Peñalvo (Ed.), *Global Implications of Emerging Technology Trends* (pp. 115–129). Hershey, PA: IGI Global. doi:10.4018/978-1-5225-4944-4.ch007

Brkljačić, T., Majetić, F., & Wertag, A. (2018). I'm Always Online: Well-Being and Main Sources of Life Dis/Satisfaction of Heavy Internet Users. In B. Bozoglan (Ed.), *Psychological, Social, and Cultural Aspects of Internet Addiction* (pp. 72–89). Hershey, PA: IGI Global. doi:10.4018/978-1-5225-3477-8.ch004

Brown, M. A. Sr. (2018). Defining Your Team. In *Motivationally Intelligent Leadership: Emerging Research and Opportunities* (pp. 1–22). Hershey, PA: IGI Global. doi:10.4018/978-1-5225-3746-5.ch001

Brown, M. A. Sr. (2018). Empowering Leaders With Tools. In *Motivationally Intelligent Leadership: Emerging Research and Opportunities* (pp. 72–96). Hershey, PA: IGI Global. doi:10.4018/978-1-5225-3746-5.ch006

Brown, M. A. Sr. (2018). Sensemaking Theory. In *Motivationally Intelligent Leadership: Emerging Research and Opportunities* (pp. 46–55). Hershey, PA: IGI Global. doi:10.4018/978-1-5225-3746-5.ch004

Brown, S., & Bousalis, R. (2018). Best Practices in K-12 Arts Integration: Curricular Connections. In *Curriculum Integration in Contemporary Teaching Practice: Emerging Research and Opportunities* (pp. 95–124). Hershey, PA: IGI Global. doi:10.4018/978-1-5225-4065-6.ch004

Brown, S., & Bousalis, R. (2018). Interdisciplinary Curriculum in K-12 Schools: Current Practices in the Field. In *Curriculum Integration in Contemporary Teaching Practice: Emerging Research and Opportunities* (pp. 125–143). Hershey, PA: IGI Global. doi:10.4018/978-1-5225-4065-6.ch005

Bullock, C. A. (2018). Collaboration: Academes, Government, and Community to Drive Economic Uplift and Empowerment. In S. Burton (Ed.), *Engaged Scholarship and Civic Responsibility in Higher Education* (pp. 1–24). Hershey, PA: IGI Global. doi:10.4018/978-1-5225-3649-9.ch001

Burdenko, E. V., & Mudrova, S. V. (2018). Indicators System as a Measure of Development Level of Knowledge Economy: Application of World Bank Methodology. In N. Baporikar (Ed.), *Global Practices in Knowledge Management for Societal and Organizational Development* (pp. 74–105). Hershey, PA: IGI Global. doi:10.4018/978-1-5225-3009-1.ch004

Burston, B., & Collier-Stewart, S. (2018). STEM for All: The Importance of Parent/School/Community Partnerships Across the K-12 Pipeline and Beyond. In K. Norris & S. Collier (Eds.), *Social Justice and Parent Partnerships in Multicultural Education Contexts* (pp. 274–288). Hershey, PA: IGI Global. doi:10.4018/978-1-5225-3943-8.ch015

Carboni, M., & Perelli, C. (2018). "Beyond" Religious Tourism: The Case of Fez. In H. El-Gohary, D. Edwards, & R. Eid (Eds.), *Global Perspectives on Religious Tourism and Pilgrimage* (pp. 71–83). Hershey, PA: IGI Global. doi:10.4018/978-1-5225-2796-1.ch005

Cascella, M., Muzio, M. R., Bimonte, S., & Cuomo, A. (2018). Nutraceuticals for Prevention of Chemotherapy-Induced Peripheral Neuropathy. In A. Verma, K. Srivastava, S. Singh, & H. Singh (Eds.), *Nutraceuticals and Innovative Food Products for Healthy Living and Preventive Care* (pp. 236–259). Hershey, PA: IGI Global. doi:10.4018/978-1-5225-2970-5.ch011

Cena, F., Rapp, A., Likavec, S., & Marcengo, A. (2018). Envisioning the Future of Personalization Through Personal Informatics: A User Study. *International Journal of Mobile Human Computer Interaction, 10*(1), 52–66. doi:10.4018/IJMHCI.2018010104

Chandiramani, J., & Airy, A. (2018). Urbanization and Socio-Economic Growth in South Asia Region. In U. Benna & I. Benna (Eds.), *Urbanization and Its Impact on Socio-Economic Growth in Developing Regions* (pp. 130–154). Hershey, PA: IGI Global. doi:10.4018/978-1-5225-2659-9.ch007

Chang, Y., Choi, S. B., Lee, J., & Jin, W. C. (2018). Population Size vs. Number of Crimes: Is the Relationship Superlinear? *International Journal of Information Systems and Social Change, 9*(1), 26–39. doi:10.4018/IJISSC.2018010102

Chaudhary, N. S., & Yadav, R. (2018). Cross-Cultural Conflicts: Concept, Causes, and Elucidations. In N. Sharma, V. Singh, & S. Pathak (Eds.), *Management Techniques for a Diverse and Cross-Cultural Workforce* (pp. 79–96). Hershey, PA: IGI Global. doi:10.4018/978-1-5225-4933-8.ch005

Chirisa, I., Mukarwi, L., & Matamanda, A. R. (2018). Social Costs and Benefits of the Transformation of the Traditional Families in an African Urban Society. In U. Benna & I. Benna (Eds.), *Urbanization and Its Impact on Socio-Economic Growth in Developing Regions* (pp. 179–197). Hershey, PA: IGI Global. doi:10.4018/978-1-5225-2659-9.ch009

Chitima, S. S., & Ndlovu, I. (2018). Incorporating Indigenous Knowledge in the Preservation of Collections at the Batonga Community Museum in Zimbabwe. In P. Ngulube (Ed.), *Handbook of Research on Heritage Management and Preservation* (pp. 396–407). Hershey, PA: IGI Global. doi:10.4018/978-1-5225-3137-1.ch019

Choudhury, D. K., & Rao, P. (2018). Determinants of FDI Inflows in Developing Countries: A Dynamic Panel Approach. In V. Malepati & C. Gowri (Eds.), *Foreign Direct Investments (FDIs) and Opportunities for Developing Economies in the World Market* (pp. 25–45). Hershey, PA: IGI Global. doi:10.4018/978-1-5225-3026-8.ch002

Cipolla-Ficarra, F. V., Carré, J., Quiroga, A., & Ficarra, V. M. (2018). Anti-Models for Architectural Graphic Expression and UX Education. In F. Cipolla-Ficarra, M. Ficarra, M. Cipolla-Ficarra, A. Quiroga, J. Alma, & J. Carré (Eds.), *Technology-Enhanced Human Interaction in Modern Society* (pp. 218–233). Hershey, PA: IGI Global. doi:10.4018/978-1-5225-3437-2.ch011

Cipolla-Ficarra, F. V., Ficarra, V. M., & Cipolla-Ficarra, M. (2018). Inverted Semanteme Into Financial Information Online. In F. Cipolla-Ficarra, M. Ficarra, M. Cipolla-Ficarra, A. Quiroga, J. Alma, & J. Carré (Eds.), *Technology-Enhanced Human Interaction in Modern Society* (pp. 263–283). Hershey, PA: IGI Global. doi:10.4018/978-1-5225-3437-2.ch013

Cipolla-Ficarra, F. V., Quiroga, A., & Ficarra, V. M. (2018). Kernel of the Labyrinths Hypertextuals. In F. Cipolla-Ficarra, M. Ficarra, M. Cipolla-Ficarra, A. Quiroga, J. Alma, & J. Carré (Eds.), *Technology-Enhanced Human Interaction in Modern Society* (pp. 122–142). Hershey, PA: IGI Global. doi:10.4018/978-1-5225-3437-2.ch006

Coffey, S. M. (2018). Unveilings Through Transformative Pedagogy: Striving for Realization of Du Bois' Educational Paradigm. In U. Thomas (Ed.), *Advocacy in Academia and the Role of Teacher Preparation Programs* (pp. 206–224). Hershey, PA: IGI Global. doi:10.4018/978-1-5225-2906-4.ch012

da Rocha, J. P. (2018). Process Outcomes. In *Political Mediation in Modern Conflict Resolution: Emerging Research and Opportunities* (pp. 155–164). Hershey, PA: IGI Global. doi:10.4018/978-1-5225-5118-8.ch004

Dahiya, K., & Dhankhar, R. (2018). Role of Nutraceuticals in Cancer. In A. Verma, K. Srivastava, S. Singh, & H. Singh (Eds.), *Nutraceuticals and Innovative Food Products for Healthy Living and Preventive Care* (pp. 176–194). Hershey, PA: IGI Global. doi:10.4018/978-1-5225-2970-5.ch008

Dasgupta, S., & Kothari, R. (2018). The Impact of Digital Word-of-Mouth Communication on Consumer Decision-Making Processes: With Special Reference to Fashion Apparel Industry. In S. Dasgupta, S. Biswal, & M. Ramesh (Eds.), *Holistic Approaches to Brand Culture and Communication Across Industries* (pp. 176–198). Hershey, PA: IGI Global. doi:10.4018/978-1-5225-3150-0.ch010

Dávila, F. A. (2018). Relationship Lending and Entrepreneurial Behavior: A Game-Theoretic-Based Modeling. In Rajagopal, & R. Behl (Eds.), Start-Up Enterprises and Contemporary Innovation Strategies in the Global Marketplace (pp. 65-86). Hershey, PA: IGI Global. doi:10.4018/978-1-5225-4831-7.ch006 de Sousa, J. C. (2018). Memory. In *Neuromarketing and Big Data Analytics for Strategic Consumer Engagement: Emerging Research and Opportunities* (pp. 92–100). Hershey, PA: IGI Global. doi:10.4018/978-1-5225-4834-8.ch006

de Sousa, J. C. (2018). Sensory and Motor System. In *Neuromarketing and Big Data Analytics for Strategic Consumer Engagement: Emerging Research and Opportunities* (pp. 68–91). Hershey, PA: IGI Global. doi:10.4018/978-1-5225-4834-8.ch005

Deka, D. B., & Jadeja, M. (2018). Childhood Sexual Abuse: Prevention and Intervention. In R. Gopalan (Ed.), *Social, Psychological, and Forensic Perspectives on Sexual Abuse* (pp. 127–146). Hershey, PA: IGI Global. doi:10.4018/978-1-5225-3958-2.ch010

Dobell, E., Herold, S., & Buckley, J. (2018). Spreadsheet Error Types and Their Prevalence in a Healthcare Context. *Journal of Organizational and End User Computing*, *30*(2), 20–42. doi:10.4018/JOEUC.2018040102

Donert, K., & Papoutsis, P. (2018). School on the Cloud: Connecting Education to the Cloud for Digital Citizenship. In K. Koutsopoulos, K. Doukas, & Y. Kotsanis (Eds.), *Handbook of Research on Educational Design and Cloud Computing in Modern Classroom Settings* (pp. 157–182). Hershey, PA: IGI Global. doi:10.4018/978-1-5225-3053-4.ch008

Downton, M. P. (2018). Preparation for Future Teaching: Authentic Activities in a Teacher Education Classroom. In D. Polly, M. Putman, T. Petty, & A. Good (Eds.), *Innovative Practices in Teacher Preparation and Graduate-Level Teacher Education Programs* (pp. 293–305). Hershey, PA: IGI Global. doi:10.4018/978-1-5225-3068-8.ch016

Drivas, G., Sotiriou, C., Bonanou, H., Saliari, S., Balafouti, M., & Tsevi, H. (2018). The Sky Is the Limit! In K. Koutsopoulos, K. Doukas, & Y. Kotsanis (Eds.), *Handbook of Research on Educational Design and Cloud Computing in Modern Classroom Settings* (pp. 101–121). Hershey, PA: IGI Global. doi:10.4018/978-1-5225-3053-4.ch006

Erçetin, Ş. Ş., & Bisaso, S. M. (2018). Migration and Refugee Crisis: Structural and Managerial Implications for Education. In Ş. Erçetin (Ed.), *Educational Development and Infrastructure for Immigrants and Refugees* (pp. 47–71). Hershey, PA: IGI Global. doi:10.4018/978-1-5225-3325-2.ch003

Erçetin, Ş. Ş., & Kubilay, S. (2018). Educational Expectations of Refugee Mothers for Their Children. In Ş. Erçetin (Ed.), *Educational Development and Infrastructure for Immigrants and Refugees* (pp. 171–195). Hershey, PA: IGI Global. doi:10.4018/978-1-5225-3325-2.ch009

Erçetin, Ş. Ş., Potas, N., Açıkalın, Ş. N., Özdemir, N., & Doğan, A. M. (2018). Municipalities and Refugee Crisis: Ansar Policies and Numbers. In Ş. Erçetin (Ed.), *Social Considerations of Migration Movements and Immigration Policies* (pp. 46–57). Hershey, PA: IGI Global. doi:10.4018/978-1-5225-3322-1.ch003

Erkekoğlu, L. C., & Madi, İ. (2018). The Hashemite Kingdom of Jordan. In S. Ozdemir, S. Erdogan, & A. Gedikli (Eds.), *Handbook of Research on Sociopolitical Factors Impacting Economic Growth in Islamic Nations* (pp. 95–121). Hershey, PA: IGI Global. doi:10.4018/978-1-5225-2939-2.ch006

Essien, E. D. (2018). Strengthening Performance of Civil Society Through Dialogue and Critical Thinking in Nigeria: Its Ethical Implications. In S. Chhabra (Ed.), *Handbook of Research on Civic Engagement and Social Change in Contemporary Society* (pp. 82–102). Hershey, PA: IGI Global. doi:10.4018/978-1-5225-4197-4.ch005

Feza, N. N. (2018). The Socioeconomic Status Label Associated With Mathematics. In I. Tshabangu (Ed.), *Global Ideologies Surrounding Children's Rights and Social Justice* (pp. 186–203). Hershey, PA: IGI Global. doi:10.4018/978-1-5225-2578-3.ch012

Fleener, J., Lu, L., Dun, J., & Mingquan, Y. (2018). Sustaining a Teacher Professional Learning Community in China Through Technology. In H. Spires (Ed.), *Digital Transformation and Innovation in Chinese Education* (pp. 80–99). Hershey, PA: IGI Global. doi:10.4018/978-1-5225-2924-8.ch005

Forge, J. (2018). Defence. In *The Morality of Weapons Design and Development: Emerging Research and Opportunities* (pp. 52–77). Hershey, PA: IGI Global. doi:10.4018/978-1-5225-3984-1.ch004

Forge, J. (2018). Justification. In *The Morality of Weapons Design and Development: Emerging Research and Opportunities* (pp. 78–93). Hershey, PA: IGI Global. doi:10.4018/978-1-5225-3984-1.ch005

Forge, J. (2018). Projectile Weapons. In *The Morality of Weapons Design and Development: Emerging Research and Opportunities* (pp. 94–117). Hershey, PA: IGI Global. doi:10.4018/978-1-5225-3984-1.ch006

Forge, J. (2018). Proportionality, Just War Theory, and Weapons Design. In *The Morality of Weapons Design and Development: Emerging Research and Opportunities* (pp. 139–154). Hershey, PA: IGI Global. doi:10.4018/978-1-5225-3984-1.ch008

Forge, J. (2018). Purposes and Means. In *The Morality of Weapons Design and Development: Emerging Research and Opportunities* (pp. 34–51). Hershey, PA: IGI Global. doi:10.4018/978-1-5225-3984-1.ch003

Fudge, M. (2018). The Inequity of User Fees and the Overreliance by Communities to Generate Revenue. In H. Levine & K. Moreno (Eds.), *Positioning Markets and Governments in Public Management* (pp. 147–158). Hershey, PA: IGI Global. doi:10.4018/978-1-5225-4177-6.ch011

Furumoto, R. R. (2018). Mexican-American Parents Using Critical Literacy to Address Climate Change. In K. Norris & S. Collier (Eds.), *Social Justice and Parent Partnerships in Multicultural Education Contexts* (pp. 187–208). Hershey, PA: IGI Global. doi:10.4018/978-1-5225-3943-8.ch010

Gabay, D. (2018). Who's Represented in Canadian Teaching and Learning Centres? In B. Blummer, J. Kenton, & M. Wiatrowski (Eds.), *Promoting Ethnic Diversity and Multiculturalism in Higher Education* (pp. 172–198). Hershey, PA: IGI Global. doi:10.4018/978-1-5225-4097-7.ch010

Garner, G. (2018). Foundations for Yoga Practice in Rehabilitation. In S. Telles & N. Singh (Eds.), *Research-Based Perspectives on the Psychophysiology of Yoga* (pp. 263–307). Hershey, PA: IGI Global. doi:10.4018/978-1-5225-2788-6.ch015

Geethanjali, P. (2018). Bio-Inspired Techniques in Human-Computer Interface for Control of Assistive Devices: Bio-Inspired Techniques in Assistive Devices. In D. Lopez & M. Durai (Eds.), *HCI Challenges and Privacy Preservation in Big Data Security* (pp. 23–46). Hershey, PA: IGI Global. doi:10.4018/978-1-5225-2863-0.ch002

Gharote, M. (2018). Common Features Between Findings in Traditional Texts and Contemporary Science: Yoga Texts and Contemporary Science. In S. Telles & N. Singh (Eds.), *Research-Based Perspectives on the Psychophysiology of Yoga* (pp. 309–315). Hershey, PA: IGI Global. doi:10.4018/978-1-5225-2788-6.ch016

Giosi, A., Zaccaro, E., & Testarmata, S. (2018). Social Responsibility, Shared Value, and Business Modelling: An Integrated Approach. In M. Risso & S. Testarmata (Eds.), *Value Sharing for Sustainable and Inclusive Development* (pp. 100–121). Hershey, PA: IGI Global. doi:10.4018/978-1-5225-3147-0.ch005

Grădinaru, C., Toma, S. I., & Marinescu, P. I. (2018). Entrepreneurial Thinking in the Educational System. In M. Risso & S. Testarmata (Eds.), *Value Sharing for Sustainable and Inclusive Development* (pp. 29–48). Hershey, PA: IGI Global. doi:10.4018/978-1-5225-3147-0.ch002

Güler, A. (2018). PKK-Related Asylum Applications from Turkey: Counter-Terrorism Measures vs. Refugee Status. In Ş. Erçetin (Ed.), *Social Considerations of Migration Movements and Immigration Policies* (pp. 117–142). Hershey, PA: IGI Global. doi:10.4018/978-1-5225-3322-1.ch008

Gupta, S. K. (2018). Sexual Abuse of Children and Adults With Intellectual Disabilities: Preventive, Supportive, and Intervention Strategies for Clinical Practice. In R. Gopalan (Ed.), *Social, Psychological, and Forensic Perspectives on Sexual Abuse* (pp. 197–206). Hershey, PA: IGI Global. doi:10.4018/978-1-5225-3958-2.ch014

Gürcan, Ö. F., & Gümüşsoy, Ç. A. (2018). Factors Influencing Effective Knowledge Transfer in Organizations. In N. Baporikar (Ed.), *Global Practices in Knowledge Management for Societal and Organizational Development* (pp. 271–292). Hershey, PA: IGI Global. doi:10.4018/978-1-5225-3009-1.ch013

Hagen, I., Kofoed, S., & Nayar, U. (2018). Yoga for Psychological Wellbeing in Modern Life and Contexts. In S. Telles & N. Singh (Eds.), *Research-Based Perspectives on the Psychophysiology of Yoga* (pp. 316–334). Hershey, PA: IGI Global. doi:10.4018/978-1-5225-2788-6.ch017

Handayani, B. (2018). The Paradox of Authenticity and Its Implications for Contemporary and "Bizarre" Tourism Campaigns. In S. Sarma (Ed.), *Global Observations of the Influence of Culture on Consumer Buying Behavior* (pp. 48–65). Hershey, PA: IGI Global. doi:10.4018/978-1-5225-2727-5.ch003

Huamaní, G. A., Fernández-López, S., Gómez, I. N., Rey-Ares, L., Rodríguez-Gulías, M. J., & Rodeiro-Pazos, D. (2018). The Role Models as Determinants of New Technology-Based Firms: An Exploratory Study. In A. Carrizo Moreira, J. Guilherme Leitão Dantas, & F. Manuel Valente (Eds.), *Nascent Entrepreneurship and Successful New Venture Creation* (pp. 272–288). Hershey, PA: IGI Global. doi:10.4018/978-1-5225-2936-1.ch013

Hucks, D., Sturtz, T., & Tirabassi, K. (2018). Building, Shaping, and Modeling Tools for Literacy Development and Civic Engagement. In *Fostering Positive Civic Engagement Among Millennials: Emerging Research and Opportunities* (pp. 22–35). Hershey, PA: IGI Global. doi:10.4018/978-1-5225-2452-6.ch002

Hucks, D., Sturtz, T., & Tirabassi, K. (2018). Insights, Next Steps, and Future Research. In *Fostering Positive Civic Engagement Among Millennials: Emerging Research and Opportunities* (pp. 65–72). Hershey, PA: IGI Global. doi:10.4018/978-1-5225-2452-6.ch005

Iguisi, O. V. (2018). Comparative Analysis of Hofstede's Culture Dimensions for West African Regions (WAF) and Nigeria. In S. Sarma (Ed.), *Global Observations of the Influence of Culture on Consumer Buying Behavior* (pp. 190–205). Hershey, PA: IGI Global. doi:10.4018/978-1-5225-2727-5.ch012

Islam, M. R. (2018). Abuse Among Child Domestic Workers in Bangladesh. In I. Tshabangu (Ed.), *Global Ideologies Surrounding Children's Rights and Social Justice* (pp. 1–21). Hershey, PA: IGI Global. doi:10.4018/978-1-5225-2578-3.ch001

Ito, K., & Hilliker, S. M. (2018). Supporting University International Students Through Supportive ESL Instruction and Corrective Feedback. In B. Blummer, J. Kenton, & M. Wiatrowski (Eds.), *Promoting Ethnic Diversity and Multiculturalism in Higher Education* (pp. 40–58). Hershey, PA: IGI Global. doi:10.4018/978-1-5225-4097-7.ch003

Iurato, G. (2018). A Brief Account of Ignacio Matte Blanco Theory and Other Related Psychoanalytic Themes. In *Computational Psychoanalysis and Formal Bi-Logic Frameworks* (pp. 114–135). Hershey, PA: IGI Global. doi:10.4018/978-1-5225-4128-8.ch003

Iurato, G. (2018). First Attempts to Formalize Some Main Aspects of Psychoanalysis: Towards a Computational Psychoanalysis. In *Computational Psychoanalysis and Formal Bi-Logic Frameworks* (pp. 136–205). Hershey, PA: IGI Global. doi:10.4018/978-1-5225-4128-8.ch004

Jacobsen, M., Friesen, S., & Brown, B. (2018). Teachers' Professional Learning Focused on Designs for Early Learners and Technology. In D. Polly, M. Putman, T. Petty, & A. Good (Eds.), *Innovative Practices in Teacher Preparation and Graduate-Level Teacher Education Programs* (pp. 417–438). Hershey, PA: IGI Global. doi:10.4018/978-1-5225-3068-8.ch022

Jensen, A. A., & Thomassen, A. O. (2018). Teachers' Reflective Practice in Lifelong Learning Programs. In Z. Djoub (Ed.), *Fostering Reflective Teaching Practice in Pre-Service Education* (pp. 25–45). Hershey, PA: IGI Global. doi:10.4018/978-1-5225-2963-7.ch002

Jiang, K., Barnett, G. A., Taylor, L. D., & Feng, B. (2018). Dynamic Co-Evolutions of Peace Frames in the United States, Mainland China, and Hong Kong: A Semantic Network Analysis. In B. Cook (Ed.), *Handbook of Research on Examining Global Peacemaking in the Digital Age* (pp. 145–168). Hershey, PA: IGI Global. doi:10.4018/978-1-5225-3032-9.ch010

Jiménez-González, S. G., Mendoza-González, R., & Luna-García, H. (2018). Guidelines Based on Need-Findings Study and Communication Types to Design Interactions for MOOCs. In F. Cipolla-Ficarra (Ed.), *Optimizing Human-Computer Interaction With Emerging Technologies* (pp. 210–231). Hershey, PA: IGI Global. doi:10.4018/978-1-5225-2616-2.ch008

Johnson, N. N. (2018). Effectively Managing Bias in Teacher Preparation. In U. Thomas (Ed.), *Advocacy in Academia and the Role of Teacher Preparation Programs* (pp. 146–160). Hershey, PA: IGI Global. doi:10.4018/978-1-5225-2906-4.ch008

Joseph, C. (2018). The Role of Government in a Liberal Market Economy: A Double-Edge Sword. In H. Levine & K. Moreno (Eds.), *Positioning Markets and Governments in Public Management* (pp. 53–61). Hershey, PA: IGI Global. doi:10.4018/978-1-5225-4177-6.ch005

Kade, D., Lindell, R., Ürey, H., & Özcan, O. (2018). Supporting Motion Capture Acting Through a Mixed Reality Application. In F. Cipolla-Ficarra (Ed.), *Optimizing Human-Computer Interaction With Emerging Technologies* (pp. 248–273). Hershey, PA: IGI Global. doi:10.4018/978-1-5225-2616-2.ch010

Karataş, S., Kukul, V., & Özcan, S. (2018). How Powerful Is Digital Storytelling for Teaching?: Perspective of Pre-Service Teachers. In D. Polly, M. Putman, T. Petty, & A. Good (Eds.), *Innovative Practices in Teacher Preparation and Graduate-Level Teacher Education Programs* (pp. 511–529). Hershey, PA: IGI Global. doi:10.4018/978-1-5225-3068-8.ch027

Kavaklı, N. (2018). Hate Speech Towards Syrian Refugees in Turkish Online Reader Comments. In C. Akrivopoulou (Ed.), *Global Perspectives on Human Migration, Asylum, and Security* (pp. 127–142). Hershey, PA: IGI Global. doi:10.4018/978-1-5225-2817-3.ch007

Kaynak, S. (2018). Pakistan. In S. Ozdemir, S. Erdogan, & A. Gedikli (Eds.), *Handbook of Research on Sociopolitical Factors Impacting Economic Growth in Islamic Nations* (pp. 293–313). Hershey, PA: IGI Global. doi:10.4018/978-1-5225-2939-2.ch015

Korstanje, M. E. (2018). Thana-Capitalism and the Sense of Reality: Lessons Unlearned. In C. Akrivopoulou (Ed.), *Global Perspectives on Human Migration, Asylum, and Security* (pp. 1–20). Hershey, PA: IGI Global. doi:10.4018/978-1-5225-2817-3.ch001

Korstanje, M. E. (2018). The Lost Paradise: The Religious Nature of Tourism. In H. El-Gohary, D. Edwards, & R. Eid (Eds.), *Global Perspectives on Religious Tourism and Pilgrimage* (pp. 129–141). Hershey, PA: IGI Global. doi:10.4018/978-1-5225-2796-1.ch008

Korstanje, M. E., & George, B. P. (2018). Emotionality, Reason, and Dark Tourism: Discussions Around the Sense of Death. In M. Korstanje & B. George (Eds.), *Virtual Traumascapes and Exploring the Roots of Dark Tourism* (pp. 1–25). Hershey, PA: IGI Global. doi:10.4018/978-1-5225-2750-3.ch001

Kougioumtzis, G. A., & Louka, D. (2018). Advocacy and Teacher Mentoring. In U. Thomas (Ed.), *Advocacy in Academia and the Role of Teacher Preparation Programs* (pp. 65–87). Hershey, PA: IGI Global. doi:10.4018/978-1-5225-2906-4.ch004

Kousar, H. (2018). Gender Violence in Academia. In N. Mahtab, T. Haque, I. Khan, M. Islam, & I. Wahid (Eds.), *Handbook of Research on Women's Issues and Rights in the Developing World* (pp. 144–155). Hershey, PA: IGI Global. doi:10.4018/978-1-5225-3018-3.ch009

Koutsafti, M., & Politi, N. (2018). Career Counseling: The "Model of Personal Career Management". In K. Koutsopoulos, K. Doukas, & Y. Kotsanis (Eds.), *Handbook of Research on Educational Design and Cloud Computing in Modern Classroom Settings* (pp. 410–429). Hershey, PA: IGI Global. doi:10.4018/978-1-5225-3053-4.ch020

Koutsopoulos, K. (2018). From Ground to Cloud: The School on the Cloud. In K. Koutsopoulos, K. Doukas, & Y. Kotsanis (Eds.), *Handbook of Research on Educational Design and Cloud Computing in Modern Classroom Settings* (pp. 1–21). Hershey, PA: IGI Global. doi:10.4018/978-1-5225-3053-4.ch001

Kovacevic, Z., Klimek, B., & Drower, I. S. (2018). Refugee Children and Parental Involvement in School Education: A Field Model. In K. Norris & S. Collier (Eds.), *Social Justice and Parent Partnerships in Multicultural Education Contexts* (pp. 139–161). Hershey, PA: IGI Global. doi:10.4018/978-1-5225-3943-8.ch008

Kratky, A. (2018). Personal Touch: A Viewing-Angle-Compensated Multi-Layer Touch Display. In F. Cipolla-Ficarra (Ed.), *Optimizing Human-Computer Interaction With Emerging Technologies* (pp. 232–247). Hershey, PA: IGI Global. doi:10.4018/978-1-5225-2616-2.ch009

Kuang, Y. (2018). Application of the "Teaching Innovation Practice Platform" in English Reading Instruction: A Case Study of a Public Middle School in Shanghai. In H. Spires (Ed.), *Digital Transformation and Innovation in Chinese Education* (pp. 249–271). Hershey, PA: IGI Global. doi:10.4018/978-1-5225-2924-8.ch014

Kubilay, S., & Yardibi, N. (2018). Refugee Parents' Preferential Values in Education. In Ş. Erçetin (Ed.), *Educational Development and Infrastructure for Immigrants and Refugees* (pp. 72–84). Hershey, PA: IGI Global. doi:10.4018/978-1-5225-3325-2.ch004

Kumar, T. P. (2018). Impact of Corporate Social Responsibility on Service Performance in Mediating Effect of Brand Equity With Reference To Banks in India. In Rajagopal, & R. Behl (Eds.), Start-Up Enterprises and Contemporary Innovation Strategies in the Global Marketplace (pp. 88-99). Hershey, PA: IGI Global. doi:10.4018/978-1-5225-4831-7.ch007

LaPlante, J. M. (2018). Unequal Opportunities and Inequitable Outcomes: Rethinking Education Finance Policy Design for a Global Society. In H. Levine & K. Moreno (Eds.), *Positioning Markets and Governments in Public Management* (pp. 209–239). Hershey, PA: IGI Global. doi:10.4018/978-1-5225-4177-6.ch016

Lau, B. T., & Win, K. M. (2018). Differentiated Animated Social Stories to Enhance Social Skills Acquisition of Children With Autism Spectrum Disorder. In V. Bryan, A. Musgrove, & J. Powers (Eds.), *Handbook of Research on Human Development in the Digital Age* (pp. 300–329). Hershey, PA: IGI Global. doi:10.4018/978-1-5225-2838-8.ch014

Lee, J. K., & Chirino-Klevans, I. (2018). Cosmopolitanism in a World of Teachers: American Student Teachers in a Chinese School. In H. Spires (Ed.), *Digital Transformation and Innovation in Chinese Education* (pp. 232–248). Hershey, PA: IGI Global. doi:10.4018/978-1-5225-2924-8.ch013

Lee, S. (2018). Expatriate Cantonese Learners in Hong Kong: Adult L2 Learning, Identity Negotiation, and Social Pressure. In D. Velliaris (Ed.), *Study Abroad Contexts for Enhanced Foreign Language Learning* (pp. 151–168). Hershey, PA: IGI Global. doi:10.4018/978-1-5225-3814-1.ch007

Lee, S. C. (2018). Mother America: Cold War Maternalism and the Origins of Korean Adoption. In F. Topor (Ed.), *Ethical Standards and Practice in International Relations* (pp. 157–186). Hershey, PA: IGI Global. doi:10.4018/978-1-5225-2650-6.ch007

Li, Y., & Wang, X. (2018). Seeking Health Information on Social Media: A Perspective of Trust, Self-Determination, and Social Support. *Journal of Organizational and End User Computing, 30*(1), 1–22. doi:10.4018/JOEUC.2018010101

Livers, S. D., & Lin, L. (2018). Elementary Teacher Candidates' Perspectives on the Teaching and Learning of English Learners. In U. Thomas (Ed.), *Advocacy in Academia and the Role of Teacher Preparation Programs* (pp. 23–41). Hershey, PA: IGI Global. doi:10.4018/978-1-5225-2906-4.ch002

López-Cózar-Navarro, C., & Priede-Bergamini, T. (2018). Nascent Social Entrepreneurship: Economic, Legal, and Financial Framework. In A. Carrizo Moreira, J. Guilherme Leitão Dantas, & F. Manuel Valente (Eds.), *Nascent Entrepreneurship and Successful New Venture Creation* (pp. 132–152). Hershey, PA: IGI Global. doi:10.4018/978-1-5225-2936-1.ch006

Lu, S. (2018). Financial Literacy Education Program Post Financial Housing Crisis: Community Based Financial Literacy Education Program. In S. Burton (Ed.), *Engaged Scholarship and Civic Responsibility in Higher Education* (pp. 49–66). Hershey, PA: IGI Global. doi:10.4018/978-1-5225-3649-9.ch003

Luyombya, D. (2018). Management of Records and Archives in Uganda's Public Sector. In P. Ngulube (Ed.), *Handbook of Research on Heritage Management and Preservation* (pp. 275–297). Hershey, PA: IGI Global. doi:10.4018/978-1-5225-3137-1.ch014

Luyombya, D., Kiyingi, G. W., & Naluwooza, M. (2018). The Nature and Utilisation of Archival Records Deposited in Makerere University Library, Uganda. In P. Ngulube (Ed.), *Handbook of Research on Heritage Management and Preservation* (pp. 96–113). Hershey, PA: IGI Global. doi:10.4018/978-1-5225-3137-1.ch005

Lytras, M. D., Papadopoulou, P., Marouli, C., & Misseyanni, A. (2018). Higher Education Out-of-the-Box: Technology-Driven Learning Innovation in Higher Education. In S. Burton (Ed.), *Engaged Scholarship and Civic Responsibility in Higher Education* (pp. 67–100). Hershey, PA: IGI Global. doi:10.4018/978-1-5225-3649-9.ch004

Mafumbate, R. (2018). Child Resilience, Survival, and Development: Voices of Orphans in Zimbabwe. In I. Tshabangu (Ed.), *Global Ideologies Surrounding Children's Rights and Social Justice* (pp. 239–252). Hershey, PA: IGI Global. doi:10.4018/978-1-5225-2578-3.ch015

Malmierca, M. J. (2018). Cloud Computing for Rural and Isolated Schools. In K. Koutsopoulos, K. Doukas, & Y. Kotsanis (Eds.), *Handbook of Research on Educational Design and Cloud Computing in Modern Classroom Settings* (pp. 376–394). Hershey, PA: IGI Global. doi:10.4018/978-1-5225-3053-4.ch018

Maroofi, F. (2018). Knowledge Management and Organizational Performance in Service Industry: Transformational Leadership Versus Transactional Leadership. In N. Baporikar (Ed.), *Global Practices in Knowledge Management for Societal and Organizational Development* (pp. 194–212). Hershey, PA: IGI Global. doi:10.4018/978-1-5225-3009-1.ch009

Mattson, T., & Aurigemma, S. (2018). Running with the Pack: The Impact of Middle-Status Conformity on the Post-Adoption Organizational Use of Twitter. *Journal of Organizational and End User Computing, 30*(1), 23–43. doi:10.4018/JOEUC.2018010102

Medhekar, A., & Haq, F. (2018). Urbanization and New Jobs Creation in Healthcare Services in India: Challenges and Opportunities. In U. Benna & I. Benna (Eds.), *Urbanization and Its Impact on Socio-Economic Growth in Developing Regions* (pp. 198–218). Hershey, PA: IGI Global. doi:10.4018/978-1-5225-2659-9.ch010

Meletiou-Mavrotheris, M., & Koutsopoulos, K. (2018). Projecting the Future of Cloud Computing in Education: A Foresight Study Using the Delphi Method. In K. Koutsopoulos, K. Doukas, & Y. Kotsanis (Eds.), *Handbook of Research on Educational Design and Cloud Computing in Modern Classroom Settings* (pp. 262–290). Hershey, PA: IGI Global. doi:10.4018/978-1-5225-3053-4.ch012

Miller, J. (2018). Causes and Ramifications of Public Pension Fund Underfunding: A Case Study of the New Jersey Pension Funds. In H. Levine & K. Moreno (Eds.), *Positioning Markets and Governments in Public Management* (pp. 114–146). Hershey, PA: IGI Global. doi:10.4018/978-1-5225-4177-6.ch010

Milović, B. (2018). Developing Marketing Strategy on Social Networks. In S. Sarma (Ed.), *Global Observations of the Influence of Culture on Consumer Buying Behavior* (pp. 66–82). Hershey, PA: IGI Global. doi:10.4018/978-1-5225-2727-5.ch004

Mosweu, O., & Kenosi, L. S. (2018). Theories of Appraisal in Archives: From Hillary Jenkinson to Terry Cook's Times. In P. Ngulube (Ed.), *Handbook of Research on Heritage Management and Preservation* (pp. 24–46). Hershey, PA: IGI Global. doi:10.4018/978-1-5225-3137-1.ch002

Mukherjee, S., & Pradeep, K. (2018). Does Internationalization of Business-Group-Affiliated Firms Depend on Their Performance? In Rajagopal, & R. Behl (Eds.), Start-Up Enterprises and Contemporary Innovation Strategies in the Global Marketplace (pp. 153-165). Hershey, PA: IGI Global. https://doi.org/doi:10.4018/978-1-5225-4831-7.ch011

Mutisya, P. M., & Conway, C. S. (2018). Quality Mentoring: A Prerequisite for Faculty at HBCUs. In C. Conway (Ed.), *Faculty Mentorship at Historically Black Colleges and Universities* (pp. 15–34). Hershey, PA: IGI Global. doi:10.4018/978-1-5225-4071-7.ch002

Nagabhushan, P. (2018). Mean Level Changes in College Students' Academic Motivation and Engagement. In *Engaging Adolescent Students in Contemporary Classrooms: Emerging Research and Opportunities* (pp. 142–174). Hershey, PA: IGI Global. doi:10.4018/978-1-5225-5155-3.ch006

Naranjo, J. (2018). Meeting the Need for Inclusive Educators Online: Teacher Education in Inclusive Special Education and Dual-Certification. In D. Polly, M. Putman, T. Petty, & A. Good (Eds.), *Innovative Practices in Teacher Preparation and Graduate-Level Teacher Education Programs* (pp. 106–122). Hershey, PA: IGI Global. doi:10.4018/978-1-5225-3068-8.ch007

Nirmala, T., & Aram, I. A. (2018). Newspaper Framing of Climate Change and Sustainability Issues in India. *International Journal of E-Politics*, *9*(1), 15–28. doi:10.4018/IJEP.2018010102

Novak, J. I., & Loy, J. (2018). Digital Technologies and 4D Customized Design: Challenging Conventions With Responsive Design. In V. Bryan, A. Musgrove, & J. Powers (Eds.), *Handbook of Research on Human Development in the Digital Age* (pp. 403–426). Hershey, PA: IGI Global. doi:10.4018/978-1-5225-2838-8.ch018

Ögeyik, M. C. (2018). Measuring Phonological and Orthographic Similarity: The Case of Loanwords in Turkish and English. In D. Buğa & M. Coşgun Ögeyik (Eds.), *Psycholinguistics and Cognition in Language Processing* (pp. 49–67). Hershey, PA: IGI Global. doi:10.4018/978-1-5225-4009-0.ch003

Oling-Sisay, M. (2018). Don't Touch My Hair: Culturally Responsive Engagement in Service-Learning. In O. Delano-Oriaran, M. Penick-Parks, & S. Fondrie (Eds.), *Culturally Engaging Service-Learning With Diverse Communities* (pp. 43–55). Hershey, PA: IGI Global. doi:10.4018/978-1-5225-2900-2.ch003

Ololube, N. P., Ingiabuna, E. T., & Dudafa, U. J. (2018). Effective Decision Making for Knowledge Development in Higher Education: A Case Study of Nigeria. In N. Baporikar (Ed.), *Global Practices in Knowledge Management for Societal and Organizational Development* (pp. 382–399). Hershey, PA: IGI Global. doi:10.4018/978-1-5225-3009-1.ch018

Oritsejafor, E. O. (2018). Enhancing Competitiveness of Public Utilities in Nigeria: The Case of the Power Holding Company of Nigeria (PHCN). In H. Levine & K. Moreno (Eds.), *Positioning Markets and Governments in Public Management* (pp. 240–252). Hershey, PA: IGI Global. doi:10.4018/978-1-5225-4177-6.ch017

Otunla, A. O., & Olatunji, O. T. (2018). Clients' Perception, Extent of Adoption, and Level of Satisfaction With Multi-Platform Advertising Media Strategies (MuPAMS): Among Business Organisations in Ibadan, South-Western Nigeria. In K. Yang (Ed.), *Multi-Platform Advertising Strategies in the Global Marketplace* (pp. 54–80). Hershey, PA: IGI Global. doi:10.4018/978-1-5225-3114-2.ch003

Owuor, N. A. (2018). Oil and Gas Discoveries in Kenya: Important Global Exploration and Production Value Chain Lessons for the Society. In M. Risso & S. Testarmata (Eds.), *Value Sharing for Sustainable and Inclusive Development* (pp. 322–337). Hershey, PA: IGI Global. doi:10.4018/978-1-5225-3147-0.ch015

Özdemir, E., & Yılmaz, M. (2018). Omni-Channel Retailing: The Risks, Challenges, and Opportunities. In A. Kumar & S. Saurav (Eds.), *Supply Chain Management Strategies and Risk Assessment in Retail Environments* (pp. 97–118). Hershey, PA: IGI Global. doi:10.4018/978-1-5225-3056-5.ch006

Panko, T. R., & George, B. P. (2018). Animal Sexual Abuse and the Darkness of Touristic Immorality. In M. Korstanje & B. George (Eds.), *Virtual Traumascapes and Exploring the Roots of Dark Tourism* (pp. 175–189). Hershey, PA: IGI Global. doi:10.4018/978-1-5225-2750-3.ch009

Paraschiv, M. M. (2018). Elif Shafak's Works: A Means of Preventing Honor Based Violence. In M. Badea & M. Suditu (Eds.), *Violence Prevention and Safety Promotion in Higher Education Settings* (pp. 36–49). Hershey, PA: IGI Global. doi:10.4018/978-1-5225-2960-6.ch003

Paravastu, N., Simmers, C. A., & Anandarajan, M. (2018). Non-Compliant Mobile Device Usage and Information Systems Security: A Bystander Theory Perspective. *International Journal of Information Systems and Social Change, 9*(1), 1–25. doi:10.4018/IJISSC.2018010101

Pathak, B. (2018). Process Documentation of Interfaith Peacebuilding Cycle: A Case Study From Nepal. In B. Cook (Ed.), *Handbook of Research on Examining Global Peacemaking in the Digital Age* (pp. 70–93). Hershey, PA: IGI Global. doi:10.4018/978-1-5225-3032-9.ch006

Pathak, S. J. (2018). Women Painters of Mithila: A Quest for Identity. In N. Mahtab, T. Haque, I. Khan, M. Islam, & I. Wahid (Eds.), *Handbook of Research on Women's Issues and Rights in the Developing World* (pp. 370–381). Hershey, PA: IGI Global. doi:10.4018/978-1-5225-3018-3.ch023

Patro, C. S., & Raghunath, K. M. (2018). Corporate Social Responsibility: A Conscientious Take. In M. Risso & S. Testarmata (Eds.), *Value Sharing for Sustainable and Inclusive Development* (pp. 75–99). Hershey, PA: IGI Global. doi:10.4018/978-1-5225-3147-0.ch004

Pérez-Uribe, R. I., Torres, D. A., Jurado, S. P., & Prada, D. M. (2018). Cloud Tools for the Development of Project Management in SMEs. In R. Perez-Uribe, C. Salcedo-Perez, & D. Ocampo-Guzman (Eds.), *Handbook of Research on Intrapreneurship and Organizational Sustainability in SMEs* (pp. 95–120). Hershey, PA: IGI Global. doi:10.4018/978-1-5225-3543-0.ch005

Perrotta, K. A., & Mattson, M. F. (2018). Using Counterstories and Reflective Writing Assignments to Promote Critical Race Consciousness in an Undergraduate Teacher Preparation Course. In U. Thomas (Ed.), *Advocacy in Academia and the Role of Teacher Preparation Programs* (pp. 42–64). Hershey, PA: IGI Global. doi:10.4018/978-1-5225-2906-4.ch003

Poli, A., Gambini, A., Pezzotti, A., Broglia, A., Mazzola, A., Muschiato, S., ... Costa, F. (2018). Digital Diorama: An Interactive Multimedia Resource for Learning the Life Sciences. In F. Cipolla-Ficarra (Ed.), *Optimizing Human-Computer Interaction With Emerging Technologies* (pp. 52–82). Hershey, PA: IGI Global. doi:10.4018/978-1-5225-2616-2.ch003

Presadă, D. (2018). Literature and Aesthetic Reading as Means of Promoting Nonviolence. In M. Badea & M. Suditu (Eds.), *Violence Prevention and Safety Promotion in Higher Education Settings* (pp. 94–109). Hershey, PA: IGI Global. doi:10.4018/978-1-5225-2960-6.ch006

Punetha, H., Kumar, S., Mudila, H., & Prakash, O. (2018). Brassica Meal as Source of Health Protecting Neuraceutical and Its Antioxidative Properties. In A. Verma, K. Srivastava, S. Singh, & H. Singh (Eds.), *Nutraceuticals and Innovative Food Products for Healthy Living and Preventive Care* (pp. 108–131). Hershey, PA: IGI Global. doi:10.4018/978-1-5225-2970-5.ch005

Puri, R., & Sengupta, P. (2018). Application of Statistics in Human Resource Management. In D. Bhattacharyya (Ed.), *Statistical Tools and Analysis in Human Resources Management* (pp. 15–37). Hershey, PA: IGI Global. doi:10.4018/978-1-5225-4947-5.ch002

Putnik, N., & Milošević, M. (2018). Trends in Peace Research: Can Cyber Détente Lead to Lasting Peace? In B. Cook (Ed.), *Handbook of Research on Examining Global Peacemaking in the Digital Age* (pp. 1–18). Hershey, PA: IGI Global. doi:10.4018/978-1-5225-3032-9.ch001

Rana, S., & Sharma, R. (2018). An Overview of Employer Branding With Special Reference to Indian Organizations. In N. Sharma, V. Singh, & S. Pathak (Eds.), *Management Techniques for a Diverse and Cross-Cultural Workforce* (pp. 116–131). Hershey, PA: IGI Global. doi:10.4018/978-1-5225-4933-8.ch007

Randa, I. O. (2018). Leveraging Knowledge Management for Value Creation in Service-Oriented Organisations of Namibia. In N. Baporikar (Ed.), *Global Practices in Knowledge Management for Societal and Organizational Development* (pp. 145–167). Hershey, PA: IGI Global. doi:10.4018/978-1-5225-3009-1.ch007

Rekun, M. S. (2018). A Swift Kick: Russian Diplomatic Practice in Bulgaria, 1879-1883. In F. Topor (Ed.), *Ethical Standards and Practice in International Relations* (pp. 49–72). Hershey, PA: IGI Global. doi:10.4018/978-1-5225-2650-6.ch003

Rodil, K., Nielsen, E. B., & Nielsen, J. B. (2018). Sharing Memories: Co-Designing Assistive Technology with Aphasic Adults and Support Staff. *International Journal of Sociotechnology and Knowledge Development, 10*(1), 21–36. doi:10.4018/IJSKD.2018010102

Samli, R. (2018). A Review of Internet Addiction on the Basis of Different Countries (2007–2017). In B. Bozoglan (Ed.), *Psychological, Social, and Cultural Aspects of Internet Addiction* (pp. 200–220). Hershey, PA: IGI Global. doi:10.4018/978-1-5225-3477-8.ch011

Sánchez-García, J. C., & Hernández-Sánchez, B. R. (2018). Nascent Entrepreneurs, Psychological Characteristics, and Sociocultural Background: Psycho-Sociocultural Background of Nascent Entrepreneurs. In A. Carrizo Moreira, J. Guilherme Leitão Dantas, & F. Manuel Valente (Eds.), *Nascent Entrepreneurship and Successful New Venture Creation* (pp. 111–131). Hershey, PA: IGI Global. doi:10.4018/978-1-5225-2936-1.ch005

Santana-Mansilla, P., Costaguta, R., & Schiaffino, S. (2018). A Multi-Agent Model for Personalizing Learning Material for Collaborative Groups. In F. Cipolla-Ficarra (Ed.), *Optimizing Human-Computer Interaction With Emerging Technologies* (pp. 343–375). Hershey, PA: IGI Global. doi:10.4018/978-1-5225-2616-2.ch015

Santos, C. E., Lima de Oliveira, D., & Freitas, M. D. (2018). The Role of Pibid in Graduation Courses: Discussing Teachers' Education. In Z. Djoub (Ed.), *Fostering Reflective Teaching Practice in Pre-Service Education* (pp. 218–234). Hershey, PA: IGI Global. doi:10.4018/978-1-5225-2963-7.ch012

Sarkar, J. (2018). Methodological Considerations for Research in Compensation Management. In D. Bhattacharyya (Ed.), *Statistical Tools and Analysis in Human Resources Management* (pp. 142–168). Hershey, PA: IGI Global. doi:10.4018/978-1-5225-4947-5.ch007

Sarofim, S., & Tolba, A. (2018). When Age, Religion, and Culture Matter: The Impact of Aging, Religiosity, and Cultural Differences on Consumers' Emotions and Behavior. In S. Sarma (Ed.), *Global Observations of the Influence of Culture on Consumer Buying Behavior* (pp. 261–278). Hershey, PA: IGI Global. doi:10.4018/978-1-5225-2727-5.ch015

Schroth, S. T., & Helfer, J. A. (2018). Differentiated Fieldwork and Practicum Experiences: Matching Teacher Candidate Assignments to Their Skills and Needs. In D. Polly, M. Putman, T. Petty, & A. Good (Eds.), *Innovative Practices in Teacher Preparation and Graduate-Level Teacher Education Programs* (pp. 306–326). Hershey, PA: IGI Global. doi:10.4018/978-1-5225-3068-8.ch017

Schwartz, H. M. (2018). States via Markets and Markets via States: Symbiosis and Change, Not Conflict. In H. Levine & K. Moreno (Eds.), *Positioning Markets and Governments in Public Management* (pp. 1–10). Hershey, PA: IGI Global. doi:10.4018/978-1-5225-4177-6.ch001

Semali, L. M. (2018). Indigenous Knowledge as Resource to Sustain Self-Employment in Rural Development. In S. Chhabra (Ed.), *Handbook of Research on Civic Engagement and Social Change in Contemporary Society* (pp. 142–158). Hershey, PA: IGI Global. doi:10.4018/978-1-5225-4197-4.ch008

Seraphin, H., & Gowreesunkar, V. (2018). On the Use of Qualitative Comparative Analysis to Identify the Bright Spots in Dark Tourism. In M. Korstanje & B. George (Eds.), *Virtual Traumascapes and Exploring the Roots of Dark Tourism* (pp. 67–83). Hershey, PA: IGI Global. doi:10.4018/978-1-5225-2750-3.ch004

Shahidi, N., Tossan, V., & Cacho-Elizondo, S. (2018). Assessment of A Mobile Educational Coaching App: Exploring Adoption Patterns and Barriers in France. *International Journal of Technology and Human Interaction, 14*(1), 22–43. doi:10.4018/IJTHI.2018010102

Sikira, A. N., Matekere, T., & Urassa, J. K. (2018). Engaging Men in Women's Economic Empowerment in Butiama District, Mara Region, Tanzania. In N. Mahtab, T. Haque, I. Khan, M. Islam, & I. Wahid (Eds.), *Handbook of Research on Women's Issues and Rights in the Developing World* (pp. 252–268). Hershey, PA: IGI Global. doi:10.4018/978-1-5225-3018-3.ch015

Silveira, D. G. (2018). Diffusion of Innovation and Role of Opinion Leaders. In S. Sarma (Ed.), *Global Observations of the Influence of Culture on Consumer Buying Behavior* (pp. 83–93). Hershey, PA: IGI Global. doi:10.4018/978-1-5225-2727-5.ch005

Simard, D. A., Martin, M., Mockry, J., Puliatte, A., & Squires, M. E. (2018). Introduction: Mental Health and Well-Being of College Students. In M. Martin, J. Mockry, A. Puliatte, D. Simard, & M. Squires (Eds.), *Raising Mental Health Awareness in Higher Education: Emerging Research and Opportunities* (pp. 1–20). Hershey, PA: IGI Global. doi:10.4018/978-1-5225-3793-9.ch001

Sosnin, P. (2018). Experimental Actions With Conceptual Objects. In *Experience-Based Human-Computer Interactions: Emerging Research and Opportunities* (pp. 47–97). Hershey, PA: IGI Global. doi:10.4018/978-1-5225-2987-3.ch003

Sosnin, P. (2018). Lack of Naturalness in Human-Computer Interactions. In *Experience-Based Human-Computer Interactions: Emerging Research and Opportunities* (pp. 9–46). Hershey, PA: IGI Global. doi:10.4018/978-1-5225-2987-3.ch002

Spaseski, N. (2018). Fractal and Wavelet Market Analysis in Pattern Recognition. In *Alternative Decision-Making Models for Financial Portfolio Management: Emerging Research and Opportunities* (pp. 254–309). Hershey, PA: IGI Global. doi:10.4018/978-1-5225-3259-0.ch007

Spaseski, N. (2018). Theory and Modelling. In *Alternative Decision-Making Models for Financial Portfolio Management: Emerging Research and Opportunities* (pp. 1–19). Hershey, PA: IGI Global. doi:10.4018/978-1-5225-3259-0.ch001

Spires, H. A., Green, K. E., & Liang, P. (2018). Chinese Parents' Perspectives on International Higher Education and Innovation. In H. Spires (Ed.), *Digital Transformation and Innovation in Chinese Education* (pp. 272–287). Hershey, PA: IGI Global. doi:10.4018/978-1-5225-2924-8.ch015

Spires, H. A., Himes, M., & Wang, L. (2018). Designing a State-of-the-Art High School in Suzhou, China: Connecting to the Future. In H. Spires (Ed.), *Digital Transformation and Innovation in Chinese Education* (pp. 191–210). Hershey, PA: IGI Global. doi:10.4018/978-1-5225-2924-8.ch011

Squires, M. E., Martin, M., Mockry, J., Puliatte, A., & Simard, D. A. (2018). Campus-Wide Initiatives. In M. Martin, J. Mockry, A. Puliatte, D. Simard, & M. Squires (Eds.), *Raising Mental Health Awareness in Higher Education: Emerging Research and Opportunities* (pp. 77–104). Hershey, PA: IGI Global. doi:10.4018/978-1-5225-3793-9.ch005

Standing, K., & Parker, S. L. (2018). Girls' and Women's Rights to Menstrual Health in Nepal. In N. Mahtab, T. Haque, I. Khan, M. Islam, & I. Wahid (Eds.), *Handbook of Research on Women's Issues and Rights in the Developing World* (pp. 156–168). Hershey, PA: IGI Global. doi:10.4018/978-1-5225-3018-3.ch010

Stępień, B., & Hinner, M. (2018). From Love to Rebuff: How Culture Shapes the Perception of Luxury Goods Among Consumers. In S. Sarma (Ed.), *Global Observations of the Influence of Culture on Consumer Buying Behavior* (pp. 24–47). Hershey, PA: IGI Global. doi:10.4018/978-1-5225-2727-5.ch002

Tantau, A. D., & Frăţilă, L. C. (2018). Trends and Conclusions for Business Development in the Renewable Energy Industry. In *Entrepreneurship and Business Development in the Renewable Energy Sector* (pp. 351–376). Hershey, PA: IGI Global. doi:10.4018/978-1-5225-3625-3.ch010

Terry, D. L., & Amudalat, E. A. (2018). Data Documentation and Informed Consent in Research. In C. Sibinga (Ed.), *Ensuring Research Integrity and the Ethical Management of Data* (pp. 127–154). Hershey, PA: IGI Global. doi:10.4018/978-1-5225-2730-5.ch008

Toma, S. I., Marinescu, P., & Grădinaru, C. (2018). Creating Shared Value in the 21st Century: The Case of Toyota Motor Company. In M. Risso & S. Testarmata (Eds.), *Value Sharing for Sustainable and Inclusive Development* (pp. 155–184). Hershey, PA: IGI Global. doi:10.4018/978-1-5225-3147-0.ch007

Travis, F. T. (2018). Long-Term Changes in Experienced Yoga Practitioners: Growth of Higher States of Consciousness. In S. Telles & N. Singh (Eds.), *Research-Based Perspectives on the Psychophysiology of Yoga* (pp. 35–51). Hershey, PA: IGI Global. doi:10.4018/978-1-5225-2788-6.ch003

Tripp, L. O., Love, A., Thomas, C. M., & Russell, J. (2018). Teacher Education Advocacy for Multiple Perspectives and Culturally Sensitive Teaching. In U. Thomas (Ed.), *Advocacy in Academia and the Role of Teacher Preparation Programs* (pp. 161–181). Hershey, PA: IGI Global. doi:10.4018/978-1-5225-2906-4.ch009

Tshabangu, I. (2018). Child Poverty and Social Inequalities in Africa: A Social Justice Perspective. In I. Tshabangu (Ed.), *Global Ideologies Surrounding Children's Rights and Social Justice* (pp. 74–87). Hershey, PA: IGI Global. doi:10.4018/978-1-5225-2578-3.ch005

Tugjamba, N., Yembuu, B., Gantumur, A., & Gezel, U. (2018). Research Study on Climate Change Education for Sustainable Development in Mongolia. In P. Ordóñez de Pablos (Ed.), *Management Strategies and Technology Fluidity in the Asian Business Sector* (pp. 192–214). Hershey, PA: IGI Global. doi:10.4018/978-1-5225-4056-4.ch012

Upadhye, B. D., & Bandopadhyay, N. (2018). The Taxonomy of Methodological Approaches in Marketing Research: Retrospect and Prospect. In Rajagopal, & R. Behl (Eds.), Start-Up Enterprises and Contemporary Innovation Strategies in the Global Marketplace (pp. 276-293). Hershey, PA: IGI Global. https://doi.org/doi:10.4018/978-1-5225-4831-7.ch021

Uvanesh, K., Nayak, S. K., Sagiri, S. S., Banerjee, I., Ray, S. S., & Pal, K. (2018). Effect of Non-Ionic Hydrophilic and Hydrophobic Surfactants on the Properties on the Stearate Oleogels: A Comparative Study. In A. Verma, K. Srivastava, S. Singh, & H. Singh (Eds.), *Nutraceuticals and Innovative Food Products for Healthy Living and Preventive Care* (pp. 260–279). Hershey, PA: IGI Global. doi:10.4018/978-1-5225-2970-5.ch012

Vallverdú, J., Nishida, T., Ohmoto, Y., Moran, S., & Lázare, S. (2018). Fake Empathy and Human-Robot Interaction (HRI): A Preliminary Study. *International Journal of Technology and Human Interaction, 14*(1), 44–59. doi:10.4018/IJTHI.2018010103

Van Deur, P. (2018). Assessing Self-Directed Learning at School Level. In *Managing Self-Directed Learning in Primary School Education: Emerging Research and Opportunities* (pp. 61–77). Hershey, PA: IGI Global. doi:10.4018/978-1-5225-2613-1.ch003

Van Deur, P. (2018). Case Study: The Relationship Between Curriculum Focus on Inquiry and Self-Directed Learning. In *Managing Self-Directed Learning in Primary School Education: Emerging Research and Opportunities* (pp. 95–111). Hershey, PA: IGI Global. doi:10.4018/978-1-5225-2613-1.ch005

Van Deur, P. (2018). Describing Self-Directed Learning in Primary Students. In *Managing Self-Directed Learning in Primary School Education: Emerging Research and Opportunities* (pp. 33–59). Hershey, PA: IGI Global. doi:10.4018/978-1-5225-2613-1.ch002

Vargas-Hernández, J. G., Almanza-Jiménez, R., Calderón, P. C., & Casas-Cardenaz, R. (2018). Organizational Learning and Performance Under the Approach of Organizational Theories. In N. Baporikar (Ed.), *Global Practices in Knowledge Management for Societal and Organizational Development* (pp. 106–125). Hershey, PA: IGI Global. doi:10.4018/978-1-5225-3009-1.ch005

Vega, J. A., Arquette, C. M., Lee, H., Crowe, H. A., Hunzicker, J. L., & Cushing, J. (2018). Ensuring Social Justice for English Language Learners: An Innovative English as a Second Language (ESL) Endorsement Program. In D. Polly, M. Putman, T. Petty, & A. Good (Eds.), *Innovative Practices in Teacher Preparation and Graduate-Level Teacher Education Programs* (pp. 48–66). Hershey, PA: IGI Global. doi:10.4018/978-1-5225-3068-8.ch004

Verma, A. K., Singh, A., & Negi, M. S. (2018). Nutriproteomics: An Advance Methodology of Nutrichemical Analysis. In A. Verma, K. Srivastava, S. Singh, & H. Singh (Eds.), *Nutraceuticals and Innovative Food Products for Healthy Living and Preventive Care* (pp. 1–23). Hershey, PA: IGI Global. doi:10.4018/978-1-5225-2970-5.ch001

Verma, J., & Verma, R. (2018). Innovation in the Provision of Medical Services in India. In Rajagopal, & R. Behl (Eds.), Start-Up Enterprises and Contemporary Innovation Strategies in the Global Marketplace (pp. 16-27). Hershey, PA: IGI Global. doi:10.4018/978-1-5225-4831-7.ch002

Verrini, A. (2018). Strategists From the Past, as Encrypted Cognitive Maps, Whose Access Code Is the Will of Learning Solutions. In L. dall'Acqua, & D. Lukose (Eds.), Improving Business Performance Through Effective Managerial Training Initiatives (pp. 196-209). Hershey, PA: IGI Global. https://doi.org/ doi:10.4018/978-1-5225-3906-3.ch009

Veselinova, E., & Samonikov, M. G. (2018). Driving Brand Equity With Radical Transparency. In *Building Brand Equity and Consumer Trust Through Radical Transparency Practices* (pp. 18–62). Hershey, PA: IGI Global. doi:10.4018/978-1-5225-2417-5.ch002

Veselinova, E., & Samonikov, M. G. (2018). Henkel: Radical Transparency and Sustainability. In *Building Brand Equity and Consumer Trust Through Radical Transparency Practices* (pp. 337–389). Hershey, PA: IGI Global. doi:10.4018/978-1-5225-2417-5.ch009

Veselinova, E., & Samonikov, M. G. (2018). The 3M Company: How to Use Radical Transparency to Generate Value for the Company. In *Building Brand Equity and Consumer Trust Through Radical Transparency Practices* (pp. 185–318). Hershey, PA: IGI Global. doi:10.4018/978-1-5225-2417-5.ch007

Vila, A. R. (2018). Latin American and Caribbean Literature Transposed Into Digital: Corpus, Ecosystem, Canon, and Cartonera Publishing. In F. García-Peñalvo (Ed.), *Global Implications of Emerging Technology Trends* (pp. 34–58). Hershey, PA: IGI Global. doi:10.4018/978-1-5225-4944-4.ch003

Vorkapic, C. F. (2018). Yoga for Children. In S. Telles & N. Singh (Eds.), *Research-Based Perspectives on the Psychophysiology of Yoga* (pp. 104–120). Hershey, PA: IGI Global. doi:10.4018/978-1-5225-2788-6.ch007

Vu, N. T. (2018). Pros and Cons of Integrating Non-Financial Services in Microfinance. In S. Hipsher (Ed.), *Examining the Private Sector's Role in Wealth Creation and Poverty Reduction* (pp. 171–199). Hershey, PA: IGI Global. doi:10.4018/978-1-5225-3117-3.ch008

Wani, K. A., Manzoor, J., Anjum, J., Bashir, M., & Mamta. (2018). Pesticides in Vegetables: Their Impact on Nutritional Quality and Human Health. In A. Verma, K. Srivastava, S. Singh, & H. Singh (Eds.), *Nutraceuticals and Innovative Food Products for Healthy Living and Preventive Care* (pp. 132-157). Hershey, PA: IGI Global. https://doi.org/ doi:10.4018/978-1-5225-2970-5.ch006

Weiss-Randall, D. (2018). DOI Theoretical Framework: Adopting Innovative Technologies. In *Utilizing Innovative Technologies to Address the Public Health Impact of Climate Change: Emerging Research and Opportunities* (pp. 144–166). Hershey, PA: IGI Global. doi:10.4018/978-1-5225-3414-3.ch005

Weiss-Randall, D. (2018). Sustainable Development. In *Utilizing Innovative Technologies to Address the Public Health Impact of Climate Change: Emerging Research and Opportunities* (pp. 167–203). Hershey, PA: IGI Global. doi:10.4018/978-1-5225-3414-3.ch006

Whitelaw, L., & Taddei, L. M. (2018). Using Reflection to Explore Cultural Responsiveness of Preservice Teachers. In Z. Djoub (Ed.), *Fostering Reflective Teaching Practice in Pre-Service Education* (pp. 166–188). Hershey, PA: IGI Global. doi:10.4018/978-1-5225-2963-7.ch009

Wongsurawat, W., & Shrestha, V. (2018). Information Technology, Globalization, and Local Conditions: Implications for Entrepreneurs in Southeast Asia. In P. Ordóñez de Pablos (Ed.), *Management Strategies and Technology Fluidity in the Asian Business Sector* (pp. 163–176). Hershey, PA: IGI Global. doi:10.4018/978-1-5225-4056-4.ch010

Woodman, K., & Kourtis-Kazoullis, V. (2018). Facebook, Tele-Collaboration, and International Access to Technology in the Classroom. In F. Cipolla-Ficarra (Ed.), *Optimizing Human-Computer Interaction With Emerging Technologies* (pp. 274–286). Hershey, PA: IGI Global. doi:10.4018/978-1-5225-2616-2.ch011

Woods, R. J., Johnson, S., & Pope, M. L. (2018). Teaching in an Anti-Deficit Pedagogical Mindset. In U. Thomas (Ed.), *Advocacy in Academia and the Role of Teacher Preparation Programs* (pp. 190–205). Hershey, PA: IGI Global. doi:10.4018/978-1-5225-2906-4.ch011

Wright, M. (2018). Cyberbullying: Description, Definition, Characteristics, and Outcomes. In F. Cipolla-Ficarra (Ed.), *Optimizing Human-Computer Interaction With Emerging Technologies* (pp. 161–182). Hershey, PA: IGI Global. doi:10.4018/978-1-5225-2616-2.ch006

Xu, D. (2018). Multimodal Semiotics in China. In H. Spires (Ed.), *Digital Transformation and Innovation in Chinese Education* (pp. 60–79). Hershey, PA: IGI Global. doi:10.4018/978-1-5225-2924-8.ch004

Yaokumah, W., & Kumah, P. (2018). Exploring the Impact of Security Policy on Compliance. In F. García-Peñalvo (Ed.), *Global Implications of Emerging Technology Trends* (pp. 256–274). Hershey, PA: IGI Global. doi:10.4018/978-1-5225-4944-4.ch014

Yaokumah, W., & Okai, E. S. (2018). Inter-Organizational Study of Access Control Security Measures. *International Journal of Technology and Human Interaction, 14*(1), 60–79. doi:10.4018/IJTHI.2018010104

Zheng, X., Liu, H., Lin, D., & Li, J. (2018). Achieving Rural Teachers' Development Through a WeChat Professional Learning Community: Two Cases From Guangdong Province. In H. Spires (Ed.), *Digital Transformation and Innovation in Chinese Education* (pp. 307–318). Hershey, PA: IGI Global. doi:10.4018/978-1-5225-2924-8.ch017

About the Contributors

Ela Burcu Ucel is a graduate of Hacettepe University, Business Administration. She had the opportunity to experience corporate life for 12 years. Then, she earned a scholarship from Izmir University of Economics and completed her PhD in organizational behavior. She has been teaching management, strategy and HRM at Izmir University of Economics since 2011. She also is an experienced trainer: she actively takes part in adult training programs in mediation, negotiation and culture. She loves teaching, writing, learning, and volunteering. Her areas of interest are gender studies, education management, human resources, and climate change. She is actively learning and teaching these topics and taking part in related research.

* * *

Jannatul Akmam completed her BA and MA from the Department of English, Jahangirnagar University, Dhaka, Bangladesh. Her area of interest includes Media and Cultural studies, Disability studies, Postcolonial Literature etc. She is working as a Lecturer of English at Jamia Ahmadia Sunnia Mohila Fazil Madrasah, Chattogram, Bangladesh. She has also worked as an Adjunct Faculty at Chittagong Government Women's College under National University of Bangladesh and Asian University for Women, Chittagong, Bangladesh. She has published couple of research papers in her area of interest.

Nuray Atsan is an Associate Professor of Management at Akdeniz University. Nuray has a BS degree in Business Administration from Hacettepe University, an MBA degree from Akdeniz University and a PhD degree in Management and Organization from Akdeniz University. Her research interests include entrepreneurship, innovation, technology transfer and managerial decision making. Nuray is Editorial Board member of the Akdeniz IIBF Journal (published by Akdeniz University, Turkey)

Soumia Boutkhil is Professor of English and gender studies at Mohammed Premier University, Oujda, Morocco. She has studied in Morocco, France and the

USA. Dr. Boutkhil is the initiator and former head of the Graduate interdisciplinary program "Gender, Society and Human Development." As a Fulbright Visiting Scholar for 2008-9 at Rutgers University, Dr. Boutkhil wrote and lectured extensively on feminine literature and women's status in Morocco with a particular focus on the problematic intersections of law and religion. Dr. Boutkhil co-founded the "Identity and Difference" research group at her university. She coedited a number of books among which Minority Matters: Literature, Theory, Society (2005), Representing Minorities: Studies in Literature and Ciriticism (2006 and 2008), and The World as A Global Agora: Critical Perspectives on Public Space (2008). North African Women after the Arab Spring: In the Eye of the Storm (2017). Over and above her academic commitments, Dr. Boutkhil is actively involved in civil society as a member of the Hijra Clinique Juridique, she currently serves as the Director of the Hijra Legal Aid clinic for migrants, refugees and asylum seekers in Oujda.

Yiğitcan Çolak was born in Konak, Izmir in 1998. He completed his primary and middle school education in Kemalpaşa Merkez Cumhuriyet Primary School, between 2004-2012. After, he went to Konak Atatürk Anatolian Medical-Vocational High School. He was trained to be an EMT between 2012-2017. After graduation, he studied western classical music as an amateur. In 2020, he started to study Economics at Izmir University of Economics. In addition, he started Logistics Management double major program at Izmir University of Economics by 2021.

Hugo Gaggiotti is an Associate Professor at the University of the West of England, Bristol, United Kingdom. The focus of Gaggiotti's writing is on the intersections between rhetoric, rituals, nomadic management and how organisations could contribute to the construction of vulnerability in particular contexts of displacement, transfiguration and liminality, like international borderlands, multinational assembly plants and ephemeral project-based work. His work has appeared in a range of interdisciplinary journals and his books include Organizational Ethnography: and Experiential and Practical Guide (in press) and Origins of Organising (2019).

Burcu Güneri Çangarlı is a Professor in Management and Organization at Izmir University of Economics. In her research, Güneri Çangarlı, explores topics such as ethics, leadership, power and politics, counterproductive work behavior. Her work has appeared in a range of international journals and edited books. In addition to scholarly research, Güneri Çangarlı is also involved in executive teaching with national and international organizations of all scales, and has taken part in a range of applied research and consultancy projects with public and private sector organizations. Since 2020 she is the Dean of the Faculty of Business of Izmir University of Economics.

Ibrahim Inan received a BS in production engineering from the University of Strathclyde – Scotland, a Ph.D. in business administration from the Cukurova University- Turkey, and an MS in psychology from the Cag University-Turkey. Ibrahim has worked as a commercial coordinator at Lesaffre Group in Turkish operation, and as a country manager at CSM's Bakery Supplies, a worldwide leader in pastry and bakery products. Ibrahim was engaged at Çağ University as an asst. prof. at the faculty of Economics and Administrative Sciences, Director of the Center for Continuing Education, and Vice-Director of the Institute of Social Sciences from 2014-2020. Ibrahim has written a book with his academic college entitled, "the world business cultures: EU countries". Ibrahim was the 2002 recipient of the "Most Successful Branch and Branch President award of the Association of Junior Chamber International (JCI) in Turkey. Currently, Ibrahim is the president of the Digital Entrepreneurship and Investment Association and works as a company consultant in business administration.

Selen Kars-Unluoglu is a Senior Lecturer in Organization Studies in the Bristol Business School at the University of the West England. Kars-Unluoglu researches the everyday experiences of change, innovation and learning in organizations. Her work is informed interpretative phenomenology and practice-based approaches. Her most recent research investigates the impact of COVID-19 pandemic on leadership and organization, which has appeared in the edited book Life after Covid: The Other Side of Crisis (Bristol University Press, 2020). She has published in International Small Business Journal, Innovation, Journal of Management & Organization, Leadership and Management Learning.

Benan Kurt Yılmaz completed her undergraduate education at Dokuz Eylül University, Faculty of Economics and Administrative Sciences, Department of Business Administration in 2005. In 2009, she received her master's degree in the field of Management and Organization at DEU. Benan Kurt Yılmaz, who completed her doctoral studies in DEU Business / Management and Organization in 2019, works in the Department of Management and Organization at Sinop University Ayancık Vocational High School. Areas of expertise; She has national and international publications and studies on organizational psychology, diversity management, equality, and discrimination in working life.

Zeynep Ozdamar Ertekin is an assistant professor of marketing at Izmir University of Economics. Her academic research concentrates on sustainability, fashion, consumption theories and macromarketing. Her work has been published in well recognized academic journals, such as Journal of Marketing Management, Journal of Macromarketing, International Journal of Consumer Studies, Journal of Global

Fashion Marketing, and Markets, Globalization and Development Review. She has 16 years of professional experience in fashion apparel industry.

Seray Begum Samur-Teraman received BA in International Relations (in English) with an honour degree at Istanbul Kultur University where she was granted a full scholarship. Then, she continued her academic career by studying for MBA. She studied Innovative Work Behaviors and Organizational Innovativeness for her MBA thesis. Then, she was admitted to the doctoral program in Marmara University, department of Management and Organization (in English) where she successfully completed and was awarded PhD degree in April 2017. Her PhD studies specifically focus on Entrepreneurial Assistance Programs in the context of Entrepreneurial Mentoring. In addition, her broader research interests include mainly Entrepreneurship, Entrepreneurial Mentoring and Coaching, Entrepreneurial Assistance/Supporting Programs, Entrepreneurial Ecosystems, Innovation-Innovative Orientation. Besides, she has studied soft skills particularly emotional intelligence from an entrepreneurial career perspective, entrepreneurial cognition, affect and creativity. She has also studied Research Methods, Advanced Statistics, and Qualitative Research Methods as part of her post-graduate studies. She has had extensive experience in data analysis, reporting and discussing. Samur-Teraman has had two research assistant positions in Business Administration departments at Istanbul Aydın University and FMV Isik University respectively. She was a vice-editor for IAU Business Review and editor for Press Academia Procedia, Global Business Research Congress Vol. 1. Until now, she has participated in several national and international conferences and published several articles in academic journals. She is currently working as an Assistant Professor for Istanbul Kültür University in the department of Entrepreneurship. She also took part as a mentor in INOSUIT project which is based on university-industry collaboration and aims to increase innovation capacity of mentee companies. She is married and can speak English fluently.

Duygu Seckin-Halac completed her Ph.D. in 2013 in Business Administration and became an associate professor of Management and Strategy in July 2020 due to the evaluation of the Interuniversity Board of Turkey. After a five-year industry experience, she has been working at Yasar University since 2010. She is still a teaching staff at Yasar University. She also completed a second master's program in Women's Studies. Her main research interest covers entrepreneurship and gender. She has published many academic papers in proceedings, books, and international refereed journals on strategic management, innovation, and entrepreneurship.

Olca Sürgevil Dalkılıç completed her undergraduate education at Dokuz Eylül University, Faculty of Economics and Administrative Sciences, Department of

Business Administration in 2003; she received her master's degrees in the field of Management and Organization at DEU in 2005 and in the field of Social Psychology at Ege University in 2007. Surgevil Dalkılıç, who completed her doctorate studies in DEU Business Administration / Management and Organization in 2008, started to work as an Associate Professor in DEU Business Administration Department, Department of Management and Organization in 2012. Between 2013-2015, she was a visiting researcher at the University of Wisconsin River Falls, College of Business and Economics. She has national and international publications about organizational psychology, human resources management, equality and discrimination in workplace, and organizational development.

Ceren Deniz Tatarlar is a Lecturer of Organization Studies at Tilburg University. Prior to her current position, she worked as a research assistant in Ege University (2014-2021) and teaching assistant in Izmir University of Economics. She received her MA degree in HRM from Ege University (Izmir, Turkey) and her Ph.D. in Business Administration with a major of Management and Organizations from the Izmir University of Economics with full scholarship (Turkey). Her research focuses on sociological and psychological aspects of organizations, self and identity studies within organizations and dark side of behavioral patterns and intentions of individuals. Prior to her academic career, she has three years-work experience in private industry as HR Assistant Specialist.

Index

J

M

N

O

P

S

T

W

www.ingramcontent.com/pod-product-compliance
Lightning Source LLC
Chambersburg PA
CBHW080501051126
54379CB00005B/137